T0305086

ROYAL HISTORICAL SOCIETY

STUDIES IN HISTORY

New Series

MANAGING THE BRITISH EMPIRE

THE CROWN AGENTS, 1833–1914

FOR MY FATHER, THE LATE ARTHUR SUNDERLAND

'AN INTELLIGENT MAN'

Ceylon Kelani Valley Railway: Yatizantota Bridge – July 1903

MANAGING THE BRITISH EMPIRE
THE CROWN AGENTS, 1833–1914

David Sunderland

THE ROYAL HISTORICAL SOCIETY
THE BOYDELL PRESS

First published 2004

Transferred to digital printing

A Royal Historical Society publication
Published by The Boydell Press
an imprint of Boydell & Brewer Ltd
PO Box 9, Woodbridge, Suffolk IP12 3DF, UK
and of Boydell & Brewer Inc.
668 Mt Hope Avenue, Rochester, NY 14620, USA
website: www.boydellandbrewer.com

ISBN 978-0-86193-267-2

ISSN 0269-2244

A CiP catalogue record for this book is available
from the British Library

This publication is printed on acid-free paper

Contents

List of Figures

List of Tables

Publication of this volume was aided by a grant from the Scouloudi Foundation, in association with the Institute of Historical Research.

Acknowledgements

Many people and institutions have helped me in the research and writing of this book. My greatest debt of gratitude lies with Dr Avner Offer, who supervised the thesis on which the book is based. Through his example and advice he gave me the tools required to carry out the research and caused me to completely rethink my approach to the Crown Agents. I would also like to thank Professor Martin Daunton, for his support for the book and his valuable comments on its contents; Professor Peter Cain, one of the examiners of the thesis, who identified its many defects and read and commented on various articles on the Crown Agents and on the original introduction to the book; Dr Colin Newbury, the second examiner; Anthony Kirk-Greene, who read and commented on the first draft of the thesis; Professor David Jeremy; Dr John Darwin; Professor Judith Brown; and those who attended the various seminars at which papers on the Agents were presented.

I am also grateful to the Economic and Social Research Council for the studentship which allowed me to study for my DPhil., and to the Crown Agents, who allowed me access to their archive. I owe much to the Crown Agents' archivist, Philip Knights MBE, who gave me important insights into the Agency, listened with patience to my wilder theories and provided me with his friendship. His predecessor, the late A. W. Abbott, through his weeding notes and extensive writings on the Crown Agents, also influenced my views. I would like to believe that he would have approved of the conclusions that I have drawn from my research.

Over the past few years, I have visited innumerable libraries and archives searching, often in vain, for information on the Agents. I must particularly thank the knowledgeable and helpful staff of the Public Record Office, the staff of the Bodleian Library, of Rhodes House Library, of the Bank of England archive, of the archive of the National Westminster Bank and in particular its archivist, Susan Snell, of Barings Bank, of Churchill College, Cambridge, of the Guildhall Library, London, and of Edinburgh University Library.

Immense help has come from individuals. Thanks go to the late Lt Col. J. A. Cameron, who permitted me to read his father's memoirs; Rowena Berry and Mrs J. A. Sibbald for their memories of their grandfather; Mrs Pamela Blake; and David Kynaston, who unselfishly gave me a copy of his notes of his interview with the late Sir George Aylwen and Scrimgeours' profit figures. I would, similarly, like to record my gratitude to the Fellows and staff of Wolfson College, Oxford; Professor Mike Gibson; Professor Barry Redding; and Christine Linehan, who prepared the manuscript for the press with patience and great skill. The jacket and frontispiece illustrations are reproduced by kind permission of the British Empire & Commonwealth Museum, Temple Meads, Bristol.

Research is a lonely business, and, finally, I would like to thank the following for their friendship and support: Mari Momose, Maurizio Grilli, Michael Farrell (for encouraging me to take a 'leap in the dark' and accept the offer of a place at Oxford), Wendy Irwin (for the Thursday lunches), Philip Burbidge and Thelma Willock.

David Sunderland
April 2003

Abbreviations

AO	Audit Office
BE	Bank of England
CA	Crown Agent
CAA	Crown Agent Archive, Sutton, Surrey
CAOG 17/24, CAR	CAs to CO, 7 Apr. 1902, CAOG 17/24, misc. 142, no. 34
CE	Consulting engineer
CO	Colonial Office
EHR	*English Historical Review*
FO	Foreign Office
GL	Guildhall Library, London
NAN	National Archive of Natal, Pietermaritzburg
NWB	National Westminster Bank
PP	Parliamentary papers
PPD	Parliamentary papers 1905, lvi (Cd 2325): F. Shelford's defence of West African railway construction
PPE	Parliamentary papers 1909, xvi (Cd 4474): Crown Agents enquiry: evidence
PPR	Parliamentary papers 1909, xvi (Cd 4473): Crown Agents enquiry: report
PPS	Parliamentary papers 1909, xlvii (Cd 4668): Royal Commission on Shipping Rings: evidence
SH	Somerset House, London
WASA	West Australian State Archives, Perth

Introduction

The British empire comprised two types of colonies. Responsible government colonies, such as Canada and Australia, possessed representative institutions, the crown retained only the right of veto on legislation and had no control over public officers, except the governor. Alternatively, in crown colonies, like Ceylon, West Africa and the West Indies, the imperial government had full control over both legislation and the local administration, which consisted of a governor and various officials advised by a legislative council or an assembly composed of appointed members and elected representatives of the local business and indigenous elites. Matters affecting the economic affairs of crown colonies were dealt with by the Treasury, which acted as the guardian of the public purse; by the Colonial Office, the source of most policy decisions; by colonial administrations and legislative councils, which provided the colonial secretary with information and policy proposals; and by the Office of the Crown Agents, which acted for the colonies as commercial and financial agent in the United Kingdom.

The origins of the Crown Agents can be traced back to the mid-eighteenth century when there were four sets of officials commonly referred to as colony agents. King's agents were appointed by the crown and resided in the colonies, where they aided and protected merchants and trade. In the United Kingdom there were grant agents, employed by the Treasury to supervise the payment of parliamentary grants, and colonial agents, representatives of local assemblies, who protected their colonies' interests and ensured that their laws were confirmed.[1] There were also private agents, appointed by governors, regiments stationed overseas and large merchant houses to look after their affairs at home and, in the case of governors' agents, to claim their employers' salaries. The first crown-appointed colony representatives were Richard Cumberland and Purbec Langham, who in 1764 became the agents of Quebec and Grenada respectively. Both colonies had recently passed into British hands as gains of the Seven Years War and, as they initially lacked elective assemblies, their colonial agents were appointed by royal warrant. Neither office, however, was secure. Langham was replaced by an assembly-appointed agent in 1770, and the Quebec assembly finally succeeded in abolishing Cumberland's agency, after numerous attempts, in 1828.

Permanent crown-appointed agents first appeared at the turn of the century, in those colonies acquired as a result of the Napoleonic Wars (*see*

---

[1] Grant agents were usually Treasury clerks. The post disappeared in 1835 when its duties were transferred to the Department for the Payment of Civil Services.

appendix 1, table 1). The revolt of the American colonies, difficulties with Canada, quarrels with the West Indies and a desire to suppress the slave trade, led the imperial government to introduce into these spoils of war a non-representative form of administration that comprised a governor and a nominated council. The agents of these colonies were thus appointed by the crown – in theory by the governor. Colonial appointment, however, was 'more . . . appearance than reality'.[2] By 1810 agents were chosen by the Colonial Office, a practice established after disputes over the appointment of Cape and Trinidad representatives. In the Cape, in 1806, the Treasury offered a newly-vacated post to their own candidate on the basis that they recruited grant agents, but gave way to the Colonial Office after a discussion of the duties of the post.[3] The Trinidad disagreement was more protracted. In 1802, on the resignation of the colony's agent, the Colonial Office nominated their own replacement. The governor objected, failed to pay his salary and when the agent resigned a few months later, appointed his own representative, the former attorney-general Archibald Gloster.[4] To cover the discharge of his duties in the United Kingdom, the colony paid Gloster £2,000 followed by a further £6,000, without the secretary of state's authorisation. The Colonial Office appointee, T. C. Marling, received nothing, and was treated 'as if [he had] been dismissed'.[5] A stand-off between the colony and the Colonial Office then ensued until 1807, when the new secretary of state brokered an agreement that the two agents would act jointly, but that all future representatives of the colonies would be chosen by the Colonial Office.[6]

The secretary of state used his patronage over agents' appointments to improve the efficiency of the Colonial Office and thus ensure his own reputation as an able minister. In general, agencies were given to serving or retired Colonial Office clerks. For serving officials they 'offered a means of rewarding long and able service', thus strengthening the department's relationship with its staff, and 'succession to them . . . [was] . . . looked forward to by the senior clerks as an advantage which they might reasonably expect'.[7] The promise of an agency was also used as a lure to encourage less efficient officials to retire.[8] Colonial Office policy after 1815 was to allow those who wished to leave the service early to do so, and the 1822 Superannuation Act permitted an officer to retire if, after allowing for his pension and the salary of his successor, there was an establishment saving.[9] Occasionally, agencies were additionally given

2   Treasury to Malta, 22 Jan. 1913, PRO, T 64/75/146.
3   L. M. Penson, 'The origins of the Crown Agents' office', EHR xl (1925), 201.
4   Castelreigh to Hislop, 4 July 1808, T 64/86, 54; Bathurst to Woodford, 17 Dec. 1801, ibid. 90.
5   Castelreigh to Hislop, 4 July 1808, ibid. 54.
6   Castelreigh to Hislop, 10 June 1809, ibid. 66.
7   CO to Treasury, 15 Mar. 1833, PRO, CO 324/147/139.
8   Ibid.
9   D. M. Young, The Colonial Office in the early nineteenth century, London 1961, 28, 63.

to those who could, or had, aided the secretary of state or his department in a private capacity.

The work of the new agents was diverse, reflecting the differing needs of the colonies. Most purchased public sector goods and made payments in the United Kingdom for the colonies, for example the salaries of officials on leave and pensions.[10] They also performed *ad hoc* services and some undertook duties similar to those performed by the old style colonial agents. The Mauritius representative, for example, supplied his employer with information on points that interested the colony 'including laws and Parliamentary proceedings' and provided help to Mauritian visitors to England.[11] The amount of work varied from colony to colony. The average annual disbursements on behalf of Sierra Leone were £3,000, as compared to Mauritius's £16,120, Malta's £41,767 and Ceylon's £51,937.[12]

Unfortunately, the standard of service provided was poor and there were complaints from the colonies. The retired Colonial Office officials and external appointees were inefficient, and the serving clerks were unable to devote adequate time to their agencies, which rarely covered the colonies that they supervised as part of their day-to-day duties. The cost of the system also came in for criticism. In 1830 the report of the Commission on the Receipts and Expenditures of Colonies stated that the business conducted by the agents of Malta, New South Wales and Mauritius was insufficient to justify the salaries paid to them.[13] The commission's conclusions were taken up by the Treasury, which in 1832 argued that the agents' duties 'could be as satisfactorily and efficiently performed by one of the present agents' working full-time at a quarter of the cost.[14] Wishing to avoid further colonial and Treasury attacks, the Colonial Office in the following year therefore reorganised the system and created a single agency. All the existing agents were dismissed apart from two, the Colonial Office clerk George Baillie and the former clerk Edward Barnard, who relinquished their other duties and were given the title 'Joint Agents-Generals for the Colonies'.[15] Two agents as opposed to one were appointed, as the work involved was thought to be too great for one man and it was felt that the increasingly similar duties of the

---

[10] PP 1822, xx.

[11] PP 1830–1, iv. 49.

[12] CAA, CA M 1; PP 1820, xii; PP 1822, xx; PP 1823, xiv; PP 1824, xvi. The Mauritius mean is for the years 1813 to 1822, Malta's for the period 1814 to 1823 and Ceylon's for the years 1814 to 1822.

[13] PP 1830–1, iv. 3, 13, 73.

[14] Treasury to CO, 10 Feb. 1832, CO 323/214/134.

[15] The dismissed agents were granted pensions and gratuities totalling £2,614. The new agency therefore involved extra expenditure in 1833 of £220 and a saving in subsequent years of £1,180 *per annum*: Treasury to CO, 28 Mar. 1833, CO 323/217/191; CO to Treasury, 15 Mar. 1833, CO 324/147/139.

Table 1
Area, population and public expenditure of the Crown Agent clients, responsible government colonies and British India, 1851, 1881, 1911

Colony	1851			1881			1911		
	Area (m. sq. miles)	Pop. (m.)	Public expen. (per capita)(£)	Area (m. sq. miles)	Pop. (m.)	Public expen. (per capita)(£)	Area (m. sq. miles)	Pop. (m.)	Public expen. (per capita)(£)
CA clients	2.037	4.0	0.673	1.291	6.0	1.1	1.253	35.7	0.49
Respon. gov. colonies	1.384	2.4	not known	6.88	7.9	4.828	7.88	20.5	6.036
British India	1.005	123.9	0.218	0.962	198.8	0.36	1.093	244.2	0.32

Source: PP 1866, lxxiii; PP 1892, lxxxvii; PP 1916, xxxii.

Notes: 1851 responsible government figures exclude those colonies that were clients of the CAs. 1851 population figures were not available for Tasmania, Vancouver Island, Honduras or British Colombia, and there is no 1851 public expenditure data for New Zealand, Queensland, St Helena, Vancouver Island, Canada or British Colombia. 1881 and 1911 public expenditure totals include gross expenditure and expenditure on public works. The 1881 population totals for crown colonies and protectorates exclude the Gold Coast, for which no figures are available.

colonial agents for those colonies in receipt of parliamentary grants would eventually be added to their workload.[16]

At first the new Agency performed its duties well and its disbursements rose rapidly, from £28,649 in 1833 to £274,567 in 1857, 21 per cent of which came from self-governing colonies.[17] As the two Agents aged and took up outside directorships, however, the quality of service fell. Responsible government colonies, which in any case wished to cut their links with the Colonial Office, began to appoint their own agents, and Ceylon threatened to withdraw its business.[18] By 1858 the Agency was in 'a state verging on bankruptcy in both means and character', with an income of £1,627 and receipts of only £2,000.[19] Not wanting to take over its role, the Colonial Office sought to recruit a new Agent who could return the Agency to its former profitability.[20] The candidate chosen, on the recommendation of the Treasury, was Penrose Julyan, who had 'the air of much intelligence and activity' and 'the appreciation and good familiarity with the class of business to which he would be introduced'.[21] Informed that his post was 'temporary and experimental', Julyan set about his task with gusto. Showing 'remarkable energy', he increased staff numbers and salaries, developed new systems of work, introduced a scale of fixed charges to pay for the changes and, finally, in 1863 renamed the Agency the 'Crown Agents for the Colonies'.[22]

From the 1860s until well into the second half of the twentieth century, the Agency supplied crown colonies with non-locally manufactured public sector stores, organised the provision of external finance, managed their investments in the UK and supervised the construction of their railways, harbours etc. In addition, it performed a personnel role, recruiting technical officers, paying colonial service pensions and some salaries, and arranging for the transport of colonial troops, and, from 1878, Indian indentured labour, and supervised the award of colonial land and mineral concessions. Until 1880, it also acted, largely in the financial sphere, for a number of responsible government colonies (see table 1 and appendix 1, table 3). Treasury concern that its issue of such colonies loans could give the impression that they carried an imperial guarantee, however, then led to this work being abandoned. It was taken over by agents-general, direct employees of the governments concerned.[23]

---

[16] Treasury minute, 26 Mar. 1833, CO 323/217/191; CO to Treasury, 15 Mar. 1833, CO 324/147/139. The parliamentary grant colonies began to use the Agents in the 1850s.

[17] Barnard to CO, 7 May 1858, CO 323/252/4453.

[18] CO to Treasury, 31 Aug. 1858, CO 323/252/9239.

[19] Barnard to CO, 7 Mar 1858, CO 323/252/4853; Julyan to CO, 26 Nov. 1879, CO 323/339/18599.

[20] Baillie had died two years earlier.

[21] Note, n.d., CO 323/252/4453.

[22] Rogers note, 5 Mar. 1870, CO 323/299.

[23] Treasury to CO, 23 Dec. 1878, T 1/7710/20021. The work of agents-general is discussed in B. Attard, 'The Australian high commissioners' office', unpubl. DPhil. diss. Oxford 1991.

Constitutionally, the Agency was an anomaly.[24] Its United Kingdom counterparts, such as the purchasing departments of the War Office and Admiralty and the accountant-general at the India Office, were part of government, and in other countries its functions were performed by colonial administrations or again by the imperial power.[25] The Crown Agents were merely under the control of the government – at first the Treasury and the Colonial Office, and, after 1880 when the Treasury expressed concern over its status, the colonial secretary of state.[26] Financially and administratively, it was an independent organisation. It covered its expenses through a system of charges for work done, transferring any surpluses to a reserve fund, which met pension costs and financed deficits. It recruited its own staff from outside the civil service, and was given a wide latitude by the Colonial Office as to how it conducted its business. Its functions were never officially laid down, except inferentially in colonial regulations, and it had no formal constitution.[27]

The Agency was managed by a Senior Agent and one or two junior Agents.[28] Each assumed responsibility for a specified part of the business and the day-to-day administration of a particular set of departments, with the division of labour changing according to personnel and the type and the amount of work undertaken.[29] Although they were 'as dissimilar as, I suppose, three men could be', they 'always managed to work amicably and to get on'.[30] As each had his own distinct area of control, there was little disagreement, and, when a departure from normal practice required a change of policy, they would discuss the matter informally and reach a mutually acceptable decision.[31] They were supported by a staff of three in 1833, thirty in 1881, 200 in 1908 and 468 in 1914, who were divided into three, and, from 1901, four classes and worked in five service and five function departments (see appendix 1, fig. 1).[32] The majority were men employed on a permanent basis, though from 1879 to 1880 the Office recruited a small number of female clerks, who were confined to the correspondence and stock and coupon

[24] Although the nineteenth-century British state ceded or delegated power to non-state bodies, it rarely made use of quasi-governmental organisations.

[25] FO to CAs, 21 Mar. 1933, CAA, M 70.

[26] Meade note, 19 July 1880, CO 323/344/10454; Herbert note, 19 Oct. 1880, ibid. The Treasury believed that it had no 'real power' over the Agents and that, if they 'chose to repudiate . . . [its] . . . interference tomorrow and set up on their own account', there was 'nothing to hinder them, except their knowledge that it is not in their interests to do so': note, 1 Nov. 1878, T 1/7710/17281.

[27] CO 885/19/223, v.

[28] From 1833 to 1879, and from 1888 to 1895, there were just two Agents.

[29] PPE, qq. 1116, 1118–20, 1123.

[30] Ibid. q. 1106.

[31] Ibid. qq. 1106, 1107.

[32] CAA, accounts, 1881; PPE, appendix 1, qq. 20, 170; PP 1914–16, xlv (Cd 7973). In 1880 the Colonial Office employed 71 staff, in 1908 there were 162, and in 1914 192: PP 1880, xlv (161), 87; PP 1909, lv (54), 112; PP 1914, lv (132), 118.

departments, and occasionally employed temporary staff.[33] The Agency also used third party firms – a shipping agent, a packing agent, a firm of solicitors, consulting engineers and a broker. Such out-sourcing enabled it to relieve itself of some of the financial liability for the work undertaken and, where the demand for the services supplied were small, reduced costs.[34]

This book seeks to add to that body of work that examines the role played by the metropolitan power in the development of colonial economies by identifying the contribution made by the Crown Agents.[35] Hitherto, historians in this field have tended to disregard the Agents, largely because of a perceived paucity of source material.[36] Those who have discussed them, often in passing, assume that their 'primary motivation . . . [was] . . . a sincere desire to serve their principals to the best of their ability' and that they performed their duties 'well and adequately'.[37] Davis and Robert Huttenback go further and estimate that the use of the Agency reduced the cost of colonial supplies by 10 per cent and flotation expenses by 1 per cent, saving colonies on average £2.5m. per year.[38] This book questions these findings. It argues that the Crown Agents, along with the Colonial Office and colonies, acted largely out of self-interest. Until the mid-1890s the interests of the Agents, Colonial Office and colonies converged and the Agency provided a high quality, though expensive service. Thereafter, changes in its finances forced the Agents to alter their priorities and to provide an excessively expensive and substandard service that was incompatible with the interests of the Colonial Office and the colonies.

---

[33] PPE, qq. 3045, 4216. If possible, the CAs avoided the use of temporary staff, whose 'identification with . . . [the Agency's] . . . interest is proportionately slight': CAs to CO, 27 Oct. 1909, CO 323/553/35347; CAs to CO, 29 July 1890, CO 323/379/14853.

[34] PPE, qq. 350, 353.

[35] R. M. Kesner, *Economic control and colonial development: crown colony financial management in the age of Joseph Chamberlain*, Oxford 1981; Robert V. Kubicek, *The administration of imperialism: Joseph Chamberlain at the Colonial Office*, Durham, NC 1969; L. E. Davis and R. A. Huttenback, *Mammon and the pursuit of empire: the political economy of British imperialism, 1860–1912*, Cambridge 1986.

[36] In fact, although a part of the Office archive was destroyed in the late 1960s, much material survives. The most important papers were retained by the Agency, while a large number of files had previously been transferred to the Public Record Office or lodged in the Agents' Liverpool store, where until 1995 they had lain forgotten. In addition, much material relating to the Office can be found in the Public Record Office Colonial Office correspondence files and in the archives of the Bank of England, the National Westminster Bank and the British Museum.

[37] R. M. Kesner, 'Builders of empire: the role of the Crown Agents in imperial development, 1880–1914', *Journal of Imperial and Commonwealth History* v (1977), 326; L. H. Gann and P. Duignan, *The rulers of British Africa, 1870–1914*, Stanford 1978, 70. See also A. W. Abbott, *A short history of the Crown Agents and their office*, London 1959 (privately printed); Davis and Huttenback, *Mammon*; Vincent Ponko, Jr, 'Economic management in a free trade empire: the work of the Crown Agents for the colonies in the nineteenth and early twentieth centuries', *Journal of Economic History* xxxi (1966), 363–77.

[38] Davis and Huttenback, *Mammon*, 188. The figures seem little more than guesses.

The theoretical basis of the book is largely derived from principal–agent theory, though other economic and organisational theories are also used. It is assumed that individuals are primarily motivated by their own self-interest, but on occasion make choices that fail to maximise their welfare, that is their income, status and power.[39] Unable to obtain and assess all relevant information, agents may 'satisfice' and chose an alternative that appears to generate a satisfactory level of return. Others may be inter-temporally inconsistent, that is, when faced with a small gain available in the short-term and a superior reward obtainable in the distant future, they will choose the inferior option, the achievement of which is relatively certain.[40] People are also influenced by social and private norms of behaviour, self-imposed standards of conduct, such as honesty and integrity.[41] Social norms are common to all members of a society and are sustained by the disapproval and approval of others and a desire to reduce decision-making costs.[42] Private norms are exclusive to the individual. Determined by conditioning, learning over time and perhaps genetic inheritance, they are supported by emotional rewards and punishments and self-interest.[43]

Given that self-interest is the primary motivating factor, there is a danger in all principal–agent relationships that the agent will take advantage of the principal through the provision of less than maximum effort or through fraudulent behaviour.[44] Such a threat particularly exists in situations of asymmetric information, where the principal is not as well-informed as the agent, and in conditions of uncertainty, when the an agent's output cannot invari-

[39] Self-interest arguably arises from each individual's desire to ensure the survival and continuation of his or her genetic inheritance: Richard Dawkins, *The selfish gene*, London 1978, 21.

[40] George Ainslie, 'Beyond microeconomics: conflict among interests in a multiple self as a determination of value', in Jon Elster (ed.), *The multiple self*, Cambridge 1986, 139–43.

[41] W. Gaerner and Y. Xu, *Rationality and external reference* (University of Nottingham, discussion papers on economics, no. 96/17, May 1996), 5–6.

[42] Jon Elster, 'Social norms and economic theory', *Journal of Economic Perspectives* iii (1989), 100. Violation of norms may lead to punishment by society, withdrawal of friendship, loss of reputation, which could reduce future gains, and feelings of guilt and shame on the part of the violator: Robert Axelrod, 'An evolutionary approach to norms', *American Political Science Review* lxxx (1986), 102–7.

[43] Gay S. Becker, 'Altruism, egoism and genetic fitness: economics and socio-biology', *Journal of Economic Literature* xiv (1976), 817–26. The rewards and punishments of altruists are respectively peace of mind and guilt. The beneficiaries of an altruist are discouraged from harming him, and an honest person will be allowed to co-operate with like-minded colleagues and thus avoid the costs of dishonesty. Through their negative acts, sociopaths would appear to increase their feelings of self-worth, which fall if no act is committed. Their vengeance discourages people from committing acts likely to harm them and their victims will often acquiesce in their wishes.

[44] Principal–agent theory is discussed in John W. Pratt and Richard J. Zeckhauser, *Principal agent theory: the structure of business*, Boston 1984; Richard M. Kreps, *A course in microeconomic theory*, London 1990, chs xvi, xvii; Paul Milgrom and John Roberts, *Economics, organisation and management*, Princeton, NJ 1992, chs v, vi.

ably be linked with inputs or effort. Where asymmetrical information and uncertainty are present, principals face two problems: adverse selection and moral hazard. Adverse selection arises from the capacity of agents to hide information, especially about their abilities, from principals prior to signing a contract. Moral hazard is the temptation for agents to pursue their own interests that are incompatible with those of their principals after a contract has been agreed. Such opportunistic behaviour will occur if the agent believes that the chances of discovery are low and/or the likely gains are greater than the loss he would suffer if his actions were revealed. Both adverse selection and moral hazard can be countered through the adoption of various strategies. Principals can recruit only agents whose abilities and honesty can be easily discovered, closely monitor their activities, or increase the financial consequences of dismissal for opportunism by paying high salaries or requiring sureties.

Existing principal–agent theory, however, has its limits. This book therefore makes the following extensions to the paradigm.

• The theory generally assumes just one principal–agent relationship. In reality, agents are usually part of a large interconnected network of associations. Often they have agents of their own and acknowledge more than one principal, who may in turn be agents. Indeed, in some cases an agent and a principal may share a principal (*see* fig. 1).

• The theory admits only to an agency problem. But, as anyone who is employed in higher education is aware, principals can also act duplicitly, and the existence or threat of such behaviour can itself promote agent opportunism, diluting the associated penalty of guilt.

• The theory assumes that agents have just one set of interests. In fact, most senior employees have organisational goals as well as purely personal interests. This book consequently divides moral hazard into institutional moral hazard and personal moral hazard. The former occurs when employees perform their duties in a way that serves their institution's interests, rather than those of the organisation's principal. The latter involves the completion of tasks by senior members of an organisation in a way that benefits them at the expense of either their employer and/or their employer's principal. Both forms of opportunism are further divided into 'quality moral hazard', which reduces the quality of the good or service supplied, and 'price moral hazard' that increases the cost or price of the good or service.

• It is proposed that a degree of reciprocity can exist between a principal and an agent regarding moral hazard, which reveals itself in two ways. A principal will be more inclined to tolerate a level of duplicity on the part of the agent if that agent is aware of, but does not divulge, moral hazard committed by the principal in his dealings with his own principal. So, for example, an employer who is defrauding clients, will accept similar dishonesty by his employees if his criminality is known to them. Secondly, like agents, princi-

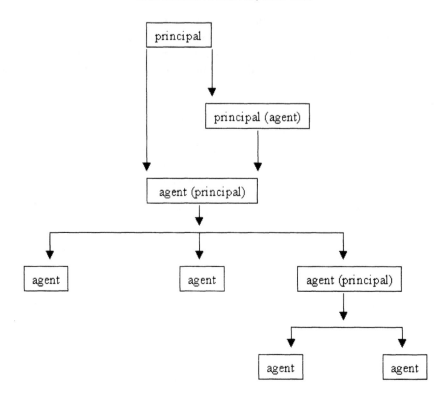

Figure 1. A network of principal–agent relationships

pals have many goals, and agent action that is damaging to one interest may benefit another. A principal will therefore allow moral hazard in one area, provided that, in return, the agent fulfils other more important goals.[45] For instance, if a principal prizes quality over price and pays an agent a commission to seek out goods, he will accept the supply of overly expensive items and the maximisation of the agent's earnings provided that the agent ensures quality. The price moral hazard will increase an agent's cost of dismissal for supplying poor quality goods, as he would lose both future earnings and the extra commission obtained through the supply of excessively expensive items. The principal's acceptance of the agent's moral hazard will also engender trust, and create an obligation for the agent to reciprocate by providing high quality goods.[46] Equally, a principal whose agents could easily

[45] The utility from the interest advanced is greater than the disutility from the interest damaged.
[46] Likewise, if the agent's performance of his duties involves a subagent, to fulfil his principal's requirements, he in turn, will attempt to stop subagent quality moral hazard, but will accept subagent price moral hazard.

commit major fraud without his knowledge, may permit minor larceny in order to prevent the theft of large sums. This book used the term 'benign moral hazard' for opportunism that is accepted by a principal; acts that are deemed unacceptable are referred to as 'malign moral hazard'.

• It is further suggested that where an agent has two principals, actions against the interests of one principal may advance the interests of the other. If this is the case, when deciding whether to act opportunistically against one principal, an agent will take into account the gains that could accrue from the principal that benefits from his dishonesty.

• Finally, and perhaps most importantly, the theory's solutions to moral hazard exclude the establishment of trust between a principal and an agent. Trust relationships involve each party adopting and maintaining high standards of behaviour derived from social and private norms, in particular that neither will take advantage of the other and that favours, including the acceptance of moral hazard, will eventually be reciprocated. Both parties monitor their own behaviour, punishing themselves with the penalty of guilt if they act dishonestly, and are aware that defaults from such norms could prove costly. Future material and emotional gains from the continuation of the relationship would be lost, as would the accompanying savings in transaction costs and the gains from future alliances with others that arise from the acquisition of a reputation for probity. If they have a shared background with their associate, withdrawal of trust could also damage their social life.

There are two types of trust. Calculative or self-interested trust develops from the strategic interaction of self-interested economic agents and is maintained as long as it serves their self-interest. Personal trust, on the other hand, arises from close relationships and a sharing of goals, and, in turn, can be split into ascribed and earned trust.[47] The former is based on the characteristics of trusting agents, such as family, ethnicity, class, religion or similar attributes. Such shared features enable economic agents to gauge the honesty of potential partners from personal experience or the ethical culture associated with the common background, and encourage a 'blind' trust that arises from individuals' unwillingness to ascribe the negative characteristics of untrustworthiness to their peers and by extension to themselves.[48] Earned trust, on the other hand, is based either on an agent's own personal experience of the individual involved or on the experience of others, and arises as a result of long relationships and face-to-face interaction. Long relationships, beginning with minor transactions involving little risk or trust, enable agents to monitor their counterparts and to discover their reputation for trustworthi-

47 Hubert Schmitz, 'From ascribed to earned trust in exporting clusters', *Journal of International Economics* xlviii (1999), 143.
48 W. W. Powell, 'Trust-based forms of governance', in R. M. Kramer and T. R. Tyler (eds), *Trust in organisations: frontiers of theory and research*, London 1996, 55.

ness from those who have had earlier dealings with them.[49] Personal contact builds emotional bonds, permits non-verbal communication, which reduces the risk of misunderstanding and allows more accurate appreciations of integrity, and facilitates gossip, strengthening reputation mechanisms. In a work environment, meanwhile, the principal's moral rhetoric and example can play a part. The success of this strategy, however, is highly dependent on the charismatic qualities of the manager, whose rhetoric cannot be fine-tuned to the needs of individuals, who, through socialisation, rapidly become aware of his exhortations to others.[50]

[49] B. Burchill and F. Wilkinson, *Trust business relationships and the contractual environment* (ESRC Centre for Business Research, University of Cambridge, working paper, no. 35), 4.
[50] Mark Casson, *Corporate culture and the agency problem* (University of Reading, Department of Economics, discussion papers in economics, no. 238, 1991), 1–6.

1

The Office of the Crown Agents

The Crown Agents were at the centre of a network of principal–agent relationships, within which individuals had their own interests and were subject to institutional and/or personal moral hazard (*see* fig. 2). They were firstly the principals of their staff and of those who provided the colonies with goods, services and capital. They themselves, meanwhile, were supposedly the agents of colonial governors, who in turn were the agents of both the Colonial Office (the agent of the wider state, the government and ultimately the electorate) and their respective colonies. In reality, however, despite the secretary of state's insistence that they acted 'not in any sense as agents of Her Majesty's government', the Crown Agents, colonies and Colonial Office all regarded the colonial secretary as the Agents' true principal.[1] He recruited them, set their salaries and service charges, had the power to dismiss them and, if he wished, to close down the Agency. The Agency thus existed to fulfil not only the interests of colonial governors, but also those of the Colonial Office. The first part of this chapter examines both sets of interest, together with those of material, service and capital suppliers, and discusses why the Colonial Office used a quasi-government agency to deliver goods and capital to colonies.

Like the Colonial Office, colonies and suppliers, the Crown Agents had their own interests and were particularly open to institutional moral hazard. They had a far greater knowledge of each service area than the Colonial Office, their output could not invariably be linked with input and effort and, given the diversity and complexity of their activities, full monitoring would have been difficult, if not impossible, and the cost would have exceeded any possible loss.[2] The second part of the chapter examines the institutional goals of the Agents and discusses how these influenced the service provided. It will be demonstrated that until the mid-1890s the methods adopted to fulfil these goals were largely compatible with the interests of the Colonial Office and colonies. A reduction in their commission and an alteration in the Colonial

---

[1]   The Agents Sir Ernest Blake and Sir Reginald Antrobus believed that they served 'two masters' and were 'under the orders of the Secretary of State': PPE, qq. 39945, 3808. See also PPE, p. 1016, and CO to Treasury, 26 Nov. 1880, PP 1881, lxiv. Depending on the work performed, the Agents also had other principals. For example, the investors who bought crown colony securities and the banks that provided colonies with short-term loans.
[2]   In 1870 the under-secretary, Sir R. Herbert, accepted that 'if the honour of the Agents were not to be trusted, it would be difficult to detect abuses': Herbert note, Sept. 1870, CO 323/299/181.

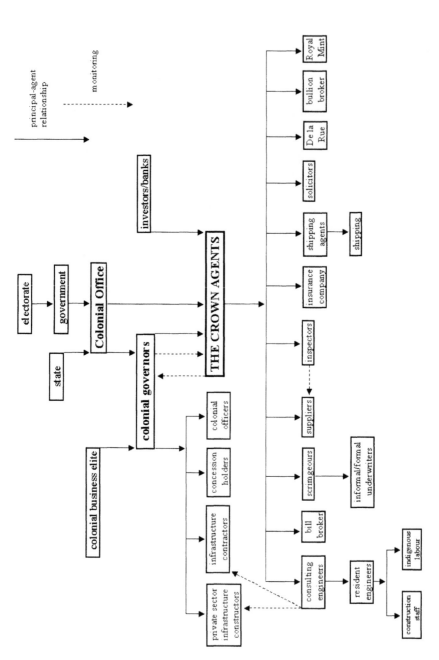

Figure 2. Colonial and Crown Agent principal–agent relationships

Office's goals then forced the Agents to adopt new means of achieving their aims, which ultimately were in the interests of neither the colonies nor the colonial secretary.

In addition to institutional moral hazard, the Agents and their staff were prone, as individuals, to personal adverse selection and moral hazard.[3] The final part of this chapter looks at the practices adopted by the Colonial Office to reduce the likelihood of impropriety on the part of the Crown Agents, and at those used by the Agents to limit opportunism by their own staff. The strategies adopted succeeded in discouraging serious fraud, but failed to halt minor misdemeanours, which both the Colonial Office and Crown Agents tolerated, aware that, by permitting such behaviour, they increased the cost of serious fraud and hence dismissal to perpetrators.

The interests of the Colonial Office, suppliers and the colonies

The Colonial Office was the agent of, and represented, the wider state and the government, which was the agent of the electorate and the principal of its MPs. The interests of the wider state were to maintain, and, if possible, increase the country's international standing. The government wished to retain the benefits of power and thus sought to satisfy the preferences of the median voter, who, seeking to maximise his utility, voted for the party that he perceived would provide him with the highest return. MPs, meanwhile, sought to maximise their party's and their own welfare. In addition to representing the state and government interests, Colonial Office officials also had their own institutional and personal goals. Like all rational employees, they wanted to maximise their income, power, prestige, convenience and security.[4] Unlike private sector workers, however, their ability to increase their pecuniary gains by individual or collective action was severely constrained and they therefore placed greater emphasis on non-pecuniary advantages, such as influence, status, prestige and the interest and importance of their tasks. Their institutional aims were thus to maintain and, if possible, increase the power and prestige of their office, and their personal goals were to maximise their own influence and the satisfaction they gained from their work.

Prior to the 1880s officials achieved state, government and their own institutional and personal goals through the retention of the crown colonies at the lowest possible cost to the British taxpayer. Colonial administrations derived their income from indirect taxes, mainly import and export duties, and receipts from the sale of crown lands, the operation of railways and such-

---

3 PPE, q. 1044.
4 Patrick Dunleavy, *Democracy, bureaucracy and public choice: economic explanations in political science*, London 1991, 148.

like. If this income failed to cover costs, funds had to be sought from the imperial Treasury in the form of subsidies or grants-in-aid. Such finance, however, was unpopular with the electorate, damaged the legitimacy of empire, and, more importantly, led to the haemorrhaging of Colonial Office power and status and officials' influence to the Treasury.

The Office's objectives then changed. It became in the state's, government's and its own interest to develop the crown colonies. The expansion of empire meant that territories had been acquired which were too underdeveloped to generate the income required to support local administrations. At the same time, if the British state wished to maintain its international standing, it was important that it exhibit a more active presence in its territories, and, if governments wanted to obtain the support of the enlarged electorate, they had to stave off growing European and American economic competition through the acquisition of new markets, new sources of raw materials and new outlets for surplus domestic funds. Development solved all these problems. Economic growth would increase the revenues of colonial governments. This would ensure an adequate British presence and avoid dependence on the imperial Treasury and the associated decline in the autonomy of the Colonial Office and of electoral support for empire. Furthermore, it would increase British imports from the colonies and primary exports, create employment and ensure high returns for those who provided the capital required to generate growth. Britain would thus maintain its international economic position, and improvements in the welfare of MPs, who had extensive colonial commercial and financial interests, commercial interest groups and the median voter would permit governments to retain power. The concomitant expansion of the Colonial Office's workload, meanwhile, would increase its power and status in government, together with the influence of its officials and the satisfaction they gained from their work. The Colonial Office, consequently, increasingly began to intervene in the economies of the crown colonies through both direct methods, such as the construction of infrastructure, and, following the creed of *laissez faire*, indirect means designed to promote private sector involvement. Its activities, though, were constrained by the need to ensure that as little as possible of the cost of development fell on the British taxpayer.

Turning to supplier and colonial goals, the interest of those who supplied goods, services and capital to the colonies was to maximise their present and future income. There was thus a danger that they would minimise costs through the provision of poor quality work, increase returns by charging excessive prices or by other means, or capture contracts through bribery.[5] Governors and local administrators, meanwhile, like the Colonial Office, wished to maximise their power, prestige, convenience and security, and

---

[5] Amongst most suppliers and service providers 'a considerable laxity of ideas over . . . [corruption] . . . prevails': Ebden note, 22 Feb. 1876, CO 537/217.

placed little emphasis on current pecuniary gains. Like the Crown Agents, however, they served two principals – the Colonial Office and their respective colonies in the form of local business elites, which, wishing to maximise their own incomes, favoured economic expansion in their colony and low taxation. Governors, as rational individuals, often found it was in their own interests to support the interests of these elites. A collaborative trust relationship with local business communities, well represented on legislative councils, was crucial for the convenience of their work and the smooth running of their colonies on which their reputation at the Colonial Office rested. It could also reap personal benefits. Elites determined their social status and reputation, both in the colony and, through extended social networks, in Britain, and could provide valuable directorships on their retirement from public service.

Given their geographical distance from the United Kingdom and from the control of the Colonial Office, and their short tenure of office, there was thus a danger that governors would commit moral hazard and support policies that, although beneficial to the local elite and by extension to themselves, would in the long term lead to unbalanced colonial accounts.[6] Moreover, they and their staff could even succumb to personal moral hazard i.e. fraud, which would cause further damage to the standing of the secretary of state and weaken the legitimacy of British rule in the eyes of both ruled and rulers. Obviously it was in the interests of the Colonial Office to minimise such behaviour. But, at the same time, it was important that in so doing it avoided damaging both its relationships with governors and local elites and governor – elite collaboration. Strong bonds of trust with governors inhibited moral hazard, the support of business elites was essential for successful colonial development, governor – elite collaboration reduced the cost of administration, and any resistance from governors and elites to Colonial Office policy initiatives could greatly increase the work of officials, lead to political embarrassment and damage the legitimacy of the empire.

The organisational form used to deliver the Agents' services was determined by the Colonial Office's wish to forward its own interests and to subsume the moral hazard of material, service and capital suppliers and colonial governors, whilst maintaining a trust relationship with the latter. Theoretically the Agents' duties could have been performed by staff in the colonies or at the Colonial Office. The former avenue was rejected because there was a likelihood that colonial governments would act only in the interests of their colonies and consume non-United Kingdom manufactures, services and capital. Use of the Agency as a monitor also allowed the Colonial Office to minimise moral hazard in the colonies that could lead to unbalanced accounts. By forcing colonial governments to obtain all non-locally produced goods through the Agents, who monitored all requisitions, and by giving the

---

6   Governorships generally lasted only 5 to 6 years, presumably to prevent the development of even stronger relationships between governors and elites.

Agents control over the construction of infrastructure, the Colonial Office prevented colonial over-expenditure. Likewise, the issue of all London loans through the Agents and their organisation of short-term borrowings from banks and colonial funds held in the United Kingdom stopped colonies raising finance without the secretary of state's knowledge.[7]

Use of the Crown Agents similarly reduced the likelihood of fraud and moral hazard by material, capital and service providers. It was far easier for the colonial secretary to monitor the activities of one British agency than those of many agents, most of whom would operate from the colonies. And, just as he used the Agents to monitor the colonies, he could use colonial governments to monitor the Crown Agents. As regards supplier duplicity, it appears unlikely that colonial governments could have established trust relationships with providers of material, capital and service. The lack of face-to-face interaction, the differences in social backgrounds and the intermittent nature of their business dealings would have precluded the development of trust. The cost of self-interested behaviour and the various safeguards necessary to protect against it, for example monitoring and litigation, would therefore have been high. The Agents, acting as trust intermediators, bridged this absence of trust. With similar backgrounds to colonial governors, with whom they often had close professional and personal relationships, they were trusted by the colonies. At the same time, long-term business relationships and often personal and family connections ensured that they possessed the trust of material, capital and service suppliers, who were less inclined to resort to duplicity. Acting for all colonies, they also accumulated experience and knowledge and could reap economies of scale and standardisation.

In theory, of course, the services could have been provided and the colonies monitored by the Colonial Office itself. This did not occur, again because it was not in that office's interests. The cost of the Agency would have had to have been met from imperial funds, and the colonies would have resented the apparent diminution of their independence, damaging their support for empire. Colonial Office officials, in any case, did not possess the skills or the inclination necessary to perform the work. They would have been unable to issue loans without giving them an implicit imperial guarantee of repayment, and, having different backgrounds and no personal links with suppliers, would have had difficulty in establishing the requisite trust relationships. The work, furthermore, was relatively mundane and politically unimportant compared to policy-making. The Crown Agents' quasi-independent status also proved useful to the Office. It reduced the damage to its trust relationship with colonies and elites that could arise from the mini-

---

[7] To provide the Agents with an incentive to ensure that all goods and loans were purchased and issued through them and monitored, purchase and issue fees were in the form of commission.

misation of colonial moral hazard and the poor performance of the Agents' services; it allowed the secretary of state to circumvent Britain's ethos of free trade and ensure that colonies consumed United Kingdom goods and capital; and it permitted the Colonial Office to behave in a self-interested manner.[8] Officials could push forward development projects with little scrutiny or interference from the Treasury, parliament or the press, offer favours to politically powerful colonial interest groups, and exercise patronage through the recommendations of candidates for Crown Agent clerical posts.

Agency interests and institutional moral hazard

The way in which the Agents performed their work was determined by their principals' interests, the methods by which these interests were fulfilled and by their own interests and goals. Any assessment of the performance of their duties must therefore be divided into two periods, the line between them drawn at the point when the Colonial Office decided to achieve its goals through the development of the crown colonies. The Agents, like their actual and supposed principals, sought to maximise their income, power, prestige, convenience and security. This was achieved through the adoption of three goals. First they wished to ensure the survival of the Agency. All were well aware of the precariousness of its existence and the uniqueness and vividness of past crises probably led them to overestimate the chances of its disappearance. In 1859 the provision of a poor service prompted many self-governing colonies to abandon the Agency, driving it to near bankruptcy. A Treasury decision, thirty years later, that the Agents should no longer act for responsible government colonies again led to a severe contraction in their business, and the loss of their work for the Transvaal in 1907 forced them to lay off staff.[9] On a more personal level, each Agent was warned in his letter of appointment that his salary was 'dependent on the contributions derived from the various colonies' and was 'liable to reduction' if incomes failed to cover costs.[10] In 1900, meanwhile, the Agents Maurice Cameron and William Mercer were informed that the secretary of state was 'unable to guarantee . . . promotion . . . as the arrangements and the organisation of the Agency may be subject to reconsideration from time to time'.[11]

The second goal was the expansion of the Agency and its income. The 'keenness' of Sir Ernest Blake, a Senior Crown Agent, was that he was

---

[8]   Acting as a 'buffer to shield' the secretary of state from colonial complaint, the Agents also ensured that his office retained its government reputation: PPE, q. 2233.
[9]   PPE, q. 2189.
[10] Herbert to Blake, 28 Jan. 1881, Sir Ernest Blake papers (c/o J. A. Sibbald, 7 Wilfred Street, Simonstown, South Africa).
[11] CO to CAs, 5 June 1900, PRO, CAOG 16/160.

'earning for the Office' and his 'great anxiety . . . [was] . . . to make the Office a success'.[12] One of his predecessor's, Sir Penrose Julyan, similarly believed that 'an office of this kind cannot stand still. It will either go on increasing or it will some day become . . . nearly extinct'.[13] A high income led to a large reserve fund, which reduced the likelihood of bankruptcy if receipts fell and ensured the payment of Agent and staff pensions. Growth enabled the Agents to acquire power and prestige and led to higher salaries and fringe benefits. It also increased the likelihood of survival. The performance of a greater number and variety of tasks made the Agents more useful to the secretary of state, and stretched and thus weakened the Colonial Office's monitoring abilities; a reputation for success, derived from growth, facilitated co-operation and satisfaction in the colonies; and organisational changes could be more easily accomplished, and headquarters occupied that generated 'that confidence and respect which a Crown Agency . . . ought to command'.[14]

Thirdly, the Agents wished to increase 'the excitement and interest of the work'.[15] As their salaries were determined by the Colonial Office, pay rises were finite. After their incomes had reached the level beyond which further increases were unlikely, they consequently placed greater emphasis on non-pecuniary activities, in particularly the adoption of more intellectually satisfying work. Most of them, as former Colonial Office clerks, had performed such work before they joined the Agency, and, if they did it well enough, they were likely to gain promotion to Colonial Office under-secretary.[16] They thus took on a greater variety of tasks, increasingly became involved in policy-making, for example decisions on the construction of infrastructure and the negotiation of concession agreements, and hived off boring routine tasks to shipping agents, solicitors etc. Further advantages of this strategy were that policy decisions were more opaque than those relating to business and therefore less subject to criticism, and that out-sourcing diffused complaint. Moreover, by gaining a greater influence on policy, the Agents could promote colonial economic expansion, which by increasing local government demand for the Agency's services increased its income.

For most of the nineteenth century, the Crown Agents achieved these goals through the provision of quality goods and services and by ensuring the

---

12 PPE, q. 1250.

13 CAs to CO, 25 July 1876, CO 323/327/8924. The same view was expressed by the Agent Sir William Mercer, who believed that 'the Crown Agents . . . have to make the Office pay and they are eager to secure business': PPE, q. 2210.

14 CAs to CO, 15 Jan. 1859, CO 323/254/587. The Agents believed that their Cannon Row building 'was not respectable and bears very unfavourable comparison with most London offices of any standing': ibid.

15 PPE, q. 1272.

16 In 1901 the Senior Agent, Sir Montague Ommanney, was appointed under-secretary of state at the Colonial Office.

full subscription of loans. The survival and growth of the Agency was dependent on colonial satisfaction with the performance of its duties. If discontented, the colonies would complain to the Colonial Office, which would be disinclined to extend the Agents' tasks, and, wishing to maintain its relationships with governors and local elites might eventually take action to restrict their independence or close down the Agency. Colonial satisfaction, in turn, depended on the provision of quality goods, services and infrastructure, and on the successful flotation of loans. Governors were easily able to monitor quality and the success of flotations and were highly averse to defective supplies and unsuccessful issues, which ultimately damaged business communities. A bias towards quality and fully subscribed loans also increased the Agency's income, which permitted growth and the performance of policy-making tasks for no fee. (As the market for the Agency's services was constrained by colonial government demand, it could not raise its income through its own direct efforts.) The premium charged for quality services led to higher purchasing earnings, and successful loan issues ensured the receipt of the whole of the Agents' issue commission and subsequent loan management fees, and, by financing infrastructure construction, increased their purchasing workload.

To ensure the provision of a quality service and fully subscribed loans, the Crown Agents occasionally acted against the interests of the Colonial Office and other principals, and, more importantly, minimised their subagents' quality moral hazard. This was achieved in a number of ways. The Crown Agents restricted competition by choosing agents with whom they often had family or social relationships. This reduced the likelihood of adverse selection, encouraged the development of trust relationships, and, as relatives could monitor their fellow agents, facilitated monitoring. Secondly, they tended to employ high status agents whose future work depended on the maintenance of their reputation for quality and probity, who relied upon the Agency for a large part of their turnover and who would go out of business if dismissed. Once recruited, these people were closely monitored by the Agents' paid inspectors, other agents or fellow principals. To increase the cost of dismissal for opportunism, they were sometimes required to provide sureties and were either paid a premium for their services or permitted to charge excessively high prices i.e. to commit benign moral hazard, which additionally helped to engender trust and quality reciprocity. Generally, they were employed for long periods – fifty years was not unusual. Long relationships allowed the Crown Agents to accumulate sufficient experience of their agents' actions to allow them to predict the existence of dishonesty, and, through repeated personal interactions, to build up social ties and a store of goodwill that encouraged trust. This also increased the cost to the agent of opportunism or providing poor quality services. Agents dismissed for impropriety would lose the future gains of subsequent transactions, both with the Crown Agents and those clients encouraged to use their services by their status as Crown Agent suppliers and service providers, and would be left with

Figure 3. Office reserve fund, 1856–1914

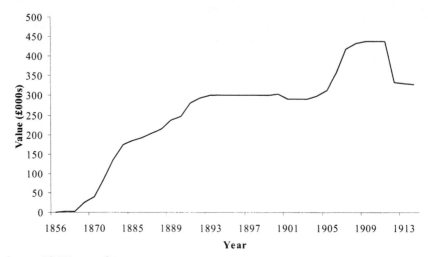

Source: CO 323 series; CA accounts.

Note: For before 1884 only figures for 1856, 1860, 1863, 1867, 1870, 1875 and 1879 are available.

physical and human capital highly specific to the Agency for which there was little market demand.[17]

These practices, of course, greatly increased the cost of goods, services and loans. Monitoring was expensive, the limited use of competition prevented the testing of prices, and high status agents charged a premium for their services. The Colonial Office and colonies, however, partly satisficing, accepted the price moral hazard, which they regarded as benign. The extra expense was far smaller than the potential cost of the supply of substandard goods, the failure of loans and the non-construction of infrastructure. Both also had difficulty monitoring costs. In 1870 the auditing of the Agents' colonial accounts passed from the auditor-general to the colonies, which, like the Colonial Office, lacked the commercial and financial expertise required to check material and loan prices.[18] Furthermore, they could be confident that the Agents, in return, would not divulge their own moral hazard – the purchase of goods from local merchants by colonial administrators and the

---

[17] Long-term relationships were particularly important in the case of firms that produced experience goods, the quality of which could only be discovered after use.

[18] Short-term contracts, promotions between colonies and long periods of leave meant that there was little continuity of European personnel, who were often of poor quality; and, in West Africa, lower grade clerks were mostly poorly trained Africans: P. H. S. Hatton, 'British colonial policy in Africa, 1910–14', unpubl. PhD diss. Cambridge 1971, 19; D. D. Bush, 'The Colonial Office and the making of British policy towards Sierra Leone, 1865–98: a case study in the bureaucracy of imperialism', unpubl. PhD diss. Cambridge 1978, 72.

Figure 4. Office account surpluses and deficits, 1864–1914

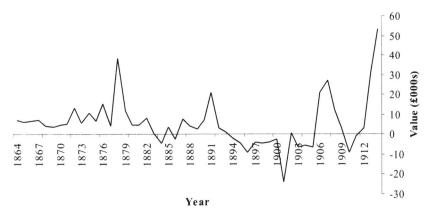

Source: CO 323 series; CA accounts.

Notes: Surplus/deficit = net receipts (total receipts – balance – transfers from Office Reserve Fund) – net expenditure (total expenditure – balance in hand – transfers to Office Reserve Fund).

Colonial Office's favouritism towards colonial businessmen such as Sir Alfred Jones.

The Agents' concentration on quality and full subscription ceased in the mid-1890s. Agency income surpluses were channelled into an invested reserve fund, which met pension costs and financed deficits. Owing to the supply of quality goods and successful loan issues, a 1886 increase in charges and economic growth in the colonies, this fund grew rapidly (*see* fig. 3).[19] Easily monitored, its growth was noted by the Treasury and in 1893 the Colonial Office, fearing criticism, told the Agents to cut their loan and other fees and allowed them to increase staff numbers and salaries. The resultant fall in income, however, was far greater than expected, and the Agents began to make losses (*see* fig. 4). The Agents' financial situation then worsened, largely due to the Colonial Office's new policy of promoting colonial development. The organisation of infrastructure construction and the adoption of other development tasks for which the Agents received no remuneration increased costs, and the Colonial Office's attempts to obtain imperial funds for infrastructure construction and the subsequent collapse of the loan market led to a halt in the issue of loans and a loss of issue income. Since there was a greater likelihood of the Agency going bankrupt than of it being closed down because of criticism from the colonies, the Agents, perhaps displaying some inter-temporal inconsistency, increasingly began to concentrate on the maximisation of their income. The moral hazard that resulted

[19] Charges were raised to offset the effect on the Agency's income of the loss in 1880 of financial work for the self-governing colonies.

greatly increased the cost of supplies, issues and infrastructure, led to the construction of poor quality railways and the failure of loans and came to be regarded by both the Colonial Office and colonies as malign. Prevented by the Agents from buying goods locally, colonial administrations began to criticise the Agents' performance, and, in 1908, the secretary of state set up an enquiry into the Agency, which recommended various organisational changes that were subsequently put into effect.

Personal moral hazard: Crown Agents and staff

As well as the risk of institutional self-interested behaviour, the Colonial Office faced the problem of personal moral hazard on the part of both the Agents and their staff. To avoid the pecuniary and political cost of major Agent fraud, it adopted a number of strategies to minimise such impropriety. To limit duplicity on the part of Crown Agent staff, it made the Agents financially responsible for any loss suffered by their clerks, an obligation that, along with their wish to provide a quality service and avoid any scandal that could lead to the Agency's disappearance, prompted the Agents to introduce their own strategies to counter opportunism.

Strategies to minimise Crown Agent personal moral hazard
The Colonial Office discouraged personal moral hazard by the Crown Agents through targeted recruitment, the provision of securities, monitoring and the payment of high salaries.[20] Of the nine men who acted as Agents from 1833 to 1914, seven had served in the Colonial Office, one, Cameron, in the colonial service and four in the colonies (see appendix 1, table 2). Before appointment, the secretary of state thus had a great deal of information about the abilities and honesty of each of them, and they turn had learnt and internalised the ethical culture of the Colonial Office and were acquainted with the current Crown Agents.[21] In addition, new Agents had some knowledge of the Agency's operations and the problems and needs of principals, and, more important for the Colonial Office, were aware of the wider political aspects of its activities.

The Agents, similarly, shared common backgrounds. Most had been brought up in upper middle-class families in the south-east of England, had professional fathers and had been educated at public schools as members of the Church of England. They, therefore, had assimilated the gentlemanly

[20] Opportunism was also probably discouraged by its likely impact on the Agents' institutional goals. Scandal could lead to criticism of the Agency and force the Colonial Office to reduce its power or even close it down.

[21] Although he never worked at the Colonial Office, Cameron was acquainted with Ommanney, who had been one of his instructors at the Royal Military Academy, and had corresponded with Blake: Sir Maurice Cameron papers (c/o Lt Col. J. A. Cameron, 22 Butterfield House, Bromyard, Herts), memoirs, 131.

ethos of fair play and honesty, though, as will be seen, what constituted honesty varied according to the norms of the society in which a gentlemen found himself, and perhaps shared the missionary zeal for the 'civilisation' of the colonies generated by the evangelical and Oxford movements.[22] They were also able to form strong trust relationships with governors and Colonial Office officials, who in many respects had similar, though far more elitist backgrounds, and with whom they had regular official and social contact.[23] All often belonged to the same clubs, and, at least Cameron and Ommanney, counted a number of governors as close friends.[24] At the same time, as will be discussed in chapters 2, 3 and 6, the Agents had close personal and professional links and shared some background characteristics with industrialists and those employed in the City. Few of the Agents had attended Oxbridge or any university, and many came from the lower ranks of the upper middle classes; in the case of Blake, from the middle classes. They were therefore able to form equally strong trust relationships with many of those who provided the colonies with capital, materials and services.

Securities were introduced at the suggestion of the Audit Office in 1830, after it was discovered that the Trinidad agent had defrauded the colony.[25] On entering the Office, each Agent was required to provide a bond of £4,000 and a further £2,000 from a third party, generally a friend or relative.[26] This at first protected only the crown colonies against loss by the Crown Agents and their staff, but from 1863, when the total amount required was increased to £10,000, responsible government clients could also claim compensation from the Agents.[27] The advantages of the bonds were that they increased the financial cost of opportunism and dismissal and added a social cost, in that the loss suffered by the third party would damage the Agent's relationship with that individual and ensure that any malpractice would probably become common knowledge in the social circles in which he moved. They also encouraged the Agents to guard against staff misdemeanour and minimised the problems of adverse selection. Only candidates with no intention of acting immorally would be willing to provide bonds, and the readiness of third parties to provide securities testified to the prospective Agent's reputation for trustworthiness. The use of sureties, however, had a number of draw-

[22] At least towards the end of his life, Blake was particularly religious: personal communication from R. Sibball to author, 25 Oct. 1994. From 1920 to 1925 Antrobus was a member of the National Assembly of the Church of England, and, for the following ten years, a member of its Central Board of Finance: *Who's who*, London 1936.

[23] J. M. Carland, *The Colonial Office and Nigeria, 1898–1914*, London 1985, 22.

[24] Cameron's governor friends included Sir Walter Egerton, governor of Nigeria and British Guiana; Sir H. G. Maccallum, governor of Lagos, Natal and Ceylon; and Sir William Maxwell, governor of the Gold Coast: Cameron memoirs, 81, 86, 103; CO 323/538. Because of the paucity of face-to-face meetings, the Agents' trust relationships with most governors were probably weaker than those with Colonial Office officials.

[25] AO to Treasury, 29 Oct. 1829, CO 323/208, 147.

[26] CO to CAs, 27 Aug. 1830, CO 324/146/260.

[27] CO to Treasury, 3 July 1863, CO 309/65/4813.

backs, and, in 1900, the Colonial Office principal clerk, G. V. Fiddes, admitted that he had 'no belief in the system'.[28] The Colonial Office failed to monitor the continued availability of third party sureties. They thus did not notice that the insurance company that provided Julyan's security had gone bankrupt until ten years after the event.[29] On the one occasion Agents were fined, the deterrent effect of the bonds was weakened by the fact that the sums were paid into the office reserve fund, and therefore, by increasing the financial security of the Agency, benefited the Agents. The bonds also failed to cover the maximum possible loss, reduced Crown Agent morale and may have discouraged potential Agents from putting themselves forward for or accepting positions.

The Colonial Office monitored the Agency's activities through the crown colonies, new Agents – though self-interest caused these to switch their allegiance to the Agency – those relatives and friends who were appointed Crown Agent clerks, and, from 1901, Sir Montague Ommanney, the former Senior Crown Agent who was promoted to permanent under-secretary of state. In addition, they required the Agents to obtain authorisation for their most important acts and to provide information on the completion of each piece of work. From 1875 to 1903 they could also physically monitor the Crown Agents, who occupied offices rented from them in Downing Street.[30] Unfortunately, most colonial complaints were sent to the geographical departments of the Colonial Office, which often did not pass them on to the general department, the direct supervisor of the Agency, and, grossly understaffed until 1900, the office failed to investigate criticisms fully.[31] Moreover, Sir Reginald Antrobus, the head of the general department and from 1898 the assistant under-secretary of state, favoured the Agents, influenced perhaps by the fact that his brother, E. G. Antrobus, was their chief clerk and accountant, and Ommanney, throughout his time at the Colonial Office, acted as their apologist.[32] On a higher level, before 1870, the Agents also had to provide the Colonial Office with monthly accounts, accompanied by the relevant documentation, which were audited by the auditor-general. The Treasury's refusal to pay for the full audit of an office not financed by the imperial government, however, meant that from 1870 only those accounts of colonies in receipt of grants-in-aid were fully audited by the government audit. The accounts of other colonies were audited by colonial accounting departments, which often lacked the personnel and expertise to scrutinise

[28] Fiddes note, 6 Mar. 1900, CO 323/452/6740.
[29] Julyan to CO, 23 Jan. 1877, CO 323/331/913.
[30] CAs to CO, 13 July 1875, CO 323/322/7847. In 1902 the Agents moved to Whitehall Gardens, and in 1916 to Millbank: Abbott, Short history, 28, 34.
[31] The Colonial Office was aware of the problem: Round note, 13 Dec. 1908, CO 323/545/10303; Bush, 'The Colonial Office', 16.
[32] During his time as under-secretary, Ommanney received a £200 per annum pension from the Agents: Hansard, 4th ser. 1904, cxxxvi. 693.

expenditure effectively.[33] As for the Agency's own accounts, those received by the Colonial Office in 1880 demonstrated 'a fictitious control over the Agents' expenditure', and, even after the Colonial Office had demanded the provision of more information, they remained inadequate.[34] Until 1905 the Agency was subject only to a protective audit, which merely ensured that money had been expended for sanctioned purposes.[35] Thereafter, a full audit was undertaken, but its effectiveness was weakened by the Colonial Office's insistence that, in order to maintain the Agency's discretion, authority for expenditure should be limited to proof that a sum had been paid.[36]

The early Agents' salaries were relatively high. In 1833 Baillie was paid £800 *per annum* and Barnard £600 *per annum*.[37] In addition, they were allowed to hold five paid directorships between them.[38] Because of the weak financial state of the Agency, however, on the appointment of Julyan and Sargeaunt, these rates were reduced to £600 and £500 *per annum* respectively on the understanding that if the new recruits brought the Agency 'into a healthy condition, the sacrifice . . . [that they] . . . had reluctantly made would be substantially acknowledged'.[39] In 1870 Julyan and Sargeaunt consequently requested major salary increases. Although they had received higher pay in 1863 to compensate them for the provision of larger sureties, they claimed that they still obtained less than their predecessors, who had performed less arduous work, and considerably lower wages than agents-general, each of whom represented just one colony.[40] Both claims were somewhat disingenuous. The salaries quoted for Barnard and Baillie included their Colonial Office pensions and the position of agent-general was not comparable to that of Crown Agent. Agents-general 'were removable at a moment's notice or whenever their political opponents are in power', and were usually men of high standing, who received no pension and had the added expense of setting up a second home in Britain.[41] The secretary of state nevertheless acted on

[33] In 1908, for example, the auditing system used in Sierra Leone, Gambia and Uganda had to be replaced as 'the native clerks to whom the actual working details are necessarily entrusted are not competent as a rule to carry out satisfactorily the procedures which such a system involves': Audit department to CO, 7 Mar. 1908, CO 323/545/8367.
[34] Blake note, 11 Feb. 1880, CO 323/343/1054; CO to CAs, 5 June 1880, ibid; CO to CAs, 12 Aug. 1884, CAA, CA M 5.
[35] CO to auditor-general, 10 July 1905, CAA, CA 73/4.
[36] Ibid.
[37] Note, 8 May 1858, CO 323/252/4453.
[38] CAs to CO, 4 May 1854, CO 323/241. If Barnard and Baillie earned the minimum directors' payment (one guinea per meeting), Barnard's directorships would have increased his income by £298 *per annum* and Baillie's by £52 *per annum*: ibid; anon, *The City or the physiology of London business*, London 1845, 81.
[39] CAs to CO, 3 Mar. 1870, CO 323/299/2437.
[40] CAs to CO, 14 May 1863, CO 309/65/4813; CAs to CO, 3 Mar. 1870, CO 323/299/2437.
[41] Note, 9 Mar. 1870, CO 323/299/2437.

the Agents' requests, increasing the Senior Agent's maximum salary to £1,200 *per annum* and that of the Second Agent to £1,000.[42]

Subsequent increases caused the Agents' annual remuneration to rise to levels far higher than those paid to their counterparts in the civil service (*see* appendix 1, table 4), although 'much lower than those of the principal officers of banks and insurance officers', who, in 1908, 'earned £3,000 or £4,000 or more'.[43] Ommanney, as colonial under-secretary, argued that the salaries were reasonable.[44] The premium over civil service incomes reflected the relative insecurity of their employment and greater responsibilities, whereas their relatively low pay as compared to the private sector was compensated by their greater security, generous pension rights and the 'recognition of their services in forms other than mere salary', that is in titular awards and status.[45] Others at the Colonial Office, though, had 'long . . . [had] . . . the impression' that the payments were 'unduly high'.[46] It was pointed out that the Agents earned more than those in equivalent posts at the India Office, War Office and Admiralty, that their position was as secure as that of most civil servants, and that much of their work was routine and required little business experience. In response, on the resignation of Sir Ernest Blake, the Colonial Office reduced the Senior Agents' salaries by £700 to £1,800 *per annum*.[47]

In fact, the salary premium earned by the Agents appears to have had little to do with job security or skill, but rather was designed to increase the cost of opportunism, with the Senior Agent's salary only being cut when, after the reorganisation of the Agency, opportunism became less likely.[48] Earnings were higher than those received by officials in the India Office, War Office and Admiralty because the work of these departments could be more easily monitored, and were lower than those in the private sector because dismissed Agents would be unable to obtain equivalent positions in the City.[49]

Crown Agent personal moral hazard

Despite the Crown Agents' non-compensatory wages and other safeguards, some Agent personal moral hazard did occur.[50] In 1872 the Agents Penrose

[42] CO to CAs, 21 Mar. 1870, CO 323/299/2437. Julyan was also given a £200 *per annum* personal allowance: ibid.
[43] CAs to CO, 10 May 1894, CO 323/396/8119; Harris note, 15 June 1908, CO 323/ 538/5221,
[44] Ommanney to Lyttelton, 15 Aug. 1904, CO 323/499/28851.
[45] Ibid.
[46] Harris note, 15 Dec. 1908, CO 323/548/45741.
[47] Hopwood to Antrobus, 29 June 1909, CO 323/562/12420.
[48] In 1870 Sir R. Herbert acknowledged that it was a 'dangerous economy to underpay an Office exposed to great temptation': Herbert note, Sept. 1870, CO 323/299/181.
[49] The War Office and Admiralty bought a restricted range of articles, the India Office shipped goods only to India and the issue of India Office loans was largely undertaken by the Bank of England.
[50] In 1870 the under-secretary Sir Robert Herbert accepted that, given 'the gains which might be made by unprincipled men in . . . [the Agents'] . . . position . . . a few hundred per

Julyan and William Sargeaunt purchased with their own funds and without Colonial Office permission the lease of the building adjacent to the Agency, which they proposed to rent to themselves in their official Crown Agent capacities.[51] Julyan later accepted commissions for the issue of several New Zealand loans without the colonial secretary's sanction, and it seems likely that the Agents favoured those relatives that they employed in their Agency and as their shipping agents and solicitors.[52]

The Agents succumbed to personal moral hazard for a number of reasons. Inter-temporally inconsistent, they may have considered only the short-term advantages of their actions. Given the small amount of money involved they could also be confident that the Colonial Office would not dismiss them for their impropriety. Equally, since any loss in the quality of the service provided was likely to be relatively small, they could discount the resulting colonial criticism, which would be correspondingly weak, or even not forthcoming.[53] As regards the possible costs of guilt and moral self-disgust that often has to be paid by those who commit such acts, Blake and Julyan appear to have possessed lax private norms, and Julyan's conscience was probably assuaged by his belief that the Colonial Office had broken its agreement to fully compensate him for rescuing the Agency.[54] By 1908, moreover, the Agency saw itself as a 'mercantile firm doing work for the government, but outside the government service'.[55] The Agents thus judged themselves by the ethical social norms of the private sector and the City, where such behaviour was common practice and accepted.

The colonies seem to have known nothing about the Agents' activities. In the case of serious misdemeanours, the Colonial Office merely reprimanded the Crown Agents responsible and sought to prevent recurrence by strengthening its safeguards, in particular by raising the Agents' wages and therefore further increasing the cost of opportunism.[56] None of the Agents were

annum additional salary . . . [will] . . . not operate to make a doubtful man honest': Herbert note, Sept. 1870, CO 323/299/181.

[51] CAs to CO, 22 Jan. 1873, CO 323/313/630. The Agents were instructed to arrange for the building to be purchased by the Agency at no profit to themselves: CO to Hunt, 31 Mar. 1873, CO 431/30/2350; Treasury to CO, 9 May 1873, CO 431/30/4348.

[52] These incidences are discussed in chapter 7 below. An early colonial agent also acted dishonestly. In 1828 it was discovered that the Trinidad agent, Henry Cutler, had defrauded the colony of £2,984: AO to Treasury, 29 Oct. 1828, CO 323/208, fos 145–6; Treasury to Hay, 15 Nov. 1828, ibid. fos 146–52.

[53] The marginal utility gained from their actions was therefore greater and more certain than the marginal utility they would lose from a reduction in quality and possible colonial criticism.

[54] Julyan to CO, 14 July 1879, CO 323/339/18599.

[55] PPR, p. vi. See also CAs to CO, 13 Dec. 1903, CO 323/393/21057. The CAs may also have absorbed the private sector's relatively greater desire for immediate gratification, which reduced their willingness to resist short-term advantages in favour of long-term goals.

[56] In 1876, for example, after the loans commissions scandal, the salaries of the Senior Agent and Second Agent were increased by £300 per annum and £200 per annum respectively on condition that no further sums were accepted: Meade note, 22 Feb. 1876,

punished, as public acknowledgement of corruption would have damaged the reputation of the colonial secretary, the social elites to which the Agents and their Colonial Office counterparts belonged and the legitimacy of the empire. As regards Agents showing favouritism towards their relatives, Colonial Office officials turned a blind eye. The Agents accepted that office's own close relationships with individuals such as Sir Alfred Jones, and a social norm of late nineteenth-century government was that it was legitimate to take no action on private knowledge which was not in the public domain.[57] It was also understood that the employment of relatives minimised staff and service provider adverse selection and moral hazard, and that any loss from preferential treatment was likely to be less than that which would follow if friends and relatives were not employed. In addition, favouritism and its loss on dismissal further increased the cost to the Crown Agents of more serious opportunism, and Colonial Office tolerance of its existence created obligations that helped to build networks of trust and reciprocity between the Colonial Office and the Crown Agents.

Strategies to minimise Crown Agent staff personal moral hazard

Compared to the staff of the War Office purchasing department, the clerks employed by the Crown Agents appear to have been relatively honest.[58] Minor corruption, however, was not unknown, and may have been accepted by the Agents in order to increase the cost of major fraud and subsequent dismissal and to build up networks of mutual trust with their clerks. Staff obtained Christmas boxes and presents from suppliers, gave information to dealers regarding the issue of stamps, and in 1907 sold thousands of unsold stamps removed from Crown Agent correspondence to dealers, receiving in return up to a third of their face value.[59] To minimise major corruption and reduce shirking, the Agents recruited only candidates whose honesty and abilities were verifiable, adopted a number of pecuniary incentives, required some staff to provide bonds, closely monitored work and attempted to create an ethical office culture. It was also made clear that any clerk discovered acting fraudulently would be dismissed and subjected to legal action under the 1899 Official Secrets Act and the 1906 Prevention of Corruption Act.[60]

CO 537/218. In 1892 wages were raised to compensate the Agents for the loss of the personal fees earned from their coolie emigration work: CAA, CA M 38. See also Ommanney to Lyttelton, 15 Aug. 1904, CO 323/499/28851.

[57] Jeffery Butler, *The liberal party and the Jameson Raid*, Oxford 1996, 362.

[58] In their report the Select Committee on War Office Contracts concluded that they had 'received evidence in some cases in which bribes were offered and . . . [had] . . . heard a few cases where bribes may have been accepted': PP 1900, ix (313), ix. Admiralty and Post Office purchasing staff also occasionally accepted bribes: Admiralty to CO, 7 June 1901, CO 323/464/19615; Post Office to War Office, 21 Apr. 1901, CO 323/470/16166.

[59] CAA, office memorandum book, vol. 1, 21 Dec. 1905; 2 Mar. 1906; 4 Mar. 1907; *Gibbons' Stamp Weekly* v (1907), pt 8, 128. All these practices were halted by Sir Ernest Blake.

[60] CAA, office memorandum book, vol. 1, 1 Jan. 1907; 4 Mar. 1907. See also PPE, q. 1044.

Provided that they kept within the Colonial Office limit on the maximum amount that could be spent on employees, the Agents had complete discretion over who should be employed and on individual staff salaries.[61] Before 1900 recruitment was 'a matter chiefly of friends of the Crown Agents and soldier clerks', 'many' from Ommanney's 'old Corps'.[62] In addition, the Agents employed candidates recommended by their own staff and by Colonial Office officials, generally 'the sons of colonial governors, [and] people who have done good work for the country' (see table 2).[63] Such recruitment was normal practice in the private sector and not unusual in the Civil Service, even after 1870.[64] Its main advantages were that it reduced search costs – the cost of discovering suitable employees – and minimised adverse selection. The Agents had personal knowledge of the capabilities and honesty of their friends and relatives, and, in the case of Ommanney, former army subordinates. They could easily discover the abilities of other soldier clerks from their army records and could be confident that their staff would recommend competent candidates, as each clerk was aware that 'he would incur a very severe responsibility if he said that he had a very smart lad he knew and that lad did not turn out smart'.[65] The possibility that their offspring could join its staff also no doubt discouraged governors and Colonial Office officials from criticising the Agency.

A further advantage of this method of employment was that it reduced the likelihood of moral hazard. Personal relationships between the Agents, staff and Colonial Office officials and the new employees increased the social cost of opportunism, and the employment of the relatives of existing clerks and army clerks, who already possessed a set of shared values, contributed to the establishment within the Agency of a culture of trust. There is evidence, however, that in their treatment of staff the Agents favoured those clerks recommended by themselves and the Colonial Office, although these may not have been the most productive members of the Agency. The punishment of such employees carried a social and political cost, their advancement a social and political gain and the resultant increase in the Agents' marginal utility was far greater and certain than any marginal utility lost through greater inefficiency and complaints from the colonies. In letters to the press

61 CAs to CO, 14 Jan. 1880, CAA, CA M 5.
62 PPE, qq. 1952, 2570. The soldier clerks had all previously been non-commissioned army officers. They were first employed by Sir Julyan Penrose, a former assistant commissary-general of the army commissariat: *British biographical index*, London 1990; PPE, q. 128.
63 PPE, qq. 117, 1656.
64 J. M. Bourne, *Patronage and society in nineteenth century England*, London 1986, 115. Although civil servants were recruited through open competition, from 1870 patronage survived in the more specialist departments, such as the Board of Agriculture, and in the Post Office until 1907. The Colonial Office and Foreign Office exercised political patronage in the appointment of governors and consuls until the end of the century: ibid. 41, 95, 187. Even today, patronage is widely practised in the City, and allegedly in the selection of quango members.
65 PPE, q. 143.

Table 2
Some family and social relationships of Crown Agents and staff

Employee	Relationship
W. Anderson, clerk, 1901–6	Son of E. G. Anderson, clerk, 1878–91
E. G. Antrobus, assistant accountant, 1879–93, chief clerk and accountant, 1893–1920	Recommended by Sir William Sargeaunt. Brother of Sir Reginald Antrobus, CA 1909–18. Grandfather, the Revd Robert Gream, was Sir Montague Ommanney's great-uncle and grandfather-in-law
Miss E. M. Blyth, lady clerk, 1895–1914	Niece by marriage of Sir Ernest Blake
Miss M. E. Boddy, lady clerk, 1879–1908, head of stock and coupon department, 1908	Recruited through 'Sir Montague Ommanney . . . [knowing] . . . someone I knew'
Miss A. E. Boddy, lady clerk, 1891–5, head of correspondence branch ,1906	Step-sister of Miss M. E. Boddy
E. J. H. Boose, clerk, 1901–21	Employed 'on the recommendation of the late Sir Robert Herbert and Sir Montague Ommanney'
J. Chadwick, Jr, clerk, 1879–99	Son of J. Chadwick, clerk, 1875–80
F. W. Deakin, City office clerk, 1886–1914	Son of W. Deakin, office keeper, 1886–1909
F. H. H. Graves, clerk, 1900–5	Recommended by Colonial Office. Son of colonial official, 'who had lost his life in the colonial service'
A. C. Knollys, clerk, 1902–5	Recommended by Colonial Office. Son of a former governor of Trinidad
A. Reeves, clerk, 1910	Recommended by Frederic Shelford, his former employer and a Crown Agent consulting engineer
A. St George Sargeaunt, clerk, 1882–3	Son of Sir William Sargeaunt
Edward Woodbine Sargeaunt, clerk, 1879–81	Son of Sir William Sargeaunt
H. F. Smith, clerk, 1894–1903, assistant cashier, 1904, head of general stores department, 1905	First cousin once removed of Sir Ernest Blake
William Henry Stanger, engineering clerk, 1873, general works inspector and chemical analyst, 1875–1902	Recommended by Sir William Sargeaunt, who, as colonial secretary of Natal, had been a colleague of his father, the Natal surveyor-general.
G. Wells, clerk, 1902–6	Recommended by Sir A. M. Rendel, his former employer and a Crown Agent consulting engineer
Norman Edward Ommanney Willis, clerk, 1892–1902	Relation of Sir Montague Ommanney

Source: memo, 5 Oct. 1908, CAOG 17/22;Wells to CAs, 6 Nov. 1901, CAOG 13/383; Boose to CAs, 4 Oct. 1919, CO 323/797/59112; PPE, qq. 2580, 3044, 3117, 113, 2792, 2796; CAA, staff register, i; CAs to CO, 7 Apr. 1911, weeded files, O/Sec 159; Minutes of the Proceedings of the Institution of Civil Engineers cliii (1902–3), 338; Sir Reginald.Antrobus, Antrobus pedigrees: the story of a Cheshire family, London 1929, 92; British biographical archive, London 1984. In 1922 E. G. Antrobus' brother married Anne Ommanney, a close relation of the CA Sir Montague Ommanney: Antrobus, Antrobus, 92.

in 1904, the Agents' clerks complained that the Agency was run by a 'family party', that salary increases and promotions went to those who least deserved them, and that 'favouritism alone rules the day'.[66]

Apart from the ex-army non-commissioned officers and the very occasional employment of men with special technical training, most of the clerks were recruited at between seventeen and nineteen years of age, immediately after leaving school.[67] The employment of young men reduced costs, contributed to the development of an Agency culture, as they were highly susceptible to influence, allowed the Agents to ensure that any clerk promoted to more difficult work possessed the required honesty and ability and, along with the rapid growth of its workload, caused the Agency to be staffed by relatively young employees, who were flexible and adaptable to change.[68] The majority had a minor public school education, which given the strong moral basis of teaching at such schools, may have increased the likelihood that they would be honest, and, since they shared a common set of values, encouraged the creation of an Agency culture.[69] 'University men' and boys recruited via the Civil Service Commissioners were avoided until the 1900s. Highly-educated clerks tended to be less efficient at routine work, 'would become desperately discontented and . . . would aspire to become Crown Agents', and were difficult to 'get rid off if they are not suitable'.[70] Those from the Civil Service Commissioners were insufficiently subservient, possessing 'a certain Trade Union feeling', and it required 'an earthquake' to dismiss them.[71] After recruitment, to prevent boredom and engrained moral hazard, male clerks were moved around the departments, staying in each for between five and ten years.[72] Few left the Office before retirement, the age of which was left open, and there were few dismissals.[73] This again encouraged the development of

66 *Pall Mall Gazette*, 17 Aug. 1904, 8; 20 Aug. 1904, 3; 1 Sept. 1904, 10. In 1909, for example, despite the Colonial Office's 'very great doubts', E. G. Antrobus, the chief clerk and accountant, was awarded a salary far above that attached to his post by his brother, the newly-appointed Senior CA Sir Reginald Antrobus: Harding note, 18 Nov. 1909, CO 323/553/37066.
67 PPR, p. viii. The engineering clerk, T. R. Marsh, and draughtsman and estimator, W. H. Lancaster, employed in respectively 1874 and 1879, had engineering qualifications; the clerk F. W. Deakin, recruited in 1895, had previously worked in the City; and the bookkeeper and accountant from 1879 to 1902, J. W. Leonard, had commercial experience: CAs to CO, 13 Sept. 1900, CO 323/453/29986; CAs to CO, 31 Jan. 1913, CO 323/608/3644; Deakin to CAs, 4 Sept. 1919, CO 323/797/55272; CAs to CO, 22 July 1902, CO 323/474/30615.
68 The average age of established male clerks in 1900 and 1910 was thirty-three and twenty-nine years respectively: *Colonial Office list*, 1900, 1910; CAA, staff register, vol. 1.
69 PPE, q. 129.
70 Ibid. qq. 23, 1180, 3930.
71 Ibid. qq. 1068, 1954.
72 Ibid. qq. 4522, 4528, 4559–67.
73 Ibid. qq. 1975, 1977. In 1886 the chief clerk finally retired at the age of seventy-four, and in 1891 the inspector of clothing and dry goods left the Office at the age of seventy-

trust relationships, though it may also have led to inflexibility and resistance to change in older employees.[74]

In the late 1890s the Agents reformed their recruitment policy. From 1900 to 1908 the Works Department employed ten clerks from the engineering sector, four of whom had previously worked in engineering companies, three for consulting engineers and three for railway companies.[75] Similarly, five clerks were obtained through the Civil Service Commissioners and, after 1901, slightly over half of the class iv clerks were recruited from those boy copyists who, during their time at the Agency, had studied for and passed the second division exam.[76] The examination gave the Crown Agents some indication of the abilities of the candidates, which, in the case of the former boy copyists, was supplemented by the Agents' own knowledge of their work. Some Class iv clerks, however, continued to be recruited through patronage, and the resultant personal jealousies that developed between these young men, known in the Office as 'nephews', and those who had passed the civil service exam affected productivity.[77] To prevent such problems and 'the suspicion of jobbery', the 1908 enquiry committee advised that all clerical staff should be appointed through competitive examinations, a recommendation put into effect in 1909.[78]

Deterrents to pecuniary moral hazard took the form of high pensions, a generous life insurance scheme and poundage. No salary premium was paid (see appendix 1, table 4) as the relatively small potential losses from fraudulent behaviour did not justify such payments, and the relatively high demand for the skills of Crown Agent clerks in industry and the City lessened the opportunity cost of dismissal. The Agents did, however, use annual salary increments to reward and punish good and bad performance and, on occasion, granted staff bonuses when their workload temporarily increased, which helped to build employee goodwill.[79] Theoretically, Crown Agent pensions

three: CAs to CO, 2 Apr. 1906, CO 323/364/5664; CAs to CO, 16 July 1891, CO 323/383/14469.

[74] Barnard, on employing the chief clerk and accountant as his assistant in 1858, commented that 'the best guarantee I have for his not abusing this trust must be the confidence which I have in him having served me faithfully for twenty two years': CAs to CO, 25 Sept. 1855, CO 323/245/9020.

[75] Schedule, CO 323/548/45364.

[76] PPR, p. viii.

[77] PPE, qq. 117, 142; CAA, CA M 82. Of the class iv clerks recruited between 1901 and 1908 three were recommended by members of the CAs' staff, three by the Colonial Office, three by the librarian of the Royal Colonial Institute and one by a supplier: memo, 5 Oct. 1908, CAOG 17/22.

[78] PPR, p. viii.

[79] Ommanney believed it 'a useful thing to be able to say to a man "you have been slack this year and I have only given you £5 as an increment" or "you have done well and I have given you £10" ': PPE, q. 4106. In 1891 and 1897 clerks earned bonuses for the extra work generated by the purchase of goods for, respectively, the British South Africa Co. and the De Beers Volunteers, and the Uganda railway: CAs to CO, 17 May 1891, CO 323/383/15937; CAs to CO, 13 Mar. 1897, CO 323/415/5386.

were granted in 'strict accordance with the rules observed in the imperial service'.[80] In reality, they tended to be 'calculated on a more favourable basis', and the Agents' discretion as regards their size helped them to establish a network of trust with their staff. Their payment also increased the cost of dismissal, particularly towards the end of a clerk's career, when further promotion was unlikely, the temptation to work less rigorously was high and the clerk's knowledge and experience increased the likelihood that any fraudulent act would be successful.

From 1895 employees also obtained generous life insurance. Previously, widows and orphans had been dealt with individually on merit, which forced the Agents to undertake the 'disagreeable duty' of investigating their pecuniary circumstances.[81] When the Colonial Office asked the Agents to slow down the growth of their office reserve fund, they proposed the establishment of a life insurance scheme, the members of which would pay respectively a fifth and a quarter of their premiums and the office reserve fund the remainder.[82] The Colonial Office at first rejected the proposal, arguing that the fund was 'public money and not the property' of the Agency, and that the Agents were seeking 'what the civil service has not got and . . . more than what any mercantile clerk gets'.[83] Nevertheless, after much discussion, it relented and authorised a slightly less generous scheme, under which existing staff and new employees earning less than £300 *per annum* contributed a quarter of their premiums and the Crown Agents and new staff with salaries over £300 *per annum* paid a third of their premiums.[84] The scheme again increased the opportunity cost of dismissal, giving the Agents 'the greatest hold over the staff possible, because men know that if there was any corruption they would lose their benefits'.[85] In addition, it discouraged Agent moral hazard, and again helped to create an Agency culture based on trust.

Poundage was the commission paid by the Inland Revenue to the Agents for the collection of tax on colonial salaries, pensions and dividends. Since the Agency was not a wholly public office, unlike other government departments, it was allowed by the Treasury to keep the payments.[86] These sums were originally distributed among the staff engaged in the collection of tax. In 1902 complaints from other employees caused the Agents to pay the actual collectors of tax only £5, and to distribute the remainder to the rest of the

[80] CO 885/19/223, iv.
[81] CAs to CO, 13 July 1893, CO 323/393/11909.
[82] Ibid.
[83] Meade to Ommanney, 17 Nov. 1893, ibid; Meade to Ommanney, 3 Mar. 1894, CO 323/393/21057.
[84] Ommanney to Meade, 24 Feb. 1894, CO 323/393/21057. Married men earning up to £300 *per annum* could insure themselves for between £500 and £1,000; those on incomes of £300 to £1,000 *per annum* for £2,000; those earning from £450 to £800 *per annum* for £1,500 to £3,000; and the CAs for £5,000 to £10,000: ibid. Sir R. Meade commented that 'the CAs open their mouths very wide': Meade note, 18 Aug. 1894, CO 323/396/8119.
[85] PPE, q. 1187.
[86] CO 885/19/223, iv.

Agency on a *pro-rata* basis.[87] The Agents also determined that any loss resulting from the carelessness or fraudulent activity of a member of staff would be directly recovered from poundage before distribution.[88] The payments amounted to roughly 4 per cent of salaries, and again increased the cost of opportunism.[89] Furthermore, they 'tended to create a healthy public opinion in the Office against members of staff who may be guilty of carelessness', that is discouraged free riding, the tendency for team members to contribute less effort than their colleagues, and gave employees an incentive to engage in 'whistle blowing', i.e. to inform management of the misdemeanours of others.

The Agency's deterrents to pecuniary moral hazard remained in force until 1909, when, on the recommendation of the enquiry, all staff were placed on civil service salaries and pension scales, a new life insurance scheme 'of a more modest character' was introduced for all new employees and poundage was treated as Agency income.[90] The Agents strongly opposed these changes, which initially were part of a proposal to make their staff civil servants. It was argued that 'if you give a man fixity of tenure absolute, fixity as regards salary and everything else to a great extent the stimulus of work is withdrawn'.[91] More important, loss of control over their staff would reduce the Agents' own power and status and 'make our clerks our masters . . . [enabling them to] . . . dictate to us what we shall do'.[92] In the event, the Crown Agents' opposition proved unsuccessful, probably because, given the reorganisation of the Agency after the enquiry, such deterrents were no longer thought to be necessary.

Other methods adopted to minimise moral hazard included bonds, monitoring and the establishment of an Agency trust relationship. At first no security was extracted from clerks, as no sum that 'they could afford would form any appreciable protection to the Crown Agents'.[93] But by 1900 bonds were supplied by fifteen members of staff, whose jobs were difficult to monitor and whose corruption or lack of effort could lead to major losses.[94] The securities varied from £100 to £5,000, depending on the employee's level of income and the potential cost of moral hazard, and had to be provided by third parties. In 1901 these securities were replaced by bonds obtained from guarantee societies, the premiums of which were met from poundage.[95] The need to provide

---

87 PPE, qq. 1150–1.
88 CAA, office memorandum book, 1 July 1901.
89 PPE, q. 1728. In 1909 poundage totalled £1,141: PP 1910, lxvi (Cd 5391).
90 PPR, p. xvi. New employees paid two-thirds of their life insurance premiums: ibid. In compensation for the loss of poundage, existing employees received a personal allowance equal to the average payments of the previous three years: ibid. p. xv.
91 PPE, q. 4069.
92 Ibid.
93 CAs to CO, 30 Nov. 1869, CO 323/308/206.
94 Blake note, 1 July 1901, CO 323/548/45364.
95 Ibid.

securities thus no longer discouraged applications for jobs, and the likelihood that theft would increase premiums and reduce the amount of poundage available for distribution encouraged 'whistle blowing'.

Monitoring was facilitated by the restriction of decision-making, the effectiveness of which was difficult to measure, to the Crown Agents; by requiring all letters and tenders entering the Agency to be opened in the presence of an Agent, who also signed all outgoing correspondence and cheques; and the employment in the 1860s of a chief clerk, a Mr Brown, 'known as the official watchdog', and in 1901 an Office secretary, who acted as the Agents' 'personal officer' and ensured that they 'should not be left in the dark as regards anything happening'.[96] In addition, much of the work of the Agency was divided into highly specialised routine procedures, which could be supervised easily and also reduced costs.[97] The inflexibility of the rules that governed these procedures, though, reduced the Agency's ability to respond to changes in its environment. The boring and repetitive nature of the work and the few opportunities for exerting judgement may also have led to poor staff motivation and low productivity, and encouraged some clerks to obtain work satisfaction through the establishment of close relationships with their colleagues, strengthening resistance to change.

Finally, the Senior Agents attempted to establish networks of trust with their staff through the provision of praise and the granting of perks that created obligations of reciprocity. Not all the Senior Agents, however, were successful in generating trust. In the 1860s and early 1900s, when the future of the Agency was unclear, the Colonial Office, wishing to avoid the complications of its disappearance, appointed as Senior Agents, Julyan and Blake, both of whom possessed unaltruistic private norms. Although ideal for rescuing a business in trouble, their aggressive and autocratic characters were poorly suited to the creation of trust and the reorganisation of moribund office procedures. Their treatment of their clerks and attempts at office reorganisation inevitably led to a collapse in morale and productivity and to much bad publicity. Yet it was not in the interests of either the Colonial Office or the other Crown Agents to intervene. For both, the survival of the Agency was paramount, and the future careers of junior Agents depended on maintaining good relations with their superior.

Julyan's poor relations with his staff first became apparent in 1863 when he dismissed the Agency's shipping and insurance clerk, a Mr Carter, whom he accused of failing to insure cargo bound for Ceylon.[98] Carter appealed to the Colonial Office, who, privately agreeing that a milder form of punishment

---

[96] *Civil Service Gazette*, 22 Feb. 1869, in CO 323/291/2424; pamphlet, ibid; CAs to CO, 9 May 1903, CO 323/483/16903; PPE, qq. 4138, 4157.
[97] Such procedures allowed the employment of less skilled workers, and increased productivity by minimising training and the time employees spent moving from task to task and in consultation with management.
[98] Note, 15 Sept. 1863, CO 323/270/9013.

would have sufficed, asked Julyan for an explanation of his behaviour.[99] In reply the Senior Agent claimed that his attempts to introduce alterations and reforms had resulted in 'that most ungovernable of all forces – passive resistance' and that he had sacked Carter as a warning to the other 'incompetents'.[100] Aggrieved at Carter's appeal to the Colonial Office, Julyan then refused to send him his outstanding pay, forcing him to take legal action, successfully, for the money.[101]

Julyan's treatment of Carter's successor as shipping and insurance clerk, F. A. Wrinkley, was equally poor. In 1868 a junior clerk, after a reprimand for being half a minute late arriving at work, sent a satirical valentine card to the chief clerk. Shown the card, Julyan decided that, as a punishment, all staff should henceforth start work a full hour earlier. This pronouncement created 'great excitement and discontent' and Wrinkley wrote to Julyan informing him that, if the decision stood, he would have to resign his post because he had such a long journey to work. In response, the Senior Agent returned his letter with the addition of the words 'Mr Wrinkley's resignation accepted'.[102] Feeling that he had been treated with 'contempt', Wrinkley approached the *Civil Service Gazette* which described the incident as a 'monstrous abuse of power' and 'an instance of petty office tyranny'.[103] Julyan's reaction was to demand the return of the letter and at a subsequent meeting with Wrinkley, at which he 'taunted and insulted . . . [him] . . . very much', dismissed him for theft of office property i.e. the letter.[104] The incident then rapidly developed into a minor *cause célèbre*. Further articles appeared in the press, and Wrinkley published a pamphlet and retained the support of a number of MPs.[105] Aghast, the Colonial Office again asked for an explanation from Julyan, only to be informed that his actions had been necessary to prevent 'insubordination' that arose from the 'jealousy and disfavour' of the 'old hands' towards 'the superior men' that he had recently employed.[106]

Blake's treatment of his staff was, if anything, worse than Julyan's. Whereas his predecessor as Senior Agent, Sir Montague Ommanney, was 'a man of even temper and great kindliness of heart and . . . a kind and considerate head of an office' and his staff were 'very contented and happy', Blake was a 'born autocrat' and 'tyrant'.[107] His low opinion of his clerks, favouritism and

[99] Ibid. Carter's defence was that the stores had been insured by another member of staff: Carter to CO, 29 Aug. 1863, CO 323/271/8619.
[100] Julyan to CO, 12 Sept. 1863, CO 323/270/9013.
[101] CAs to CO, 4 Aug. 1864, CO 323/275/7323.
[102] Pamphlet, CO 323/291/2424.
[103] *Civil Service Gazette*, 22 Feb. 1868, ibid.
[104] Pamphlet, ibid; Julyan note, 18 June 1868, CO 323/290/6634.
[105] *Civil Service Gazette*, 29 Feb. 1868, CO 323/291/2424; Julyan to Adderley MP, 22 June 1868, CAA, CA M5.
[106] Julyan to CO, 20 June 1868, CO 323/290/6634.
[107] *The Times*, 25 Aug. 1925, 13; PPE, qq. 122, 1978, 4064; character sketch by A. W. Abbott, CAA, CA M 64. Abbott joined the Agency three years after Blake resigned. Even

personal vendettas greatly reduced morale and at times reached absurd proportions. For example, believing that the first office secretary kept him 'in the dark about all important matters', he encouraged Crown Agent staff to circumvent him, refused to provide his room with heat and then decided, without consultation, that he should no longer have his own office.[108] Further disillusionment was engendered by his encouragement of older class iii and iv clerks 'to move on' to avoid the classes being composed of 'responsible mediocrity', his abolition of minor benign staff moral hazard and his attempts to reduce costs. The latter led to an increase in workloads, long hours of 'depressing and wearisome' unpaid overtime, particularly during loan flotations, and low or non-existent annual increments in salary.[109]

Relations between employers and staff reached their nadir in 1904, when several clerks wrote anonymous letters to *The Times* and the *Pall Mall Gazette* in which they complained of favouritism and the lack of rules regulating salaries, increments and promotions.[110] Later correspondence called for the establishment of an independent enquiry into staff conditions, which 'must promise each individual . . . that whatever they say will not be used against them . . . [as] . . . failing this no member would care to bear the wrath of the Senior Agent for fear of instant dismissal'.[111] In response, Blake set up an internal enquiry composed of Carmichael, the chief clerk, and representatives of each class of clerks.[112] He was, however, reluctant to implement its recommendations, fearing a dilution of his power, an upsurge of moral hazard and the response of the Colonial Office who 'take it upon themselves to

before he became Senior CA, Blake 'was not an easy man to live with': Anderson to Keith, 7 Aug. 1905, Arthur Berriedale Keith papers, Edinburgh University, Gen 144/3/24.
[108] He also unfairly complained about his work (later dismissing the criticism as 'a joke'), refused to provide his room with running water and, after promising that he would be made a CA 'in a few years', created the post of head of engineering, the holder of which was almost certain to become an Agent: Keith to Mercer, 29 Mar. 1905, Keith papers, Gen 144/3/58a; Keith note, 30 May 1905, Gen 144/3/56; Keith note, 27 Nov. 1903, Gen 144/3/69. In 1905 Keith returned to the Colonial Office, even though, in so doing, he took a 50% salary cut and was denied the seniority that he had accumulated before joining the Agency: Keith to Mercer, 29 Mar. 1905, Gen 144/3/58a; Anderson to Keith, 7 May 1905, Gen 144/3/24. Similarly, Blake ensured that the deputy head of the works department, who had done 'good work for many years', but with whom he 'did not get on at all well', stayed on 'a relatively low wage': PPE, q. 1079; CAs to CO, 31 Jan. 1913, CO 323/608/3644; Harris note, 5 Jan. 1913, ibid.
[109] PPE, qq. 1078, 4010, appendix vi; Alford note, 21 Jan. 1908, CAOG 16/12. Between 1904 and 1908 17 members of staff resigned. The clerk Alford claimed that between June and October 1907 he had worked overtime on 109 working days, staying until after 6.30 p.m. on sixty days, and after 7.00 p.m. on forty-four days, the equivalent of a full month's work: Alford note, 21 Jan. 1908, CAOG 16/12. Overtime was unpaid, as Blake believed that otherwise 'your staff will create overtime': PPE, q. 4073.
[110] *The Times*, 30 Aug. 1904, 10; *Pall Mall Gazette*, 17 Aug. 1904, 8; 20 Aug. 1904, 3; 26 Aug. 1904, 2.
[111] *Pall Mall Gazette*, 1 Sept. 1904, 10.
[112] PPE, q. 4084.

criticise our work and to be our masters'.[113] In the event, only a few of the suggestions were put into effect and then only after the announcement of the 1908 enquiry.[114]

Composed of rational self-interested individuals, the Colonial Office, colonial governors, Crown Agents and those who supplied the colonies with goods, services and capital all had their own interests and were prone to moral hazard. In order to fulfil its own interests – the reduction of the cost of colonial administration to the British tax-payer – the Colonial Office had to minimise opportunism on the part of colonial governments, suppliers, brokers and service providers. This was achieved through the employment of the Crown Agents, whose quasi-governmental status allowed the Office itself to indulge in self-interested behaviour. The Agents, however, had their own institutional goals – the wish to ensure the survival and growth of their Agency and to increase the satisfaction they gained from their work. As the Colonial Office monitored their performance through the colonies, these goals were met through the fulfilment of those colonial needs that could easily be monitored by governors and produced a monetary gain for the Agency. The Agents therefore provided colonies with high quality goods and fully subscribed loans, as quality and subscription were easily monitored and the quality premium and full subscription increased Agency commissions. Unfortunately, the fulfilment of these goals necessarily caused other needs to be left unfulfilled. The practices adopted to minimise that supplier and broker dishonesty that militated against the provision of quality goods and successful issues greatly increased the cost of articles and loans. Until the mid-1890s these extra costs were accepted and the Agency's moral hazard regarded as benign by the colonies and Colonial Office. Satisficing, both realised that the higher costs arising from the supply of quality goods and fully subscribed loans were less than the opportunity cost of the provision of defective articles and the failure of issues. It also allowed them to reciprocate the Agency for its acceptance of their own moral hazard. The reduction in Crown Agent fees, and the Colonial Office's adoption of a policy of development as a way of achieving its interests in an altered environment, then forced the Agents to modify their own strategies. Efforts to maximise their income involved a clamp-down on colonies purchasing local goods, led to the construction of poor quality railways and the failure of loans, and raised the cost of materials and infrastructure above the opportunity cost of the supply of defective articles and works. As a result, their moral hazard began to be regarded by the colonies and Colonial Office as malign and in need of attention.

Minor personal moral hazard on the part of Agents and Crown Agent staff was, similarly, regarded as benign. The Colonial Office and the Agents took

---

113 PPE, qq. 4092, 4073.
114 PPE, q. 4073.

steps to limit major fraud that were largely successful. Small improprieties at the Agency however, were accepted by the Colonial Office, which realised that tolerance prevented more substantial financially and politically damaging moral hazard. Likewise, the Agents appear to have turned a blind eye to minor Colonial Office and staff opportunism, concentrating on discouraging major fraud by their clerks.

2

Supply Monopoly and the Purchase of Goods

The Agents' purchasing role was based on its monopoly of the supply of government stores not manufactured within colonies, and, from 1904, in adjacent colonies, which, unofficially accepted from the earliest days, was placed in the colonial regulations in 1874. Under this ruling, acquisitions rose from £414,500 in 1887 to £4.4m. in 1914 (*see* fig. 5). The existence of the monopoly was largely a result of the undeveloped state of crown colonies. Particularly in the early period, few dependencies could produce the goods required themselves and most lacked a merchant community. Purchases, consequently, had to be obtained from overseas. Given the meagre nature of crown colony revenue due to the relative absence of economic activity, it was crucial that the articles bought were subject to neither colonial nor supplier moral hazard. The former would lead to over-expenditure, and the latter to the provision of goods that were excessively priced, and, more important, of poor quality. Undeveloped colonies lacked the facilities for the repair of defective articles, and the real cost, and, to the local business community, the opportunity costs of obtaining replacements was high. The use of the Crown Agents theoretically minimised such dangers. The Agents were experienced buyers and monitored all purchases thus preventing colonial moral hazard. Until 1863 the sanction of the secretary of state had to be obtained before they undertook any transaction. As orders increased, this was relaxed and only requisitions for goods valued at more than £100 or not authorised by a relevant colonial law or ordinance had to be submitted to the Colonial Office. The use of the Agents also had other advantages. They prevented orders being 'thrown [into] the hands of the World at large', thus ensuring purchase within the United Kingdom, had low administrative costs and could purchase materials in bulk, at a discount and from manufacturers, eliminating the retail premium.

The Crown Agents, however, had their own agenda. Until the mid-1890s it was in their own interests to turn a blind eye to colonial violations of the monopoly regulation and to purchase high quality goods. Acceptance of colonial moral hazard helped to establish strong trust relationships with governors. The quality bias, meanwhile, maximised Agency income, as the premium charged for superior materials led to higher earnings, and reduced the likelihood of criticism in the colonies. Governors were able to monitor quality effectively through use, had little knowledge of prices, but were highly averse to defective supplies, which reduced colonial revenues and damaged their reputation for fiscal competence. The Agents consequently adopted a

Figure 5. Crown Agent purchases, 1887–1914

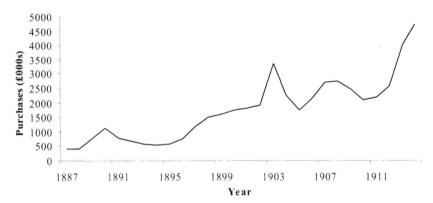

Source: CO 323 series; CA accounts.

Note: Annual purchases = annual purchasing commission x 100.

purchase procedure that ensured the provision of quality but expensive goods.[1] The fall in the Agency's income from the early 1890s and the growth in their workload then forced them to adjust their priorities. Fearful for the survival of the Agency, they became more concerned with the maximisation of their income than with quality. Colonies were forced to purchase all their supplies from the Agency, and more goods were bought from wholesalers and fewer through competition. As a result, the already high prices of Agent supplies rose even further. This chapter concentrates on the prices paid for supplies. An examination of colonial circumvention of the Agency's monopoly is followed by an investigation of the Agents' purchasing proce-dure and the policy change of the mid-1890s. The other charges that made up the cost of goods – freight rates, packing fees and so on – are discussed in the chapter 3.

---

[1] In 1902 Sir Frederick Lugard, then governor of Northern Nigeria, stated that, as it was in the Agents' 'interest that no complaints of quality should be made, . . . they naturally go to expensive firms': Lugard to the earl of Scarborough, 17 Dec. 1902, earl of Scarborough papers, Rhodes House, Oxford, MS Afr. s 87, 3. Both Sir Reginald Antrobus, when under-secretary of state, and his colleague C. P. Lucas accepted that the Agents were 'inclined to insist on a rather better article than was absolutely necessary': Antrobus note, 26 June 1905, CO 87/174/2283; PPE, q. 1609. See also Uganda railway committee to CAs, 2 Jan. 1900, CO 537/62; director of public works to high commissioner, 15 Aug. 1904, CO 446/41/1089; Olivier to CO, 10 Sept. 1900, CO 137/612/31704; West African Mail, 29 Apr. 1904, 29.

Local purchase

The monopoly regulation, as acknowledged by the Agents, was 'frequently violated' (see table 3). Although some colonies, such as British Guiana, openly flouted the ruling, most were circumspect. Northern Nigeria purchased materials secretly. For example, Sir Frederick Lugard bought 'a good deal of cement and corrugated iron' from the merchants Maciver & Co. in 1902, and attempted to arrange for the import of a range of goods from the Royal Niger Company.[2] The Federated Malay States, whilst professing that all its materials were bought from the Agents, did nothing to prevent its staff from using merchants. In 1905, when the railway storekeeper was discovered purchasing stores privately, C. P. Lucas, the assistant under-secretary of state, concluded that 'probably all government officials' in the colony 'were aware of the system of local purchase and ignored the fact that it was going on'.[3] Moreover he suspected that the attempts by the governor and railway manager to defend the storekeeper, whose dismissal the Colonial Office had demanded, were motivated by a recognition that they were 'responsible for the system, and are therefore uncomfortable at the feeling that a minor official has had to bear all the consequences'.[4] Other colonies circumvented the ruling through perceived loopholes. Orders were placed with local manufacturers in the full knowledge that the firms would subcontract the work to British companies. In 1905, for instance, it was discovered that an ironwork contract awarded by the Straits to the Penang Foundry had been sublet to merchants, who in turn had passed the order to Messrs Dorman Long & Co.[5] In 1901 an order for steel, given by the Central South Africa Railway to two Johannesburg firms, was sublet to a London manufacturer, who, via merchants, placed the order with a German company.[6] Until the War Office stopped the practice in 1859, many colonies also bought non-military goods from local military storekeepers, or exploited the understanding that goods could be purchased from merchants if required urgently.[7] In 1907, for example, Southern Nigeria claimed that, owing to a series of emergencies, it had been forced to buy 59 per cent of its supplies privately in the first six months of the year.[8]

---

[2] Lugard to Scarborough, 17 Dec. 1902, Scarborough papers, MS Afr. s. 87, 3. Lugard halted negotiations on discovering that the company's prices were, in many cases, higher than those of the Agents: Scarborough to Watts, 30 Oct. 1903, MS Afr. s. 94, 10.
[3] Lucas note, 19 Sept. 1907, CAOG 14/66.
[4] Ibid.
[5] CAs to CO, 29 Mar. 1905, CO 273/313/10076.
[6] PPE, appendix ix.
[7] War Office to CO, 28 Feb. 1859, CO 323/215/2278; Sells Commercial Intelligence, 16 Mar. 1904, 7.
[8] Auditor-general to CO, 11 Dec. 1907, CO 520/53/43256; Egerton to CO, 30 May 1908, CO 520/61/22421. Six months later, after a Colonial Office reprimand, merchant purchases had fallen from £10,806 to £161: ibid.

Table 3
Local purchase

Colony	Purchasing strategy
British Guiana	In 1906 merchant purchase 'had been going on for years' and only 19% of supplies came from the Agency.
Central African Railway	In the half year July to December 1903, only 70% of stores were bought through the Agents.
Ceylon	In 1908 the colony had 'for some years' purchased items such as paper, stationary and medicines locally.
Gold Coast	In 1900,an Accra clerk was discovered to have ordered large amounts of goods privately.
Hong Kong	The public works department in 1899 obtained only 53% of its stores from the CAs. In 1907 it purchased drugs and other goods privately.
Jamaica	The colony never made requisitions for necessities such as cement, clothing and saddlery, and the value of its annual orders varied enormously.
Mauritius	In 1869 the colony bought many stores direct.
Natal	In 1881 the Harbour Board appointed its own purchasing agent.
Sierra Leone	In 1908 the colony admitted that it was 'a long established practice' for goods such as timber, cement, bricks, galvanised iron etc to be purchased from local merchants.
Southern Nigeria	By 1907 the colony purchased only small quantities and low value goods from the CAs, obtaining 'the greater part of its supplies from India and Zanzibar'.
Straits	In 1904 17 % of supplies came from merchants.
Trinidad	In 1906 'all articles in common use' had been privately obtained for 'over forty years'. Only 'special articles and heavy goods', stationery and uniform material were bought from the Agents.

Source: British Guiana to CO, 23 Nov. 1906, CO 111/553/45547; British Guiana to CO, 19 Dec. 1906, CO 111/553/820; Sierra Leone to CO, 5 Jan. 1908, CO 267/501/2645; Trinidad to CO, 21 Dec. 1906, CO 295/438/806; Anderson to CAs, 24 Aug. 1909, CAOG 14/66; CO 131/33, appendix 21; CAs to CO, 2 May 1907, CO 129/350/15681; CAs to CO, 7 Apr. 1906, CO 54/704/12406; B. Guest and J. M. Sellers (eds), *Enterprise and exploitation in a Victorian economy: aspects of the economic and social history of colonial Natal*, Pietermaritzberg 1985, 32; *British and South African Export Gazette*, 5 Aug. 1904, 49; CAs to CO, 31 Dec. 1900, CO 96/366/21; CAs to CO, 14 Jan. 1897, CO 520/21/38039; CAs to CO, 22 July 1869, CO 167/521/8222.

Colonial failure to comply fully with the regulations meant that in some colonies the Agents provided their services at a loss. In 1906, for example, the Agency supplied British Guiana with £223,514-worth of miscellaneous and free services, but received in return only a £100 annual contribution and commission for the purchase of just £6,720-worth of goods, which together covered only 1/20th of the cost of their work for the colony.[9] Until the late 1890s the Agents were perhaps unaware of the extent of local purchase, as, to minimise costs, they failed to closely monitor colonial acquisitions. It was also in their interests to tolerate the colonies' duplicity. The Colonial Office was unlikely to discover the purchases, and, following the reciprocal norm of their trust relationships with governors, acceptance reduced the likelihood that colonial governments would object to their own moral hazard, the supply of expensive quality goods. Their parlous financial situation and the breakdown of their relationships with governors, however, then forced them to improve their monitoring procedures and to inform the Colonial Office of the colonies' actions.[10]

The Colonial Office, believing that it was 'a perfect farce to have a rule standing, if the adopted system is in direct contradiction of it', generally forced the guilty colonies to abandon local merchants.[11] The only exceptions were where high freight rates or the proximity of foreign suppliers made local purchase advantageous, and where enforcement was likely to damage severely the Office's bonds with both governors and local business elites and governor–elite collaboration. In West Africa, Colonial Office sanction of local purchase was initiated by the malign moral hazard of the main shippers, which led to high freight rates. The region's shipping trade was dominated by Messrs Elder Dempster, owned by Sir Alfred Jones, and the German Woermann Co., who ensured the exclusive use of their ships by requiring merchants to pay a 10 per cent primage on the cost of their freight, which was only refunded at the end of each six-month period if they had shipped in conference lines.[12] Like other rings, Elder Dempster and Woermann set excessive charges, but refused to grant the Agents special rates, allegedly fearing criticism from local firms.[13] They also further increased the cost of colonial freight by refusing to ship from London, forcing cargo to be trans-ferred to Liverpool, and charging a premium of 5s. per ton on goods loaded at Cardiff.[14]

[9] CAs to CO, 25 Jan. 1907, CO 111/558/3191. A similar situation existed in Jamaica in 1900: CAs to CO, 11 May 1900, CO 137/615/14855.
[10] Monitoring involved comparing year-on-year expenditure, searching the colonial press for reports of local purchase, investigating all invoices sent to them for payment and asking those suppliers whom they trusted to tell if they received private colonial orders: CAs to CO, 15 July 1901, CO 129/308/24442; CAs to CO, 17 July 1905, CO 54/696/25236.
[11] Lucas note, 29 Aug. 1906, CO 295/437/31840.
[12] PPS, qq. 4306–24.
[13] CAs to CO, 15 Sept. 1908, CO 96/474/34032.
[14] Freelands to CAs, 26 Sept. 1901, CAOG 12/126; Trigge to Scarborough, 4 Jan. 1908, Scarborough papers.

The Agents, however, were reluctant to charter steamers. From 1896 the conference deemed that, if they made even one shipment to any West African colony by a chartered vessel, they would lose all their West African rebates, which, between 1896 and 1905, averaged £4,274 *per annum*.[15] Chartering would therefore 'lay . . . [them] . . . open to charges of having sacrificed the interests of some particular colony in favour of some other colony'.[16] Moreover, the Agency did not have enough cargo to make chartering cost-effective (unless goods were allowed to accumulate, which led to delay and more criticism), and there were few tramp steamers willing to ship goods regularly to West Africa. The region had a reputation for unhealthiness and possessed few adequate harbours so that cargoes had to be transhipped at sea into small lighters, which were largely owned by Jones who again charged high rates for using them.[17]

In an attempt to circumvent the high rates, the Colonial Office allowed all the West African colonies to invite local tenders for the supply of coal and cement; Southern Nigeria, in 1906, to obtain kerosene oil from merchants; and Sierra Leone, in 1908, to purchase both kerosene and timber in this way.[18] Merchants imported these goods in sufficient quantities to make the chartering of ships cost-effective, and, as the successful merchant and not the colony would organise shipment, it was believed that Elder Dempster would have no grounds for withholding rebates.[19] In the case of kerosene oil, merchants were also able to transport the oil in wood, rather than in the more expensive steel drums demanded by the conference.[20] Unfortunately, the adoption of local purchase only succeeded in replacing one form of malign moral hazard with another. The coal purchased was often unsatisfactory and occasionally obtained from America, and most of the coal and cement contracts were won by Elder Dempster.[21] The company used coal as ballast and thus was able to incorporate an extremely low freight rate in its tenders, and, from the early 1900s, would only carry cement manufactured by the Burham cement company, which, in return, gave Jones a monopoly of its West African supply.[22] The coal sold by Elder Dempster was at first relatively cheap, but then gradually rose in price, particularly after the Agents,

---

[15] CAs to CO, 25 Aug. 1905, CO 147/177/30737.
[16] CAs to CO, 15 Sept. 1908, CO 96/474/34032.
[17] Freelands memo, 3 Feb. 1904, CO 323/491/10117; Freelands to CAs, 12 Mar. 1908, CO 520/69/9463. The CAs also believed that if they chartered and were then forced to return to the conference, there was a possibility that it could 'take an antagonistic attitude and raise rates still further': CAOG 17/24, CAR.
[18] CO to Lagos, 4 Mar. 1903, CO 147/168/6513; Egerton to CO, 4 Dec. 1906, CO 520/38/47545; CO to Sierra Leone, 16 Apr. 1908, CAA, CS 4 SL.
[19] Sierra Leone to CO, 5 Jan. 1908, CAA, CS 4 SL.
[20] Egerton to CO, 4 Dec. 1906, CO 520/38/47545.
[21] CAs to CO, 22 Dec. 1904, CO 147/172/43182; Shelford to CAs, 24 Nov. 1904, CO 267/474/41570.
[22] PPS, 70, qq. 5041–3, 10697, 10793.

concerned about quality and, perhaps wishing to obtain income from the transactions, insisted that it be inspected before it left Britain.[23] All attempts by merchants to undercut Elder Dempster's tenders failed, partly because of Jones's lax private norms. A relatively low bid from Messrs Miller Bros, telegraphed to the Lagos government in 1904, was intercepted by Jones, who controlled the telegraph service between West Africa and Europe and undercut Miller's price. In 1905 a further low tender was disclosed to Jones by the chief accountant of the Lagos railway, who no doubt was well rewarded for his breach of confidentiality.[24]

Purchase from local merchants was, secondly, permitted where colonies could genuinely obtain goods more advantageously from the United States. Although the monopoly ruling forbade colonial governments from purchasing directly or through merchants or manufacturers in the United Kingdom, it failed specifically to prohibit them from obtaining materials from the United State or the continent of Europe. In 1899 this loophole was tested by the Straits, who, experiencing long delays in the delivery of goods, requested permission to buy direct from America and Europe.[25] The Agents vehemently rejected the proposal. It was argued that the delays were temporary and not serious, the result of the 1897 engineering lockout and the South African War.[26] More important, it was wrong for British colonial government funds to be used to 'promote foreign industries . . . in direct competition with British manufacturers'.[27] The goods purchased would also be more expensive and of a lower standard than those available in the United Kingdom. Foreign firms provided relatively poor quality articles, were reluctant to provide bespoke goods, were unwilling to accept English contracts, which were, in any case, difficult to enforce in foreign courts, and often refused to allow inspection, which, if it occurred, was costly and troublesome. On the other hand, the Colonial Office officials C. P. Lucas and Sir R. Herbert both favoured the proposal. Herbert believed that American firms, with their standardisation of design, superior machinery and better distributed and more industrious labour force, could produce goods more rapidly, at a lower cost and to a similar standard than their British counterparts.[28] Lucas agreed, though arguing that colonies should only be allowed to deal with the United States direct, and should obtain European goods through the Crown Agents.[29] Chamberlain, however, supported the Agents, and ruled that all

---

23 CAs to CO, 15 July 1912, CO 520/118/22144.
24 PPS qq. 4328–30; extract, 4 Feb. 1905, John Holt & Co. papers, Rhodes House, Oxford, MS Afr. s. 1525, 9/8. Prices remained high until the inter-war period.
25 Straits to CO, 1 Oct. 1899, CO 273/249/29830.
26 CAs to CO, 8 Dec. 1899, CO 273/253/34283.
27 Ibid.
28 Herbert note, 29 Dec. 1899, ibid.
29 Lucas note, 20 Dec. 1899, ibid.

materials should be purchased through the Office, and that foreign goods should be supplied by them only in exceptional circumstances.[30]

The decision was short-lived. In 1900, in reply to the Agents' criticism of local purchase, Jamaica claimed that many articles could be obtained more cheaply and rapidly from the United States.[31] Furthermore, it was pointed out that lighthouse oil and some other goods supplied by the Agents were actually manufactured in America, and that their price thus included the freight from the United States to England and from England to Jamaica.[32] At first the Colonial Office rejected the colony's demands for direct purchase from America, but then, in 1902, altered its stance, and ruled that the colony should be allowed to buy from the United States those articles that could be better obtained there, for example oil, timber, foodstuffs and typewriters.[33] Those goods that could be bought as well or better in Canada were to be purchased there too, but materials that were roughly the same price, whether supplied from the United States or England, 'in view of the great sacrifice the British consumer is making for the West Indies in the matter of sugar', were to be bought by the Agents in England.[34] The policy was subsequently extended to British Honduras, and, in 1904, incorporated into the new monopoly ruling, which specifically stated that supplies should not be purchased directly in Europe, but made no mention of the United State.[35]

Thirdly, the Colonial Office sanctioned local purchase where failure to do so was likely to damage its relationship with governors and elites and governor – elite collaboration. In Transvaal and the Orange River colony the purchase of public goods by the Agents after the South African War led to strong protests from both the Johannesburg Chamber of Commerce and the legislative council.[36] Although the Colonial Office was convinced that supplies could be obtained more cheaply through the Agency, warnings from the governor of 'serious political consequences' if nothing were done, caused them to accept a compromise.[37] It was agreed that tenders would be called simultaneously, on identical specifications and forms of tender, from merchants and through the Agents, and contracts awarded by the local tender board to the firms that offered the best terms.[38] The only condition stipulated by the Colonial Office was that all the goods purchased came from Britain. The result was that the majority of tenders were subsequently won by

---

30 Chamberlain note, 20 Dec. 1900, ibid; CO to Straits, 11 Jan. 1900, ibid.
31 Olivier to CO, 10 Sept. 1900, CO 137/612/31704.
32 Director of public works to colonial secretary, 25 Aug. 1899, ibid. See also *Jamaica Daily Telegraph*, 5 Nov. 1906, 6.
33 CO to Jamaica, 27 Mar. 1902, CO 137/631/7724.
34 Ibid.
35 PPE, qq. 1570–1.
36 Milner to Lyttelton, 14 July 1904, CO 291/71/24790; Chamber of Commerce to Milner, 19 July 1904, CO 291/71/28531.
37 Milner to Lyttelton, 15 Aug. 1904, CO 291/72/30822.
38 CO to Transvaal, 20 Aug. 1904, CO 291/74/26378.

local merchants, towards whom, according to the Agents, the tender board was biased.[39]

Political expediency similarly led the Colonial Office to allow a degree of merchant purchase in Trinidad and British Guiana.[40] In Trinidad warnings from the governor in 1906 that an attempt to impose the monopoly regulation on the colony would lead to discontent and would be opposed by the legislative council, caused the Colonial Office to rule that merchants were 'entitled to any business where the difference in cost does not compensate for the inevitable delay in getting things from England'.[41] In British Guiana the Agents' insistence, again in 1906, that the government should increase its Agency purchases, partly to finance the various free services provided to the colony, led to political turmoil.[42] The issue of an instruction to this effect, after the Agents had assured the governor that nothing would be done until he had discussed the matter with the local business community, worsened the situation.[43] The mood in the colony becoming so hostile that the Combined Court threatened to refuse to pass the vote for government supplies unless the instruction was withdrawn.[44] As British Guiana was not a true crown colony and financial control rested with the Combined Court, the Colonial Office had no alternative but to withdraw the order, although in return the colony agreed to increase its annual contribution to the Agents.

United Kingdom purchase

Owing to the Agents' reluctance to publicise prices and the destruction of all their purchasing files in the mid-1970s, no official price statistics survive. Nevertheless, it seems clear that the Agency paid excessive prices for goods. The press and, from the late 1890s, governors bombarded the Colonial Office with examples and a comparison of Crown Agent and War Office prices clearly demonstrates the high cost of Agency purchase. Of the sixteen articles common to both the Agents' list of sample prices distributed to colonies in 1906 and the 1906 *War Office vocabulary*, whose prices, unlike those of the Agents, included a percentage for inspection, packing and departmental

---

[39] In 1906–7, for instance, the Central South African Railway's CA purchases fell by 72%: *British and South African Export Gazette*, Aug. 1908, 697.

[40] In 1912 the secretary of state also allowed the Egba territories of Southern Nigeria to purchase goods through a private agent in the United Kingdom, accepting that under an 1893 treaty their commercial transactions came within the scope of 'internal affairs': Takema N. Tamuno, *The evolution of the Nigerian state: the southern phase, 1898–1914*, London 1978, 93.

[41] CAs to CO, 8 Nov. 1906, CO 295/438/806; Elgin note, 7 Nov. 1906, CO 295/439/40955.

[42] *The Argosy*, 6 Oct. 1906, 5; 10 Oct. 1906, 3; 17 Oct. 1906, 3.

[43] British Guiana to CO, 23 Nov. 1906, CO 111/553/45547.

[44] Ibid.

Table 4
Comparison of Crown Agent and War Office prices, 1906

Article	Crown Agent price (s. d.)	War Office price (s. d.)	Crown Agent price premium (%)
axle grease	15s. per cwt	11s. 5d. per cwt	24
bunting	5d. per yard	3.25d. per yard	35
drums for oils, 10 gallon	3s. 4d. each (black)	2s. 6d. each (red)	25
duck, white	8.5d. (28")	7d. (27")	18
glue, best scotch	48s. per cwt	20s. 9d. per cwt	57
linseed oil, boiled	1s. 10d. per gallon	1s. 4.5d. per gallon	25
linseed oil, raw	1s. 9d. per gallon	1s. 9d. per gallon	–
oakum	17s. 6d. per cwt	16s. 5d. per cwt (white)	6
soap, hard yellow	21s. per cwt	17s. 6d. per cwt	17
soap, soft	17s. per cwt	12s. 9d. per cwt	25
tallow	30s. per cwt	31s. 9d. per cwt	– 6
tar, coal	3.5d. per gallon	3.25d. per gallon	7
tar, Stockholm	1s. 3d. per gallon	9d. per gallon	40
turpentine	2s. 11d. per gallon	1s. 11d. per gallon	34
waste, cotton, coloured	25s. per cwt	24s. 6d. per cwt	2
waste, cotton, white	34s. per cwt	26s. 3d. per cwt	23

Source: *War Office vocabulary*, 1906; CAA, CA circulars and papers, list of current prices, Sept. 1906.

Note: The War Office obtained certain of its goods from its own ordinance factories, the price of which thus excluded manufacturers' profits.

charges, fourteen could be obtained more cheaply from the War Office (*see* table 4).[45] Prices were high because the Agents believed that it was 'of more importance to attend to quality than mere concerns of price'.[46] They consequently adopted a purchasing procedure that discouraged supplier adverse selection and moral hazard that could damage quality. Prices may also have been increased by dishonesty on the part of the suppliers and by the very nature of crown colony demand.

[45] The *War Office vocabulary* was a catalogue.
[46] Barnard to CO, 7 Nov. 1851, CO 323/239/9270. See also CAs to CO, 6 Sept. 1895, CO 152/199/15905, and notes on the preparation of indents, CAOG 12/71.

Purchasing procedure

Until 1829 colonial agents bought goods from the private sector. The fraudulent activities of the Trinidad agent, Henry Cutler, then prompted the Colonial Office and the Treasury to require that all agents, 'where . . . practicable', obtain supplies from public departments, in particularly the War Office, Admiralty and Stationery Office.[47] Moreover, to prevent overexpenditure of imperial funds, when buying crown colony supplies from the private sector, the agents were to request at least three tenders from respectable tradesmen and to place orders with the lowest tenderer.[48] Unfortunately, neither instruction was a success. Despite constant Treasury and Colonial Office reminders, Barnard rarely asked for tenders for articles of low value, of 'special and somewhat unusual kind' or from suppliers 'known to be respectable'.[49] The purchase of goods from public departments, meanwhile, led to a sharp decline in the quality of materials supplied and in the speed of provision. The Agency had little power over government officials and colonial purchases made up only a small proportion of the heavy workloads of the departments. Unlike commercial firms, 'who would depend on us for their business', they therefore had 'no particular interest or desire to execute orders' in a rapid and efficient manner.[50] In addition, they charged high commissions, their delayed payment systems created confusion in the colonies and increased the Agents' administrative costs, while the Stationery Office's refusal to pack by colonial department forced orders to be split and repacked.[51]

Recruited to save the Agency from bankruptcy, Sir Penrose Julyan campaigned against the use of government departments, and in 1859 the Colonial Office gave the Agents permission to buy all supplies from the private sector, except ordinance stores, armaments and stationery.[52] At the same time, however, the Treasury tightened its purchasing restrictions.[53] If a colonial administration required an order to be placed with a particular firm in the United Kingdom or requested that colonial firms be invited to tender, the Crown Agents had to comply.[54] Otherwise, stores over £100 in value had

---

[47] CO to Treasury, 30 Apr. 1829, CO 323/211, 120; note, n.d., CO 323/239/8663.

[48] Treasury to CO, 15 Oct. 1851, CO 323/239/8663; note, 24 Feb. 1858, CO 54/339/1810.

[49] Barnard to CO, 7 Nov. 1851, CO 323/239/9279; CAs to CO, 23 Dec. 1859, CO 323/254/12679.

[50] CAs to CO, 5 Feb. 1859, CO 323/254/1366.

[51] Ibid; CAs to CO, 5 Jan. 1870, CO 137/453/209. The War Office, Admiralty and Stationery Office set commissions of 5%. The Stationery Office charged the India Office a commission of only 2.5%: CAs to CO, 1 July 1868, CO 54/439/6968.

[52] CO to CAs, 12 Feb. 1859, CO 323/254/1366. Ten years later, after much resistance from the Stationery Office, the ban on the private purchase of stationery was also lifted: CAs to CO, 30 Aug. 1870, CO 323/299/9468.

[53] With regard to representative colonies, these instructions were to be applied 'as far as possible': Treasury instructions, 1860, CO 323/337/16885.

[54] Colonies could choose firms that had given 'satisfaction' in the past and, from 1904, 'for other reasons': *Colonial Office list*, 1903, 1906.

to be bought through open competition, and, before buying lower value goods, the Agents had to obtain tenders from three or more tradesmen. Competition could only be avoided in the case of medicines, which had to be bought from the Society of Apothecaries.[55]

Not surprisingly, the Crown Agents were reluctant to adopt these instructions. As they received no commission if a colonial firm won an order but would be blamed if the goods supplied were of poor quality, they generally discouraged colonies from requesting colonial tenders. If their advice was rejected and a colonial and a United Kingdom firm each submitted identical tenders, they awarded the contract to the United Kingdom company, which was judged to have greater experience.[56] Colonial choice of United Kingdom contractors was also resented. This was regarded as the first step towards colonial purchase, and it was believed that it would encourage the bribery of colonial purchasing staff and again lead to the provision of poor quality goods.[57] The Agents consequently often refused to comply with colonies' requests, insisted that the named company take part in a tender if the amount of the work rendered 'competition desirable' or refused to accept complete responsibility for any goods supplied by such a firm.[58] As a result, few colonies, particularly in the early part of the period, took up the opportunity to name contractors.

The Agents, similarly, were opposed to the use of competition. The call for tenders facilitated monitoring of their activities by the Colonial Office and colonies and cut Agency income, as the tender process increased costs and the lower prices reduced their earnings from commission.[59] It also made supplier moral hazard and the provision of poor quality goods far more likely. The use of a greater number of suppliers increased the risk that ineffective companies would win contracts, made inspection during manufacture difficult and prevented the development of long-term relationships that helped to generate trust.[60] Over the years therefore and particularly after 1880 and the loss of Treasury control, the Agents increasingly made less use of competition. Articles worth under £100 were rarely subject to tender, supposedly

---

55 Treasury instructions, 1860, CO 323/337/16885.
56 Barry to CAs, 18 Aug. 1909, CAA, EM 261/10; PPE, qq. 1894–5, 3965. In comparison, both the India Office and the self-governing colonies gave preference to local manufacturers.
57 There is some evidence that bribery occurred. In 1909, for example, a Southern Nigerian public works department engineer asked two firms for 'advances', presumably in return for requesting their use, and, in 1910, a firm offered to pay the Ceylon medical storekeeper a commission in return for orders: Round note, 19 Oct. 1909, CO 520/85/34355; CO to CAs, 24 Apr. 1900, CO 54/667/12323.
58 CAs to CO, 8 Sept. 1888, CO 323/371/18103; Sells Commercial Intelligence, 27 Apr. 1904, 13; PPR, q. 1723. For example, CAs to CO, 10 Apr. 1889, CO 323/375b/7270; CAs to CO, 16 Sept. 1903, CO 111/539/34608. The Admiralty always used any firm specified by an ordering department: PP 1901, xl (Cd 581), q. 1794.
59 CAs to CO, 8 July 1927, CO 323/985/19.
60 Note, 28 Dec. 1859, CO 323/254/12679.

because large wholesalers were reluctant to bid for small orders, and, if the regulation were implemented, the Agents would have to resort to firms of inferior standing or higher price retailers.[61] Likewise, they gradually added to the circumstances under which competition for goods over £100 could be avoided. Thus, by the end of the century tenders were not called for such articles when they were required urgently, if their price had recently been determined by competition, a consulting engineer had advised that tenders should not be requested or the Agents had a standing order with a particular firm, which in return charged a discounted price.[62] Consequently, of the almost £1m.-worth of orders processed for the West African railways from 1898 to 1900, most of which were over £100, only 58 per cent were put out to competition.[63]

Even when tenders were called, there was generally no open competition.[64] Invitations were merely sent to those on the Agents' lists of suitable firms, inclusion on which was tightly controlled.[65] Colonial companies were not eligible: the Agency lost its commission if such companies won an order, it was unaware of their commercial reputations and their appearance on lists could be regarded by colonies as an attempt to intervene in local matters.[66] British firms also found it difficult to gain access. The existence of the lists was not advertised, and all applicants had to furnish references from a government department, English railway company or large steamship company, and, from 1911, engineering firms had to pass an inspection of their works by one of the Agents' external inspectors.[67] All references were checked, and, unless they were uniformly excellent, the company's application was disallowed. The helmet manufacturer, Messrs J. Ellwood & Sons, for example, was rejected in 1902 because it had executed just one order for the War Office in only 'a fairly satisfactory manner', and in 1904, when it reapplied, had provided the War Office with 'fairly satisfactory supplies', which was deemed 'not good enough'.[68] Ellwoods was not alone. Other firms also failed to get on to the lists, despite the fact that many regularly manufactured for other

[61] CAs to CO, 23 Dec. 1859, ibid.
[62] Enclosure a, Apr. 1901, CO 323/474/13685. For example, CAs to CO, 16 Dec. 1903, CO 295/421/45347; CAs to CO, 8 May 1901, CO 446/18/16066.
[63] PPD, table 3.
[64] The only exception was the purchase of materials for the Uganda railway, which was constructed by the Foreign Office. Fearing parliamentary criticism, the Treasury insisted on supplies being obtained through public advertisement, and, from 1904, large running orders: Treasury to Uganda Railway Committee, 7 Nov. 1895, CO 537/50/79; Treasury memo, 18 Nov. 1895, CO 537/50/156; memo, 5 Oct. 1908, CAOG 17/22.
[65] Memo, 5 Oct. 1908, CAOG 17/22.
[66] PPE, qq. 2043–4, 2074. After the enquiry, which recommended the greater use of colonial firms, the Agents reversed this policy, though there continued to be complaints of insufficient representation: PPR, p. xxiii.
[67] *Sells Commercial Intelligence*, 23 Mar. 1904, 15; CAs to Barrett, 20 June 1895, CAA, file 99; 1911 report, file 53.
[68] War Office to CAs, 1 Apr. 1902, CAOG 12/123; note, 21 May 1904, ibid.

government departments, colonial agent-generals and, in some cases, the Agents themselves as subcontractors to listed firms.[69] In theory, any rejected firm could appeal to the secretary of state.[70] But few did so, fearing that this would damage the prospects of future applications and reduce the chance of obtaining other government department contracts or Crown Agent list company subcontract work.[71] Furthermore, from 1901, all appeals were dealt with by the under-secretary of state, Sir Montague Ommanney, who, as a former Senior Crown Agent, was thought unlikely to reverse the Agents' decisions.[72]

In comparison, the India Office kept no lists, and obtained the majority of its goods, 62 per cent in 1924/5, by tender through public advertisement.[73] The War Office, from the 1860s, and the Admiralty used lists, but did far more than the Agents to encourage new applicants.[74] The War Office advertised annually and periodically asked the Woolwich store to recommend firms.[75] The Admiralty advertised, obtained copies of the War Office list and occasionally sent officials to 'a certain district to see whether we can find any additional suitable firms'.[76] Although both asked for customer references, neither specified the type of reference required, the War Office accepting 'practically . . . everybody . . . who appears to be a competent contractor'.[77] As a result, War Office lists contained approximately 10,000 firms, as opposed to the Agents' 3,000, 1,000 if the companies that appeared on more than one list are taken into account.[78]

Even inclusion on a Crown Agent list, however, did not guarantee orders. Neither the War Office nor the Admiralty placed limits on the number of companies asked to tender; the War Office sent invitations to all the firms on its lists as a matter of course.[79] The Agents, on the other hand, only asked a small number of companies on the relevant list to bid for each contract, basing their choice, in the case of engineering orders for example, on the

---

[69] *Sells Commercial Intelligence*, 16 June 1904, 7; 23 Mar. 1904, 15.
[70] Memo, 5 Oct. 1908, CAOG 17/22.
[71] *Sells Commercial Intelligence*, 31 Aug. 1904, 7.
[72] Ibid. The director of the Nyasaland Railway Co. regarded an appeal to Ommanney as 'an appeal to the Crown Agency in another form': PPE, q. 557.
[73] PPE, q. 409; PP 1924–5, xxi (711), 7.
[74] PPE, q. 1938.
[75] PP 1901, xl (Cd 581), qq. 4312–13, 84.
[76] Ibid. qq. 1778/9, 2470, 2475.
[77] Ibid. qq. 2780–1; PPE, q. 2293. The War Office also required a banker's reference, and the Admiralty inspected works: PP 1901, xl (Cd 581), qq. 2780–1, 2471.
[78] PPE, q. 2293; memo, 5 Oct. 1908, CAOG 17/22. A 1904 Parliamentary paper that contains the number of tenders received for nineteen contracts for a variety of goods worth over £500, the value at which all list firms were supposedly tendered, suggests that the average number of companies per CA list was eight: PP 1904, lxxviii (Cmd 194). The 1901 cement list, the only survivor, contains seventeen firms, nine of which appear to have been available for tender: memo, 3 Dec. 1900, CAOG 12/126.
[79] WO 254/6, 1378, Jan. 1908.

recommendation of the consulting engineer who drew up the tender specification.[80] In 1901, for goods worth between £100 and £500 it would often 'suffice to invite only a few firms from a list'.[81] Of those companies that were permitted to submit a tender, many rarely received an order. Both the Agents and their engineers, who recommended successful engineering tenders, theoretically picked the lowest tender submitted. In reality, the most competitive bid was chosen only if the tender was judged to fulfil all the colonies' requirements and the tenderer was believed to have sufficient experience and to produce well designed goods.[82] Orders, consequently, tended to be awarded to a small coterie of suppliers that produced quality goods. The iron company Messrs Walter MacFarlane & Co., for instance, was succesful in 94 per cent of the seventy-one applications which it submitted between 1883 and 1888, and, of the fifty orders for cement supplied to Ceylon betweem 1894 and 1901, 60 per cent were fulfilled by just three companies, and 30 per cent by just one.[83]

Goods purchased without tender were obtained from a small number of wholesalers and manufacturers and from the War Office. Theoretically, the Agents, like the India Office, War Office and Admiralty, did not use wholesalers, whose goods were relatively expensive, owing to the wholesaler commission, and were more likely to have been produced abroad.[84] In reality, wholesalers were regular suppliers of materials, as their specialist purchasing skills ensured quality and their use minimised delay, and, by reducing administration costs and increasing prices, maximised Crown Agent income. The largest group of articles purchased through wholesalers were 'Birmingham goods', that is hardware and metal articles manufactured largely in Birmingham.[85] These were bought by Messrs V. & R. Blakemore, a firm which had worked for the Agents since the 1860s and which depended on the Agency for a large part of its income. This company, which in 1896 obtained approximately 6.7 per cent of total purchases, bought goods without tender and again used a small number of suppliers (see table 5).[86] In return, it earned a commission of 2.5 per cent for packed items and 5 per cent for articles packed and stored in its Birmingham warehouse.[87] Its use was the subject of

[80] CAs to CO, 26 Jan. 1901, CO 137/623/3351; Preece to CAs, 23 Aug. 1907, CAOG 10/53.

[81] Enclosure a, Apr. 1901, CO 323/474/13685.

[82] CAs to CO, 8 Dec. 1899, CO 446/4/34286; Reed to CAs, 6 Apr. 1901, CO 537/68.

[83] Schedule, n.d., CAOG 12/126; schedule, Oct. 1888, CO 323/371/18103. See also enquiry, q. 1640, CO 131/33.

[84] PPE, qq. 1711, 2471; Sells Commercial Intelligence, 9 Mar. 1904, 7; 8 June 1904, 13.

[85] CAOG 17/24, misc. 142, nos 21, 17, 30; Blakemore to CAs, 12 Aug. 1904, CO 323/492/29753.

[86] CAs to CO, 28 Feb. 1902, CO 323/474/8579.

[87] Enclosure a, Apr. 1901, CO 323/474/13685. Although profit figures have not survived, the lucrative nature of the business is reflected in the estate of Villiers Blakemore, who, when he died in 1884, left £26,190: SH, probate records.

Table 5
Value of goods purchased from the largest non-tender suppliers, 1885, 1895, 1905, 1914 (£)

Company	1885	1895	1905	1914
V. & R. Blakemore	27,623 (47)	39,224 (120)	41,719 (70)	69,673 (89)
Grindlay & Co.	2 (1)	971 (8)	13,289 (143)	18,974 (111)
Howard & Sons	4,425 (40)	14,365 (76)	12,264 (39)	10,862 (24)
Millington & Co.	2,485 (45)	2,962 (69)	6,432 (50)	3,060 (27)
Milns & Co.	9,288 (42)	17,548 (125)	16,647 (47)	6,069 (44)
Saunders & Co.	17,208 (63)	13,062 (112)	26,106 (52)	10,871 (46)
Waterlow & Sons	15,410 (72)	14,987 (117)	38,113 (76)	59,600 (84)
Totals (% of total purchases)	76,441 (18%)	103,119 (18%)	154,570 (9%)	179,109 (4%)

Source: BE, C 98/7202; C 98/7211–12; C 98/7221–22; C 98/7227.

Note: The annual figures are the totals of cheques paid to each company drawn on the Agents' general account and may be underestimates. The bracketed figures, except for the totals, are the number of cheques drawn, each of which may represent an order or part of an order.

much criticism. In 1900 the Colonial Office clerk A. Sewell argued that there was no reason why the Agents themselves should not purchase such goods and that the company's remuneration was excessive.[88] Ten years later, a Birmingham firm complained that, like its fellow companies, it had never been employed by Blakemores, even though it regularly supplied the India Office, War Office, Admiralty and many agents-general, and, in 1904 it was claimed that the company failed to pass manufacturers' discounts on to the Agency.[89] In their defence, the Agents argued that Blakemores' use of a small number of producers ensured uniformity of pattern, and that the firm's staff were 'skilled experts in the hardware trade', could thus buy to better advantage than themselves and were a better judge of quality.[90] Nevertheless, in 1902, to avoid 'questions', the Agents arranged for the company to include its own commission in the price quoted for articles.[91] They also made less use of the firm, perhaps preferring to use the commission agent Grindlay & Co., whose purchases on behalf of the Agents grew rapidly during the period (*see* table 5).[92]

[88] Sewell, 11 Oct. 1900, CO 137/613/31708.
[89] Hart to CO, 15 Jan. 1902, CO 323/481/2189. Blakemores insisted that the firm had been used: Blakemore to CAs, 20 Aug. 1904, CO 323/492/29753.
[90] CAs to CO, 28 Feb. 1902, CO 323/474/8579; CAOG 17/24, CAR.
[91] CAOG 17/24, CAR.
[92] The fall in Blakemores' share of total purchases may also be related to the growth in purchases of railway material.

Other goods purchased through wholesalers were timber, furniture, miscellaneous domestic goods, paper and drugs. Timber was bought from Leary & Co., who obtained a brokerage of 1 per cent.[93] Furniture came largely from J. Schoolbred & Co. and S. J. Waring & Sons, both of whom had premises in Oxford Street, London.[94] Miscellaneous domestic goods were often bought from the Army & Navy Stores.[95] Paper was supplied by Messrs Saunders, who produced a small proportion of what was needed themselves, purchasing the remainder from other manufacturers, from whom they obtained a commission of 5 per cent.[96] Although the Agents claimed that the firm's 'expert knowledge' allowed them to 'secure the lowest price', others believed the paper to be 'far too expensive' and that the Agents to be 'particular friends' of the company.[97]

As the quality of medicines was difficult to determine and the supply of inferior goods could lead to death, all drugs were bought from the Society of Apothecaries.[98] Criticism of the society peaked in 1905 and 1907, when, respectively, Ceylon and British Guiana sent the Agents price comparisons that clearly indicated that drugs could be purchased far more cheaply privately.[99] Of the 522 items available in British Guiana from two private companies, for example, 73 per cent could be obtained at prices on average between 10 per cent and 15 per cent lower than those of equivalent articles purchased from the society.[100] The Agents declared the comparisons invalid. The prices, which were highly volatile, were collected at different times. The drugs available in Ceylon were supplied in bulk and the cost of sorting them into packages or bottles therefore was borne by the customer. In addition, it was argued that, as contracts were given to the lowest tenderer, irrespective of the quantities required, private firms deliberately kept the price of rarely used medicines low, but those of common drugs high. The two types of quinine available in British Guiana, for example, were 7 per cent and 39 per cent more expensive than that obtained from the society. Merchant drugs were also of an inferior quality to those supplied by the Apothecaries, a claim confirmed, in the case of the British Guiana drugs, by the colony's surgeon-general, who tested a number of samples.[101] Criticism, however, continued, forcing the Agents to change their policy. In 1908, declaring that improved methods of preparation and grinding had reduced the cost and improved the

93 CAs to Lagos, 22 Apr. 1912, CAOG 17/25.
94 CAs to Nigerian Railway, 3 Mar. 1914, CAOG 12/102; CAs to CO, 21 Aug. 1901, CO 291/31/29427.
95 PPE, q. 4352a.
96 CAs to CO, 4 Dec. 1906, CO 54/704/44711; Mercer's notebook, CAA, CA M 16.
97 Mercer's notebook, CAA, CA M 16; Sells Commercial Intelligence, 3 June 1908, 20.
98 CAs to CO, 14 Sept. 1867, CO 54/429/9030.
99 CAs to colonial secretary, 22 Nov. 1905, CO 54/696/41765; CAs to CO, 30 Apr. 1907, CO 111/558/15683. See also CAs to CO, 6 Sept. 1895, CO 152/199/15905.
100 CAs to CO, 30 Apr. 1907, CO 111/558/15683.
101 CAs to CO, 1 Apr. 1908, CO 111/564/11749.

quality of private supplies, they proposed that for a given period and as an experiment Ceylon should be allowed to purchase drugs through selective tender.[102] The trial led to 'a very substantial saving in cost', and the quality of the supplies, which the Agents had insisted should conform to British Pharmacopoeia definitions and be periodically tested, was found to be satisfactory.[103] The Agents, under pressure from the Colonial Office, thus extended competition to other colonies, though they appear to have purchased a large majority of supplies from just one firm, Howard & Sons.[104]

The remainder of the goods purchased without tender came from well-known manufacturers, and from the War Office. Manufacturers included Waterlow & Sons, who supplied colonial stationery; Millingham & Sons, from whom the Agents obtained envelopes; and Bickford & Sons, a fuze manufacturer.[105] The War Office supplied arms, ammunition and ordnance stores, the value of which, in 1911, amounted to £30,000.[106] Use of the War Office was compulsory and designed to ensure that it and its contractors continued to manufacture in peacetime on a scale that would allow rapid expansion in time of war.[107] The Agents strongly opposed the use of the War Office, as its general incompetence and its complex method of ordering materials greatly increased costs.[108] In addition, when goods were not available in the War Office store, there was often a long delay whilst they were bought from trade or manufactured, and for this the Agency was blamed.[109] The Agents also feared that colonial governments could be given permission to pass warlike store requisitions to local ordnance officers, rather than themselves. A proposal in 1903 that this should occur was strongly resisted by the Crown Agents, who regarded it as 'an attack on their business'.[110]

In their complaints to the Colonial Office, the Agents stressed the size of the War Office's purchasing commissions – 5 per cent for goods from the office's ordnance factories and 5.5 per cent for those specially bought in. They also argued that War Office prices were between 12 and 28 per cent higher

---

[102] CAs to CO, 31 July 1908, CO 323/538/28422.
[103] Ibid; circular, n.d., CO 323/553/40707.
[104] Circular, n.d., CO 323/553/40707; CAs to CO, 25 Mar. 1912, CO 554/7/9360.
[105] CAs to CO, 25 Mar. 1912, CO 554/7/9360; indent notes, CAOG 12/71.
[106] Lucas note, 25 July 1911, CO 323/581/19985.
[107] Ibid.
[108] CAs to CO, 1 Jan. 1907, CO 323/527/118. The Office required four copies of each order, as opposed to the trade's one, queried the 'smallest variation' in wording from its catalogue, provided only one supply invoice, forcing copies to be made and required payment between three and six months after goods were shipped: ibid; indent notes, CAOG 12/71.
[109] CO to CAs, 2 Jan. 1911, CO 323/577/456.
[110] CAs to CO, 12 Feb. 1903, CO 323/483/5971; Round note, 18 Feb. 1903, ibid. The Colonial Office believed that ordnance store purchase would eliminate delay, and, as store heads would buy goods direct, lead to more satisfactory purchase, and allow colonies to know the final cost immediately, thus reducing budgeting problems: CO 323/483/5971. The proposal was not put into effect.

than those quoted by private suppliers, a claim queried by the principal clerk at the Colonial Office, F. R. Round, who believed that, given the large quantities supplied, the War Office could probably purchase goods more cheaply than the Agency.[111] Nevertheless, in 1911, the Colonial Office gave the Agents discretion to order ordnance stores elsewhere when there was reason to believe that serious delay or expense would arise from supply by the War Office, and, on occasion, where cost was excessive gave them permission to order armaments elsewhere.[112] The Agency also occasionally bought military stores privately without Colonial Office authorisation.[113]

Suppliers

Whether they supplied the Agents with goods through 'competition' or direct purchase, the companies used had many characteristics in common. All were well-established firms with a reputation for quality and large sales that reflected customer satisfaction. They also had close trust relationships with the Agents, which again discouraged the provision of poor quality goods. Trust was generated by a number of factors. The purchasing procedure ensured that companies would regularly obtain colonial contracts and have a long working relationship with the Agency. It also seems likely that the Agents allowed some benign price moral hazard, permitting suppliers to charge excessive prices for their goods, a practice that strengthened trust, and, as the premium would be lost if companies were dismissed for opportunism, discouraged the provision of poor quality goods. Other inducements were certainly offered. In 1904, for example, the Agents allowed Messrs Saunders to distribute to the colonies, at the Agency's expense, a book of standard paper samples and a price list.[114] The Agents and their engineers, furthermore, possessed personal and social links with suppliers, which also helped to reduce adverse selection and added a social cost to quality moral hazard. Sir Montague Ommanney, for instance, had numerous manufacturers as friends, Sir Ernest Blake was the son-in-law of Alfred Blyth, one of the Agency's marine engine manufacturers and at least two consulting engineers were directors of list firms (see table 6).[115]

---

[111] See table 4. CAs to CO, 3 Nov. 1906, CO 323/517/40711; Round note, 18 Feb. 1903, CO 323/483/5971.

[112] CO to CAs, 1 Aug. 1911, CO 323/581/19985; CO to War Office, 23 July 1913, CO 129/404/24135.

[113] War Office to CO, 30 June 1911, CO 323/581/25250; War Office to CO, 25 July 1911, CO 323/581/24960.

[114] The Agents' claim that this would encourage paper standardisation was treated with some suspicion by the Colonial Office, which regarded the Agency's relationship with the firm as 'curious': note, 6 Dec. 1906, CO 54/704/44711.

[115] CAA, office memorandum book, vol. 1, 21 Dec. 1905; I. M. Blake family history, Blake papers; *Post Office London directory*, 1859; CAs to Natal, 24 Feb. 1872, CO 179/109/2146; CAs to CO, 14 Nov. 1865, CO 54/408/11068. The company owned by Alfred Blyth was Messrs J. and A. Blyth of Limehouse. Sir J. F. Flannery, one of the Agents' naval architects was a director of Callenders Cable & Construction Ltd, which was successful in at least two

Table 6
Commercial activities of some of Sir Montague Ommanney's friends

Friend	Commercial activity
Sir Charles Bagot	Director of the University Life Assurance Society.
Sir Francis Henry Evans	Partner of Messrs Donald Currie & Co., who were managers of the Union Castle Shipping Co.; director of Thames & Mersey Marine Insurance Co. and Compagnie Internationale des Wagons.
James Hall	Frederic Shelford's uncle; partner of Messrs Palmer Beckwith & Co., shipbrokers and owners.
Edward Bell Knobel	Son married Sir Montague Ommanney's niece; managing director of Ilford Ltd.
Sir Charles Rugge Price	Director of Rock Life Assurance Co.
Herbert de Stern	Senior partner in Herbert Stern & Co.
Sir Thomas Storey	Chairman of Storey Bros. & Co.; director of Bickershaw Colliery; Darwen & Mostyn Iron Co.; Lancashire Banking Co.
Lord Strathcona	Director of Bank of Montreal; Canadian Pacific Railway Co.; Commercial Cable Co.; Hudsons Bay Co.; London & Lancashire Life Assurance Co.; London & Canadian Loan & Agency Co.
Sir Frederick Wigan	Senior partner of Wigan & Co., hop merchants; director of Azoff Coal Co. Ltd; Union Assurance Society; Ragliari Gas & Water Co. Ltd; Milwall Dock Co.

Note: The people listed were guests at the weddings of Ommanney's sons and daughters.

Source: *Who was whom* (CD-ROM); *British biographical index*; Shelford press cuttings; *Directory of directors*, 1899.

That these trust relationships masked fraud on the part of both Agents and engineers, as claimed by some critics, seems doubtful. Purchasing recommendations made by consulting engineers went unmonitored until 1909, when the Colonial Office, wishing to protect them from 'approaches by contractors', required them to provide reasons for their choices.[116] Even so there is no evidence of engineer fraud, which was discouraged by their high fees, their dependence on the Agency for a large part of their income and (as will be discussed in chapter 4) their own strong trust relationships with the Agents. Similarly, there is no proof of personal dishonesty on the part of the Agents, nor, beyond the acceptance of Christmas boxes, on the part of their clerks. Malfeasance by Agents and Agency staff was discouraged by a range of strategies adopted by both the Colonial Office and the Agents. The Agency also introduced staff monitoring procedures specifically designed to guard against

tenders: *Directory of directors*, London 1908; CAOG 19/295; CAOG 19/161. Major General E. H. Harding, the military stores consulting engineer, was a director of the Chilworth Gunpowder Co. Ltd, which again supplied the Agents: *Directory of directors*, London 1889.

[116] CO to CAs, 20 Oct. 1909, CO 96/488/32376; Ellis note, 16 Oct. 1909, ibid.

Table 7
United Kingdom imports from crown colonies, 1880–1914, as percentage of total imports

Colony	1880	1914
Ceylon	30	29
Gold Coast	84	70
Jamaica	53	38
Mauritius	17	31
Sierra Leone	72	70
Straits	26	11
Trinidad	35	29

Source: PP 1894, xcii (Cd 7526); PP 1916, xxxii (Cd 8329).

fraud. On arrival, tenders were stamped, initialled, recorded in a date book and placed in a locked box, and, when the box was opened at the end of the tender period, ticked off against their date book entries. Late tenders were only accepted with the special permission of a Crown Agent, and all decisions made by purchasing clerks were checked by a deputy head, and, in the case of orders, by a Crown Agent.[117]

Suppliers, similarly, tended to be British and to a lesser extent located in the south-east. In 1911 just £2,185 of orders were inspected overseas.[118] In comparison, the India Office, from 1898/9 to 1914/15, obtained between 1.6 per cent and 10 per cent of its stores from countries other than the United Kingdom, and the War Office, except for certain war materials, always allowed foreign manufacturers to tender, and only favoured British contractors if the price difference was 'negligible'.[119] Foreign purchase was primarily discouraged by the Colonial Office's general support for British preference, motivated by a fear of the loss of British colonial markets, which, in the case of a number of crown colonies, appears to have been well grounded (*see* table 7). Although Crown Agent purchases in 1899 accounted for only 6.2 per cent of imports into crown colonies from the United Kingdom, it was believed that government purchase of British goods set an example that would be followed by the private sector.[120] Other factors that discouraged overseas purchase include the relatively high associated administration costs, the lower commission earned on the cheaper goods obtained and the risk that

---

[117] CAOG 17/24, CAR. Not all these procedures were fully adopted. In 1902, for example, the new office secretary discovered that late tenders were considered up to the time an order was placed with a supplier without any reference to an Agent, a practice that he believed to be 'objectionable' and 'a farce': Keith note, 12 Jan. 1904, Keith papers, Gen 144/3.
[118] 1913 report, CAA, file 53.
[119] PP 1904, lxvii (Cd 1915), 87; PP 1908, lxxv (Cd 3969), 105; PP 1913, xlviii (Cd 6783), 88; PP 1916, xxi (Cd 8343), 144; PRO, WO 254/3, 532, 27 Aug. 1907.
[120] PP 1904, lxxviii (264); PP 1914–16, lxxix (Cd 7786).

the materials bought would be of a substandard quality.[121] There was probably also a fear of criticism from the press, which was were strongly pro-British.

Foreign firms were invited to tender for crown colony supplies under four specific circumstances. Firstly, where the Agents wished to encourage British firms or cartels to reduce prices. In 1904, for example, the Agency explicitly warned members of the rail cartel that an advert for rails for the Federated Malay States was to be placed in the United States press, and that any suitable American tenders would be accepted.[122] The Agency, though, generally went to great lengths to avoid carrying out such threats. When it was found, in the case of these rails, that the second lowest tender was from the United States, 'every effort' was made to induce British tenderers to reduce their prices, and a manufacturer, who underbid the Americans, was encouraged to offer a more suitable port of shipment.[123] Orders were placed abroad only when the cartel remained intransigent, the Agents then using the order to encourage members of the ring to lower their prices in the future. In 1901, for instance, after placing a cement order in Germany, the Agents warned the secretary of the Associated Portland Cement Co., the cement cartel, that, unless prices were reduced, 'our business . . . which is already very large and likely to increase, will most assuredly go abroad'.[124] On the whole this strategy was successful. In 1904 the threat of foreign purchase caused the rail cartel to reduce prices from £5 10s. to £5 2s. 6d. per ton, and, when an order was placed in the United States and the cartel realised 'we were in earnest', to £4 14s. per ton.[125]

Second, foreign goods were purchased where it was clear that a very distinct advantage would accrue to a colony, generally interpreted as a price difference of more than 10 per cent, or where there was likely to be a lengthy delay in delivery, due to a strike or other causes.[126] The Agents in 1900, for example, purchased Jamaican railway carriages in the United States, because 'long deliveries' were offered by British firms, and, in 1912, obtained cement from America to avoid the London dock strike.[127] Overseas tenders were also invited where a particular country produced articles that were not available in Britain, or were more advanced than those manufactured by domestic firms, for example electrical engineering goods.[128] An exception was electric

---

[121] *Sells Commercial Intelligence*, 9 Mar. 1904, 7; 1911 report, CAA, file 53. The cost of inspecting foreign purchases in 1911 was £119, but the fee charged was only £60: 1913 report, CAA, file 53.
[122] CAs to CO, 7 Sept. 1904, CO 273/304/31241.
[123] Ibid.
[124] CO to CAs, 5 June 1901, CO 520/10/15284.
[125] Memo, 16 Mar. 1904, CO 323/492/10117.
[126] CO to CAs, 12 July 1904, CO 273/304/23875; memo, 19 Feb. 1926, CAOG 12/97; Chamberlain note, 20 Dec. 1902, CO 273/253/34283.
[127] CAs to Cooper, 8 May 1900, CO 137/623/3351; CAs to CO, 15 July 1912, CO 323/591/22145.
[128] Federated Malay States to CAs, 30 Aug. 1901, CO 273/276/39738.

light carbons, which, though superior products could be obtained from Germany, were purchased from the General Electric Co. from 1911 on the advice of the Admiralty, which wanted to ensure their continued production in the United Kingdom on the 'grounds of imperial defence'.[129]

The Agents' distrust of foreign suppliers was matched, though to a lesser extent by their, and their consulting engineers' suspicion of northern manufacturers. Fifty-three per cent of the firms listed in the *Board of Trade Labour Gazette* as having won Crown Agent orders between 1910 and 1914 had addresses in the south and south-east. Even if allowance is made for those companies that gave their headquarters rather than their works location, this finding still suggests a strong southern preference.[130] In certain sectors the bias was highly pronounced. A study of the orders placed for shallow draft steamers designed by the Crown Agent's naval consultant, for example, revealed that the vast majority went to relatively expensive London yards.[131] The preference of Agents and engineers for southern suppliers was probably related to the ease with which they could form relationships of trust with their owners. It seems likely that they shared far more social and cultural characteristics with southern than northern manufacturers, and that they met them, in both a social and a professional capacity, more frequently. Raised and firmly settled in the south, the Crown Agents also no doubt possessed a strong loyalty to the region, and may have wished to help its relatively unsuccessful industrial economy. In 1870, for example, they recommended the immediate construction of a Ceylon steamer 'in the interests . . . of the poor unemployed artisans in the East End of London'.[132] The consulting engineers, similarly, were based in the capital, and may have been discouraged from recommending northern firms by the long distances that had to be travelled to inspect the finished goods, which carried a high time opportunity cost that the Agents' relatively low fees only partly compensated. As regards the preference for southern shipyards, the Agency's naval consultant, Sir Edward Reed, was an architect for the navy, which predominantly favoured London constructors, while the Agents believed that 'North country and Scottish firms' used 'inferior materials and workmanship' and that their vessels had high maintenance and repair costs that offset any saving in price.[133]

---

[129] CAs to CO, 26 Jan. 1911, CO 323/577/2738. In the case of the Transvaal, whose business the Agents took over in 1901, the Office for some years sent repeat orders to foreign firms used by the previous administration: memo, 1 Feb. 1930, CAOG 12/97.

[130] Only 37% of the successful tenderers came from the north, Midlands and south-west, 9% from Scotland and 1% from Wales and Ireland: *Board of Trade Labour Gazette*, 1910–14. It is interesting that today the Agents display a marked northern bias.

[131] Robert V. Kubicek, 'The design of shallow draft steamers for the British empire, 1868–1906', *Technology and Culture* xxxi (1990), 449.

[132] CAs to CO, 2 Feb. 1870, CO 54/459/1353.

[133] CAs to Natal, 24 Feb. 1872, CO 179/109/2146.

Other factors that raised prices

Despite the Agency's acceptance of some price moral hazard, there is the possibility that exceptionally greedy suppliers may have set unacceptably high prices without the Agents' knowledge. Prices were unofficially monitored through the Agents' consulting engineers, many of whom were directors of commercial companies and were familiar with average price levels through their other consulting work (see table 8), by those companies with which they had trust relationships, by former Crown Agents, former Colonial Office officials and governors, some of whom took up directorships on retirement, and, from 1900, by clerks who had previously been employed by suppliers.[134] It was nevertheless claimed that manufacturers failed to provide colonies with full trade and cash discounts and export allowances.[135] This accusation appears to be supported by the addition in 1907 of a note on all Crown Agent tender forms that specifically warns all suppliers that failure to provide normal rebates would cause them to be struck off the Agency's lists.[136] The use of competition also increased the likelihood of the establishment of rings of list members, as the small number of firms invited to tender would have ensured that each member would have regularly won a contract and made agreements easier to reach. According to the writer E. D. Morel and the ex-governor Sir F. A. Swettenham, rings of list members were common, particularly where large goods, such as locomotives, were put up to competition.[137] The Agents accepted that industry rings existed, but claimed that the Agency was largely unaffected by their activities.[138] This seems unlikely. The Agents' chemical suppliers, Howard & Sons, appear to have had numerous agreements with competitors, many of their manufacturers of track fittings were in official or unofficial pacts and, until the 1920s, the

---

134 The clerk, C. E. Williams, had previously worked for the Vulcan foundry and Messrs Carruthers; E. Owen had been employed at the Atlas works; H. E. Wimperis at Sir W. G. Armstrong, Whitworth & Co.; and H. Horsburgh at Messrs Bell & Morcom, Messrs Clark & Standfield and at the Norman Portland Cement Co.: schedule, CO 323/548/45364. The CAs bookkeeper and accountant from 1879 to 1902 had 'commercial and financial experience in the Mediterranean and Eastern trades': CAs to CO, 22 July 1902, CO 323/474/30615.

135 *Hansard*, 4th ser. 1904, cxxxv. 1331, 1337. See, for example, CAs to CO, 9 Nov. 1906, CO 54/704/41348.

136 Ceylon to CO, 30 July 1857, CO 54/339/2283; Federated Malay States railway manager, 8 May 1905, CAOG 14/66; *Sells Commercial Intelligence*, 3 June 1908, 20. The warning appears to have had little effect. In 1910, for instance, a letter from Thorneycroft & Co. to its British Honduras agent revealed that the firm was 'in the habit of quoting full list prices to the CAs': CAs to CO, 31 Mar. 1910, CO 123/266/16375.

137 PPE, q. 860; E. D. Morel to Antrobus, Mar. 1904, Morel papers, British Library of Political and Economic Science, London School of Economics, F (9).

138 The Agency circumvented a blasting powder cartel by placing orders with firms outside the ring; the rail and cement associations through the purchase of foreign goods; and the American paraffin cartel through the use of British companies: CA memo, 16 Mar. 1904, CO 323/492/10117.

Table 8
Commercial links of selected consulting engineers

Consulting engineer	Link
Sir John Wolfe Barry	Director of Brazilian Submarine Telegraph Co. Ltd; London Platino-Brazilian Telegraph Co.; Western & Brazilian Telegraph Co.; Rock Life Assurance Co.; Eastern Extension, Australasian and China Telegraph Co. Ltd; Eastern Telegraph Co. Ltd; Eastern & South African Telegraph Co.; Globe Telegraph & Trust Co. Ltd; Western Telegraph Co. Ltd; River Plate Telegraph Co. Ltd
Sir John Coode	Director of Alliance Economic Investment Co. Ltd
Robert Elliott-Cooper	Director of New Sharlston Collieries Co. Ltd; Royal Sheba Co. Ltd
Sir Fortescue Flannary	Director of Peterson's Water Tube Boiler Co. Ltd; Callenders Cable & Construction Co. Ltd; Henry Pooley & Son Ltd; Suburban Gas Co. Ltd
Charles Hutton Gregory	Director of Morgan Crucible Co. Ltd
John Clark Hawkshaw	Director of Anglo-Norwegian Aluminium Co. Ltd
Sir William Preece	Director of British Coalite Co.; London Electric Supply Corp. Ltd
Sir Robert Rawlinson	Director of Tredegar Iron & Coal Co. Ltd
Sir Edward Reed	Former manager of the engineering company J. Whitworth Ltd; chairman of Earl's Co. (1871); director of Delta Metal Co. Ltd; Goodwins Jardine & Co. Ltd; Hopcroft Furnace Co. Ltd
Sir Alexander Rendel	Brother was London manager and later vice-chairman of the shipbuilding and engineering company Armstrong Whitworth & Co.
Sir William Shelford	Wife's brother was the shipowner and broker James Hall who, with Sir Charles Palmer and his brother John Hall, was a partner in Palmer Hall & Co.; director of Roller Bearings Co. Ltd
Major General Harding Steward	Director of Chilworth Gunpowder Co. Ltd

Source: *Directory of directors*, 1889, 1890, 1899, 1904, 1908; *Dictionary of national biography: missing persons*, Oxford 1993; *Dictionary of national biography*, Oxford 1993; *Newcastle Daily Chronicle*, 29 Dec. 1904, in Shelford press cuttings.

Agency lost large sums from a pact between stamp and note printers.[139] Furthermore, in the inter-war period, the belief that the Agents would never buy large amounts of goods overseas, led some cartels to charge the Agency far higher prices than their other clients.[140] The Steel Sleeper Association and the Switches and Crossings (Export) Association, for example, used the Agents as a milch cow, charging them far higher prices than any other customer, and using the profits earned to cross-subsidise more competitive work.

Prices were raised further by a number of miscellaneous factors. Individual colonies generally purchased small amounts of materials at any one time and were reluctant to accept low cost standard articles. As a result the Agents were often denied rebates on bulk purchases, faced relatively high delivery charges and were unable to enter long-term contracts under which goods were supplied for a set period at a set price.[141] Colonies also had a tendency to mark goods 'urgent' to avoid delay, forcing the payment of a premium for rapid delivery.[142] In 1902 the Agents asked colonial governments only to use the term if the need was genuine, but to little effect; in 1911, 90 per cent of Lagos textile, blanket and cap orders continued to be described as 'urgent'.[143] The Agents, meanwhile, when buying materials for public works, were reluctant to take advantage of any fall in price by purchasing all the articles required for a project at one time, a strategy which would also have gained them a bulk purchase discount. Instead, they preferred to buy goods as they were needed, as large one-off purchases could lead to criticism if prices subsequently fell further, tied up capital for no return and led to high storage and deterioration costs.[144]

The new purchasing policy

From the late 1890s the Agents' use of competition declined, due to their dire financial situation and colonial development and the expansion of empire, which increased the demand for goods. Although their workload had grown, they were reluctant to increase staff numbers. More staff would plunge them further into debt and lead to criticism from the Colonial Office. Moreover,

---

[139] Howard & Son, 20, 21 Nov. 1891, Howard & Son papers, London Metropolitan Archive, ACC 1037/93, 125; 21 Aug. 1902, ACC 1037/94, 30; ACC 1037/92, 234, 237; ACC 1037/94, 240; J. F. Hargrave, 'Competition and collusion in the British railway track fittings industry: the case of the Anderton foundry, 1800–1960', unpubl. PhD diss. Durham 1992, appendix A3.74. The agreement between stamp and note printers is discussed in chapter 9 below.

[140] Hargrave, 'Competition', 301.

[141] CAs to CO, 27 Jan. 1908, CO 273/342/3102. The adoption of long-term contracts was further discouraged by their speculative nature.

[142] Notes, CAOG 12/71.

[143] Notes, 13 Nov. 1911, ibid.

[144] CAs to CO, 3 Mar. 1905, CO 273/313/6939. For an exception to this policy see CO to CAs, 30 May 1911, CO 879/104/951, no. 158.

Figure 6. General department productivity, 1902–14

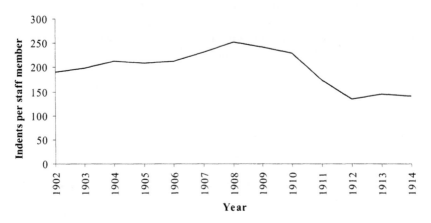

Source: CAOG 12/40, nos 1, 22.

Note: Pre-1901 figures are not available.

the work arising from railway projects rose and fell, as schemes started and were completed, and there was a risk that the general rise in colonial purchases would prove short lived. New principals could become self-governing colonies and railway construction was bound eventually to slow down or come to a halt. There was thus the danger that an expansion of the office would be followed by a fall in the workload, leaving the Agents with an expensive establishment to maintain and eventually to dismiss and compensate.[145] The rise in orders was therefore met through greater productivity (*see* fig. 6). More goods were purchased from wholesalers and without competition, and various other practices adopted 'which need not be mentioned'.[146] As a result, the Agents' costs fell, prices and their commission income rose, there was an increase in 'misinterpretations and omissions' and longer delays.[147]

The colonies were unwilling to accept the consequences of the policy change. The extra expense was too great to be offset by a slight increase in taxation and could no longer be avoided through the use of colonial merchants. Owing to the expansion of merchant communities, the greater circulation by United Kingdom manufacturers of catalogues and price lists and, in West Africa, medical advances that permitted native clerks to be replaced by Europeans, governors could also monitor prices and costs more easily. Quality, meanwhile, was no longer of paramount importance. Colonial development meant that defective goods could often be repaired within colo-

---

[145] PPS, q. 10824; CAs to CO, 26 Sept. 1904, CO 291/74/26378.

[146] Memo, 4 Jan. 1908, CAOG 12/40, no. 7.

[147] Ibid; note, 7 Oct. 1902, CO 885/8/151.

nies and improvements in communications had reduced the opportunity costs of obtaining replacements from Britain. Colonial criticism of the Crown Agents therefore increased.

Developed colonies called for the abandonment of the Agency monopoly. It was argued that materials could be purchased more cheaply from local merchants, and numerous comparisons of prices were produced to prove this point. The Agents disputed the claims, arguing that the price comparisons were invalid. The merchant goods whose prices were quoted were of a relatively poor quality; purchased earlier or later than the most recent Agent delivery, during which time the price or freight rate respectively had risen or fallen; were of different sizes or weight; or had prices set artificially low to entice first-time customers.[148] Their own comparisons, however, were equally inadequate, failing to include the full cost of goods or the hidden expenses of supply by the Crown Agents.[149] It seems likely that the monopoly prevented merchants from buying goods in bulk and passing the savings on to the customer, reduced colonial taxation revenues, restricted competition, disturbed government–commercial relations and discouraged British manufacturers from establishing a strong colonial presence.[150] On a more basic level, because of the long delays in delivery, colonies had to determine their future requirements for goods, which could prove difficult and lead to shortages or surpluses that would deteriorate or have to be sold off at discounted prices.[151] They were similarly unable to view articles before purchase, increasing the likelihood of the supply of unsuitable goods, and had to establish stores, which, if building, staff, insurance, cartage, deterioration expenses and the opportunity cost of the capital tied up in stock were taken into account, could add between 10 and 15 per cent to the price of materials.[152]

Other colonies sought to limit the Agents' discretion as regards prices. The Colonial Office permitted colonial governments to state on requisition forms the maximum price that they wished to pay for each item required and the expected cost of the entire order.[153] Before purchase the Agents could thus

---

[148] CAs to CO, 22 Feb. 1906, CO 273/322/6421; CAs to CO, 13 July 1909, CO 54/729/23483; CAs to CO, 5 Apr. 1905, CO 291/89/11401; CAs to Sierra Leone, 20 July 1911, CAA, CS 4 SL; memo, n.d., E 283/1; CAs to colonial secretary, 22 Nov. 1905, CO 54/696/41765. The Agency, for example, supplied cement in 400lb casks, whereas merchants used 375lb and 387lb barrels: CAs to CO, 22 Feb. 1906, CO 273/322/6461; CAs to CO, 21 Feb. 1902, CO 137/631/7725.

[149] Memo, n.d., CAA, CS 4 SL; Freelands to CAs, 12 Oct. 1908, ibid; Sierra Leone to CO, 13 Aug. 1908, ibid.

[150] *Demerara Daily Chronicle*, 13 Jan. 1883, 2; *Sells Commercial Intelligence*, 9 Mar. 1904, 7. CA purchases in 1889, 1899 and 1913 accounted, respectively, for 9.48%, 15.3% and 13.8% of total crown colony public expenditure: PP 1914–16, lxxix (Cd 7786); PP 1904, lxxviii (264); PP 1914, lx (Cd 7510); CAA, accounts, 1889.

[151] Egerton to CO, 28 May 1906, CO 520/35/22223.

[152] CAs to Jamaica, 14 Feb. 1905, CO 137/648/5954; *The Argosy*, 26 Sept. 1906, 2; Round note, 18 Feb. 1903, CO 323/483/5971.

[153] Example requisition form, CAOG 12/71.

Figure 7. General department orders per indent, 1906–29

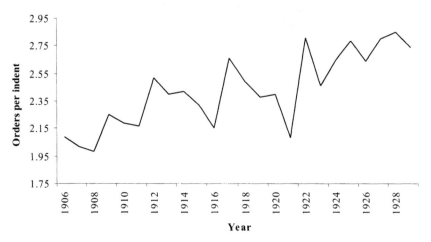

Source: CAOG 12/40, nos 6, 22.

compare the order price with the estimate and colonial maximum, and, if the former were excessive, refer back to the colony for instructions. In the event, to avoid the concomitant increase in costs and the delay and colonial criticism that resulted from referrals, the Agents only went back to a colony if the total cost of requisition articles exceeded the prices quoted by 25 per cent, the order was not urgent and there was no doubt as to the articles required.[154] In many cases, orders, even then, were not queried. For instance, in 1901, the Agents failed to contact Jamaica, even though passenger cars required for the colony's railway were 80 per cent more expensive than the estimate.[155] Attempts by the colonies to force the Agents to comply with the initiative were largely unsuccessful. A 1902 agreement that involved each colonial government laying down limits by which it would permit prices to be exceeded before referral became necessary was abandoned two years later for goods under £10.[156] The Agents claimed that the large number of referrals had led to long delays in delivery. Likewise, a plan put forward by Northern Nigeria in 1907 for the Agency to reduce the quantities of goods purchased if prices exceeded the maximum price set met with strong Agent resistance and was eventually rejected by the Colonial Office.[157]

---

[154] CAOG 17/24, CAR. The India Office, after determining the price of an order, always telegraphed India for approval: PP 1896, xv (Cd 8258), q. 2633.
[155] CO to Jamaica, 25 Apr. 1902, CO 137/631/7724. See also CAs to CO, 4 May 1900, CO 147/152/14525.
[156] CAs to CO, 19 Oct. 1904, CO 323/492/36051; CAs to CO, 28 Nov. 1904, CO 323/492/40471.
[157] CAs to CO, 18 Apr. 1907, CO 446/67/13734.

Figure 8. General department average indent and order values, 1910–29

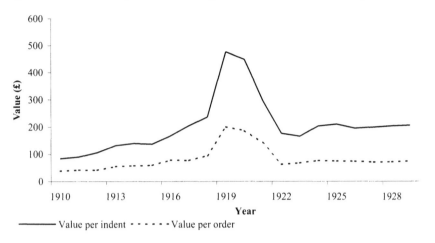

Source: CAOG 12/40, nos 22, 27–47.

Competition returned to favour only after the 1908 enquiry and the employment of the former Colonial Office under-secretary, Sir Reginald Antrobus, as Senior Agent. He, presumably, had been instructed to increase the use of public tenders. At the same time the Agency's income rose, and the enquiry's recommendation that its reserve fund should be redistributed to the colonies through lower fees constituted a further incentive to raise costs and increase staff numbers. Greater standardisation of goods ordered also reduced the risk that an unknown contractor would supply poor quality articles.[158] By 1911 the Agents had begun to invite tenders for paper and drugs and, by 1914, for enamelled wire and electroplate.[159] In 1914 furniture orders were passed to manufacturers for the first time, even though the Agents thus obtained 'less commission, as the money value is less'.[160] Other goods also began to be put up to competition and to be supplied by manufacturers. In the general purchasing department, productivity fell (*see* fig. 6), and indents, which usually contained demands for a large variety of articles, were split into smaller company orders, suggesting that there was less use of merchants, who generally supplied large combinations of goods (*see* fig. 7). Similarly, the value of company orders grew to a lesser extent than that of indents, reflecting a greater reliance on competition, which slowed order price rises (*see* fig. 8).[161] None the less, the supplier base continued to be relatively

---

158 CAs to CO, 15 Nov. 1912, CO 323/591/36350.
159 CAs to CO, 7 Oct. 1911, CO 323/577/32800; memo, 29 Apr. 1914, CAOG 16/25.
160 H.S. [*sic*.] to Mercer, 15 Jan. 1904, CAOG 12/102.
161 The slow rise in order prices is also reflected by the price lists that the Agents distrib-uted to colonies from 1906. Of the thirty-five articles supplied in both 1907 and 1911, the

Table 9
Purchases by the Crown Agents and India Office, 1910–14

	Crown Agents	India Office
Percentage of goods categories with three or more orders, of which 100% were obtained from one supplier	16.1	10.8
Percentage of goods categories with three or more orders, of which 70% were obtained from one supplier	31	18.7
Percentage of goods categories with three or more orders, of which 50% were obtained from one supplier	60	55

Source: *Board of Trade Labour Gazette*, 1910–14.

Note: The CAs had 168 goods categories with more than three orders and the India Office 203.

restricted. Analysis of successful tenders published in the *Board of Trade Labour Gazette* from 1910 to 1914, indicates that the Agents gave orders to only 468 firms during the period, most relatively large and well-known, and that in the case of 16 per cent of categories of goods all the orders went to just one supplier (*see* table 9).[162]

Given the danger of colonial and supplier dishonesty, it was in the interests of the Colonial Office to ensure that all public sector goods not manufactured in colonies should be supplied by the Agents. In reality, until the 1890s, the Crown Agents succumbed to benign moral hazard and accepted colonial and supplier self-interest. The colonies purchase of goods from local merchants was accepted by the Agents, as, following the reciprocal norm of their trust relationship with governors, they could be confident that the colonies in return would be inclined to accept their own duplicity. This involved the supply of quality goods, which further reduced the likelihood of colonial criticism and maximised their income. Quality was assured by the minimisation of that supplier self-interest that led to the provision of poor quality materials. Articles were bought with no or limited competition from large-scale British companies, many based in the south-east, that had had long relationships with the Agency, and, in some cases, were wholesalers. In addition the Agents permitted some benign supplier price moral hazard in the belief that this would strengthen their trust relationships with the companies involved and encourage the provision of quality goods. There may also have been,

price of 46% fell (57%, if seven types of canvas are excluded): CAA, CA circulars and papers. By comparison, the Board of Trade wholesale price index rose during the same period from 106 to 109.4: B. R. Mitchell, *British historical statistics*, Cambridge 1988, 728.
[162] Of the most commonly used firms (the most successful in each category) 85% had a credit rating of at least £2–3,000: *Credit index*, 1895/6.

unbeknown to the Agency, some further fraud on the part of suppliers. The result of the policy was that the prices paid for supplies were excessive. The Colonial Office and colonies, nevertheless, accepted the extra expense. Both had difficulty monitoring prices, fully accepted the quality criteria of evaluation actively promoted by the Agents and cared little about the additional cost, aware that it was relatively small when compared to the opportunity cost of substandard goods. The Agents' failure to enforce the monopoly regulation also allowed some low quality purchases to be made from colonial merchants, while for governors, criticism of an Agency that monitored their activities could carry a high personal cost.

The Agents' moral hazard became malign from the 1890s and the adoption of their income maximisation policy. The restriction of competition led to even higher prices and the clamp-down on self-seeking behaviour in the colonies, now regarded as malign, meant that colonies could no longer avoid the extra costs. Because of changes in the environment in which they operated, governors were also able to monitor prices more easily and were less concerned about quality. Faced with the possibility of unbalanced budgets, colonial governments began to question the purchasing monopoly and to criticise the Agents' prices. Such complaints, together with criticism of the Agents' activities in regard to infrastructure and issue, contributed to the eventual decision by the Colonial Office to reform the Agency.

3

Service Provision: Costs, Delay, Quality

Purchasing quality goods and adopting practices designed to limit adverse selection and moral hazard on the part of suppliers did not necessarily lead to the provision of perfect articles. Even carefully chosen and highly paid firms could be tempted to act dishonestly, and impropriety by the companies that packed and shipped goods could lead to supplies arriving in a colony in a damaged condition. Moreover, the goodwill earned by the provision of quality merchandise could easily be lost if those employed to insure cargoes and deal with associated legal matters performed their duties poorly. Consequently, where possible, the Agents monitored the manufacture of supplies, inspected completed articles and restricted competition in their choice of service providers, who earned high fees and formed trust relationships with the Agency, often based on family and professional ties. Inevitably, these practices, along with the Agents' purchasing commission, increased the cost of supplies. Furthermore, monitoring and the employment of high status engineers contributed respectively to delays in the delivery of goods and to the provision of unsuitable articles. Delay, however, was regarded by colonies as less important than the quality of the goods supplied and could be blamed by the Agents on a range of factors over which they had no control. The supply of unsuitable goods was relatively rare. These externalities of their self-interest were therefore disregarded by the Agents, though some action was taken to minimise delay.

Purchasing commission, inspection and packing fees

The Agents' purchase of goods was at first remunerated from an annual lump sum paid by the larger colonies, the size of which varied according to the amount of work undertaken.[1] The adoption of private sector purchase in 1860, which along with colonial development increased the Agents' workload, then prompted the Colonial Office to allow the Agency to charge those smaller administrations that did not pay a lump sum a commission of 5 per cent, 3 per cent for paper, and for large orders and for goods supplied to colonies suffering temporary economic depression between 2 and 2.5 per cent.[2]

---

[1] CAs to CO, 2 Apr. 1886, CO 323/364/5663.
[2] Ibid; CAs to CO, 18 May 1860, CO 323/256/5092; CAs to CO, 21 June 1871, CO 107/143/6154. The 5% commission was the same as that charged by other government

Lump sum payments, however, remained unchanged and in many cases failed to cover costs, forcing the Agents to make up the shortfall from the large fees that they earned from their issue of loans. In 1880 the loss of the responsible government colonies greatly reduced this income, and the Agents began to make losses on their purchasing work. Fearing Crown Agent bankruptcy, the Colonial Office in 1886 therefore allowed the annual contributions to be used to cover the cost of a number of services for which no charge had previously been made, and the Agents' purchase work for all colonies to be remunerated by a universal 1 per cent commission.[3]

Although the commission was generally treated as Office income, when, in exceptional circumstances, the Agency was required to undertake additional purchasing duties that added to its workload, it was distributed to the Agents or their staff. For example, in 1891, the £450–£460 earned for the purchase of goods for the British South African Telegraph Account, the De Beers Volunteers and the British South Africa Co. was paid directly to the clerks involved.[4] The commission was charged on the value of goods shipped i.e. the cost of the article, the shipping agent's fee and insurance and freight, and, according to the Agents, was relatively moderate.[5] It was certainly lower than the commissions set by the War Office, Admiralty and Stationery Office, who in 1896 charged respectively 5 per cent, 10 per cent and 5 per cent.[6] It was also less than most colonial merchant fees, which, owing to their small turnovers, colonial presence and high colonial capital charges, varied between 2.5 and 10 per cent, though many merchants claimed that they would be willing to complete government purchase for little or no profit, for the prestige value and to facilitate bulk purchase.[7]

Compared to private railway companies and the India Office, however, the Crown Agents' commission was relatively high. A comparison made in 1901 by the Uganda Railway Committee of the Agents' remuneration for the purchase of materials for the Uganda railway with the expenses of five

purchasing departments and took account of the small economies of scale that accrued from dealing with the restricted orders of these colonies.

[3] CAs to CO, 21 June 1871, CO 107/143/6154; PPS, q. 10755. A commission was preferred over an annual fixed sum, as it took account of fluctuations in business, and, for the colonies, was a fairer form of remuneration.

[4] CAs to CO, 17 Apr. 1891, CO 323/383/15937. In 1896 the Agents received a third and their staff two-thirds of the £1,491 earned during that year from the purchase of Uganda railway materials: CAs to CO, 13 Mar. 1897, CO 323/415/5386. The practice led to a widespread belief that the Agents were paid by commission rather than by salary: see, for example, *Hansard*, 4th ser. 1904, cxxx. 945.

[5] CAs to CO, 29 July 1912, CO 323/577/34999.

[6] PP 1896, xv (Cd 8258), q. 11745.

[7] Ibid; PPE, q. 3675; CAs to Anderson, 27 Dec. 1905, CAOG 14/66; *The Argosy*, 6 Oct. 1906, 5. In addition, during shipment many merchants charged interest on the cost of an order and freight: *Daily News*, 27 Apr. 1904, 6. The claim that government work would allow merchants to reduce their fees is supported by Holt to Deemin, 20 July 1908, Holt papers, MS Afr. s 1657, 1, jd/4b, 37.

comparable Indian railway companies and one Egyptian company, found that the Agency's remuneration far exceeded the costs of the private companies. Whereas the Agents' average annual charge was £4,807, that of the railway companies varied between £1,087 and £3,733, and averaged £2,460 per annum.[8] The Agents argued that the Ugandan railway business was 'extremely onerous and responsible', and claimed, somewhat disingenuously, that it charged the railway committee a lower fee than its usual principals, who additionally paid an annual contribution.[9] The committee was unconvinced, but nevertheless let the matter drop, as the majority of the railway materials had been purchased, and it was feared that if the complaint was pursued, the Agents could quit and some difficulty might be experienced in finding a replacement.[10]

The expenses of the India Office, which was financed from the revenue of the government of India, for the purchase and packing of goods and the organisation of shipping amounted, in 1878-9, to 0.17 per cent, and, in 1887–8, to 0.14 per cent.[11] The office's expenses were lower than those of the Crown Agents partly because its orders were far larger and it therefore had lower associated administration costs. In 1924–5, for instance, the average India Office order was £350 as compared to the Agents' £76 and, in 1907, each purchasing employee of the Crown Agents administered £18,682 of goods per year, as opposed to the £50,561 per annum dealt with by each member of the India Office's purchasing staff.[12] In addition, the Agents' work was more difficult than that of the India Office, owing to the larger number of principals, each with their own different needs and preferences, the necessity of ensuring that expenditure had been sanctioned by the Colonial Office and inadequate completion of order forms, due to the relatively poor quality of colonial staff.[13]

Yet, even if the greater and more difficult workload of the Agents is taken into account, their commission still appears to have been too high, particularly if the great increase in purchases from 1886 and the accompanying fall in administration costs is taken into account. The fee was excessive, partly to maximise the Agency's income and its reserve fund and partly to offset the cost of those services for which the Agents received no remuneration. When the charging structure was first introduced, these services were either not undertaken by the Agency or involved very little work and, given the difficulty of calculating their cost, it had been decided that no charge should be

---

8 Memo, 27 Mar. 1901, T 1/9660A/7003. The annual purchases of the railway companies were roughly the same as those of the Agents. The Uganda Railway Committee organised the construction of the Ugandan line.
9 CAs to Uganda Railway Committee, 8 Jan. 1901, CO 537/68.
10 Note, 4 Apr. 1901, CO 614/9/49.
11 PP 1896, xv (Cd 8258), qq. 11714–16.
12 PPE, appendix iv, vii, q. 424; PP 1924–5, xxi (711), 9; CAOG 12/40, nos 27–47.
13 PPR, p. vii.

made.[14] Thereafter, the number of services and the work involved grew, partly because of economic expansion in the colonies and partly because of the Agents wish to increase the interest of their tasks and the size and power of the Agency.[15]

To ensure the supply of quality goods and to avoid colonial criticism, the Agency closely monitored acquisitions through inspection and, to prevent damage during shipment, repacked supplies. Because of the importance of inspection, the Colonial Office allowed the cost to be recouped directly from the colonies rather than through the Agency's commission. The latter would have encouraged the Agents to minimise inspection in order to maximise profits, and the greater size of the commission would have made the cost of inspection more observable and more likely to be subject to Treasury or parliamentary criticism. Until 1904 inspection was undertaken by freelance inspectors and the Agency's consulting engineers, whose use allowed the Agents to avoid financial responsibility for the supply of defective goods.[16] Thereafter the Agents employed salaried full-time inspectors and established a specialist department that co-ordinated engineering inspection. In the case of engineering goods, a large proportion of the materials was examined before production commenced, and all goods were looked at during and after manufacture.[17] Other articles, such as cement and coal, were examined after production, and clothing, textiles, boots, military supplies and miscellaneous goods such as wagon covers and twine were transported to the Agents' London packers' warehouse for appraisal.[18]

Colonial criticism of the inspection process centred around three complaints. It was firstly argued that inspection was excessive, and that the use of leading firms, with highly effective inspection departments of their own, whose reputation and business would be damaged by the supply of poor quality goods, made the practice unnecessary.[19] A view supported by the limited amount of inspection undertaken by other public bodies. The War Office inspected only steel and small arms during production, though all delivered goods were examined, and the Admiralty and India Office usually inspected goods on delivery.[20] The Agents, however, claimed that inspection prevented fraud, and that 'even the best firms' could not, 'under the stress of

---

[14] CAs to CO, 1 Mar. 1907, CO 273/332/7781.

[15] The Colonial Office resisted all requests for additional remuneration. In 1907 it considered the introduction of a charge for correspondence and a universal annual lump sum payment, but decided that the matter should 'rest for the present': note, 11 Mar. 1907, ibid; Fiddes note, 11 Mar. 1907, ibid.

[16] Legally, inspectors and consulting engineers were employed and paid by the colonies.

[17] CAOG 17/24, CAR.

[18] PPE, qq. 4851, 4918, 4727, 1468; CAs to CO, 14 Feb. 1919, CO 323/797/10073.

[19] PPE, q. 1028; CAs to CO, 4 Mar. 1889, CO 18/214/4807. The Central South Africa Railway became so disgruntled that, in 1905, it requested that only certain articles be examined: *British and South African Export Gazette*, 1 June 1905, 1407.

[20] PP 1901, xl (Cd 581), qq. 448, 2328; PPE, qq. 431, 2481, 2491.

competition, be relied upon to turn out their best work'.[21] If inspection occurred only in the colonies, many defects would fail to be discovered, owing to the poor quality of local examiners, and there would be long and costly delays whilst defective articles were replaced.[22] In addition, suppliers would raise prices or no longer tender for crown colony orders, as they would have to employ a local agent to protect their interests, meet the cost of trans-porting replacement goods to the colony and defective articles back to the United Kingdom, and would suffer delays in payment, which occurred only after the acceptance of an article.[23] As regards the form of inspection adopted, the transport of clothing etc. to London ensured a minute and detailed examination, prevented the substitution 'through carelessness or fraud' of uninspected for inspected goods, and was often cheaper than sending an inspector to the supplier.[24] Works inspectors could obtain an accurate assessment of production costs that could be used in subsequent contract negotiations, and reduced delays, as their monthly progress reports allowed the Agency to send reminders to laggardly contractors.[25] Inspection visits to factories also strengthened agent–supplier trust relationships, and the rela-tively low cost of replacing partially completed articles prevented long and costly disagreements over the replacement of defective goods.[26]

A further criticism of inspection was that it was too expensive. The Colo-nial Office clerk J. F. N. Green stated in 1910 that the fees charged 'are not and never have been justifiable', and, in 1907, commented that the Agents' reduction of motor vehicle charges, in response to criticism, was 'virtually' an admittance of overcharging.[27] Likewise Lord Lugard, in 1902, accused inspec-tors of charging 'exorbitantly', and Western Australia, in 1889, believed the cost to be 'extraordinary great'.[28] Freelance inspectors' fees varied according to their status and the quantity of goods to be inspected.[29] Although no

---

[21] CAOG 17/24, CAR. The Agents' inspectors discovered a number of cases of fraud. In 1908 a contractor was found to be using a false inspectors' stamp to pass substandard goods: Ommanney to O'Callaghan, 4 Apr. 1898, CO 537/54. In 1892 a cotton waste manufacturer was found to have mixed cotton waste, rejected by an inspector, with the replacement waste: Bowring to Stanger, 11 Jan. 1892, CAA, file 20.

[22] CAOG 17/24, CAR. Colonial inspectors, aware of the high cost of rejection, could also be tempted to lower their standards.

[23] CO to Milner, 20 Aug. 1904, CO 291/74/26378.

[24] Memo, 23 Nov. 1908, CAOG 17/22.

[25] CAOG 17/24, CAR.

[26] Ibid. enclosure c; Crown Colonist, 1933, 371–2. In addition, the presence of inspectors stopped the supply of goods manufactured abroad. They could also often suggest useful improvements in design and production.

[27] Green note, 9 Sept. 1910, CO 323/564/22512; CAs to CO, 10 May 1907, CO 273/332/16717.

[28] Lugard to Scarborough, 17 Dec. 1902, Scarborough papers, MS Afr. s 87, 3; CAs to CO, 4 Mar. 1889, CO 18/214/4807. See also the British and South African Export Gazette, 5 Aug. 1904, 33.

[29] CAs to CO, 2 June 1904, CO 323/492/19809. To increase the cost of poor quality work,

record of their size survives, it seems likely that they were set relatively high to compensate for the temporary nature of the work, to attract men of 'proved ability and tried integrity' and to increase the cost of dismissal due to opportunism.[30] There was also a certain amount of inspector moral hazard. In 1912, for instance, it was discovered that the general works inspector for many years had charged the daily expenses fee of 4 guineas, available only where goods were to be inspected 'at any great distance', each time he had worked outside central London.[31]

On taking over inspection, the Agency continued to charge these rates, adopting, where inspectors were paid different amounts for the same work, the highest rate charged.[32] Furthermore, it decided that those fees that took the form of a percentage value of the work inspected should be calculated according to the FOB or CIF cost of goods ie. inclusive of packing and freight or packing, freight and insurance charges, arguing that the examination of packing formed an important part of the inspection process and that delivery and insurance expenses were often not known.[33] As a result, the fees introduced by the Agents in 1904 were far higher than those set by the India Office. For instance, the Agency charged 1.5 per cent for the inspection of clothing, as compared to the India Office's 0.958 per cent, and for railway materials between 1.5 per cent and 2.5 per cent, as opposed to the India Office's 1.334 per cent and the South Punjab Railway Company's 0.5 per cent.[34] Its profits from inspection similarly were large, between 1905 and 1909 amounting to between 50 per cent and 68 per cent for clothing inspection and between 12 per cent and 42 per cent for the examination of engineering goods.[35]

Finally, prior to 1904, inspection was not totally effective, and colonies were occasionally supplied with defective goods. For example, in 1904 iron-work intended for the Lagos Court House was found to have ill-fitting joints; timber destined, in 1901, for the Gold Coast Government House was discov-

the fee for a second inspection when a first had proved unsatisfactory was met by the manufacturer: CAs to Austin, 29 Apr. 1884, CAOG 12/120.

[30] CAs to CO, 4 Mar. 1889, CO 18/214/4807.

[31] Stanger to CAs, 13 Mar. 1912, CAOG 12/68. In 1901 the Agents strongly suspected that their naval architect, Sir Edward Reed, combined CA inspection with private work: CAs to Reed, 20 Sept. 1901, CAOG 10/36.

[32] CAs to CO, 2 June 1904, CO 323/492/19809.

[33] CAs to CO, 24 Dec. 1901, CO 137/623/45494; Carmichael to chief clerk, 15 Nov. 1926, CAOG 17/123. FOB = freight on board; CIF = carriage, insurance and freight. In 1926 the Agents accepted that the practice could not be justifed: Carmichael to chief clerk, 15 Nov. 1926, CAOG 17/123.

[34] CAs to CO, 2 June 1904, CO 323/492/19809; PP 1896, xv (Cd 8258), qq. 11716, 11726; South Punjab Railway Co. to Uganda Railway Committee, 28 Jan. 1901, CO 537/69/436.

[35] But for the high start-up costs, the continued use of consulting engineers to inspect highly remunerative bridgework and electrical contracts and the provision of a variety of services for no fee, engineering profit margins would have been even higher: CAOG 12/40, no. 5; reports 1905–9, CAA, file 53.

ered to be of poor quality; and springs supplied to Ceylon, in 1902, were of a higher resisting power than requested.[36] The Agents argued that mistakes in inspection were inevitable, given the number and complexity of the goods inspected, the need to limit the inspection of urgent goods to speed supply, the tendency for faults only to become apparent during use and, in the case of large orders, the small proportion of items that it was cost-effective to spot-check.[37] It was also claimed that defects were often due to bad or unskilful use, with the colonial officer responsible blaming the Agents to avoid censure.[38] A more likely explanation is inspector moral hazard, due to the low cost of opportunism and poor monitoring. For the freelance inspectors, dismissal involved neither the loss of certain future earnings nor a claim for damages, as the Agents, to avoid problems in recruiting inspectors, discouraged colonies from seeking financial retribution. It was also unlikely that any moral hazard would be discovered. The Agents monitoring of inspection was generally ineffective owing to the expense involved, which could not be recouped from the colonies, their physical distance from the inspectors, their lack of engineering experience and expertise and their reluctance, except on rare occasions, to obtain external advice.[39]

In 1904, fearing that criticism could threaten the existence of the Agency, in need of extra income and perhaps wishing to increase the size of the Agency and enhance their own status, the Agents established an engineering inspection department and appointed a permanent clothing inspector.[40] The new section consisted of a chief inspector and, by 1908, thirteen headquarters staff and twenty-seven external inspectors based in ten cities.[41] By increasing the cost of opportunism and improving monitoring, the department greatly

---

[36] PPE, q. 659; CAs to CO, 21 Oct. 1901, CO 96/386/37044; Gregory to CAs, 31 Dec. 1903, CO 54/691/728. In 1902 the governor of Southern Nigeria pronounced inspection to be 'utterly useless and futile, and the fees paid money thrown away': CAs to CO, 8 Dec. 1902, CO 520/17/50883.

[37] Gregory to CAs, 31 Dec. 1903, CO 54/691/728; CAOG 17/24, CAR.

[38] In 1905 pipes supplied to Hong Kong were found to have been subject to inappropriate treatment in the colony, which the Colonial Office concluded had then 'tried to throw the blame on the CAs': CAs to CO, 5 Mar. 1907, CO 129/342/8325; note, 7 Mar. 1907, ibid.

[39] The Agents checked their inspectors' explanations of poor inspection only in 1901, when they passed samples of bungalow materials and hoes respectively to the War Office chief surveyor and chief general stores inspector: CAs to CO, 21 Oct. 1901, CO 96/386/37044; CAs to Uganda Railway Committee, 10 Jan. 1901, CO 537/68.

[40] CAs to CO, 15 June 1904, CAOG 16/25. Leather goods continued to be inspected by a freelance until 1927: CAs to CO, 29 Sept. 1927, CO 323/977/12. The creation of the department was made possible by the move to Whitehall Gardens, which increased office space.

[41] Schedule, CO 323/548/45364. The ten locations were Barrow-in-Furness, Birmingham, Glasgow, Leeds, London, Manchester, Middlesborough, Newcastle, Newport and Sheffield. By 1912 the Office employed forty-two external examiners: CAs to CO, 6 Feb. 1912, CO 323/591/3806. The new inspectors were recruited largely from the ranks of freelance inspectors, but also from private engineering. Of the inspectors employed between 1904 and 1909 52% had previously worked in an engineering company, with half of those who

reduced inspector moral hazard. It also allowed the Agents to monitor the progress of goods through the manufacturing process, which reduced delays, gave them a better knowledge of the character and methods of suppliers and enabled them to take on highly lucrative inspection work for the Egyptian War Office and the Sudan Government Reserve.[42]

After inspection, those goods examined at the Agents' London packers' warehouse were repacked, as were materials likely to be damaged in transit, military goods and articles provided by firms for a number of colonies, which had to be split and in some cases then combined with other articles into packages. Packing was undertaken by Messrs Hayter, Howell & Co., later Messrs Hayter & Hayter, who were first employed by Julyan in the 1860s, having previously packed for the War Office and, apart from work for China and the British South Africa Co., depended wholly on the Agents for their livelihood.[43] The firm's remuneration took the form of a fee per package, which in 1907 averaged 13s. and made it possible for it to earn a profit of on average 16 per cent *per annum* between 1902 and 1907.[44] Critics of the Crown Agents questioned the need to repack goods and the size of the fees charged. Although in 1885 the firm adopted a cheaper form of packaging, which reduced some costs by 25 per cent, 'none but the best materials' continued to be used, and the firm 'regarded cost as a secondary consideration to that of thorough protection'.[45] There were also some complaints of poor packing, and of the company's lack of understanding of conditions in the crown colonies.[46] On the recommendation of the enquiry, the firm's duties in 1909 were taken over by the Agents, who, much to the consternation of the Colonial Office, paid the Hayter brothers compensation in the form of a 'salary' of £1,200.[47] The Agents improved the efficiency of the work, reducing total charges by 5 per cent and, by 1912, had accumulated profits of £880.[48]

left between 1904 and 1914 returning to the private sector, a trend that may have led to clashes of interest: CAA, record of inspectors; 1913 report, file 53.

[42] CAs to CO, 18 Jan. 1904, CO 323/492/2218; Mercer to Western, 20 Nov. 1908, CAOG 12/109.

[43] CAs to Natal, 2 Aug. 1865, CO 54/408/7482; CAs to CO, 3 Apr. 1909, CAOG 17/125; PPR, appendix xii, 221.

[44] Hayter to CAs, 4 Nov. 1908, CAOG 17/22; Hayter to CAs, 2 Nov. 1908, ibid. In the case of goods ordered by the Anglo-French boundary commission in 1907, the cost of packing varied from 2.9% to 5% of value: CO 431/121/1669, 12, 14.

[45] Hayter to CAs, 20 Aug. 1885, CAOG 16/15; CAs to CO, 10 Sept. 1885, ibid; PPR, appendix xii, 221.

[46] Ceylon to CO, 30 July 1857, CO 54/339/2203; public works department to high commissioner, 15 Aug. 1904, CO 446/41/10789; CAs to CO, 6 Sept. 1895, CO 152/199/15905.

[47] CAs to CO, 20 Aug. 1910, CO 323/564/25751; Green note, 25 Aug. 1910, ibid; note, 25 Aug. 1910, ibid.

[48] CAs to CO, 28 May 1913, CO 323/608/18225.

Shipping, insurance and legal fees

The final four components of Crown Agent prices were the fee paid to the shipping agent, the insurance charge, the cost of shipment and, occasionally, a legal charge. Until 1860 the transport of goods to the colonies was organised either by the public department that had supplied them, or, in the case of commercially bought items, by a private agent.[49] With the introduction of private purchase, freight was wholly arranged by a commercial company. The Agency's shipping department merely advised colonies on the despatch of stores, forwarded bills of loading and administered the insurance of cargoes.[50] The Agents claimed that they lacked the experience necessary to undertake the duties involved themselves, and that the exclusive use of CIF contracts, under which freight was arranged by the suppliers, would increase prices as contractors lacked the negotiating experience and the economies of scale of a professional agent.[51] The Crown Agents' first shipping agent was Messrs W. A. Wrinkley, whose business was monitored by the Agency's shipping and insurance clerk F. A. Wrinkley, the son and brother of the firm's owners.[52] Wishing to gain revenge on F. A. Wrinkley for the damage he had inflicted on the Agency on his dismissal and aware that mutual trust had been irrevocably broken, the Agents replaced Wrinkleys with Messrs J. & R. B. Freelands in 1868.[53] This company worked for the Agents until 1911, and its long relationship with the Office and almost total dependence on crown colony work, which increased the potential cost if their services were to be dispensed with, no doubt encouraged it to perform its duties honestly and adequately. As with Messrs Wrinkley, there was a personal link between the company and the Agents, which again facilitated monitoring, strengthened trust and increased the social cost of dishonesty. The son of Sir William Sargeaunt, A. St George Sargeaunt, was employed by the company in 1883 as a clerk, became one of the partners in 1888, at the age of twenty-four, and, in 1907, on the death of the firm's founder, John Freeland, became senior partner.[54] Likewise, in 1899, the son of Sir Ernest Blake, Ernest Stephen Blake, after gaining a Cambridge degree and two years experience in a shipbroker's and a merchants' office, also joined the company as a clerk, becoming, as a result of a prior agreement between his father and the childless John Freeland, a partner at the age of

49 CAs to CO, 5 Feb. 1859, CO 323/254/1366.
50 PPR, p. xix.
51 CAOG 17/24, CAR. Smaller articles were occasionally posted to colonies by contractors: PPE, q. 4503.
52 Wrinkley to CO, 27 May 1868, CO 323/291/2424.
53 CO to CAs, 9 Aug. 1911, CAOG 17/41; PPS, q. 10685. To organise shipments from Liverpool, Freelands in turn employed a further shipping agent, Messrs Greenshields Cowie & Co.: CAA, M 120.
54 CAs to CO, 28 Oct. 1911, CO 323/577/34999; PPE, qq. 4283–311.

twenty-eight.[55] Although both Sargeaunt and Blake obtained large shares of the firm's profits, neither took an active part in its day-to-day operations.[56] Sargeaunt dealt with the company's 'finances', and Blake, whom the principal clerk at the Colonial Office, J. Anderson, regarded as 'pretty useless', helped supervise shipments.[57] The bulk of the work was carried out by John Freeland and Thomas Holt, a long-time employee who was made a partner on the announcement of the 1908 enquiry.[58]

The fees paid to the company appear to have been relatively high. To avoid suggestions that it had an interest in the cost of the freight obtained, the firm, unlike other shipping agents, was remunerated according to weight, and, in the case of packages, the number of parcels shipped.[59] Where large quantities of goods were to be transported to a particular colony, a uniform charge of 6d. per ton was adopted.[60] In addition, for the arrangement of passages for colonial officers, the firm received a commission from the shipping companies concerned, which some believed it had no right to retain.[61] The size of the fees paid was the subject of much criticism. In 1901 the Uganda Railway Committee, on discovering that the company's commission for the arrangement of shipments to Uganda was double that charged by the India Office's shipping agent and private Indian and Egyptian railway companies, asked for an explanation.[62] In 1905 the Tanjong Harbour Board complained of fees, which it claimed amounted to 1 per cent of the cost of the goods shipped.[63] In 1909, meanwhile, a parliamentary question drew attention to the fact that, whereas in 1904/5 the India Office paid its shipping agent £4,185 for the transport of £4.5m. of stores, the Agents paid Freelands £9,189 for the shipment of goods to the value of between £2.1m. and £2.5m.[64]

Freelands denied that they made excessive profits, claiming that, in the case of large shipments, they often charged lower fees than those laid down by the Agency, and that their profits in 1908 amounted to only 30–35 per cent of receipts.[65] Charges were relatively high because crown colony freights involved a great deal more work than those of the India Office and private railway companies. The Agents shipped from many ports to a relatively large

---

[55] Blake to CAs, 11 Sept. 1911, CO 323/577/34999. In 1891 Sir Ernest Blake also employed a parlourmaid named Ellen Freeland: PRO, census records, RG 12/548.

[56] In 1908, a year before he retired, Sargeaunt obtained 43% of the profits and Blake 18%: Holt to Antrobus, 14 Oct. 1911, CAOG 17/41.

[57] PPE, q. 4511; CAs to CO, 28 Oct. 1911, CO 323/577/34999.

[58] CAs to CO, 28 Oct. 1911, CO 323/577/34999.

[59] Freelands to CAs, 12 Sept. 1908, CAOG 17/22.

[60] Memo, 24 Sept. 1908, ibid.

[61] PPR, p. xix; PPE, q. 1028.

[62] CAs to Uganda Railway Committee, 6 Nov. 1900, CO 537/62; Uganda Railway Committee to CAs, 17 Dec. 1900, ibid.

[63] Board to CAs, 21 Aug. 1907, CAOG 17/22.

[64] Question, 13 May 1909, CAOG 17/20.

[65] PPE, qq. 4392–9; Freelands to CAs, 12 Sept. 1908, CAOG 17/22.

number of colonies, each served by its own lines and with its own water and harbour conditions and customs duties, all factors that had to be taken into account when negotiating rates. Furthermore, the Office transported a great variety of relatively small goods, many delicate or with difficult dimensions, which necessitated the negotiation of special rates and the employment of storage inspectors to ensure that they were correctly stowed.[66] The firm also performed more duties than most other shipping agents. For example, it corresponded with contractors to ascertain the weight and measurement of stores, supervised the arrival and loading of goods to ensure prompt delivery and settled post-voyage disputes and insurance claims.[67]

In fact, the firm appears to have made relatively large profits; in 1908 between 48 per cent and 70 per cent of receipts.[68] On learning of the enquiry's recommendation that their business be transferred to the Agents, the company offered to cut its charges substantially; and, when the Agency did take over the work, it was able to absorb custom entry fees and 20 per cent of the cost of bills of lading, and to abandon its own 1 per cent commission on shipping charges.[69] The firm's profits were high because the amount of work involved in organising crown colony freights was not as great as claimed. The decision that most freight should be shipped by conference lines rather than ships chartered by tender, as in the case of the India Office, greatly reduced the firm's workload. Similarly, although the company's role was far greater than that of the India Office's agents, who merely received tenders for freight, it was not greatly different from that of other shipping agents.[70] The manager of the Bombay Railway Co., when asked by the Uganda Railway Committee to comment on Freelands' claims, stated that the firm had 'unduly magnified its duties', which were much the same as those performed by his own agents.[71] The committee also pointed out that most Uganda goods were purchased on FOB terms, that contractors automatically supplied weight and measurement statements and that few Ugandan shipping contracts had ended in disputes.[72]

The Agents accepted the firm's fees, probably because its high charges increased their own commission, they wished to increase the cost of dismissal due to poor performance or corruption and they realised that it was necessary to pay the company a premium for its 'vast amount of information and experience of crown colony shipments'.[73] They may also have had difficulty monitoring the firm's remuneration. At the 1908 enquiry, the deputy head of the shipping branch admitted that his staff did not 'know anything about ship-

---

66 Freelands to CAs, 12 Sept. 1908, CAOG 17/22; memo, 23 Nov. 1908, ibid.
67 Freelands to CAs, 9 Oct. 1900, CO 537/62.
68 CAs to CO, 3 Apr. 1909, CAOG 17/41; Holt to Antrobus, 14 Oct. 1911, ibid. On his death in 1907 John Freeland left £25,357: SH, probate records.
69 Note, 19 May 1909, CO 323/553/11712; CAs to CO, 29 July 1912, CO 323/577/34999.
70 CAs to CO, 29 July 1912, CO 323/577/34999.
71 Begbie to Uganda Railway Committee, 12 Nov. 1900, CO 537/68.
72 Uganda Railway Committee to CAs, 17 Dec. 1900, CO 537/62.
73 PPS, q. 10637.

ping', and kept no detailed records of the amounts paid to the firm.[74] A more important factor, though, was probably the Agents' family connections with the company and personal self-interest.

The Agents' links with Freelands lasted until 1911. In its 1909 report, the committee of enquiry into the Office recommended that, to prevent duplication of work, the firm's duties should be taken over by the Agency.[75] Both the Agents and the company were in contact with suppliers, and it was believed that amalgamation would eliminate much correspondence. The Agents strongly opposed the proposal, claiming that they lacked the requisite office accommodation, would be unable to obtain the best rates, as they lacked Freeland's experience and expertise, and that shipping brokers restricted special terms to 'those in their line of business and no other'.[76] It was also argued that, as a Crown Agent shipping department would lack the company's profit motive, the quality of work performed would be lower. Some at the Colonial Office, however, suspected more personal motives for the Agents' opposition. J. F. N. Green, in 1911, for example, noted that the Agents adopted 'with energy and promptitude' those recommendations that led to an increase in emoluments, but 'flatly denied' to take notice of a proposal that would 'disadvantage relations'.[77] Eventually, after much pressure from the Colonial Office, the Agents complied with the enquiry's recommendation, agreeing to employ the whole of Freelands' staff.[78] Although some at the Colonial Office believed that the directors of the firm had no claim to compensation, the Agents agreed to pay Sargeaunt £150, John Freeland's sister, who had received a pension from the company, £500, and Blake, who subsequently became a farmer, £1,500.[79] Holt, whose case was 'altogether different from the others, in that he is the one who has really done the work', was given £2,500 and appointed head of the new shipping department.[80]

In theory Freelands, like the India Office's shipping agents, chartered ships through open competition.[81] In reality, the company chartered only when large, irregular orders had to be shipped and generally used conference lines.[82] By 1904 the firm collected rebates from ten rings, and had agreed schedules of

---

[74] PPE, q. 4587. Although the head of the department may have known 'something of the technicalities': ibid.

[75] PPR, p. xx.

[76] Memo, 23 Nov. 1908, CAOG 17/22.

[77] Green note, 4 Feb. 1911, CO 323/577/3364.

[78] CAs to CO, 3 Jan. 1912, CO 323/591/333.

[79] Blake to Antrobus, 11 Sept. 1911, CAOG 17/41; Anderson note, 21 Nov. 1911, CO 323/577/34999; CAs to CO, 29 Nov. 1911, ibid.

[80] CAs to CO, 28 Oct. 1911, CO 323/577/34999.

[81] PPS, 380.

[82] Freelands to CAs, 23 Apr. 1903, CO 323/492/6877. All the Uganda railway materials, for instance, were shipped in chartered vessels: ibid.

rates with thirteen others.[83] Where chartering was adopted, the particulars of freight available were advertised only in their own office, rather than, as was the case with other shipping agents, in the Shipping Exchange, and contracts were almost always won by the same firms.[84] Critics of the Agents argued that the company's method of engaging freight was unfair, and led to the payment of high rates. In 1903 a complaint by the shipping company Temperley Carter & Burke that they had never been invited to tender for the conveyance of goods to Ceylon, led to a House of Lords motion on the subject.[85]

Freight was engaged in this way, firstly because there was often no competition for cargo. Many routes were served by only one company, tramp steamers often failed to sail during periods of poor trade or particular seasons when no return cargo was available and the small amounts shipped by the Agents often discouraged firms from bidding for contracts.[86] In addition, chartering and tendering increased Freeland's workload and costs, and the associated adverse selection, low cost of dismissal and weak trust relationships meant that chartered ships provided a poor service, often damaging or losing materials, which was particularly disastrous when freights were uninsured.[87] Chartering also led to delays, as the tendering process took time and the small amount of freight shipped meant that cargoes had to be left to accumulate until the chartering of a steamer became cost-effective. Conferences, on the other hand, offered a regular service, superior passenger accommodation, previously the subject of 'very frequent' complaint, and usually gave the Agents very favourable rates, and, occasionally, allowed them to charter without loss of rebate.[88]

As regards those conferences that set excessive rates, the Agents argued that the support of lines that wished to break up the monopolies was a futile

---

[83] Freelands note, 3 Feb. 1904, CO 323/492/10117.

[84] Freelands to CAs, 30 Mar. 1903, CO 323/492/6877.

[85] Temperley to Grey, 21 Mar. 1903, ibid. Freelands pointed out that Temperleys made very few trips to India and Ceylon, often failed to tender when steamers were chartered and, when they did tender, were outbid: Freelands to CAs, 23 Apr. 1903. ibid. In 1909 the Northern Nigerian governor, Sir P. Girouard, negotiated the contract for the shipment of Baro–Kano railway material himself 'afraid that if left to the CAs and their shipping brokers we would not do too well': Girouard to Lugard, 25 Jan. 1908, Lord Lugard papers, Rhodes House, Oxford, MS Brit. Emp. s. 63.

[86] Freelands to CAs, 23 Apr. 1903, CO 323/483/11332; Freelands memo, 3 Feb. 1904, CO 323/491/10117.

[87] Freelands to CAs, 30 Mar. 1903, CO 323/492/48717; Freelands memo, 3 Feb. 1904, CO 323/492/10117.

[88] PPS, qq. 10582, 10953. In South Africa, in 1904, the Agents were charged 16s. per ton for the transport of goods to the Transvaal, whereas ordinary merchants paid 25s. per ton: Transvaal Leader, 22 July 1904, 8. Critics argued that such rates were obtained at the expense of merchants, who were charged correspondingly higher rates: PPS, q. 10707. Blake (q. 10711) denied the accusation, claiming that government shipments were not 'sufficiently large to influence the price', and that the lower rates partly reflected the heavy and bulky nature of crown colony cargoes, particularly railway materials.

exercise. The independent lines either failed to compete, or, if it captured a significant part of the trade, usually joined the ring and raised its charges. Shippers who supported such lines thus lost their conference rebates without any real return.[89] The Agents, consequently, generally discouraged the support of independent lines. In 1905, for example, when a German and English company attempted to break the P & O and British India Co. India/ Ceylon conference, the Agents strongly advised the Colonial Office to stay with the ring, which doubled and then trebled its rebate and was wholly British.[90] Likewise, in 1904, when the Colonial Office wished to support the Houston line in its attempt to compete against the South African conference, the Agents recommended the continued use of the ring, as private enquiries had discovered that Houston had entered the market with a view to joining the conference.[91]

In the case of the West African conference, the Crown Agents were highly critical of its co-organiser, Elder Dempster, which charged unacceptably high rates. Nevertheless, despite the damage it inflicted on local economies and the likelihood of colonial complaint, they did little to support those who challenged the ring. They gave cargo neither to the Princes line nor to the General Steam Navigation Co. when those companies tried to enter the West African trade in 1891 and 1894 respectively.[92] And, although they initially recommended that support should be given to Messrs Symons, who attempted to break Elder Dempster's monopoly in 1906, they subsequently agreed with the Colonial Office that nothing should be done.[93] Their passivity was related to the Colonial Office's close relationship with Sir Alfred Jones, and its obvious wish that they should not act against his business interests. Office officials were well aware that, through his myriad businesses, Jones could affect the success of their development policy and help them in other ways, and that good relations with him could reap political and personal benefits.[94] They thus blocked any Agency attempt to

---

[89] Note, 26 June 1905, CO 323/504/21723.

[90] Ibid; CAs to CO, 20 June 1905, CO 323/504/21289.

[91] CA memo, 4 June 1904, CO 323/492/6877, appendix e.

[92] P. N. Davies, *The trade makers: Elder Dempster in West Africa, 1852–1972*, London 1973, 103–4.

[93] CAs to CO, 3 Oct. 1906, CO 96/449/36668; CAs to CO, 12 June 1907, CO 96/461/ 20929.

[94] Besides his shipping and banking companies, Jones had interests in West African mines, quarries, mills, timber, tramways, lighterage and river boat companies, repair and engineering workshops, ship construction and cold storage and victualling facilities. He also owned the African Direct Telegraph Co. and was the founder of the Liverpool West African Syndicate, president of the British Cotton Growers Association and the Liverpool Chamber of Commerce, and a member of the influential Joint West African Committee of the United Kingdom Chamber of Commerce: M. Sherwood, 'Elder Dempster and West Africa, 1891–1940: the genesis of underdevelopment', *International Journal of the African Historical Society* xxx (1997), 255. In 1899 Jones lent the government twenty of his ships to transport Boer war troops to the Cape and prisoners to St Helena and gave heavily to

reduce his power.[95] Having a relationship of trust with the office, the Agents accepted the favouritism in the knowledge that officials tolerated their own moral hazard, and were unlikely to respond to colonial criticism of their inaction. They may also have been fearful of antagonising Jones, who, in addition to his connections with the Colonial Office, had close relationships with some governors, and, through the journalist and former employee E. D. Morel, could ensure that his views appeared in the press.[96]

As well as organising shipments, Freelands also dealt with the insurance of freight. From 1899 to 1908, on average, approximately £1.5m., 68 per cent of crown colony shipments, were insured.[97] Since the imperial government had long since dispensed with insurance, which it did not believe was cost-effective, the goods of those colonies in receipt of imperial finance were not protected against loss or damage.[98] Other colonies, generally the more affluent, specifically instructed the Agents not to obtain cover, and some, such as the Seychelles, only insured goods over a given value.[99] Insurance cover was provided by the London Assurance Corporation, which was exclusively used by the Agents from 1858.[100] Until 1891 each shipment was covered by a separate policy negotiated by Freelands.[101] Thereafter, an open continuous policy operated, the premiums of which were negotiated annually

---

charity: David Hollett, *The conquest of the Niger by land and sea: from the early explorers and pioneer steamships to Elder Dempster*, Abergavenny 1995, 230. He helped Chamberlain in his Cardiff constituency in the 1903 election, prompting the merchant Holt to comment that 'C has made friends with the mammon of unrighteousness', and financially supported the Unionist cause. He gave to the daughter of Sir Montague Ommanney on her marriage a necklace, muff chain and silver cutlery, held a dinner for Sir Francis Hopwood to 'welcome' his appointment as under-secretary of state, and, according to Major James Carmichael, the Agents' head of engineering, had Winston Churchill, the colonial parliamentary under-secretary, 'in his pocket': Holt to Morel, 30 Nov. 1903, Morel papers, F (8); *Barnes and Mortlake Herald*, 18 Nov. 1899, in F. Shelford, album of press clippings, Rhodes House, Oxford; invitation, 9 Oct. 1907, Sir Francis Hopwood papers, Bodleian Library, Oxford, MSS Southborough, box 2; Kirk to Scarborough, 19 Sept. 1907, Scarborough papers, MS Afr. S. 96, 12.

95 See also CAs to CO, 7 Sept. 1905, CO 96/434/32224.

96 Jones made the governor of Southern Nigeria, Sir Ralph Moor, a director of the African Steamship Co. on his retirement, invited West African governors to numerous banquets and allowed invalid colonial officials to recuperate at his Canary Isles hotel: W. I. Ofongoro, *Trade and imperialism in Southern Nigeria, 1881–1929*, New York 1929, 191, 375. Morel wrote about West Africa in the *Liverpool Daily Post*, the *Manchester Guardian* and later in his own paper, the *West African Mail*, in which Jones invested £500. He acknowledged that Jones 'knew of my press associations and often utilized them to his advantage': Catherine Ann Cline, *E. D. Morel, 1873–1924: the strategies of protest*, Belfast 1980, 11, 12, 291. In his 1902 book *Affairs of Africa* and many of his press articles he was highly critical of the Agents (see ch. xi).

97 CAs to Seychelles, 4 Oct. 1893, CAOG 11/134.

98 CO to Treasury, 30 May 1900, CO 446/12/15680.

99 CAs to Seychelles, 1 Jan. 1894, CAOG 11/134; note, 25 May 1906, CAOG 17/7.

100 Memo, n.d., CO 323/492/26361.

101 CAA, A. Jeffries, 'A short history of the CAs' insurance fund', typescript, c. 1960, 4.

by John Freeland, after independent advice from 'unofficial contacts at Lloyds', presumably his insurance broker brother and former partner Alex Freeland.[102] In return for this service and dealing with claims, Freelands received a proportion of the brokerage.[103] The charges agreed, again appear to have been excessively high. In 1905 it emerged that the rates on shipments to the Transvaal were greater than those paid by private merchants.[104] The insurance expert engaged in 1912 to advise the Agents on their own insurance scheme, meanwhile, believed that the Office paid 'a good deal too much' to London Assurance, which made a 'handsome profit', amounting between 1899 and 1908 to 64 per cent of payments.[105] Given their well-packed cargoes, use of high class steamers and the propriety of their principals, the Agents were a low risk and should have been charged lower than average premiums.[106]

The Agents kept no detailed records of premiums and claims, and thus may have had difficulty in monitoring the performance of London Assurance.[107] They were, nevertheless, confident that use of the firm benefited the colonies. It was claimed that the company offered colonial governments favourable rates, rapidly and liberally settled claims and that its acceptance of an open policy freed them from the payment of stamp duty.[108] The Agents' loyalty to the company, however, may also have been motivated by self-interest. High brokerage increased the Agents' and Freelands' commissions, the operation of an open policy greatly reduced their administration costs and the acceptance of some price moral hazard increased the cost of dismissal for corruption or poor performance. In addition, in 1899 and 1900–4 respectively, the Senior Agents, Sir Montague Ommanney and Sir Ernest Blake, were, in their private capacities, directors of the company.[109] Blake claimed that the directorships were a source of 'a great many ideas on the operation of the Office', and allowed him to monitor not only London Assurance, but also, through information provided by his fellow directors, the Agency's shippers, railway consulting engineers and the City institutions that purchased crown colony stock.[110] This argument is supported by his and Ommanney's regular attendance at directors' meetings, their decision to sit

---

102 Ibid. 5, 21; probate records, SH; *City of London directory*, London 1894, 84.
103 CAs to CO, 8 Nov. 1913, CO 323/608/38729.
104 CAs to CO, 14 Feb. 1905, CO 291/89/5105.
105 Owen to Cameron, 8 Nov. 1909, CAOG 17/42; Jeffries, 'CAs' insurance fund', 14. A similar view was expressed by the CA clerk W. E. James, who in 1904 proposed that the Agency set up its own insurance scheme: James to CAs, 18 Oct. 1917, CO 323/773/6917.
106 Cameron to CO, 21 Dec. 1909, CAOG 17/42.
107 Cameron to Owen, 2 Nov. 1909, ibid.
108 Memo, n.d., CO 323/492/26361; Lucas note, 4 Mar. 1905, CO 291/89/5105; Ommanney note, 6 Feb. 1905, ibid.
109 Neither the published directors list nor the company's directors' minutes make any mention of their official positions: London Assurance papers, GL, MS 18728, vols il, l.
110 PPE, qq. 4030, 4032.

on the firm's marine subcommittee and the careers of their fellow directors.[111] Privately, the Colonial Office supported the Agents' connections with the company, of which, at least unofficially, they were aware, and which, as the Agents were not civil servants, were not prohibited.[112] However, in 1904, under pressure from parliament, the secretary of state forced Blake to resign his directorship.[113]

The Agency's own relationship with London Assurance came to an end in 1911, when the Agents, in a further attempt to avoid the implementation of the 1908 enquiry's recommendation that their profits and reserve fund income be redistributed to the colonies, set up their own insurance scheme. The original intention was to transfer Agency profits and reserve fund income to an insurance fund, which would also receive premium profits and meet all claims.[114] The Colonial Office, however, believed that such transfers would merely lead to 'the piling up of the reserve fund under a different name' and would 'obstruct the position of both funds'.[115] The Agents, claiming that without office and reserve fund income the scheme would be unable to cover all crown colony cargoes, insisted that the transfers should be permitted, and, after much discussion, the Colonial Office relented, though with the proviso that the money was to be treated as an interest-bearing liability.[116] It was also decided that, to reduce the threat of bankruptcy, the risks of the new scheme should be shared with London Assurance at least for the first few years, and that the existing scale of charges paid by the colonies should be retained.[117]

Finally, in the case of large engineering contracts, the colonies were charged a small legal fee. The Agents' legal business was undertaken by solicitors, as it was believed that, given the small volume and the variety of the work, a legal department would not be economically viable.[118] Until 1889 the Agency employed three firms of solicitors, but thereafter used only one, Messrs Sutton, Ommanney & Rendel, whose partners included the uncle and

[111] From his appointment to his resignation, Ommanney attended every board meeting: London Assurance papers, MS 18728, vols il, l. Blake was present at 58% of meetings: ibid. In 1901, of Blake's twenty-four fellow directors, 58% were directors of banks, 46% merchants and 21% directors of railway companies: *Stock Exchange official intelligence*, London 1901; *Directory of directors*, London 1901.

[112] Memo, n.d., CO 323/492/26361.

[113] *Hansard*, 4th ser. 1904, cxxxviii. 877. Ommanney had resigned in 1900, on becoming under-secretary of state.

[114] CAs to CO, 24 Feb. 1910, CO 323/564/5727.

[115] Harris note, 26 Mar. 1910, ibid.

[116] CO to CAs, 10 May 1910, ibid.

[117] Jeffries, 'CAs' insurance fund', 26. By 1914 the insurance fund had an insured value of £3.7m.: CAA, S 203/5.

[118] CAA, CA M 120. Besides dealing with purchasing matters, the solicitors also drew up colonial loan ordinances and construction and employment contracts, acted for the Agents in any action brought by or against the Agency, recovered money from members or ex-members of the Colonial Service and provided the Agents and colonies with legal advice.

brother of Sir Montague Ommanney and, from 1903 and 1913 respectively, his son and nephew too.[119] This firm undertook certain routine duties for a reduced fee, but charged a high remuneration for others. The solicitors Messrs Birchalls, asked by the Colonial Office to comment on a bill for work completed for the Straits in 1913/14, found the charges to be between £40 and £50 too high and warned that 'in the event of it being strictly taxed, . . . [it] would probably be disallowed'.[120] For much of the period, the firm's close bond of trust with the Agents and its high fees appear to have encouraged the firm to perform its services satisfactorily. From 1906, however, its work became the subject of some complaint. In that year it was discovered that the company, unbeknown to the Agents or the Colonial Office, had obtained an extra fee from a colonial client, while a scandal in 1913/14 led the Agents to demand the resignation of the partner H. B. Rendel.[121] The Colonial Office, meanwhile, began to regard the company as 'dilatory and its work desultory and unsatisfactory'.[122] Business carried out for the Straits in 1912 was performed 'very indifferently', and the resulting arbitration case was 'practically given away . . . owing to . . . mismanagement'.[123] It seems likely that the decline in standards of work began with Ommanney's promotion to the post of under-secretary in 1901 and the subsequent weakening of the Agency's links with the firm, but that the Agents, unwilling to damage their own trust relationship with the Colonial Office, took no action. After Ommanney's retirement in 1907 and the disappearance 'of . . . [the firm's] . . . great protector', however, the Agency began to employ other solicitors, and, by 1913, the company was only used for the recovery of money from colonial officers.[124]

Delay and the provision of unsuitable goods

The Agents were subject to numerous complaints about delay and some criticism of the supply of unsuitable goods. The 1901 enquiry received seventy-one specific examples of late delivery from seventeen colonies and protectorates and, in the 1908 enquiry, the ex-governors Sir H. A. Blake, Sir F. A. Swettenham and Sir H. A. Wilson all drew attention to the problem.[125]

---

[119] CAA, MC 77; *Law list*, 1880–1914. The services of the solicitor T. E. Allen were dispensed with in 1885, and those of Messrs Bircham & Co. in 1889: *Colonial Office list*, 1880–8.

[120] CAs to Ommanney, 28 Jan. 1916, CO 273/447/7217. In 1895 Barbados refused to pay a bill that it considered excessive: CAs to CO, 16 Apr. 1895, CO 28/238/6581.

[121] Blake to Lucas, 23 July 1906, CO 54/704/27221; CAA, MC 77. The relevant 1913–14 file has been destroyed. Blake to Lucas, 23 July 1906, CO 54/704/27221. There may have been a further scandal in 1901/3: CAA, weeded files, a85.

[122] Anderson to Fiddes, 20 Mar. 1916, CO 273/453/16054.

[123] Ibid; Fiddes note, 8 June 1916, ibid.

[124] Fiddes note, 6 Sept. 1923, CO 323/902/19475; CAs to CO, 26 Apr. 1923, CAOG 17/64; CAA, S/Gen.

[125] CAOG 17/24, misc. 142; PPE, qq. 832–5, 980–1, 2387.

Delays were not only frequent, but also relatively long. A survey by the government of Gibraltar in 1900 found that the Junior Army & Navy Stores could supply a kitchen range and linoleum from England within forty and seventeen days respectively, as compared to the Agents' eighty to ninety days and eighty-three days.[126] Delay occurred at every stage of the acquisition process, and, to avoid colonial criticism, the Agents made great efforts to speed orders. It was far less damaging to colonial economies, however, than the delivery of defective goods, and the Colonial Office treated the resultant complaints far less seriously.[127] The Agents, consequently, only sought to reduce delays where their actions were unlikely to affect the quality of supplies or greatly increase their costs.

In the period before purchase, delay arose from a number of factors. To reduce costs, the Colonial Office ruled that orders had to be sent by mail rather than telegraph.[128] This slowed delivery and meant that requisitions arrived in large batches from several colonies, which took time to process. On opening the orders, it was often found that they had been incorrectly prepared, requested a wide range of articles, set impracticable limits on expenditure, specified the use of a particular inefficient firm or failed to separate the contents according to the Crown Agent departments that handled them.[129] Orders were also subsequently altered, and all or some had to be passed to the secretary of state for approval which, depending on the Colonial Office's workload, could itself take weeks. In an attempt to eliminate these problems, the Crown Agents advised colonies that technical orders should be completed or checked by engineers.[130] In 1902 a series of explanatory notes on order preparation and sheets of sample prices were distributed, and two years later storekeepers were asked to number articles consecutively on requisitions to aid identification and checking.[131] Pressure was also successfully placed on the Colonial Office to reduce the number of requisitions requiring its sanction.[132]

Further delays occurred during purchasing and manufacture. The use of manufacturers as opposed to wholesalers increased the time taken to supply goods. The government departments used before 1860 had little incentive to speed orders.[133] Private firms often failed to meet deadlines and generally gave colonial requisitions low priority, owing to their small size and bespoke

---

126 CAOG 17/24, misc. 142, no. 2.
127 In 1874 Meade commented that 'I had much rather . . . that the colony should incur some extra delay in processing articles through the Agents than open so serious a mistake as permitting unrestricted local purchase': Meade note, 4 Feb. 1874, CO 267/326.
128 CAOG 17/24, CAR.
129 CAs to CO, 26 Feb. 1901, CO 446/18/7388; indent notes, CAOG 12/71; Ezechiel note, 27 Feb. 1902, CO 446/26/8156.
130 CAs to CO, 2 Jan. 1866, CO 167/494/127.
131 Indent notes, CAOG 12/71; CAs to CO, 18 Apr. 1904, ibid; CAA, G 844/5.
132 Circular, 26 Feb. 1904, CO 323/492/8389.
133 CAs to CO, 13 July 1859, CO 54/348/7051.

nature.[134] All Crown Agent contracts contained penalties, which usually took the form of a fixed or percentage fine for every day or week delivery was delayed.[135] Yet, like the War Office, India Office, Admiralty and the private sector, the Agents implemented these clauses only when suppliers had displayed negligence or bad faith, and even then merely imposed part of the fine, the size of which, in the case of engineering goods, was determined by the consulting engineers.[136] Fines were believed to disrupt trust relationships with suppliers and to either discourage them from tendering, forcing the employment of replacements who were more likely to act opportunistically, or to cause them to reduce the quality of their goods or increase the size of their tenders in order to offset the possibility of a fine.[137] Unlike their counterparts, the Crown Agents were also unwilling to remove late deliverers from their lists: this, they claimed had the same affect as fines. Likewise they hesitated to terminate contracts and buy by default, as this merely meant more delays.[138]

Instead, they promoted bulk purchase for the colonies and standardisation, ensuring that they were represented on the engineering standards committees and, in the early 1900s, slashing the number of patterns offered.[139] They also used administrative solutions to speed orders. Inspectors wrote monthly reports on the progress of engineering goods and, once a delivery date had passed, the contractor was sent constant reminders.[140] Wishing to minimise their costs, though, the Agents failed to make the most of the information available, and, as they themselves admitted, their reminder system was 'slipshod'.[141] Until 1907, although Freelands contacted suppliers a few weeks before contract deadlines and obtained accurate delivery dates in order to book freight, they failed to inform the Agency if a deadline would not be met, except in the case of urgent orders.[142] Similarly, the Agency only discovered

---

[134] CA circular, Dec. 1908, CAOG 12/39.

[135] The fines varied from £5 to £10 per day, £30 to £50 per week and from 1% to 2% of the value of work in arrears per week: CAA, CAOG 19/713, 53; 19/609, 7; 19/721, 8; 19/568; 19/87; 19/521.

[136] PP 1901, xl (Cd 581), qq. 431, 1816, 4357; PP 1901 xl (Cd 580), appendix 5/b; CAOG 17/24, CAR; Rendal to CAs, 25 Mar. 1901, CO 537/68.

[137] CAs to CO, 11 Oct. 1900, CO 137/615/33187; CAs to CO, 6 Sept. 1900, CO 137/615/29265.

[138] Purchase in default occurred only in extreme cases, for example, CAs to Uganda Railway Committee, 11 Oct. 1900, CO 537/62; CAs to CO, 6 July 1901, CO 137/623/23380; CAOG 17/24, CAR; PP 1901, xl (Cd 581), q. 1816; PP 1901, xl (Cd 580), appendix 5 (b).

[139] CAs to CO, 27 May 1902, CO 323/474/21017. From 1900 to 1903 the Agents reduced the number of paper types available by 205, and in 1908 cut the number of blue serge patterns from sixty to nine: Saunders to CAs, 24 May 1900, CAOG 12/37; circular, Dec. 1908, CAOG 12/39.

[140] PPR, p. xx; Mercer to CO, 7 Apr. 1902, CAOG 17/23, misc. 142, no. 34; CAs to CO, 3 Apr. 1909, CO 323/353/11712.

[141] PPR, q. 4700.

[142] PPE, qq. 4853, 4410.

that a firm had failed to deliver when it received Freeland's monthly report on shipments.[143] The Office then sent recalcitrant suppliers reminders, which were issued at the same time each month. In theory, therefore, over a month could pass before a contractor received a first reminder from the Agency.[144]

Finally, delivery times were lengthened by inspection, the transport of textiles etc. to London for examination and despatch difficulties. In the early days goods often had to wait weeks before a ship was scheduled to sail to the purchasing colony.[145] Throughout the period, the Crown Agents could only arrange freight when the whole order was completed, as the transport of individual items was not cost- effective and led to confusion.[146] Until 1859, when using mail steamers, they also had to apply for freight by letter to the Colonial Office, which then contacted the Admiralty, which wrote to the shipping company. The reply was then directed backwards along the same route and often arrived after the mail ship had sailed.[147]

Given the quantity of goods purchased by the Agents, colonial criticism of the supply of inappropriate articles was minimal. The Crown Agents argued that few of the complaints were warranted. It was claimed that colonies often mistakenly ordered the wrong item, that because of high staff turnover materials requested by one colonial officer were often received by his successor, who had a different view of colonial requirements, and that colonial purchasing staff, wanting to use local merchants, often deliberately made false allegations.[148] A number of criticisms, however, were genuine and sometimes appear to have been the result of poor design work by the Agents' consulting engineers. To ensure quality and protect themselves against future complaint, the Crown Agents recruited high status consultants, who, wishing to gain the commercially valuable kudos of working for colonial governments, accepted their offers of employment with alacrity. Yet, once employed, many expended little time or effort on their designs. Much of the work was routine and unexciting, and the fees paid were relatively poor, took the form of a commission on the cost of the finished article, which often bore little re-

---

[143] PPE, qq. 4700, 4744, 4266–8.

[144] From 1907 the works and general departments automatically checked the order file ten and fourteen days respectively after the contract deadline had passed, to ascertain whether the bills of lading had been received from Freelands. If not, a reminder was sent that same day to the supplier, who was required to provide reasons for the delay, and, in the case of engineering goods, to pass the explanation to the local inspector, who commented on its veracity before sending it on to the Agency: PPR, qq. 4682–3, 4854.

[145] For example CAs to CO, 30 Apr. 1856, CO 59/325/3794.

[146] Circular, 11 Aug. 1904, CAA, G 844/5.

[147] CAs to CO, 17 Jan. 1859, CO 323/254/595. After complaints, the CAs were allowed to contact the Admiralty direct: Admiralty to CO, 2 Feb. 1859, CO 323/254/1162.

[148] CAOG 17/24, CAR; Reed to CAs, 30 Aug. 1900, CO 96/385/9930. In 1904, for example, Ommanney concluded that a Hong Kong complaint regarding the supply of incorrect prison uniforms was motivated by 'a determination to discredit . . . [the Agents] . . . and to force supplies into the hands of local merchants': CAs to CO, 27 Jan. 1904, CO 291/74/3207.

lation to the time and work involved in its design, and were only received after the often long-delayed decision to construct had been reached.[149] Because of their age and the arrogance concomitant with success, some of the consultants also failed to fully research local environmental conditions and were unwilling to experiment with new technologies that if unsuccessful could damage their reputations. The Crown Agents' naval consultants John A. Welch and Sir Edward Reed, for example, respectively opposed the use of the compound engine and iron hulls, and such was the antagonism of the Agents' telegraphic expert, William Preece, towards wireless telegraphy that the Colonial Office sent design work to their own consultants.[150] In addition, a number of consulting engineers lacked the relevant expertise and, despite their status, were often poorly regarded by their peers. For example, Reed, who was principally involved in designing tropical shallow draft steamers for the Agents, was actually an expert in deep water warships and, according to an obituary, was 'never . . . a sound man', favouring 'wild schemes in a very remarkable way' and making 'tremendous mistakes with a light heart'.[151]

In their provision of the various supply services, the Agents acted in their own interests and did their best to minimise the adverse selection and moral hazard likely to lead to poor performance. They thus restricted competition in the choice of agents and employed firms with which they had social, professional or family links, thus facilitating monitoring and the formation of trust relationships and adding a social cost to dishonesty. Moreover, to guard against the supply of poor quality material, they inspected goods both during and after manufacture. Inevitably, the lack of competition increased the cost of services, which was further raised by the setting of high fees or the acceptance of benign price moral hazard. Excessive remuneration increased the cost of dismissal for the provision of a poor service, and where the Agents had a family or professional link with a company, as with Freelands and the London Assurance, conferred upon them a personal benefit. The colonies and Colonial Office, having difficulty monitoring fees, wishing to reciprocate the Agents' acceptance of their own duplicity, and, favouring a quality service, none the less, tolerated the extra expense. Likewise, as discussed in chapter 1, the Colonial Office turned a blind eye to the excessive fees paid to the relatives of Crown Agents and to London Assurance, aware that the benefits of nepotism and secondary monitoring outweighed any financial loss

---

149 Reed to Ommanney, 1 Nov. 1898, CAOG 10/36; Reed to CAs, 2 May 1901, ibid.
150 Kubicek, 'Shallow draft steamers', 434. Preece believed 'very strongly' that wireless telegraphy 'is not and cannot be a commercial business': Preece to CAs, 4 Oct. 1900, CAOG 10/3. He continued to hold this view despite mounting evidence to the contrary: Preece to CAs, 2 Jan. 1901, ibid; Preece to CAs, 15 July 1903, ibid; CAs to CO, 12 May 1905, ibid; Preece to CAs, 6 Nov. 1906, CAOG 10/6.
151 The Engineer, 2 Dec. 1906, in CAOG 10/36.

and that the Agents accepted their self-seeking behaviour. As with prices, this complacency lasted until the end of the century. The improvement in colonial monitoring capabilities, brought about by economic growth, the increase in colonial criticism of fees and the Colonial Office's fear of political embarrassment then led to widescale reform.

4

The Department System of Infrastructure Construction

Although most crown colonies were rich in natural resources and agricultural potential, lack of the infrastructure such as railways, harbours and wharves required to transport machinery inland and exports overseas discouraged businessmen from investing in them. If a colony were to develop economically, therefore, it was crucial that it build a transportation network, which, by facilitating the movement of soldiers and administrators, would also help to maintain the political stability required by capitalists. Equally, it was important that the network actually promoted economic growth and that its cost was kept to a minimum. Most railways were built with borrowed funds that were to be repaid from the additional taxation reaped from the economic activity generated, and, if they were owned by the government, operational revenues.

Most of the railways built in the crown colonies were constructed from the mid-1890s, largely in West Africa and by the department system of construction (*see* table 10). Earlier networks had been built by contractors or private enterprise (*see* chapter 5). The term 'department system' was something of a misnomer. Theoretically, the infrastructure was built by the constructing colony's public works department. In reality, the involvement of such bodies varied according to their experience and expertise. In the developed colonies, the public works department completed most of the work, which was monitored by the Agents' consulting engineers. In less developed colonies, however, and particularly in West Africa, where in 1895 few railways had been built and the country, moreover, was unsurveyed, the consulting engineers were 'practically the contractors'.[1] Where this was the case, the construction process followed a basic pattern. After the Colonial Office had decided to investigate the possibilities of construction, the consulting engineers organised a reconnaissance survey, which determined possible route(s), and, from approximately 1906, a far more detailed location survey, which set the exact direction of the line. Using the information collected, they then created designs and estimated the likely cost and economic viability of the project. Their report was sent to the Crown Agents, who added their own comments, before passing it to the Colonial Office, which decided whether the scheme should go ahead. If approval was given, the consulting engineers

---

[1]   CO to Egerton, 6 Jan. 1905, CO 147/172/42513.

Table 10
Railway construction projects supervised by the Crown Agents, 1871–1914

Colony	Mileage, 1871	Mileage, 1880	Mileage, 1895	Mileage, 1914
West Africa	0	0	0	1,632
Ceylon	74	136	158	375
West Indies	25 (Jamaica)	62	203	115
Other	66 (Mauritius)	167	417	351
Total	165	365	778	2,473

Source: PP 1882 lxxiii; PP 1894, xcii (Cd 7526); PP 1901, lxxxvi (Cd 751); PP 1905, xcvi (Cd 2679); PP 1918, xxv (Cd 9051).

Notes: 'Other' includes Mauritius, Hong Kong, Fiji, Cyprus, Nyasaland and Natal. Natal ceased to be a crown colony in 1894. The Federated Malay States have been omitted as the construction of its lines was not supervised by the Agents.

recruited a resident engineer and a support staff, who travelled to the colony, and, under their direction, built the railway, using indigenous labour.[2] On completion of the line, the consulting engineers supervised its operation and maintenance, recruited its personnel and advised the Agents on the purchase of rolling stock.

In more developed colonies, the consulting engineers adopted a far less 'hands-on' approach. The local public works department undertook the location survey and sent the results, together with their cost and receipt estimates and their design, to the consulting engineer.[3] If, after examining the material, the consultant believed the project worthwhile, he worked on improvements to the design, generally in consultation with the colonial engineer, who was often recalled to Britain for the purpose.[4] Occasionally, experts were called in. During the design of the Penang tramway, for example, a Swiss cable railway specialist was consulted.[5] If the consulting engineers and the colony were unable to agree, the consultant either acquiesced, or, if he believed his objection to be important, allowed the Colonial Office to make the final decision. Very occasionally, he might recommend that the opinion of further

[2] Report, 30 Dec. 1910, CO 520/109/1087; CEs to CAs, 14 July 1897, CO 267/434/15737.
[3] In the case of the Kowloon water scheme, the heavy workload of the Hong Kong public works departments caused the survey to be completed by a private firm: CAs to CO, 25 Apr. 1901, CO 129/308/11497.
[4] CAs to CO, 10 July 1908, CO 129/350/24882.
[5] Gregory to CAs, 21 Nov. 1911, CAOG 10/51.

Table 11
Cost overruns on miscellaneous works, 1881–1921

Works	Over estimate (%)
Southern Nigeria	
Departmentally built railways	+ 47
Old Calibar quay wall, 1904	+ 19
Lagos harbour, 1908–21	+ 37
Gold Coast	
Departmentally built railways	+ 54
Accra law courts, 1896–7	+ 21
Accra harbour works, 1907–9	+ 22
Other	
Sierra Leone departmentally built railways	+ 11
Penang harbour works, 1901	+ 10
St Lucia harbour improvements, 1881	+ 42
Colombo drainage scheme, 1903	+ 13

Source: Old Calibar quay wall: CO 520/26/726; Lagos harbour: evidence, CO 776/1, 412; Accra law courts: CO 96/281/14588; CO 96/301/2669; Accra harbour: Coode to CAs, 8 June 1907, CO 96/461/20474; CAs to CO, 25 May 1909, CO 96/488/17770; Penang harbour: Coode to Straits, 26 Dec. 1901, CO 273/285/8569; St Lucia harbour improvement: Coode to CAs, 20 Sept. 1899, CAOG 10/11; Colombo drainage scheme: schedule, CO 54/685/34786; CAs to CO, 20 July 1903, CO 54/685/27072; Southern Nigeria, Sierra Leone and Gold Coast railways: see appendix 2.

experts be sought.[6] The design and the consulting engineer's critical report on the project were then sent to the Agents and to the Colonial Office. If the scheme was authorised, the public works department organised construction, under the general guidance of the consultant, who provided advice and monitored progress.

The lines built in West Africa under the department system were the subject of much complaint from the Colonial Office, the colonies themselves, parliament and the press.[7] The work was relatively expensive when compared either with the pre-construction estimates (*see* table 11) or with French or German lines (*see* appendix 2, tables 1 and 2).[8] Furthermore, once completed, the railways were often uneconomic, receipts failing to cover costs (*see* table 12). They were also of poor quality.[9] Many had poorly

[6] CAs to CO, 21 July 1900, CO 129/302/23718; CAs to CO, 2 Feb. 1897, CO 96/301/ 2669; CAs to CO, 29 June 1905, CO 54/696/22587.
[7] *The Times*, 17 Oct. 1903, in CO 96/412/39602; Morel, *Affairs of Africa*, 30–3; *Hansard*, 4th ser. 1906, lvxvii. 658/9; 5th ser. 1910, xviii. 1494.
[8] Sir Robert Herbert defined 'Crown Agent railways' as 'the most expensive that can be made': Herbert note, 20 Nov. 1899, CO 446/8/30397.
[9] In 1912 a proposal for the Nigerian railways to be renamed the Nigerian Government

Table 12
Profit and loss on African and other crown colony railways, 1901, 1911 (£)

Colony	Net profit/loss	
	1901	1911
West African lines		
Gold Coast	−16,179	97,751
Lagos	130,131	not known
Northern Nigeria	Not known	−80,008
Sierra Leone	−11,753	−12,823
Other crown colony lines		
Ceylon	177,629	357,067
Cyprus	not known	−6,313
Hong Kong	not known	−40,790
Jamaica	−77,307	4,258
Mauritius	25,688	27,230
Straits	15,503	not known
Trinidad	4,360	20,626

Source: *Stock Exchange Official Intelligence*, 1913, p. xc.

Notes: Profit and loss is net of working costs and capital interest charges. The figures are unsatisfactory, as they fail to indicate whether competitive transport rates were set. On a macro level, the railways will have reduced transport costs and promoted economic development. In the Gold Coast, for example, railway rates were equal to 11.3*d*. per ton, as compared to the hand cart's 22*d*. per ton and head loading's 20 to 60*d*. per ton: Gould, *Transportation pattern in Ghana*, 25.

constructed earthworks and cuttings, defective drainage and badly laid track. Working expenses were therefore high and large amounts of money had to be spent in improving, and, in some cases, relaying track. In the early 1920s, for example, Lagos and the Gold Coast spent, respectively, £1m. and £418,000 improving line alignment.[10] Railways and other works constructed by the more developed crown colonies, on the other hand, were relatively less expensive (*see* appendix 2, table 3), and of a better quality. Nevertheless, they were still more costly than similar works elsewhere (*see* appendix 2, table 3), and the standard of construction was again subject to criticism.[11]

Railways was abandoned amid fears that the NGR initials would cause the line to be known as the 'No Good Railway': note, 2 May 1912, CO 520/118/27127.

[10] Sir W. de Frece, *The failure of officialdom: the disastrous record of government railway building*, London 1923, 6; *Hansard*, 4th ser. 1925, clxxxii. 37.

[11] The Ceylon railway, for instance, cost 16% per mile more than Indian lines, which were themselves considered expensive: *Papers laid before the legislative council of Ceylon*, 1895, 1, appendix 1. The colony, in 1903, complained of the poor quality of the Uda Pussellawa

Previous histories of West African railways have usually concentrated on individual lines and have largely dealt with the political machinations that led to the decision to commence projects or on the operation of the completed lines.[12] Those few writers who have examined the actual construction process, often in passing, have blamed the high costs and poor quality of the lines on the African environment.[13] This chapter argues that all those involved in the construction process acted in their own interests, and that it was this that led to the high cost and poor quality of the work. The first section identifies why the Crown Agents, Colonial Office and consulting engineers adopted the department system and examines the traditional explanations for the inadequacies of the lines built. The tendency for the use of the department system to increase the cost of schemes, and to lead to the construction of unprofitable, poor quality lines is then described.

Adoption of the department system

The Agents claimed that the department method of construction was widely used, and that, for example, the Canadian Pacific railway, Indian lines and many Argentinian extensions had been built in that way.[14] In fact, this method of building seems to have been unique to the crown colonies.[15] Until

railway, calling for an independent engineer and an enquiry to be appointed to investigate the line, and, in 1904, criticised defects in the Colombo coaling jetties, which required them to be closed during bad weather: CE to CAs, 12 Nov. 1903, CO 54/685/42223; *Times of Ceylon*, 22 Sept. 1904, in CO 273/313/6870.

[12] For example J. R. Best, *A history of the Sierra Leone railway, 1899–1949*, London 1949; R. J. Harrison Church, *The evolution of railways in French and British West Africa*, Lisbon 1952; M. F. Hill, *Permanent way: the story of the Uganda and Kenya railway*, London 1950; Francis Jaekel, *A history of the Nigerian railway*, i, ii, London 1997; T. N. Tamuno, 'Genesis of the Nigerian railway', *Nigeria Magazine* lxxxiii (1964), 279–92; lxxxiv (1965), 31–43; Carland, *Colonial Office*; R. E. Dummett, 'Joseph Chamberlain, imperial finance and railway policy in British West Africa in the late nineteenth century', *EHR* xc (1975), 289–306; Kesner, *Economic control*, 105–15.

[13] Anthony Burton, *The railway empire*, London 1994, 209; Gould, *Transportation pattern in Ghana*, 24; Gann and Duignan, *The rulers of British West Africa*, 279.

[14] PPD, 10.

[15] In responsible government colonies lines were constructed by the private sector, contractors or local government. Indian railways were built by private companies until 1869, when the government took over construction. From the mid-1880s the private sector was again used, though state construction continued: J. Kerr, *Building the railways of the raj, 1850–1900*, Oxford 1995. In French West Africa lines were largely built by the private sector. The Dahomey and Togo railways were built and run by private companies, assisted in the early stages by government loans: C. Newbury, *The western slave coast and its rulers*, Oxford 1961, 143. In the case of the Dahomey line, the road bed was laid by the government and the permanent way by the Dahomey Railway Co.: CO 879/86/765a, no. 1. The Konakry–Niger line was initially constructed by contractors and, after the cancellation of their contract, by military engineers: ibid. no. 2. In Argentina the term 'department system'

the 1890s it was rarely used and generally disparaged by the Agency which believed that it allowed colonial governments to add to schemes, or to suspend or speed up construction if revenue contracted or early completion was required, and thus resulted in expensive and unsatisfactory work.[16] The Agents, along with their consulting engineers and the Colonial Office, however, then underwent something of a conversion, and began to endorse the system, both in West Africa and elsewhere.[17] Their support was variously ascribed to colonial reluctance to use contractors, the high cost of contractor-built lines, the harsh local conditions and the small size of some of the projects, which it was thought would discourage reputable contracting firms from tendering.[18] A far more important factor, however, was self-interest.

In the case of the Crown Agents, this took the form of a desire to escape their parlous financial situation, avoid criticism and assist and expand the business of their West African consulting engineer. In order to avoid further Agency losses, it was important that a construction method was adopted that ensured that they dealt with all orders for building materials. Such orders were profitable, owing to their size and uniformity and consequent low attendant processing costs, and ensured that the Agents were remunerated for their supervision of projects. The department system guaranteed such purchases.[19] Conversely, private firms always obtained their own materials, and the Colonial Office often permitted contractor supply.[20] Colonies that adopted private sector or contractor construction were also sometimes reluctant to pay the Agents a special fee for their supervisory work. In 1906, for example, the Agency's request to be paid for the Singapore harbour improvement scheme resulted in a 'storm of indignation' in the colony, and the payment was only made after a lengthy correspondence.[21]

---

was used to describe private construction by means of contractors using piecework gangs of labourers: Shelford to CAs, 14 Mar. 1906, CAOG 10/96.

[16] CAs to CO, 15 Mar. 1888, CO 54/580/5172.

[17] Coode to CAs, 9 Feb. 1899, CAOG 10/11.

[18] CAs to CO, 15 Mar. 1888, CO 54/580/5172; CAs to CO, 24 Aug. 1906, CO 54/704/31404; Eyles to CAs, 27 Nov. 1906, CO 54/704/45246. The advantages and disadvantages of the use of contractors are discussed in chapter 5 below.

[19] Between 1897 and 1901 the Agents bought materials to the value of £2.1m. for the West African railways: Kubicek, *Administration of imperialism*, 63.

[20] Supply by contractors ensured that price rises were absorbed by the contractor rather than the colony, and, by increasing the size of small contracts, made them more attractive to tenderers and increased competition: CAs to CO, 26 May 1908, CO 96/474/19021; memo, 7 Mar. 1904, CAOG 10/96. The contractors who built the 1902 Ceylon Farmagusta harbour improvement scheme, the 1903 Singapore harbour project and the 1908 Straits lagoon wet dock all used their own materials, and those who constructed the 1880 Ceylon Nawalapitya–Nanu railway and 1906 Gold Coast Accra–Akwapim line provided all non-permanent way goods: CAs to CO, 16 Dec. 1903, CO 273/313/44688; CAA, CAOG 19/130; 19/283; 19/172; 19/106.

[21] CAs to CO, 26 June 1906, CO 273/322/23110; Stubbs note, 27 June 1906, ibid.; CAs to CO, 1 Mar. 1907, CO 273/332/7781. See also CAs to CO, 7 June 1918, CAOG 17/124; CAs to CO, 15 Dec. 1906, CO 273/322/46189.

Secondly, the department system gave the Agents greater control over the building process, which appeared to reduce the likelihood of poor quality lines and colonial criticism, and for two of the Agents provided personal gain. The Senior Crown Agent, Sir Montague Ommanney, was the father-in-law of the engineer Frederic Shelford, who, from 1899, as his father's partner, and, from 1905, on his own account, was the Agency's railway consulting engineer for West Africa.[22] Meanwhile, one of the 'greatest friends' of Sir Maurice Cameron, the Agent in charge of engineering, was Thomas Shelford, Frederic Shelford's uncle.[23] In 1890, when a Straits engineer, Cameron had shared a house with Thomas Shelford and his wife, and, from 1895 to his death in 1900, Shelford financed Cameron's £10,000 Colonial Office security bond.[24]

Self-interest similarly motivated the consulting engineers and the Colonial Office in their support for the system. For the former, department construction offered huge rewards. The engineers earned nothing for lines built by private firms that received no colonial support, and the fees and expenses obtained for the supervision of government-supported private builders and contractors were usually far lower than those for the organisation of department construction. As private lines were operated by the construction company, they also lost their post-construction fees. In addition, control over construction ensured that their designs were built to the highest standards, and prevented the 'loss of professional reputation and the chance of re-employment' as well as social awards, such as knighthoods, that were of great importance to the late nineteenth-century engineering profession.[25]

The Colonial Office, lacking technical and business expertise, generally followed the advice of the Agents and their consultants as regards the method of construction. But it too gained from the adoption of the system. The use of contractors inevitably meant delays before the work could begin, for, in order to allow a fair comparison of tender offers and the monitoring of the building process, it was essential that a location survey was undertaken and a specification drawn up before a contract was put out to competition. Such surveys and specifications, along with the contractual preliminaries, could take up to two years, and, in the meantime, the secretary of state would be subject to intense pressure from outside interest groups, for whom delay

---

[22] *Liverpool Daily Post*, 26 June 1899, in Shelford press cuttings. Ommanney closely followed his son-in-law's career and wished to see him prosper. In 1905 C. P. Lucas informed the governor, Sir Matthew Nathan, that he had passed his earlier letter, which had praised Shelford, on to Ommanney 'as it would be sure to please him': Lucas to Nathan, 20 Jan. 1905, Sir Matthew Nathan papers, Rhodes House, Oxford, MS Nathan 334.

[23] Cameron memoirs, 112.

[24] Ibid; CAs to CO, 28 Feb. 1900, CO 323/452/6740.

[25] CAs to Ellis, 11 Mar. 1910, CO 96/501/6424; D. H. Porter and G. C. Clifton, 'Patronage, professional values and Victorian public works: engineering and contracting the Thames embankment', *Victorian Studies* xxxi (1988), 192.

meant lost profits.[26] Department construction, also, through Crown Agent supply, ensured the purchase of British construction materials, reduced the likelihood of clashes between constructors and local populations, which could easily escalate into political problems, dispersed responsibility for the final works and avoided the legal proceedings that usually followed a contractor's demand for compensation and extras, which in turn drew public and parliamentary attention to overexpenditure.[27]

Cost

The Crown Agents and consulting engineers claimed that the underestimation and high cost of works was the result of a variety of factors. Owing to the lack of funds and the Colonial Office's wish to minimise losses if lines failed to pay, railways were built piecemeal, to no overall plan.[28] Only short lengths of track were therefore constructed at any one time, depriving engineers of economies of scale, and, with no knowledge of ultimate destinations, it was difficult to lay down cost-effective alignments.[29] Construction was also affected by unforeseen events and conditions and often had to be completed urgently, while estimates were occasionally made worthless by inflation.[30] The problems of the West African lines were blamed almost wholly on the harsh environment. It was argued that much of the country traversed was mountainous and crossed by myriad rivers and streams, necessitating the construction of costly viaducts, bridges, earthworks and cuttings; the

[26] One of the most influential pressure groups was the British Cotton Growing Association, the president of which was Sir Alfred Jones. The association believed that railways would facilitate the establishment of West African cotton plantations. Inevitably, Jones's involvement in the association was motivated by self-interest. The cotton, harvested at different times from other West African crops, would provide his ships with a valuable return cargo: Sherwood, 'Elder Dempster', 264. Jones's influence on the Colonial Office and Crown Agents is discussed in chapters 2 and 3 above and chapter 9 below.

[27] In 1893 Chamberlain stated that the construction of the Uganda railway would benefit 'the working classes of this country . . . as the whole of the work will . . . be done in this country': Hansard, 4th ser. 1893, xx. 602.

[28] Lucas note, 18 May 1898, CO 54/650/10809; Church, Evolution of railways, 99.

[29] In 1902 the consulting engineers estimated that constructing the Bo–Baiima line in two sections would add at least 2% to the cost of the line: CAs to CO, 15 Sept. 1902, CO 267/464/38653.

[30] CAs to CO, 14 Jan. 1901, CO 267/460/1746. For example, the high cost of the Tarkwa–Obuassi line was supposedly the result of pressure from the Ashanti Goldfields Corporation, which part-financed the line, for it to reach its mines rapidly: Shelford to CAs, 3 May 1905, CO 96/434/17000. See also Butler note, 4 Feb. 1908, CO 520/69/3965. The high cost of the Kelani Valley line, Penang harbour and the Colombo drainage scheme was allegedly caused by, respectively, the quantity of rock encountered, the character of the sea bed and the difficult nature of the ground: CAs to Ceylon, 25 Aug. 1903, CO 54/685/31774; Coode to Straits, 26 Dec. 1901, CO 273/285/8569; CAs to CO, 6 Jan. 1906, CO 54/704/713.

Freetown to Songotown railway, for example, had eleven viaducts in its first twenty miles alone.[31] Heavy rainfall meant that slips and washouts were a common occurrence, and the unhealthy nature of the climate resulted in a high death and invalidity rate and constant changes in European personnel, which had 'a disastrous effect on cost, progress and quality of work'.[32] From 1898 to 1904, each construction post on the Sierra Leone, Gold Coast and Lagos railways, for instance, was filled by 5.45, 4.31 and 3.84 employees respectively.[33] Similarly, the dense tropical forest that extended 150 miles from the coast increased clearing costs, and, owing to rapid regrowth, maintenance costs, and made surveying difficult, leading to poorly aligned lines.[34] There was also a shortage of ballast, the crushed stone on which tracks rested, and indigenous labour, particularly skilled workers, which meant that men had to be brought from neighbouring colonies and more Europeans had to be employed to train and supervise them. To build the Gold Coast railway, for example, 13,000 labourers were brought to the colony, mostly from Lagos.[35] In addition, the lack of wharfage made the landing of materials difficult, the absence of roads and paths necessitated the use of just one base and precluded the transport of materials in advance of the railhead and, in the case of the Sekondi–Kumassi and Freetown–Songotown lines, progress was held up by native revolts.

It cannot be denied that the type of environment did increase costs, although these fell over time as engineers learned how to overcome many of the natural problems, labour became more skilled, landing facilities were established and lines extended inland, where the country was more open and the climate healthier.[36] However, it seems unlikely that the environment was the only reason for the high cost of the track laid. British lines were more expensive than those built by the French in West Africa, which were constructed by similar methods, and in the case of French Guiana, in far more harsh conditions.[37] Moreover, the difficulties of construction in West Africa had long been known and should have been factored into estimates; some of the drawbacks were offset by advantages, such as starting construction from the coast – 'just everything when building a railway'; and there is some

---

[31] CO evidence, CO 766/1.
[32] Ommanney note, 1 Feb. 1902, CO 147/163/3313.
[33] PPD, 21.
[34] Report, 28 May 1906, CO 520/38/22507.
[35] PPD, 18.
[36] PPD, 21.
[37] Church, *Evolution of railways*, 97, 104, 105; *West African Mail*, 11 Aug. 1905, 470. They were also more expensive than those built in similar or worse conditions elsewhere. The Perak railway, for instance, which was the same length and on the same latitude as the Tarkwa–Kumassi line, but built through more difficult country, with over four times the rainfall, thicker forest and a greater shortage of ballast, was constructed for 22% less and to a far higher standard than the Tarkwa railway: Federated Malay States to CO, 28 Jan. 1905, CO 96/427/5543.

evidence that Shelford 'bolstered up and magnified' some of the environmental problems.[38] In 1908, for example, he attributed a 20 per cent rise in the cost of the Tarkwa–Prestea line to a doubling of labour costs, which the Gold Coast governor and the open lines and transport managers all denied had occurred. Shelford himself later admitted that he had exaggerated.[39]

The true reason for the high cost of West African and other lines was self-interest. The Crown Agents, like their consulting engineers, wished to maximise their own income and to avoid colonial criticism. They thus cared little about high expenditure, which increased Agency and company earnings, and, provided that capital repayments were covered by receipts, was unlikely to lead to colonial criticism. On the other hand they were highly averse to the construction of poor quality lines which could prompt damaging complaint. Along with their engineers, they consequently encouraged the adoption of high technical standards of construction, and, through targeted recruitment and the payment of high wages, sought to discourage that adverse selection and moral hazard that could damage quality. Such policies, along with the very nature of the department system, resulted in the construction of expensive works.

The standard of construction

In West Africa the official technical standard set by William Shelford was one that allowed for speeds of up to 15 miles per hour.[40] Similarly low standards were laid down in other crown colonies, in French and German territories and in the United States and Canada. Gauges, the distance between track rails, were narrow, and the lines had high gradients and sharp curves. Instead of avoiding hills through detours, tunnels or heavy earthworks and natural features via long radius curves, track ascended inclinations and had small radius curves.[41] Other features of construction and operation were reduced to a minimum. There were few stations and little rolling stock, stone bridges were replaced by steel trestles and certain features, such as fencing and platforms, were dispensed with altogether. The completed railways were sufficient for the low traffic levels of most undeveloped colonies, could easily be improved as traffic increased and had low operating and capital costs.[42]

38 *West Africa*, 7 Nov. 1903, 503; PP 1909, xvi (cd 4474), q. 519. Building a line from the coast permitted raw materials to be transported to the point of construction by rail rather than, more expensively, by other means.
39 Gold Coast to CO, 2 Oct. 1908, CO 96/472/39103; Shelford to CAs, 3 Feb. 1909, CO 96/488/5213. See also CO 147/177/34063.
40 PP 1905, lvi (cd 2325), p. 23.
41 E. R. Calthrop, 'Light railways in the colonies', *Proceedings of the Royal Colonial Institute* xxix (1897–8), 100; Walter L. Webb, *Economics of railway construction*, London 1910, 230, 283–5.
42 Shelford to CAs, 1 Nov. 1907, CO 520/52/39371; CEs to CAs, 19 Mar. 1903, CO 54/685/12279.

The latter allowed longer lines to be built, which increased the traffic catch-ment area and revenue, and, if development subsequently led to the estab-lishment of new trade routes, track could be cheaply and easily redirected and/or replaced.

The Crown Agents and consulting engineers were opposed to such rail-ways which, rapidly constructed and requiring relatively few building mate-rials, generated little purchasing commission, fees and expenses, and increased the likelihood of poor line performance and criticism from the colonies. Apart from the first railways, they generally recommended construction to a much higher standard, and, from the 1900s, advised that earlier sections be improved.[43] The only exception to this policy was when it appeared that a colony would have difficulty covering the debt charges on a quality line. In such cases the Agents occasionally asked consulting engineers to reduce standards.[44] For example, in the case of the Tarkwa–Kumassi line, the Agency required Shelford to reduce rail and sleeper weight, and the number of stations.[45] Usually, however, a compromise was achieved. Where a 3' 6" gauge could not be afforded, it was suggested that earthworks and bridges be constructed for a 3' 6" line, but that a 2' 6" track be laid, which would allow the railway to be upgraded easily in the future.[46] Moderate gradients were adopted only on a track that was likely to carry the heaviest traffic, usually the outward line.[47] Temporary bridges were constructed prior to their subsequent replacement by stone structures, particularly on railways with relatively few rivers and streams, where the upkeep before replacement would not lead to serious inconvenience or expense.[48] In the case of the Baro–Kano line, it was proposed that good secondhand permanent way materials be purchased from the Beira railway.[49]

The Agents and consulting engineers justified these recommendations by arguing that the capital savings on lines built to a low standard were relatively small. For example, the adoption of a 2' 6" as opposed to a 3' 6" gauge reduced costs by only 10 per cent and if the cost of transporting, sawing and seasoning were taken into account, native wood sleepers were no cheaper than their

[43] Shelford to CAs, 23 Oct. 1908, CO 520/70/39569.
[44] Report, 30 Oct. 1897, CO 96/301/25787.
[45] Ibid. The original standard was later implemented.
[46] CAs to CO, 22 June 1906, CO 520/38/22507; CAs to CO, 25 June 1906, CO 96/449/23032.
[47] CAs to CO, 21 Aug. 1906, CO 96/449/30967; Strachey note, 22 Mar. 1909, CO 520/84/8675.
[48] Shelford to CAs, 21 June 1906, CO 96/449/23032; Shelford to CAs, 21 Jan. 1907, CO 520/51/3975; CAs to Shelford, 15 May 1900, CO 96/366/22488; Shelford to CAs, 29 May 1900, ibid.
[49] CAs to CO, 7 Feb. 1907, CO 446/67/4832; CAs to CO, 28 Apr. 1903, CO 67/136/15662.

Table 13
The impact on lines of a lower standard on operating costs
and carrying capacities

Pioneer feature	Impact on operating costs.
Corrugated iron pipes	Increased incidence of costly washouts and slips.
High gradients and sharp curves	Increased danger of derailment, collision and flood. Required relatively more tractive force, which increased fuel consumption and wear and tear on permanent way and rolling stock. Greater length of track to be maintained and operated. Reduced train speeds and number of carriages.
Incomplete earthworks	Higher maintenance costs.
Light rails	Less durable than heavy rails; light engines essential.
Narrow gauge rolling stock	Relatively expensive and small. More prone to breakdown than broader gauge counterpart. Smaller trucks increased empty haulage and siding needs.
Narrow gauge track	Comparatively unsafe and subject to costly accidents. Truck size has little effect on administration and supervision, the largest component of working costs.
Native wood sleepers	Shorter lifespan and required more maintenance than steel sleepers.
Restricted station accommodation	Loading difficulties.
Trestle bridges	More likely to collapse than stone bridges.

Source: Shelford to CAs, 19 Sept. 1907, CO 520/52/34138; Shelford to CAs, 27 Sept. 1907, CO 520/52/34939; Calthrop, 'Light railways', 101; F. Shelford, *Some features of the West African railways*, London 1912, 41; W. J. Busschau, 'Some aspects of railway development in Natal', *The South African Journal of Economics*, i (1933), 411; CAs to CO, 5 May 1898, CO 54/650/7732; Webb, *Economics*, 230, 283–5.

Notes: The life of light rails could be prolonged by the careful laying of sleepers. Although high gradients increased the length of track to be maintained and operated, as traffic rates were set according to mileage, the extra costs were partly offset by additional receipts: Webb, *Economics*, 230, 283–5.

steel counterparts.[50] Moreover, any capital savings were offset by high operating costs, and the lines had small carrying capacities (*see* table 13). Given that consulting engineers had estimated high traffic on most West African lines, the railways would therefore have to be upgraded after only a short period, which, owing to the resultant disruption of traffic, would prove rela-

[50] Shelford to CAs, 1 Oct. 1895, CO 96/263/17259; report, 28 May 1906, CO 520/38/22507. See also CAs to CO, 28 Mar. 1878, CO 54/516/3829. To prevent linkages with French metre gauge lines 2' 6" and 3' 6" were chosen as standard thoughout West African: CAs to CO, 31 Oct. 1895, CO 147/101/19160.

tively expensive.[51] However, not all the experts supported this thesis. It was claimed that it took many years before the slightly higher operating costs of low standard railways offset their lower capital cost, and, provided specially designed light rolling stock with uniform axle load were used, a 2' 6" line had the same carrying capacity as a standard gauge railway.[52] More important, as both the Agents and their engineers were aware, the consulting engineers had deliberately exaggerated traffic estimates in order to encourage the construction of lines. Even if low standard railways did, indeed, have relatively low traffic-carrying capabilities, it was therefore highly unlikely that the lines would have to be upgraded.

Recruitment and remuneration of consulting engineers, resident engineers and indigenous labour

To avoid adverse selection, the Crown Agents and their engineers recruited subagents whose abilities could easily be discovered, and to counter self-interested behaviour paid them salaries which discouraged the rapid completion of work, and a premium above their market rate, thus raising the cost of dismissal for opportunism or slacking. These strategies, however, though helping to ensure quality construction, again greatly increased the cost of the works.

Consulting engineers

In the 1870s the Agents acted as their own consulting engineers, designing and supervising schemes themselves.[53] It was then decided that such work was 'not the business of a Crown Agent' and professional consultants began to be employed.[54] When recruiting new consulting engineers, the Agents canvassed their existing engineering consultants for recommendations, thus avoiding the problem of adverse selection and adding a social cost to opportunism.[55] They tended to select men at the top of their profession, who had been involved in works of similar size to those in the crown colonies and for whom the cost of the poor performance of their duties would be high, leading

---

[51] In the case of narrow gauge and light rail lines, an upgrade would also lead to a break in gauge and rail weight with other railways, which would increase operating costs, as goods and passengers would have to be transferred at junction stations and duplicate rolling stocks maintained: CAs to CO, 21 Feb. 1911, CO 446/101/6011; Selborne note, 13 Dec. 1897, CO 54/641/23524; *Papers laid before the legislative council of Ceylon*, 1895, xxv. 3. Junction transhipment would also lead to delay, which would discourage inter- and intra-colony trade and could prove calamitous where stores were urgently required for military purposes: CAs to CO, 21 Feb. 1911, CO 446/101/6011; CAs to CO, 28 Oct. 1897, CO 54/641/23524; report, 28 Feb. 1905, CO 446/47/12976.

[52] E. R. Calthrop, *The economics of light railway construction*, Leeds 1896, 23.

[53] Antrobus note, 4 Jan. 1908, CO 323/548/45741.

[54] Ibid.

[55] E. C. Baker, *Preece and those who followed: consulting engineers in the twentieth century*, Brighton 1980, 3.

to the loss of their commercially valuable high status.[56] Such men, however, were often over-qualified for the projects for which they were retained and, as a result, sometimes expended little effort on the work.[57] Most were employed for long periods, often between twenty and thirty years. Long-term relationships promoted trust, reduced adverse selection, and enabled the engineers to acquire valuable experience of the department system and of the conditions in the particular colonies in which they worked. Confident of re-employment, they also kept 'themselves up to date' in matters that had a bearing on construction in the colonies, and were willing to provide governors and the Colonial Office with free *ad hoc* advice.[58]

For the post of West African consulting engineer, the Crown Agents recruited Sir William Shelford, whose family connections with the Agents and the Colonial Office generated trust, added a social cost to poor quality work and further minimised adverse selection.[59] Unfortunately, these advantages were partly offset by Shelford's lack of building experience in Africa.[60] He was also in poor health, and much of the work was completed by his son, Frederic, who, when he became a partner in the firm in 1899, was just twenty-eight and had been an associate member of the Institution of Civil Engineers for only two years.[61] Frederic Shelford's engineering skills were rated poorly by the Colonial Office. The clerk A. Fiddean commented in 1905 that 'no one has much confidence in . . . [him]'.[62] Nevertheless, on his

---

56 PPE, q. 1420. Of the nineteen engineers who served as presidents of the Institution of Civil Engineers between 1851 and 1913, fourteen were CA consulting engineers: Garth Watson, *The civils: the story of the Institution of Civil Engineers*, London 1988, appendix.

57 In the case of the 1907 Lagos harbour scheme, the consulting engineers subcontracted the more mundane dock design, inspection and construction work to another far less prestigious firm: report, 28 May 1907, CO 520/51/197158.

58 CAs to CO, 10 Aug. 1905, CO 323/504/2864. In 1903 the consulting engineer Osbert Chadwick, for instance, wrote, for no fee, a memo for the secretary of state on the contribution of high water rates to the Trinidad riots: CAs to CO, 9 Apr. 1903, CO 295/421/13253.

59 Ellis note, 3 Mar. 1909, CO 96/488/4266.

60 Shelford did, though, have some overseas experience, having reported on railway schemes in Italy and Argentina, advised the Newfoundland government on engineering matters and supervised the construction of the Winnipeg to Hudson Bay railway: *Dictionary of national biography*, Oxford 1912, 304.

61 Anna E. Shelford, *The life of Sir William Shelford*, London 1909 (privately printed), 116; *The Engineer*, 6 Oct. 1905, 343; Institution of Civil Engineers, *List of members, 1897*, London 1897.

62 Fiddean note, 16 Feb. 1909, CO 96/488/3152. For example, in 1905, C. Strachey stated that Shelford's proposal to extend a possible Southern Nigerian line was 'moonshine'; in 1907 an official found his contradictory schemes for the provision of water for locomotives to be 'a little difficult to follow . . . [they] do not tend to increase one's confidence in . . . [his] . . . opinion'; in 1908 F. G. A. Butler believed Shelford's rejection of a Niger footbridge was 'a brilliant flight of imagination, rather than a serious argument'; and, in 1910, the clerk W. D. Ellis commented that 'it is . . . true that it is difficult to ascertain the best route . . . in bush country, but I must say Shelfords' and their engineers appear singularly unsuccessful':

father's death in June 1905, he was retained as consultant engineer on the West African railway, largely on the insistence of Ommanney and a 'partnership' with the Crown Agent engineer Sir Benjamin Baker, and, on Baker's death, Robert Elliott Cooper, was established.[63] These, however, appear to have been marriages of convenience, entered into merely to satisfy the Colonial Office, with neither 'partner' having much involvement in construction.[64]

The Agents paid their consulting engineers a set fee plus expenses for their pre-construction work; for the supervision of construction, a further fee plus expenses in developed countries. In West Africa they paid a salary and expenses, and, from 1905, a fee based on estimates.[65] The payment of expenses as well as a set fee discouraged the engineers from minimising quality in order to maximise their income, and the adoption of salaries removed the temptation introduced by fees to speed construction, again by reducing quality. Both the method and the size of the remuneration were the subject of criticism. Fees were usually determined after a project had been completed, owing to the difficulty of estimating the work involved before building commenced.[66] Consequently, once Colonial Office authorisation had been given, consulting engineers had an incentive to add to works.[67] In 1905, in an attempt to prevent such abuse, the Agents reminded all their consultants that estimates should include all costs, should not be altered without Colonial Office authority and any excess should be brought to the notice of the Agency immediately.[68]

Strachey note, 26 Apr. 1905, CO 520/32/868; note, 5 Nov. 1907, CO 520/52/37693; Butler note, 1 Oct. 1908, CO 520/70/35423; Ellis note, 19 Oct. 1910, CO 96/501/31724. Shelford's 1911 application for a concession to build light railways in Uganda was turned down by the Colonial Office: Shelford to CO, 10 July 1911, CO 879/107/965, no. 221. Sir P. Girouard had an equally low opinion of Shelford's capabilities: Girouard to Lugard, 25 Jan. 1908, Lugard papers, MS Brit. Emp. s. 63. The journal *West Africa* believed him to be 'incompetent' and prone to 'incredible inefficiency and bungling': *West Africa*, 24 Oct. 1903, 446; 19 Dec. 1903, 644.

[63] Ommanney note, 20 Aug. 1904, CO 323/492/28934. Baker was a former employer and close friend of Sir William Shelford: *Minutes of the Proceedings of the Institution of Civil Engineers* clxiii (1905–6), 385.

[64] Antrobus note, 13 Feb. 1908, CO 96/474/4194; Elliott-Cooper to CAs, 7 June 1915, CAOG 10/55.

[65] The salary continued to be paid for six months after construction had been completed to give the consulting engineers time to wind down their business, and salaries and fees were occasionally supplemented by commissions for the inspection of plant and materials: CAs to CO, 22 May 1905, CO 96/434/17542. See, for example, Coode to CAs, 10 Jan. 1900, CAOG 10/11; Straits to CO, 9 Nov. 1899, CO 273/249/33676.

[66] CAs to CO, 10 Aug. 1905, CAOG 10/97.

[67] CAs to CO, 20 July 1903, CO 54/685/27072; evidence, CO 766/1, 79; CAs to CO, 28 June 1901, CO 147/158/22311; Grindle note, 25 Jan. 1899, CO 267/449/1979.

[68] CAs to CO, 10 Aug. 1905, CO 323/504/28564.

In West Africa, unconstrained by contractual time limits and penalty clauses or the opportunity cost of slow construction, Shelford appears to have exploited the payment of salaries, and deliberately slowed progress in order to maximise remuneration. The Colonial Office noted that he had 'a strong tendency', whenever asked for an opinion on a comparatively minor point, to say that he 'must consider it as one part of a very big question, and that, in the meantime, nothing should be done'.[69] His construction methods, similarly, slowed progress. Little plant was used, because machinery was allegedly expensive when compared to the cost of labour and its efficient use was impeded by the thickness of the forest and by the unsophisticated nature of the West African labourer, who, if given a wheelbarrow 'would probably fill it . . . and put it on his head'.[70] Consequently, rock was bored by hand rather than by mechanical drill, trees felled by axes and ropes instead of by machine, tree stumps that could have been blasted were 'grubbed' up, and earth was dug by picks and hoes rather than spades or steam shovels, and moved away from cuttings by basket, as opposed to wagons running on rails.[71] Shelford also failed to use the spoil removed from cuttings to build up embankments, as was 'the invariable rule', preferring to dump cutting material and obtain embankment earth from specially dug borrow pits.[72] He rarely built temporary diversions around heavy earthworks and viaducts to prevent their construction slowing down tracklaying.[73] Clean broken stone ballast, time-consuming to produce, rather than sand and gravel was insisted upon, and embankments were raised to their full height immediately, not in stages, which would have reduced the loss and the need to replace ballasting material.[74]

Although the Agents were confident that the idea that slow construction increased his remuneration 'had never crossed . . . [Shelford's] . . . mind', in 1905 his salary was replaced by a fee. This was set according to a percentage payment scale based on the estimated cost of work, and paid in annual instalments, with a small proportion held over until after completion.[75] The new fee eliminated the benefits of slow construction, increased estimates and thus reduced cost overruns and criticism, and prevented Shelford from effectively

[69] Butler note, 11 July 1907, CO 520/51/24142.

[70] F. Shelford, *Some features of the West African railways*, London 1912, 11, 45.

[71] Ibid. 11; F. A. Talbot, *Railway wonders of the world*, i, London 1913, 66–7; Jaekel, *History of the Nigerian railways*, ii. 6.

[72] Shelford, *Features of the West African railways*, 11; Talbot, *Railway wonders*, 67. If not drained, the pits became breeding grounds for disease-carrying mosquitoes: *West Africa*, 15 Aug. 1903, 171–3.

[73] It was claimed that the practice was impracticable in forest or on soft ground, though it was successfully adopted by the Northern Nigeria public works department when it constructed the Baro–Kano line: A. R. Seymour, 'Tropical railway', manuscript, Rhodes House, Oxford, c. 1925 6. See also CAA, CAOG 18/630, 13.

[74] CAA, CAOG 18/630, 13; Shelford, *Features of the West African railways*, 11, 28.

[75] CAs to CO, 22 May 1905, CO 96/434/17542; CAs to CO, 21 Mar. 1907, CO 520/51/10316.

maximising his income since the Colonial Office would refuse to authorise excessive estimates. It also eliminated the relatively high costs of salary negotiation, and increased the Agents' control over the building process, as the payment made after completion could theoretically be retained if the line was not up to standard.

As regards the size of remuneration, it was claimed that the fees and salaries paid to consulting engineer were higher than those paid by private clients or other government departments, and that Shelford was paid a great deal more than any of the other engineers employed by the Agency. The Agents, supported by Sir Montague Ommanney, strongly defended themselves against all three charges. The pay of consulting engineers was generally 'absurdly' below that received from private clients, particularly if the far greater correspondence was taken into account.[76] In many cases, this appears to have been the case, though the engineers' lower profits were offset by the absence of costly site visits, the size and regularity of crown colony income and the commercial value of their position, which in turn attracted private business. On other occasions consulting engineers appear to have been paid far above private rates. For example, to produce a report on the Johannesburg water supply scheme, J. Mansergh received a fee of 7,000 guineas plus expenses for himself and a servant, fees of 2,000–2,500 guineas for two assistants and a 500 guinea fee for his wife and a servant, who would accompany him during his two-month stay in the colony. Chamberlain commented that other engineers would 'jump at the opportunity for only a third of the sum'.[77]

The second and third charges appear to be borne out by a 1907 comparison of Crown Agent and Foreign Office fees (see table 14), which shows that the Agents' consultants earned more than Messrs Rendal & Robertson, who constructed the Uganda railway which was built by the Foreign Office under the department system, and that Shelford's remuneration was greater than that of Messrs Gregory Eyles & Waring, who worked in the Far Eastern crown colonies. Although the Agents claimed that Shelford's relatively high fees were due to his closer supervision of West African construction, the Colonial Office believed that the firm was 'addicted to asking too much' and was paid 'too liberally', and, on one occasion, noted that Sir Maurice Cameron awarded the company higher fees than his colleague Sir Ernest Blake.[78] After Ommanney's retirement, the Agents accepted that the firm was too highly paid, and their fees were progressively reduced to the point where the Colonial Office feared that they were in the danger of being treated illiberally.[79]

---

[76] Ommanney note, 1 May 1906, CO 323/517/2000; Cameron note, 4 June 1904, CO 273/304/18280; Ommanney note, 28 Jan. 1905, CO 87/174/2283.
[77] CAs to CO, 27 Oct. 1902, CO 291/46/44512; Chamberlain note, 31 Oct. 1902, ibid.
[78] Antrobus note, 13 May 1909, CO 96/488/4266; note, 12 Feb. 1909, CO 96/488/4172. The CAs denied the charge: CAs to CO, 5 Mar. 1909, CO 96/488/7934.
[79] Blake note, 7 Sept. 1909, CO 96/488/7934; CAs to CO, 19 May 1908, CO 520/69/18125; CAs to CO, 4 Feb. 1909, CO 96/488/4172; Antrobus note, 13 May 1909, CO 96/488/4266.

Table 14
Construction fees paid to Crown Agent and Foreign Office railway consulting engineers, 1897–1906

Consulting engineer	Cost of works supervised (£m.)	% of salary to cost	% of expenses to cost	% of total remuneration to cost
Shelford & Son (CAs, West Africa)	4	0.6	0.9	1.54
Messrs Gregory Eyles & Waring (CAs, Far Eastern colonies)	5.8	0.2	0.28	0.49
Messrs Rendal & Robertson (Foreign Office, Uganda railway)	4.9	0.074	0.075	0.149

Source: PP 1907, lvi (103); CO 323/527/8695.

Fees and salaries were high to maximise the cost of dismissal for poor construction and to generate trust. In addition, remuneration was increased by the employment of high status engineers, who were much in demand; the consulting engineers' asset specificity i.e. knowledge of crown colony conditions etc.; and the high opportunity cost of colonial visits by the consultants' staff. The Agents were also poor negotiators, finding 'haggling . . . very unpleasant', and argued that if they forced a consultant to accept a lower salary and he refused, it would be difficult to obtain a replacement willing to take responsibility for the designs: the creation of fresh plans would increase costs and lead to delay.[80] They also had great difficulty, particularly in West Africa, in accurately forecasting project workload, and monitoring fees, for which there was no set scale, and, more importantly, expenses.[81] The latter were a particular bone of contention with the Colonial Office, which strongly suspected that out-of-pocket claims were artificially inflated.[82] Consequently the Agents occasionally placed limits on expenses, and in 1909 introduced a combined personal fee and expense commission.[83]

Resident engineers

To avoid principal–agent problems among construction staff, the Agents insisted that resident engineers be appointed by the consulting engineers,

[80] CAs to CO, 22 May 1905, CO 96/434/17542; CAs to CO, 3 June 1901, CO 54/672/19122.
[81] CAs to CO, 3 June 1901, CO 54/672/19122.
[82] Darnley note, 4 Aug. 1906, CO 87/176/26414; Strachey note, 18 Jan. 1904, CO 520/26/40785; Butler note, 21 Apr. 1908, CO 446/77/12798.
[83] CAs to CO, 24 Mar. 1898, CO 96/325/6640; Blake note, 7 Sept. 1909, CO 96/488/7934.

who generally chose experienced, though often unqualified, men, with whom they subsequently had long relationships.[84] Demands from the colonies that Indian or army engineers, or directors of local public works or open line departments be employed were generally resisted. The recruitment of Indian engineers and army officers would lead to 'delay and difficulties', while Indian engineers were believed to be poorly trained.[85] It was acknowledged that the employment of local officials would have advantages. They were trusted by colonial governments, and would therefore be less likely to be the objects of criticism, and their appointment would improve the morale of other colonial technical staff.[86] However they brought the risk of poor quality construction. Most lacked the necessary experience or qualifications for such posts, and would be too preoccupied with their regular duties to concentrate fully on construction.[87] They would thus delegate tasks, leading to a division of responsibility, which would weaken one of the incentives, the certainty of punishment, that encouraged the provision of satisfactory work. There was also a danger that they would place greater weight on the views of the colonial government, on whom their future livelihood depended, than on those of the consulting engineer.[88] Furthermore, if allowed to devote all their time to new works, they would have to be replaced by someone inevitably less effective, and, when they returned to their posts, would suffer from low morale and poor motivation.[89]

The employment of resident engineers from the United Kingdom again raised costs. Unlike the directors of public works or open lines, they had little knowledge of local conditions or labour rates, and had no sense of shared endeavour with the colony.[90] They were also prone to illness and were often resented and distrusted by colonial officials, who withheld help and information.[91] Resident engineers were blamed, for example, for the defective

[84] Neither of the two resident engineers regularly appointed by Shelford, W. Bradford and P. Hayton, were qualified: Shelford, *Life of Sir William Shelford*, 117; Institution of Civil Engineers, *List of members*, London 1895–1905.

[85] CAs to CO, 16 Dec. 1904, CO 147/172/42513; CAs to CO, 21 Feb. 1900, CO 446/12/5881.

[86] CAs to CO, 5 Jan. 1911, CO 96/512/447.

[87] Ibid; CAs to CO, 20 Mar. 1897, CO 96/301/5899.

[88] CAs to CO, 20 Mar. 1897, CO 96/301/5899.

[89] CAs to CO, 5 Jan. 1911, CO 96/512/447.

[90] PPE, q. 893. The Northern Nigerian governor, Sir P. Girouard, reported that the engineers working on the Baro–Kano railway, which was built by the public works department, 'worked like slaves', as they regarded the line as 'our railway' rather than 'a Shelford extension': Girouard to Lugard, 25 Jan. 1908, Lugard papers, MS Brit. Emp. s. 63. The Agents argued that local knowledge could be acquired rapidly: CAs to CO, 2 July 1901, CO 273/276/22964.

[91] CAs to CO, 2 July 1901, CO 273/276/22964. In 1901 the Jamaican public works department appears deliberately to have failed to disclose to the consulting engineer employed to improve the colony's railway the sharpness of the line's curves, with the result that the locomotives designed proved useless: Cooper to CAs, 6 Feb. 1902, CO 137/631/7724.

bridge foundations on the Kowloon–Canton line, the inadequacies of the Lagos electric light scheme and the Kumassi bridge collapse, which killed three people.[92] It would appear, though, that on some occasions they were unfairly blamed for mistakes made by the consulting engineers. On receiving a damming independent report on the Southern Nigerian line in 1912, for example, the Colonial Office clerk, C. Strachey, commented that it was 'hardly worthwhile to start a controversy with the consulting engineers . . . [as] . . . they will, as usual, put it all down to local staff, and we can be sure that we will get little satisfaction nor apology from them'.[93]

The level of remuneration paid to resident engineers and to United Kingdom construction staff, and the method of payment, was inevitably the subject of criticism. The payment of salaries and the lack of bonuses for rapid completion, which the Agents believed led to poor workmanship, along with the fact that engineers were employed only for the duration of the construction of a project, led to idling.[94] Moreover, on a number of lines, the resident engineer appears to have unilaterally extended schemes. On the Lagos railway the resident engineer constructed, according to Shelford, one bridge that was unnecessary, another that was too large and a further bridge that was 'open to doubt'.[95] The salaries of construction staff were also believed to be excessive. In West Africa they were were generally three times those paid in the United Kingdom and, in 1897 in Lagos, slightly higher than those of South American railway engineers.[96] In addition, workers were allowed four months paid leave per year, free passage to and from the colony, free medical attention, and invalidity and widow allowances. Moreover, consulting engineers, unbeknown to the Agents, manipulated leave regulations to ensure that staff, on completion of works, were dismissed only after they had taken their leave.[97] Those who had performed satisfactorily could also expect to be employed by the consulting engineers on future construction projects, or recommended by them for posts in colonial open line and public works departments.[98]

[92] CAs to CO, 13 Oct. 1908, CO 129/350/37429; Preece to CAs, 2 Mar. 1898, CO 147/137/6746; Butler note, 7 Dec. 1903, CO 96/412/43070.
[93] Strachey note, 17 Apr. 1912, CO 520/118/10211.
[94] CAs to CO, 21 Aug. 1895, CO 147/101/14697.
[95] Robinson note, 12 Jan. 1906, CO 147/179/1066. The resident engineer in charge of the Stann Creek railway in British Honduras improved the alignment of the line, undertook heavier works than contemplated and constructed four trestle bridges without giving 'any indication that he had become involved in works of this size': Shelford to CAs, 27 May 1908, CO 123/260/2049.
[96] Report, CO 147/168/8585, 35.
[97] Shelford to CAs, 4 Sept. 1896, CAOG 13/282; CO to CAs, 16 May 1899, ibid; CAs to CO, 27 Apr. 1905, CO 267/481/14136.
[98] Shelford to CAs, 24 May 1903, CO 96/412/16349; Shelford to CAs, 30 Dec. 1910, CO 520/109/1087.

Salaries were generous in order to increase the cost of poor construction and dismissal and to promote trust, and because they were paid by the constructing colony, which deprived the consulting engineers of the restraint they would have exercised had they been obliged to meet payments from their own fees. In West Africa high incomes were also required to attract sufficient workers to projects, and to prevent those appointed from being poached by mining companies when they arrived in the colony. In the event, the monetary rewards and perks often proved an insufficient lure. Shelford sometimes found it difficult to recruit experienced assistant engineers, and there were a number of colonial complaints about the poor quality of the people employed.[99]

Indigenous labour

Indigenous workers were recruited by colonial administrations, either individually, or, in the case of earthworks, through native subcontractors, who agreed to complete a certain amount of work for a given fee.[100] Colonial officials, through their trust relationships with local chiefs and their ability to organise the import and repatriation of workers, ensured a good supply of quality labour, and prevented friction between local residents and construction workers.[101] Employing members of their own family or tribe, with whom they had strong relationships, subcontractors could attain higher levels of productivity and higher standards of work than European foremen, and, unlike foremen, if ineffective, could be easily dismissed.[102] The use of both colonial officers and subcontractors, however, greatly increased labour costs, which in West Africa were further raised by the rapid starts to construction, the general scarcity of labour and, in the Gold Coast, competition from the mines (*see* table 15). Wishing to maintain their bonds of trust with tribes, local administrators ensured that labourers obtained more than 'fair' terms and that agreements continued even when conditions had been broken. In Northern Nigeria they also demanded that workers be paid by the day, which added to administration costs and, to prevent the disruption of agriculture, stipulated that natives could be employed for only two months, which increased training costs and weakened labour effectiveness.[103] Meanwhile,

---

99 Egerton note, 3 Sept. 1905, CO 147/177/34063; CAs to CO, 24 Feb. 1897, CO 147/122/4233; CAs to CO, 4 Mar. 1903, CO 147/168/8585. Recruitment was difficult, owing to the temporary nature of the work, the harsh and unhealthy climate, the Agents' refusal to countenance the payment of rapid completion bonuses and the general shortage of engineers, due to the worldwide boom in railway construction: Hemming note, n.d., CO 147/101/11613; CAs to CO, 9 Aug. 1897, CO 147/122/17479; CAs to CO, 21 Aug. 1895, CO 147/101/14697.
100 Shelford, *Features of the West African railways*, 11.
101 Memo, Jan. 1904, CAOG 10/96; PP 1924, viii (Cmd 2016), 9.
102 CAOG 18/119, 133.
103 Shelford, *Features of the West African railways*, 79; W. Oyemakindo, 'Railway construc-

Table 15
Unskilled labour rates in West Africa, 1904

Colony	Rate per day (s. d.)
Dahomey	6.5d.
Gold Coast	1s. 3d.
Kayes Niger	5.25d.
Lagos	1s.
Sierra Leone	10d.

Source: PPD, 22.

Note: 1904 exchange rate: 1 franc = 8.75d. The French rates are 'unofficial'.

although the use of subcontractors reduced the expense of finding and employing individual workers, the subcontractors' profit margin increased overall labour costs.[104]

The nature of the department system

The Ronaldshay Committee, appointed in 1924 to investigate African railways, concluded that the department system was 'the most unsatisfactory of all' the methods of construction, and that 'it was largely due to this system that the early railways were both costly and defective'.[105] The system increased costs in a number of ways. Correspondence between consulting and resident engineers led to high administration expenses and delays, and, as the consulting engineers often had difficulty understanding problems from written descriptions, resulted in poor quality construction.[106] The system, by enabling location surveys to be carried out during construction rather than before building commenced, as occurred when contractors were used, also led to hurried surveys, particularly if construction was 'treading on . . . [the surveyor's] . . . heels'.[107] Findings were consequently incomplete and insufficiently considered, with the result that alignment and gradients were poor and expenditure high.[108] It was later claimed that pre-construction surveys were ruled out by the administrative urgency with which the railways were

tion and operation in Nigeria, 1895–1911: the labour problems and socio-economic impact', *Journal of the Historical Society of Nigeria* vii (1974), 307, 317.
[104] Report, 15 July 1903, CO 67/136/28061; Meade note, 19 Aug. 1903, ibid.
[105] PP 1924 viii (Cmd 2016), 6–7. The committee added (p. 7) that 'in the circumstances it may well be doubted whether private enterprise or contractors would have done much better'.
[106] Report, CO 446/107/10210.
[107] Hammond to committee, 25 Aug. 1923, CO 766/1, 32.
[108] The Ronaldshay Committee believed that inadequate surveys were one of the main reasons for the excessive cost of the lines: PP 1924, viii (Cmd 2016), 6.

built. Yet there were usually months and often years before building commenced when surveys could have been undertaken. A more likely explanation for their use is that the Crown Agents and consulting engineers suspected that a realistic estimate based on a separate location survey would reduce the likelihood of the Colonial Office authorising the railway and, when the department system was not certain to be adopted, perhaps feared that a survey would allow the work to be put out to contract. Separate surveys were also against the interests of the Colonial Office. They took up to two years to complete, and in the meantime officials would be subjected to intense pressure from outside interest groups for whom delay was costly.[109]

Location surveys during construction were eventually abandoned in about 1904, when the Agents and their engineers, having discovered that 'the level is a more economic excavator than the spade' and under some colonial pressure, began to argue against them.[110] However, even pre-construction surveys often contained imprecise information. Since under the department system there was no need for detailed results for monitoring purposes, they were completed relatively rapidly, often by poorly qualified people, and were underfunded.[111] The Dominican Rossea harbour project, for example, was surveyed by William Shelford's eldest son, a ship's captain, who coincidentally was sailing to the island, and the Lagos breakwater by a public works department engineer with no surveying or estimating experience.[112]

Other drawbacks of the department system were the high cost of Crown Agent materials, and the insistence of the Colonial Office that construction staff use inadequate colonial medical facilities, which contributed to the high invalidity and death rates.[113] The system also discouraged the constructing colony from being 'alive to the needs of economy'.[114] Provided costs were likely to be covered by receipts, colonies generally wished works to be as extensive as possible. Long railways, for example, increased merchants' profits, and, by increasing colonial prosperity, improved the status and career prospects of the governor. Consequently, colonies, after Colonial Office approval had been obtained, tended to add to works, a practice that would have been inhibited by the use of contractors, who would have made claims for extras and compensation.[115] On completion of lines, colonies similarly had a

[109] CO 766/1, evidence, 67.

[110] CAs to CO, 13 Nov. 1906, CO 520/38/41943; CAs to CO, 25 Nov. 1907, CO 520/52/41328; report, 28 Dec. 1904, CO 147/177/1241.

[111] CO 766/1, evidence, 325.

[112] Shelford, *Life of Sir William Shelford*, 118; Antrobus note, 27 Apr. 1901, CO 147/158/5790.

[113] Meade note, 25 Aug. 1895, CO 147/122/18148; Antrobus note, 28 Aug. 1897, ibid.

[114] Ezechiel note, 12 Dec. 1901, CO 147/158/42531. See also Herbert note, 14 June 1900, CO 879/93/845, 138, and T 1/9581/16676/9505.

[115] According to the CA, Sir William Mercer, such additions were one of the major reasons for cost overruns: evidence, CO 766/1, 73. Additional works on the Singapore, Kowloon–Canton and Madawachecki–Talai Manaar railways increased costs by 20%, 37%

tendency to place costs, which they would have had difficulty meeting from revenue, on to the capital account. In 1904, for instance, Lagos attempted to charge the cost of locomotive repair, fencing and a traction engine to capital expenditure.[116]

Unprofitable lines

A further strategy adopted by the Agents and consulting engineers to maximise their incomes was to encourage Colonial Office authorisation of lines, which led to the construction of uneconomic railways. Colonial Office approval was encouraged in three ways. First, in West Africa, Shelford was continually recommending to the Colonial Office that it sanction reconnaissance surveys, and to encourage acceptance appears to have underestimated their cost.[117] Such surveys promoted discussion, and, if they were published, led to pressure for construction from outside bodies. This, along with the high cost of the survey helped to commit the secretary of state to the project.[118] On completion of a location survey, Shelford then usually advised the Colonial Office that, to save expenditure and avoid subsequent delays, the surveyors should be allowed to stay in the colony and investigate a possible extension of the line. The cost of the second survey, as acknowledged by the assistant under-secretary, C. P. Lucas, again helped to commit the Colonial Office to construction.[119]

Secondly, the consulting engineers often underestimated, or, according to the Agents, took 'an optimistic view' of the cost of lines. This encouraged construction and, by reducing likely debt charges, improved the expected profitability of projects. Low estimates were the result of minimising the potential difficulties of construction. In his 1895 Lagos–Otta report, for example, Shelford claimed that there was 'splendid ballasting material' in the Ogun river bed and at Otta.[120] In fact, material could only be found at Abeokuta, approximately seventy miles inland; the Lagos–Otta line conse-

and 5% respectively: CAs to CO, 24 Nov. 1904, CO 273/304/40128; Barry to CAs, 15 Oct. 1907, CO 129/342/37695; CAs to CO, 9 June 1909, CO 54/729/19297.

[116] Ezechiel note, 31 Mar. 1904, CO 147/172/11204; CAs to CO, 6 Sept. 1904, CO 147/172/31164; Shelford to CAs, 6 Sept. 1904, CO 147/172/32056. See also CAs to Ceylon, 25 Aug. 1903, CO 54/685/31774.

[117] CAs to CO, 12 Feb. 1903, CO 446/34/5822; Antrobus note, 25 June 1902, CO 147/163/16292; CAs to CO, 2 Dec. 1901, CO 147/158/42531; Mercer note, 12 Feb. 1898, CO 96/325/2259.

[118] Lucas note, 25 Aug. 1906, CO 96/449/30967. The surveys also increased the incomes of consulting engineers.

[119] Ibid. See, for example, CAs to CO, 13 Nov. 1906, CO 520/38/41943; CAs to CO, 12 Feb. 1907, CO 446/67/5423; CO to CAs, 10 Aug. 1899, CO 147/146/15785; CAs to CO, 29 July 1901, CO 147/958/26276.

[120] Survey, 16 Jan. 1895, CO 147/101/3321.

quently remained unballasted until the railway finally reached the quarries in 1899.[121] Items were also simply omitted from expenses. For instance, the estimate for the Accra harbour works failed to include accommodation costs, and that for the Accra–Kpong line expenditure on a harbour for the unloading of construction materials.[122] What is more, estimates often contained inadequate margins for contingencies, used approximated quantities, particularly for bridges and rolling stock, underestimated land prices, where these were determined by the consulting engineers, took no account of the rise in labour costs that would result from the project's own demand for workers and assumed an excessively low exchange rate.[123]

Thirdly, the Agents and their engineers overestimated the likely returns from lines, which encouraged Colonial Office authorisation and strengthened the Crown Agents' case for the construction of railways to an excessively high standard. Although they took account of administrative and political factors and the views of the constructing colonies and outside pressure groups, the Colonial Office, in deciding whether construction should go ahead, leaned heavily on the advice of consulting engineers and the Crown Agents. In 1907, when it was suggested in parliament that the consulting engineers gave 'advice in order to get work', J. F. N. Green accepted that the engineers 'in a very limited sense' influenced decisions to construct.[124] Sir Montague Ommanney went further and admitted that 'consideration is, in the great majority of cases, whether the line will pay, about which the consulting engineers have more to say than anybody else'.[125] Generally the Colonial Office accepted the optimistic conclusions of the Agents and their consultants. Belonging to a culture that regarded state economic planning as unnecessary and even pernicious, Colonial Office administrators had few guidelines for judging the likely success of schemes. The idea of the use of transport for development purposes was relatively new, and the perceived success of the policy in the United States and Canada had created the impression that the construction of railways automatically led to growth.[126] Yet, even when they were less than convinced by the consulting engineers'

121 Shelford to CAs, 13 Dec. 1898, CO 147/138/23134.
122 Note, 12 Jan. 1906, ibid; CAs to CO, 26 Nov. 1904, CO 273/304/40128. See also Coode to CAs, 8 June 1907, CO 96/461/20474; CAs to CO, 10 Aug. 1899, CO 96/347/21190.
123 CAs to CO, 11 Nov. 1901, CO 273/276/39770; Elliott note, 7 Aug. 1903, CO 67/136/28061; Treasury to CO, 31 Oct.1903, T 1/100186/18832/16865.
124 Hansard, 4th ser. 1906, clxvii. 658; Lucas note, 8 Dec. 1906, CO 323/516/45203; Green note, 21 Dec. 1906, CO 323/516/46914.
125 CO to CAs, 3 Jan. 1907, CO 323/516/46914, marginal note. In his parliamentary answer to the question, Churchill stated that the Agents provided only technical information and, after a project had been authorised, only provided advice 'if advice is necessary' on the construction of works: Hansard, 4th ser. 1906, clxvii. 659.
126 Walter Pflaumer, 'The politics of transport policy in Nigeria, 1890–1914: a case study of economic planning in the colonial period', unpubl. Phd diss. Yale 1982, 285; Kesner, Economic control and colonial development, 106.

figures, since they wished the lines to be constructed, they were still highly receptive of recommendations that reinforced their preference. In the case of the Sierra Leone Freetown–Songotown line, for instance, Chamberlain admitted that he was 'distrustful' of the traffic estimates produced by Shelford, as he had 'no solid basis to go upon', but, nevertheless, was prepared to sanction the line.[127]

Recommendations made by the Agents and their consultants were usually excessively optimistic. Most of the consulting engineers' reports predicted that proposed lines would cover both working and debt charges immediately. Where this was not the case, it was usually forecast that increases in traffic would ensure that the loss was only temporary and that, in the meantime, any shortfall would be offset by increased tax revenues on the trade fostered by the line, and that, in colonies without railways, valuable experience of construction in the region would be gained.[128] Occasionally, when it seemed that a railway they had disparaged would be built, the consulting engineers improved their forecasts of profitability. After the completion of the Freetown–Songotown line, for example, Shelford claimed that an extension to Rotifunk, which he had previously declared would not be profitable, would be a financial success.[129] When a completed line failed to pay, they continued to insist that their forecasts would be fulfilled, or used the failure to encourage further construction, warning that the line would remain unremunerative unless another extension was built.[130] Shelford, for instance, claimed that the Lagos–Otta line, which was not expected to cover debt charges, would be successful if an extension were built to Ibadan.[131] On completion of the Otta–Ibadan section, which covered neither its own costs nor those of the original section, he advised that the two sections would pay only if a further extension was built.[132] Likewise, in Sierra Leone, he warned the Colonial Office that, unless the Freetown–Songotown line was extended, 'the money spent will be more or less thrown away', causing C. Harris to conclude that 'we have gone so far that we cannot stop'.[133] The Crown Agents usually accepted their consultants' conclusions, generally questioning them only when they believed them overly pessimistic. It was argued, for example, that in his Lagos–Otta report Shelford had underestimated traffic levels and the

[127] Chamberlain note, 3 Sept. 1895, CO 267/422/14724.
[128] Report, 9 Aug. 1906, CO 96/449/30967; CAs to CO, 31 Oct. 1895, CO 147/101/19160.
[129] Their previous report had allegedly been based on inaccurate import figures and a false assumption that the railway would not capture the river traffic of the area: CAs to CO, 11 Dec. 1897, CO 267/434/26730.
[130] Shelford to CAs, 15 Feb. 1904, CO 267/474/5871; Shelford to CAs, 24 Nov. 1904, CO 267/474/41570.
[131] CAs to CO, 31 Oct. 1895, CO 147/101/19160.
[132] Ezechiel note, 27 Aug. 1901, CO 147/158/26276.
[133] Read note, 21 Dec. 1899, CO 267/449/33390; Harris note, 20 Jan. 1890, ibid.

freight rate that could be borne by the region, and that in his Tarkwa–Kumassi report he had again assumed excessively low rates.[134]

Consulting engineers arrived at their conclusions after determining the interest rates of the loan initially taken out to finance the project and the working expenses of the scheme, and comparing the result with the likely immediate and future revenues. Interest charges were based on the estimated cost of the line, and working expenses on the operating costs of similar railways.[135] Revenues comprised import, export, passenger and government receipts. Although the methods adopted varied according to the information available, export estimates were generally calculated using the export figures of the nearest port, surveyors' road traffic counts, or the results of the multiplication of the average per square mile yield of the main crops grown by the number of square miles likely to be served by the railway, from which home consumption, the average population per square mile multiplied by the assumed annual *per capita* consumption, was subtracted.[136] Total exports were then multiplied by the freight rate that the consulting engineers believed the exports could bear, which was generally below that charged by competing forms of transport. Import estimates were based on import figures or the import traffic of a similar railway, which were again multiplied by a given freight rate. Passenger revenues were calculated using population figures, surveyors' road traffic counts and the passenger rates of similar lines. To calculate future receipts, the expected per acre crop of the product likely to be grown was multiplied by the acreage of the estimated cultivation area and a set freight rate, and added to an estimate of the natural increase in traffic, generally the recent traffic growth of a similar line.[137]

Estimates of profitability made by consulting engineers tended to be wide of the mark. Debt charges were based on underestimated construction costs, and working expense calculations used figures from dissimilar lines and, in the case of extensions, often assumed that in the first instance the line would be worked at a reduced cost by existing open line staff.[138] As regards receipts, the Agents believed the statistics used to be 'vague and problematical', and even Shelford accepted that they were 'necessarily indefinite'.[139] All calculations were based on a single assumed freight rate, which took no account of the different goods to be carried. Surveyors' traffic counts were limited, extending over at most only one week, undertaken as a secondary activity

134 CAs to CO, 10 Aug. 1899, CO 96/347/21190; CAs to CO, 31 Oct. 1895, CO 147/101/19160.
135 Report, 23 Oct. 1906, CO 520/38/41943.
136 Ibid; report, 15 Nov. 1899, CO 267/449/33390.
137 Report, 28 Feb. 1905, CO 446/47/12976.
138 Report, 9 Aug. 1906, CO 96/449/30967.
139 CAs to CO, 19 Apr. 1905, CO 446/47/12976; Shelford to CAs, 28 Sept. 1911, CO 96/512/34704.

and taking no account of seasonal variations in movement.[140] The information obtained from African chiefs and merchants, who often regarded the surveyors as European interlopers and railways as a potential military or commercial threat, was often inaccurate or false.[141] Many figures, meanwhile, were obtained from dubious sources; a forecast £30,000 saving in administrative and military costs resulting from the construction of the Baro–Kano line, for instance, was based on a letter from the governor of Northern Nigeria, in which he stated that such a saving 'may be conjectured'.[142] In addition, the consulting engineers assumed that all existing and future traffic would be transported by rail, and dismissed factors such as the possibility of competitive price reductions by road, river and head load carriers, the low value given to time in African culture and, in some cases, a preference for existing forms of transport.[143] In the case of the Lagos–Otta line, Shelford assumed that the railway would win the whole of the river Ogun traffic.[144] In the event, the river carriers undercut the railway's freight rate and the line failed to capture the trade, even when it introduced retaliatory rate cuts.[145] Likewise, in the case of future returns, projections were based on little evidence, and took no account of the possible unwillingness of indigenous farmers to grow new crops, the lack of the roads that were necessary for motor transport or the problems of perishability.[146]

Quality

In West Africa, and, to a lesser extent, in some other colonies, railways were shoddily built. The Lagos–Ibadan line, when handed over to the colony, was only half ballasted, had temporary earthworks and an incomplete drainage system and telegraph network, while the Sekondi–Tarkwa line was half-ballasted, had an uneven track and was 'a long way . . . from being in safe working order'.[147] The poor quality of lines was due to a number of factors,

---

[140] Bradford to Shelford, 26 Dec. 1894, CO 147/101/2665; Bradford to Shelford, 16 Jan. 1895, CO 147/101/3321.

[141] Bradford to Shelford, 24 Jan. 1895, CO 147/101/5136; note, 29 Oct. 1908, CO 96/472/39103.

[142] Antrobus note, 2 Oct. 1905, CO 446/47/12976.

[143] MacGregor to Chamberlain, 30 Mar. 1900, CO 147/148/13099; Mercer note, 15 Dec. 1897, CO 267/434/26730.

[144] CAs to CO, 31 Oct. 1895, CO 147/101/19160.

[145] MacGregor to Chamberlain, 30 Mar. 1900, CO 146/148/13099.

[146] Roads and motor transport were of particular importance in West Africa, as bullock transport was slow and expensive owing to the poor quality of the animals raised in the country, the heavy wagons used and the reluctance of natives to adopt this form of transport: CAA, CAOG 18/630, 18. In Southern Nigeria and parts of the Gold Coast, bullocks and other pack animals fell prey to the tsetse fly and were impracticable.

[147] Gold Coast to CO, 16 June 1906, CO 96/443/24376; Daniel note, 31 May 1904, CO 96/423/11628; Shelford to CAs, 11 Mar. 1904, ibid.

including the employment of United Kingdom engineers with little knowledge of local conditions and, in West Africa, the harsh environment and the
inexperience of Frederic Shelford. Despite the Agents various strategies to
combat opportunism, there was also a degree of self-interested behaviour.

The Agents' initial ignorance of the poor quality of the lines and the existence of moral hazard was the result of poor monitoring. The supervision of
activities in the colonies was difficult and potentially costly, and the Crown
Agents, no doubt, were confident that careful recruitment, the payment of
salaries and premiums and the establishment of trust relationships would
prove sufficient to prevent opportunism. In so far as it existed monitoring
took various forms. The Colonial Office and Agents perused the quarterly
reports and, from 1896, the bi-annual reports and quarterly statements on the
progress of works prepared by the consulting engineers and, in the case of the
Agents, all correspondence between consulting and resident engineers.[148]
Copies of these letters were likewise passed to the governor of the colony
where the work was being done. Governors also received works accounts and
theoretically could inspect sites themselves.[149] Consulting engineers, meanwhile, followed progress via works visits and through the resident engineer,
who was in constant correspondence with the consultant and each month
prepared progress summaries, and, in turn, monitored the construction
staff.[150] Finally, before each line was handed over to the colony, it was
inspected by an engineer or the manager of that colony's railway department.[151]

Many of these strategies were ineffective. The Colonial Office trusted the
advice and information provided by the consulting engineers, implicitly
accepting that 'when an expert is called in, one is very much in his hands' and
believing that the engineers' reputation was 'a sufficient safeguard against
fraud'.[152] The office, in any case, lacked the technical expertise and experience, time and inclination, to judge the accuracy of the information
provided, which, to minimise criticism, was perhaps deliberately presented by
the consulting engineers in a highly technical and lengthy form. Colonial
and other criticisms of construction from 1901 onwards were also usually
dealt with by Sir Montague Ommanney who, before joining the Crown
Agents had specialised in architecture. Unwilling either to criticise his
former employer or his son-in-law, he generally supported the consulting

---

148 Shelford to CAs, 16 Oct. 1896, CO 147/108/21605.
149 CAs to CO, 18 Oct. 1901, CO 267/460/36490.
150 CO to Egerton, 6 Jan. 1905, CO 147/172/42513.
151 CAs to CO, 18 Oct. 1901, CO 267/460/36490.
152 Harris note, 26 Jan. 1899, CO 267/449/1979; CAs to CO, 27 Aug. 1909, CO 129/
359/28826. Similar views were expressed in Butler note, 27 May 1908, CO 520/69/18125;
Lyttelton note, 1 Apr. 1905, CO 525/10/9841; Butler note, 22 Mar. 1907, CO 96/461/9405;
Meade note, 22 Aug. 1895, CO 147/101/14697. They also prevailed in other government
departments: Roy Macleod, *Government and expertise: specialists, administrators and professionals, 1860–1919*, Cambridge 1988, 10.

engineers.[153] A suggestion that, when technical disputes arose between the consultants and the colonies, the secretary of state should seek the advice of the War Office ordnance department was rejected on the ground that such referrals would only increase friction.[154]

Equally the Crown Agents accepted information provided by the consulting engineers in good faith. The Agents were unwilling to expend the Agency's income on more stringent supervision and thus did not employ any supervisory engineers and rarely sought outside help.[155] Construction was therefore monitored by Cameron and Blake through their consulting engineers' reports and correspondence and a variety of secondary sources.[156] Unfortunately, neither possessed the necessary time and abilities to rigorously scrutinise their consultants' actions. Sir Maurice Cameron had no experience of railway construction, though he was an engineer and no doubt gained a great deal 'on the job'.[157] Sir Ernest Blake, who managed the West African railway projects as 'they were more a question of policy than of engineering', had no engineering expertise whatsoever and did 'not pretend to deal with engineering matters'.[158]

[153] Kubicek, The administration of imperialism, 41. Even in 1908 Ommanney continued to think of himself as a CA, using the term 'we' when referring to the agency in the enquiry: PPE, q. 1881.

[154] Green note, 8 Dec. 1909, CO 323/553/39753; Harris note, n.d., ibid.

[155] The CAs appear to have checked the advice of consulting engineers on only three occasions: CAs to CO, 19 Dec. 1904, CO 273/304/42851; CAs to CO, 29 June 1905, CO 54/696/22587; CAs to CO, 31 Oct. 1895, CO 147/101/19160. They even seem to have failed to peruse the consulting engineers' accounts thoroughly. In 1903 Shelford's mistaken inclusion of his Gold Coast charge in his accounts for Nigeria and Lagos went unnoticed: CAs to CO, 9 Feb. 1903, CO 147/168/5330.

[156] The clerk A. Reeves was a former employee of Baker and Shelford: CAs to CO, 7 Apr. 1911, CAA, weeded file, o/sec/159. The clerk G. Wells and the head of the works branch and later the engineering inspection branch, A. M. Heath, had worked for Sir A. M. Rendel, and the clerks W. Eraut and G. R. Lock had previously been employed by non-CA consulting engineers: Wells to CAs, 6 Nov. 1901, CAOG 13/38; PPE, q. 164; schedule, CO 323/548/45364. Both Ommanney and Cameron had social contacts with the engineering profession, and Ommanney's uncle and father-in-law, Octavius Ommanney, was the deputy chairman of the Contract Corporation, which undertook the construction of railways and other public works at home and abroad: Banking almanac and directory, London 1865, 263. The CAs' consulting engineers no doubt also monitored themselves, most having social and professional relationships. For example, Sir William Shelford was a former employee, and, from 1888, a neighbour of Sir John Fowler, who had been in partnership with Sir Benjamin Baker, who, in turn, had at one time been an employee of Sir John Hawkshaw: Shelford, Life of Sir William Shelford, 106; Dictionary of national biography, Oxford 1901, 1912, 1927. Sir John Coode had served his articles with the father of Sir A. M. Rendel, who was the uncle of J. M. Dobson, and James Mansergh had worked with Sir Robert Rawlinson, who had trained with Sir John Hawkshaw: Minutes of the Proceedings of the Institution of Civil Engineers clxi (1904–5), 350; cxvii (1923–4), 448.

[157] Before joining the Agents, Cameron had been deputy colonial engineer and surveyor-general in the Straits, where his work had entailed the construction and maintenance of roads, bridges and public buildings: Cameron memoirs, 85.

[158] PPE, q. 1123.

Monitoring by the consulting engineers and within colonies was equally poor. Close supervision of constructing staff by the consulting engineers would have increased their costs and reduced the profits they made from their expenses. They also 'had a difficulty in ascertaining the exact state of works'.[159] The Agents believed that, based in London, they could exercise only 'a limited control', and W. D. Ellis dismissed their efforts as 'distinctly futile'.[160] The monthly summaries of progress omitted details, such as the specific cost of items of work, and the contents were not checked, allowing, as C. Harris pointed out, resident engineers to omit or falsify facts.[161] Given their connection with the building process, consulting engineers, in any case, were unlikely to draw attention to any errors on the part of construction staff or irregularities that came to light, a point acknowledged by Frederic Shelford himself, who in 1908 admitted that he was 'reluctant to criticise . . . [the British Honduras resident engineer] . . . as we sent him to the colony'.[162] As for site visits, these were relatively rare. William Shelford, for example, never visited West Africa, and his son made only three trips between 1897 and 1907.[163] Although Shelford believed that visits were 'of considerable value . . . [and] often result in savings in cost and other advantages far in excess of the comparatively small sum involved', the Colonial Office regarded them as 'expensive luxuries'.[164]

In the colonies, the long periods of leave and high invalidity and mortality rates meant that there was a high turnover of resident engineers, which made the supervision of construction staff difficult. Governors, meanwhile, were asked not to intervene in the construction process.[165] Theoretically this ruling was intended to ensure that lines were built according to the agreed standards, that consulting engineers could be held directly responsible for works and to avoid delays, but in reality it was probably a crude attempt to prevent colonial criticism of construction.[166] Inevitably, it resulted in much resentment on the part of colonial governments, which felt that they had no control over the construction of their own infrastructure, and led to a number of bitter clashes between governors and resident engineers.[167] At first the

---

[159] Shelford to Nathan, 30 Oct. 1903, Nathan papers, MSS Nathan 310.
[160] CAs to CO, 16 Dec. 1904, CO 147/172/42513; Ellis note, 2 Nov. 1911, CO 96/512/34704.
[161] Harris note, 13 Nov. 1899, CO 96/347/20621.
[162] Shelford to Swayze, 26 May 1908, CO 123/260/20495. Similar points were made by Antrobus and W. Egerton, the governor of Southern Nigeria: Antrobus note, 23 Feb. 1905, CO 96/427/5543; Antrobus note, 19 Dec. 1904, CO 147/172/42359; CO to Egerton, 6 Jan. 1905, CO 147/172/42513.
[163] Shelford, Life of Sir William Shelford, 116.
[164] Shelford to CAs, 6 Oct. 1908, CO 123/260/37841; Butler note, 26 Sept. 1907, CO 96/461/34132. See also note, 3 Aug. 1908, CO 123/260/20495.
[165] CO to Gold Coast, 30 Mar. 1900, CO 96/347/20621.
[166] Harris note, 13 Nov. 1899, ibid.; CAs to CO, 17 Apr. 1901, CO 267/460/13520; CAs to CO, 17 Aug. 1899, CO 96/347/21804.
[167] CO to Straits, 26 July 1901, CO 273/276/22964; CAs to CO, 20 July 1904, CO 273/

Agents refused to reconsider the policy, claiming that colonies had countless opportunities to influence and monitor building and actually chose 'to assume the attitude of helpless spectators'.[168] Later, pressure from the Colonial Office caused them to relax the rules slightly. In Lagos in 1902 correspondence between consulting and resident engineers also went through the office of the open lines manager, who, on behalf of the governor, could inspect the site at any time.[169] In 1906 resident engineers were also placed under an obligation to 'furnish direct to the colonial government any information required', to follow the governor's wishes in all matters 'effecting the use of works when completed', provided that they were consistent with sound engineering, and to refer to the colony questions that would effect colonial relations with indigenous populations.[170] Governors, though, were still discouraged from intervening in the construction process unless the matter was urgent.[171]

Finally, the inspection of completed lines was also unlikely to be overly critical. Inspection engineers were appointed by the consulting engineers and, in the case of the Ibadan–Oshogbo line, Frederic Shelford acted as inspector.[172] Similarly, open line managers were unlikely to criticise consulting engineers who had recruited them, advised the colony on their salaries, and on whom they would depend for selection if they wished to move to a post in another colony. Attempts by the Colonial Office to introduce some form of independent inspection were rebuffed by the Agents and their consultants. In 1901, wishing to avoid a proposed Lagos enquiry into the working of the Lagos–Ibadan line, Shelford suggested the appointment of an 'independent' inspector, ideally the resident engineer Mr Bradford, who had a long association with the firm.[173] But when the Colonial Office attempted to put the proposal into effect and appoint an engineer to visit West Africa each dry season to report on 'the condition and management of lines', it met with strong opposition. The Agents and Shelford, whose own candidate was now no longer available, claimed that an inspector would be expensive, difficult to recruit and 'introduce a disturbing factor in the organisation of the construction of works and working of lines'.[174] Undeterred, the Colonial Office resubmitted the proposal, stressing that the engineer would merely inspect open lines, but was advised that the appointment should be postponed until the

---

304/25655; Sierra Leone to CO, 14 Aug. 1900, CO 267/453/28625; CAs to CO, 4 Aug. 1899, CO 96/347/20621; CAs to CO, 17 Aug. 1899, CO 96/347/21804; Shelford to CAs, 7 Mar. 1902, CO 147/163/10897; CAs to CO, 17 Apr. 1902, CO 147/163/15038.

[168] CAs to CO, 20 July 1904, CO 273/304/25655; CO to Straits, 26 July 1901, CO 273/276/22964.

[169] CO to Egerton, 6 Jan. 1905, CO 147/172/42513.

[170] CAs to CO, 19 Oct. 1906, CO 96/449/38627; memo, Feb. 1906, CAOG 10/97.

[171] Memo, Feb. 1906, CAOG 10/97.

[172] CAs to CO, 9 Jan. 1907, CO 520/51/1283.

[173] Ezechiel note, 22 Dec. 1902, CO 96/400/49668; Ommanney note, 27 Jan. 1903, ibid.

[174] Ibid; Shelford to CAs, 18 Aug. 1902, CO 96/400/34890.

Gold Coast line was open. The Agents and Shelford would then have greater experience of line operation, and could more easily recruit the most able candidate.[175] In 1904, with the completion of the line, the Colonial Office therefore raised the matter again, only to find that both Shelford and the Agents had, in the meantime, decided that such an appointment was inadvisable.[176]

The inadequacy of the Agents' monitoring procedures encouraged consulting engineers and their staff to succumb to self-interested behaviour, which both increased costs and reduced quality. The Hon. C. Williams, a member of the Lagos legislative council, declared in 1905 that the colony's line had been built 'by people intent on filling their pockets by a system that lends itself to a gigantic swindle'.[177] The West African merchant John Holt believed William Shelford and his son to be 'knaves and fools', and wrote of the 'jobbery' that characterised construction.[178] Although such claims were no doubt an exaggeration, there are numerous examples of inefficiency on the part of construction staff. When the Kumassi bridge collapsed in 1903 it was because the resident engineer had taken its foundations only 3' below the bed of a dry stream that adjoined the main river of the region.[179] In 1900, in Lagos, three foremen were dismissed for dishonesty, in the following year the Gold Coast medical account was found to contain entries for the purchase of champagne and claret and in 1902 the assistant accountant of the Tarkwa line was convicted of fraud.[180]

Consulting engineers, and particularly Shelford, were similarly less than honest.[181] In 1907 Messrs Preece and Cardew were accused by the Straits governor of 'trying to do a little job, and put some business the way of other clients', when, after completing a report on the construction of the Tanjong

---

175 CAs to CO, 29 Nov. 1902, CO 96/400/49668.

176 It was argued that the secretary of state would find it difficult to recruit a sufficiently experienced engineer at a reasonable salary and that such an engineer would constitute 'a special commission of enquiry', which, given the lack of any 'grave emergency' could not be justified: Shelford to CAs, 2 Feb. 1904, CO 96/423/5157.

177 *West African Mail*, 27 Jan. 1905, 1046.

178 Holt to Morel, 23 Nov. 1902 and 22 Apr. 1903, Holt papers, MS Afr. s. 1525, 18/14.

179 F. G. A. Butler commented that 'one would have thought that even a slight experience of West Africa would have suggested that there was an enormous difference between a stream in the dry season and the same stream in flood': Butler note, 7 Dec. 1903, CO 96/412/43070.

180 Pflaumer, 'Politics of transport policy', 107; CAs to CO, 25 July 1900, CO 147/152/24141; resident engineer to Shelford, 27 Aug. 1901, CO 96/386/42608. See also Fiddean note, 25 June 1906, CO 267/490/27768, and CAs to CO, 30 Oct. 1906, CO 267/490/40090. Such practices were encouraged by the refusal of some colonies to prosecute. This had a 'mischievous and demoralising effect' on the rest of the staff: CAs to CO, 3 Dec. 1901, CO 96/386/42608.

181 Malfeasance on the part of consulting engineers was not uncommon: Sir John Rennie, *An autobiography of Sir John Rennie*, London 1925, 432. The renowned engineer Bazalgette, for example, was perfectly willing to recommend contractors in return for a percentage of their profits: Porter and Clifton, 'Patronage' 320, 344.

Pagar dock generating station, they passed valuable information on to a company that wished to supply electricity to the dock.[182] More important, in 1900 Shelford arranged with the Ashanti Goldfields Corporation, part financier of the Tarkwa–Obuassi line, for his resident engineer, construction staff and presumably himself to receive substantial bonuses if the line arrived at the company's mines by 31 May 1901.[183] Despite informing the company that the Colonial Office had no objection to the payments, he failed to tell either the Office or the Crown Agents about it, because, he claimed, it was 'unofficial', an explanation Butler found 'unworthy'.[184] In the event, the line reached the mines in early January 1901, but at great cost; extra labour was imported from Lagos, the line was poorly constructed and a number of bridges subsequently collapsed.[185]

On other lines Shelford's disregard of quality was motivated by the fact that the marginal utility he obtained from failing to produce the best possible lines was greater and more certain than the marginal utility lost.[186] By caring little about quality, he gained financially. The resultant large number of open lines calls for advice increased his line supervision workload and income and, when the construction of a new line was authorised by the Colonial Office, by rapidly completing his current work and making himself available, he ensured that the project would not be given to a rival firm.[187] Also consulting engineers were never held financially responsible for defective construction.[188] In theory Shelford's gains should have been offset by a fear of damage to his reputation for quality, the loss of future colonial and commercial work and eventually his standing within his family and local society. This may not have happened because of inter-temporal inconsistency. A more likely expla-

---

[182] Anderson to Cameron, 21 Mar. 1907, CAOG 10/53. The Agents and consulting engineers denied the accusation: CAs to Anderson, 18 Apr. 1907, ibid.

[183] Shelford to CAs, 10 Oct. 1904, CO 96/424/36637.

[184] Ashanti Goldfields Corporation papers, GL, MS 14164/1, no. 141; Butler note, 20 Feb. 1905, CO 96/423/5720; Shelford to CAs, 10 Oct. 1904, CO 96/424/36637. Supported by Ommanney, Shelford was merely reprimanded for his behaviour: Daniel note, 12 Nov. 1904, ibid; Shelford to CAs, 10 Oct. 1904, ibid; CO to CAs, 5 Jan. 1905, ibid. Shelford had a close trust relationship with the corporation. In January 1903 the secretary arranged for a complimentary article on Shelford to appear in the press: Raw to Shelford, 23 Jan. 1903, Ashanti Goldfields papers, MS 14172/180. In March 1903 Shelford renegotiated, without Colonial Office authorisation, a legally binding railway sidings agreement that the corporation regarded as excessively generous to the Gold Coast: Raw to Shelford, 10 Mar. 1903 ibid. MS 14172/183; MS 14164/2, no. 42.

[185] Report, 3 May 1905, CO 96/434/17000; Butler note, 20 Feb. 1905, CO 96/423/5720; West Africa, 12 Sept. 1903, 284.

[186] Gold Coast to CO, 16 June 1906, CO 96/443/24376; Daniel note, 31 May 1904, CO 96/423/11628; Shelford to CAs, 11 Mar. 1904, CO 96/423/11628.

[187] Shelford to CAs, 11 Mar. 1904, CO 96/423/11628.

[188] Demands by Ceylon for a lawsuit to be issued against the engineer La Tobe Bateman for gross negligence in the design and construction of the Malayakander reservoir, for example, were rejected because victory would be 'doubtful' given the technical nature of the dispute: CO to Ceylon, 20 July 1888, CO 54/580/14242.

nation is that his private norms allowed him to discount the social and family costs of his actions, and that, after the death of his father, the professional deterrents became far less important. He worked, and for the foreseeable future could expect to work, exclusively for the Crown Agents and, in any case, probably only intended to remain in the engineering profession for a limited period. In 1910 he successfully applied for an East African cocoa fibre concession. Five years later, at the age of forty-four, he retrained as a barrister and from 1917 practised at the parliamentary bar. He then bought and managed a Nyasaland tea plantation.[189] His failure to build the best possible lines was also unlikely to lead to the loss of colonial work. The Crown Agents rarely sacked consulting engineers found to have acted irresponsibly, as dismissal made other reputable firms reluctant to undertake projects for them, and, given his relationship with Ommanney, it seems unlikely that the Agents would even have contemplated such action as regards Shelford.[190] Moreover, poor construction could easily be ascribed to environmental or other factors. When questioned about the state of the Lagos–Ibadan and Sekondi–Tarkwa lines, for instance, Shelford claimed that it was common practice for principals to take over works before 'the finishing touches have been added', and argued that open line departments were using him as a scapegoat to escape blame for poor maintenance, inadequate inspection and their failure to trial rolling stock.[191]

The Agents were motivated in their choice of the department system by institutional and personal self-interest. The system not only held out the promise of quality construction, but increased the workloads of both the Agents and their West African consulting engineer, a friend and relative. Once construction began, the Agency and the engineer further exploited their positions. Both underestimated the cost and overestimated the returns of lines in order to encourage Colonial Office authorisation of works, and insisted on the adoption of high standards of construction. To avoid quality moral hazard, meanwhile, construction staff and indigenous labour were highly remunerated and Shelford was paid a salary, rather than a fee, which caused him to retard the rate of construction. The result was that the final cost of lines far exceeded initial estimates and receipts were less than expected. Moreover, inadequate monitoring led to opportunism, which further increased costs and contributed to poor construction.

The possibility that interest charges on loans raised to finance many West

189 East Africa to CO, 23 Dec. 1910, CO 879/107/965, no. 24; CO to East Africa, 18 Feb. 1911, ibid. no. 74; Elliott-Cooper to CAs, 7 June 1915, CAOG 10/55; *The Engineer*, 6 Aug. 1943, 111; *The Times*, 2 Aug. 1943; Shelford press cuttings, clipping, c. 1920.
190 Note, 14 Oct. 1908, CO 129/350/37429; CAs to CO, 24 Nov. 1904, CO 273/304/40128.
191 CAs to CO, 24 Nov. 1904, CO 273/304/40128. For example CAs to CO, 27 Nov. 1903, CO 96/412/43070; CAs to CO, 24 Nov. 1904, CO 273/304/40128; note, 28 Jan. 1908, CO 129/350/2398; CE to CAs, 12 Nov. 1903, CO 54/685/42223.

African railways would not be covered by line receipts began to emerge from 1900.[192] Facing high taxes and railway tariffs and concerned about the poor quality of lines and the consequent high running costs and frequent disruption of service, local business communities and governors began to bombard the Colonial Office with complaints. Shelford ordered his construction staff not to speak to the press, dismissed any newspaper criticism as 'inspired by contractors', deliberately misrepresented the size of original estimates and tried, but failed, to persuade the Colonial Office to allow receipts from the working of partly completed lines to be used to reduce capital costs.[193] Taking a more positive approach, the Crown Agents attempted to reduce the likelihood of high costs and slow construction: consultants were reminded that estimates should include all expenditure, location surveys began to be undertaken before costs were estimated, Shelford's salary was replaced by a fee and greater government intervention was permitted in the construction process.

Their actions were to no avail. The Colonial Office, fearing the prospect of unbalanced budgets and perturbed at parliamentary suggestions that 'successive Secretaries of State have connived at . . . [the] . . . abuses of [consulting engineers]', began to seek to replace the department method of construction.[194] In 1903 it was proposed that bids should be sought from contractors for the extension of the Lagos line beyond Ibadan. Although Ommanney strongly opposed the suggestion, Chamberlain felt that 'the system of department construction has been tried and the result is that estimates are always exceeded' and required Shelford to produce a report on the criteria that would be needed to judge contractor bids.[195] Unfortunately, by the time the report was submitted in 1904 Chamberlain had been replaced as secretary of state by the less forceful Alfred Lyttelton, who, faced with Shelford's critical views, abandoned the proposal. A similar fate befell a further Colonial Office initiative – that, in the case of sanitary works, the consulting engineers should be replaced by a special engineer based in West

192 None of the British West African lines covered their costs. Comparisons with other colonies are difficult, owing to differences in government freight rate policies, but it would appear that a number of other lines performed poorly, although the Natal and Porto-Novo to Sakete were deemed a success: Busschau, 'Railway developments in Natal', 419; Newbury, The western slave coast, 145–6.

193 PPD; West Africa, 20 June 1903, 452; Shelford to CAs, 26 Oct. 1903, CO 96/412/39602; Daniel note, 13 Feb. 1904, CO 96/423/3797; Ezechiel note, 23 Feb. 1900, CO 147/152/4983.

194 Lucas note, 8 Dec. 1906, CO 323/516/45203.

195 Ommanney note, 12 Aug. 1903, CO 147/168/23850; Chamberlain notes 13, 22 Aug. 1903, ibid. Two months earlier Chamberlain had commented 'I am not at all satisfied with the result of government construction in Africa and shall not be until I find that private enterprise produces worse results': Chamberlain note, 11 June 1903, CO 96/412/19242. In the following year the parliamentary under-secretary, Winston Churchill, informed the new secretary of state that 'if you employ the Crown Agents [to build the Lokoja–Baro extension] the proposal is doomed': Randolph S. Churchill, Winston Churchill, ii, London 1969, 580.

Africa and directly responsible to the secretary of state.[196] The Agents, supported by Ommanney, vigorously opposed that suggestion too, arguing that a sufficiently experienced engineer would be costly, difficult to recruit, have problems keeping abreast of technical developments in the United Kingdom and would be resented by the local public works departments.[197] Consequently the proposal was dropped. As will be seen in the next chapter, however, experiments with other methods of construction did go ahead, with varying degrees of success.

[196] CAs to CO, 2 Dec. 1903, CO 96/412/43553.
[197] Ibid.

5

Construction by Contractor, Private Sector and Public Works

The first crown colony railways were built in the 1850s and 1860s in dependencies with valuable raw materials relatively close to the coast and with easily traversable landscapes. In such colonies the rewards and the cost of proposed lines could be relatively easily and accurately predicted and investors were willing to support their construction. As there was little likelihood of cost overruns, the work was carried out by contractors employed by colonial governments, or by private individuals, who, confident of future profits and able to meet the relatively large capital needs, financed construction themselves, though often with the aid of colonial subsidies. The decision to build was generally made by the colony and Colonial Office with little input from the Agents and their engineers, and construction was directed by public works departments. The Agency's role was merely to prevent adverse selection and moral hazard on the part of contractors and private enterprise. After the failure of the department system in the late 1890s, the Colonial Office again experimented with contractors and the private sector, but from approximately 1911 turned to construction by public works department.

This chapter examines how the Agents sought to overcome opportunism by contractors and the private sector, and how, after the failure of the department system, they sought to prevent the reinstatement of these building methods and to block construction by public works departments. It concludes with an assessment of the supervision by consulting engineers of completed and operating lines.

Construction by contractor

Construction by contractor was widely used by the crown colonies until the mid-1890s, when the Crown Agents began to favour the department system. To prevent duplicity on the part of contractors, the Agents adopted a policy of targeted recruitment, sought to ensure that the Crown Agents supplied building materials and rolling stock, required contractors to provide bonds and closely monitored construction. In most cases, invitations to tender were sent only to reputable firms, that, in the opinion of the consulting engineers could produce work of the requisite quality. Invitations for the 1906 Singapore harbour improvements, for example, were sent to nine companies

134

selected from the Admiralty list of contractors.[1] Colonial demands that local firms be allowed to tender were generally dismissed, on the grounds that they usually lacked sufficient construction experience and financial backing, that, if the contract awarded was inclusive of the supply of construction materials, the use of an English purchasing contractor would increase prices and that the rejection of a local firm could lead to unpleasantness.[2] Exceptions occurred when the contract was so small as to be completely unattractive to British contractors or when there was a large local firm.[3] The successful tender was chosen on the grounds of cost and suitability by the consulting engineers, who, at least in the case of railway construction in the 1870s and 1880s, showed a bias towards two firms, Messrs Faviell and Messrs Reid & Mackay, and thus gained the advantages of long-term mutual trust.[4] Their recommendation was passed to the Crown Agents, the Colonial Office and the colony for approval, which always appears to have been given.

In order to increase their commission income, the Agents invariably advised the Colonial Office not to allow the contractors to supply construction materials and rolling stock. It was said that contractors would buy cheap poor quality goods, and that the large size of inclusive contracts deterred small construction firms from tendering, which, by reducing competition, increased contract prices. It was also argued that contractors tended to buy rolling stock before construction was completed and thus failed to benefit from any subsequent price falls, as well as forcing the constructing colony to meet high maintenance and storage costs.[5] The Agents' pleas, however, were often ignored and inclusive contracts were relatively common.

A number of financial incentives and bonding strategies were adopted. To ensure quality work and to generate trust, the Agents advanced a proportion of the cost of the plant required to the contractors, and, where a contract included the supply of construction materials, a certain percentage of the cost of all or particular materials. The builders of the Colombo harbour works, for instance, obtained advances of up to 50 per cent of the cost of materials and

1   Coode to CAs, 12 Feb. 1906, CO 273/322/5743.
2   CAs to CO, 19 Dec. 1904, CO 273/304/42851; Cameron to Lucas, 19 Dec. 1904, ibid; CAs to CO, 20 Feb. 1877, CO 54/510/2092; CO to Ceylon, 8 Jan. 1891, CO 54/598/535.
3   CO to Ceylon, 8 Jan. 1891, CO 54/598/535; CAs to CO, 23 Mar. 1881, CO 137/502/5146. In the case of the 1881 Jamaican railway extension, the Agents allowed US companies to tender, the Colonial Office arranging for the British ambassador in Washington to make 'confidential enquiries' into the background of applicants: CAs to CO, 23 Mar. 1881, CO 137/502/5146; Meade note, 24 Mar. 1881, ibid. Applications were received from the USA.
4   CAs to CO, 19 Oct. 1881, CO 137/502/18295. Faviell's honesty was demonstrated to the Agents in 1862 when the company repulsed an approach for the Ceylon Kandy–Colombo line by rival tenderers, who had 'tried to induce . . . [the firm] . . . to combine with them in an arrangement which should be beneficial to all': CAs to CO, 26 Nov. 1862, CO 54/372/11556.
5   CAs to Gregory, 17 Sept. 1861, CO 54/364/8630; CAs to CO, 28 June 1862, CO 54/372/6483.

plant and/or 10 per cent of the contract sum.[6] The practice also encouraged firms to tender for contracts, and thus promoted competition. In return, contractors and a third party were usually required to provide a security set at a level sufficient 'to exclude men of straw', though 'not . . . too high as to deter men of moderate but sufficient means' from tendering.[7] The bonds, which were returned only on the satisfactory completion of a project, increased the financial penalities of opportunism or poor quality work, added a social and reputation cost, in that unsatisfactory work would harm the third party; and, by discouraging dishonest contractors from tendering when open competition was adopted, reduced the problem of adverse selection. In addition, 10 per cent of each payment to the contractor was usually deducted and paid into an invested guarantee fund until a specified total was reached, generally some proportion of the contract sum. This fund was not made over to the contractor until satisfactory completion of the project, generally half immediately after construction and the remainder twelve months later.[8] Contracts also included fines for each day or week works remained unfinished after the completion date, occasionally obliged contractors to pay the inspection cost of all materials that failed the Agents' inspection process and required the contractor to maintain the finished line for a set period after completion, a proviso which further discouraged poor construction.[9]

Monitoring was undertaken by the Agents' consulting engineers and their teams of engineers based in the constructing colony.[10] Demands by colonies for local public works departments to perform this role were resisted by the Agency. It was argued that they lacked the necessary experience in construction, and that supervision by consulting engineers allowed them to be held professionally responsible for their plans and designs, and ensured that these were not misunderstood or altered by contractors.[11] The engineers followed the progress of works, inspected construction materials both during and after manufacture, approved suppliers of articles, ensured, where a particular manufacturer was specified, that this company was used, and checked the prices of articles purchased against the invoices supplied by the contractors.[12] In the colony, their teams of engineers monitored the completion and quality of work, ensured that local materials were obtained from the areas specified in the contract, and inspected articles, such as cement, on arrival and before

6 CAA, CAOG 19/109. See also CAOG 19/455, 16; 19/283, 19.
7 CAs to Gregory, 17 Sept. 1861, CO 54/364/8630. Sums varied from £5,000 to £8,000. See, for example, CAA, CAOG 19/130; 19/172.
8 CAA, CAOG 19/655, 13; 19/106.
9 CAA, CAOG 19/455, 44, 45.
10 In the case of the Ceylon Colombo–Kandy railway, the team comprised a chief resident engineer, a chief assistant, two assistant engineers and seven junior assistant engineers: CAs to CO, 9 Apr. 1863, CO 54/382/3493.
11 CAs to CO, 23 Mar. 1881, CO 137/502/5146.
12 CAA, CAOG 19/172, 25; 19/106; 19/455, 37, 39, 44–6.

use.[13] Any infringement of the contract was dealt with by the consulting engineers, who, as well as monitoring the work, also acted as arbitrators. Their use thus avoided the cost, delay and supposed bias of English courts, but perhaps deterred many firms from tendering.[14]

The Crown Agents began to oppose the use of contractors from the early 1890s and until 1906 offers from contractors to construct railways were always rejected.[15] Harbour work might be put out to contract but only when the consulting engineers were unable to recommend a suitable resident engineer to supervise department construction, local opinion strongly favoured the use of a contractor or the project was financed by the Treasury (which usually put pressure on the Colonial Office to open the schemes to competition).[16] The main reason for this *volte face* was the Agents' wish to maximise income and quality. The contract system carried the risk that the building materials and/or the rolling stock required for a project would be supplied by the successful contractor. Past experience had also taught the Agents that the use of contractors could lead to poor quality work.[17] To avoid criticism, they usually had to chose the lowest and therefore probably poorest quality tender, and, once a contract had been signed, could not allow the route or design to be altered for fear of subsequent heavy claims for extras, even if new information became available that improved alignment.[18] There was also the danger, in the case of lump sum contracts, under which contractors performed work for a set fee, that contractors would reduce standards in order to increase profits, or, if conditions proved worse than expected, minimise losses.[19]

In its advice to the Colonial Office, the Agency stressed that the use of contractors could lead to the construction of very expensive and thus unremunerative works. It was pointed out that when contractors were used, colonies had to pay for preliminaries, for example the drawing up of contracts, the tender process and so on, and lost the contractor's profit margin and that portion of the income earned from opening completed sections of unfinished

13 CAA, CAOG 19/455, 39, 40, 44; 19/435, 31.
14 Round note, 21 May 1912, CO 96/524/14964. The Agents believed that it would 'be in vain to expect a decision in this country against contractors over a question of time, unless they were glaringly at fault and the opposite side free of all shortcomings': CAs to CO, 23 Apr. 1867, CO 167/502/4043.
15 Paulings, for example, offered to construct the Sekondi–Kumassi line for £6,650 per mile: Paulings to CO, 9 Jan. 1901, CO 879/67/652.
16 CAs to CO, 30 Jan. 1900, CO 54/667/3252; CAs to CO, 19 Feb. 1898, CO 54/650/3933; memo, 8 Dec. 1905, CAOG 10/63; Treasury to CO, 31 Oct. 1903, T 1/100186/18832/16865; Treasury to CO, 19 June 1900, T 1/9581/16676/9505.
17 In 1882 the Agents were accused of professional incompetence when the contractor they had employed to construct the Natal main and Northern Coast lines, built a series of bridges that were discovered to have structural faults. The colony had to spend £50,000 on rebuilding and strengthening the bridges, and £19,000 on a deviation around a particularly dangerous viaduct: Guest and Sellers, *Enterprise and exploitation*, 56.
18 Memo, 7 Mar. 1904, CAOG 10/96.
19 Ibid.

lines to traffic.[20] Colonies also had to employ a resident engineer to monitor construction in the colony, and a consulting engineer, whose fees, though below those paid under the department system, were still high. Although the consultant had far less to do during construction, his workload at the start and end of projects was relatively heavy, owing to the need to prepare a specification and deal with contractors' demands for compensation and extras.[21] In addition, if a lump sum contract was adopted, when conditions proved more favourable than expected, colonies lost all or part of the contractor's contingency margin, which, in West Africa, because of lack of knowledge of local conditions, could be high.[22] Furthermore, although worse conditions than forecast would benefit the colony, there was always the possibility that they would lose any gains in subsequent claims by the contractor for compensation and extras, which often had to be settled through time-consuming and costly arbitration and litigation.[23] For example, in 1885 Ceylon had to pay the builders of the Nawalapitiya–Nanu Oya line £95,600 compensation; in the early 1880s Jamaica paid a total of £62,422 to the constructors of the Old Harbour–Porus and Ewarton branch lines; and, in 1883, the builders of the Natal Durban–Pietermaritzburg–Verulum lines put in a compensation claim of £228,000, which, after two years hard negotiation was eventually reduced to £17,461.[24] There was also the danger, particularly in West Africa, where the lack of knowledge of conditions made the setting and evaluation of tenders difficult, that the contractor would be forced into bankruptcy, leaving the colonial government to complete the line itself. Colonies could even fail to benefit from competition, as it was often difficult to attract firms of good standing to a project, owing to English contractors' reluctance to 'trespass on one another's reserves'. Further disincentives were the small size of many of the contracts, especially if the Colonial Office insisted on government supply of materials; the potentially hazardous nature of the country, especially in West Africa; and, according to the contractor Paulings, the Agents' insistence that every detail of the work should be priced, which increased the cost of tendering.[25]

The Agents, however, exaggerated the disadvantages of using contractors and failed to highlight the advantages. As confirmed by the Treasury, claims for compensation and extras were relatively rare, and numerous projects in the colonies had been satisfactorily completed without such demands.[26] The

---

[20] Ibid; PP 1924, viii (Cmd 2016), 9.

[21] CAs to Shelford, 8 Jan. 1909, CO 96/488/4266; Coode to CAs, 9 Mar. 1901, CAOG 10/11; CAs to CO, 15 Mar. 1901, CAOG 10/11.

[22] In the case of the Ceylon Northern extension, built in well-surveyed country, put up to competition but constructed by the department system, the lowest tender was 12% higher than the eventual completed cost: CAs to CO, 22 Dec. 1905, CO 54/696/45174.

[23] Memo, Jan. 1904, CAOG 10/96.

[24] PPD, 32–4, 35; CAs to CO, 7 Aug. 1884, CO 179/155/13461.

[25] Liverpool conference, CO 147/168/27225, 14; evidence, CO 766/1, 334.

[26] Herbert note, 14 June 1900, T 1/9581/16676/9505. The contractors for the Ceylon

problem of contingency margins could be partly overcome through the use of schedule contracts, under which the rates for the various classes of work to be completed were set and contractors were paid sums calculated at the agreed rates for the work actually performed. From the 1900s the Crown Agents themselves used these contracts, which ensured that the amounts lost, if conditions were less favourable than expected, were less than the sums lost under a lump sum contract when conditions were unexpectedly good.[27] In addition, contractors had specialised plant, which they moved from project to project, a great deal of experience of construction in particular areas, and highly experienced, good quality engineers, who were attracted by the permanent nature of the employment offered.[28] They also purchased cheaper though poorer quality materials than the Crown Agents, ensured delivery by enforcing penalties and, since they wished to move on to the next job promptly, offered staff bonuses for rapid construction.[29]

The Colonial Office embargo on using contractors for railway construction came to an end in 1906, by which time it was disillusioned with the department system and wished to explore the possibilities of using contractors. Under pressure from the Gold Coast, the Colonial Office required the Agency to put the Accra–Akwapim line up to competition.[30] The Agents, feeling their livelihood threatened, appear to have deliberately set out to sabotage the experiment. The contract was inadequately advertised, with the result that only five applications were received.[31] The three highest tenders, all from reputable firms with tropical experience, were rejected as too expensive, and the lowest tender was considered unrealistic.[32] The contest was won by a Mr Murphy, whose tender was 19 per cent below the consulting engineers' estimate.[33] An Irish tramway entrepreneur, Murphy had no experience of overseas railway construction and no large-scale United Kingdom experience.[34] Moreover, his design had been put together by the resident engineer on the Lagos extension, who left the project when Murphy reneged on his

Colombo–Kandy and Peradeniya–Nowalpitiya lines were both paid bonuses by the colony: PPD, 34.

[27] Contingency margins could also have been avoided through the use of 'time and line' contracts, under which contractors received a set commission based on the estimated cost of works, which rose if savings were made and fell if costs were exceeded.

[28] PP 1924, viii (Cmd 2016), 9; report, 29 June 1904, CO 267/474/23391. Between 1883 and 1923 Messrs Paulings built 5,000 miles of African railway: evidence, CO 766/1, 335. Consulting engineers used plant for just one scheme and then donated it to the constructing colony.

[29] Howard to committee, 25 Aug. 1923, CO 766/1.

[30] Chamberlain note, 16 June 1903, CO 147/165/13757.

[31] Christian F. Tsey, 'Gold Coast railways: the making of a colonial economy, 1879–1929', PhD diss. Glasgow 1986, 60; Shelford to CAs, 23 Sept. 1908, CO 96/474/35026.

[32] Shelford to CAs, 23 Sept. 1908, CO 96/474/35026.

[33] The other tenders were respectively 7%, 16% and 21% higher and 60% lower than the estimate: ibid.

[34] Ibid; The Times, 24 Apr. 1910.

agreement to make him a partner.[35] Not surprisingly, the line was expensive to construct, finished late and was poorly built (lacking sufficient bridges, ballast and earthworks).[36] Moreover, Murphy had opened sections of the unfinished line to traffic and 'pocketed the receipts', and his agents had tampered with the 'fidelity' of local officials.[37] The experiment was regarded by the Colonial Office as a failure and not repeated.[38]

Private construction

The private construction and operation of lines occurred in a range of colonies. In order to encourage construction and establish trust, concessionaires were given capital and interest guarantees, which allowed them to issue stock at par rather than at a discount, land and mineral concessions, subsidies on the working of the finished lines and government assurances that no competing railway would be sanctioned or built within a given period.[39] To ensure compliance with the contract, the constructing company, in return, was required to provide the Crown Agents with securities, the whole or part of which were returned on the completion of, respectively, the entire line or particular sections in the time laid down. Overruns and the suspension of the operation of a line led to the withdrawal of the whole or part of the working subsidy.

The Agents were generally strongly opposed to this form of construction, which directly reduced their income. The construction incentives attracted applicants with impracticable proposals or company promoters, who, after floating the company to build the line, lost interest in the project.[40] They could also prove costly. In India in the 1850s and 1890s, government 5 per cent guarantees on the cost of privately built lines resulted in excessive construction and operating costs and by 1910 the payment of £5m. in guarantees.[41] Likewise, there was a possibility that profit guarantees would

35 *The Times*, 28, 30 Apr. 1910.
36 Note, n.d., CO 96/512/14867; Fiddes note, 22 Jan. 1911, CO 96/512/41542.
37 Fiddes note, 22 Jan. 1911, CO 96/512/41542.
38 Ibid.
39 In the case of the 1888 Jamaican railway, the colony paid for the track, which cost approximately £100,000, and gave the constructing firm one square mile of crown land for every mile of railway built: PP 1913, lviii (287), 28. Similar incentives were offered in India, Russia and Latin America: P. Luntinen, *Railway on the Gold Coast: a meeting of two cultures*, Helsinki 1996, 21.
40 To discourage frivolous West African applications, the Agents required concessionaires to deposit the cost of the survey with them: CAs to CO, 15 Feb. 1906, CO 879/92/844, no. 48.
41 Equal to one-third of the cost of the lines: Kerr, *Railways of the raj*, 17; A. K. Banerji, *Aspects of Indo-British economic relations, 1858–98*: Oxford 1982, 54. The size of the

discourage economy in the operation of lines, concessions would prove more lucrative than expected, land grants, by interfering with 'native' rights, would lead to unrest, and that a company with a capital guarantee would go bankrupt.[42] For instance, Jamaica sold its railways for £800,000 in 1888 and twelve years later had to buy them back at a cost of £1.5m. plus £87,363 of unpaid interest when the purchasing company ran into difficulties.[43] In addition, the routes of lines built in this way tended to serve the interests of the promoter rather than the colony, and private extensions to government lines led to running power and rolling stock difficulties, and, if a different gauge was adopted, discouraged intra-colony trade. Sometimes the companies involved lacked construction experience and built poor quality lines, and, unable to borrow money as cheaply as colonial governments, tended to set high traffic rates. Furthermore, the colonies received none of the profits from the operation of the lines, though they could be forced by public opinion to subsidise uneconomic lines, as occurred, for example, with the Barbados railway.[44]

The Agents invariably advised against proposals for private works, particularly in West Africa.[45] In 1896, however, the Foreign Office insisted that a railway from Blantyre to Port Herald in Nyasaland be built privately. The Agents again attempted sabotage. The Foreign Office was urged to allow the protectorate to build the line itself, and the decision to grant the Shire Highlands Railway Co., the firm permitted to construct the railway, 3,200 acres of land was strongly opposed.[46] In an attempt to encourage the company to abandon the scheme, the Agents delayed negotiations on the contract, insisted that construction be supervised by consulting engineers and a resident engineer whose salaries were to be paid by the firm and that a standard of construction be adopted that was far higher than that believed to be necessary by the company's own eminent engineering consultant.[47] After construction had commenced, the Agents and consulting engineers sent the Colonial

payments led many lines from 1869 to be built by public works departments and the reduction of guarantees to 4% or less: Kerr, *Railways of the raj*, 20.

[42] CAs to CO, 15 Feb. 1906, CO 879/92/844, no. 48; Shepstone to CO, 22 Sept. 1874, CO 879/7/72, no. 3.

[43] PPD, 35. In 1900 the Demerara Railway Co. almost had to abandon construction, owing to lack of funds, but was saved by extra concessions from the government: CO 884/6, no. 102.

[44] Shelford to CAs, 26 July 1901, CO 879/67/652; Shelford to CAs, 30 July 1902, CO 96/400/32395; Ommanney note, 11 June 1900, CO 96/365/4865; PP 1907, lvi (103), 6.

[45] The Agency opposed the construction of three Gold Coast railways, a Trinidad floating dock and even a Gold Coast road: CAs to CO, 13 Feb. 1900, CO 96/365/4865; CAs to CO, 5 Aug. 1902, CO 96/400/32395; CAs to CO, 4 Mar. 1903, CO 96/412/8537; CAs to CO, 6 Jan. 1905, CO 295/435/451; CAs to CO, 20 Aug. 1898, CO 96/326/18875.

[46] CAs to FO, 15 Dec. 1896, PRO, FO 2/689; CAs to FO, 14 July 1902, FO 2/693; CAs to FO, 27 June 1902, ibid.

[47] CAs to FO, 27 June 1902, FO 2/693; CAs to FO, 7 Aug. 1902, ibid. The company believed that the appointment of a resident engineer – not a condition when railways were constructed privately in India – was 'an entire waste of money': PPE, q. 3541.

Office a barrage of complaints that listed the company's failure to meet standards, its disregard of original drawings, its supposedly unstable financial standing, its use of the uncompleted line for traffic and its alleged dishonesty as to the causes of delay and the condition of the completed works.[48]

When the firm made an application to build an extension, the Agents, whose 'plain hostility' and 'distinct prejudice' were now obvious even to the Colonial Office, raised numerous objections.[49] In particular, they insisted that a clause in the new contract, which required the company to construct the line to the satisfaction of the resident engineer, should specifically require his approval of the height of the track.[50] Sir J. D. Rees, the chairman of the British Central Africa Co., which owned the Shire Highlands Railway Co., believed the addition unnecessary and an attempt 'to thwart them'.[51] The Colonial Office agreed, the assistant under-secretary, H. W. Just, regarding the Agents' conduct to be in 'thorough disrepute'.[52] The secretary of state, the earl of Elgin, consequently wrote a conciliatory letter to Rees and, his patience 'nearly exhausted', informed the Agency that he 'must insist on there being no more difficulties manufactured'.[53] The Agents' response was to ask the Shire Highlands Railway Co. whether it accepted Rees's agreement that the clause covered the track height, behaviour that C. Harris found 'incredulous' and 'improper'.[54] To Sir Bradford Leslie, the company's engineering consultant, however, the Agents' motives were clear – they disliked private construction, and held an 'ambition that no independent people should be allowed to construct railways in a crown colony'.[55]

Public works

Until 1906 construction by the public works departments of a colony, without supervision by a consulting engineer, had occurred only in the Federated Malay States, in Jamaica in 1901 and in Natal in 1883. The Federated Malay States had a long tradition of local construction, and an attempt to force the colony to adopt the department system for the Johore line ended in failure: the resident engineer, an official of the local public works department,

---

[48] Shelford to CAs, 20 Mar. 1905, CO 525/10/9841; Harris note, 22 Feb. 1905, CO 525/10/3340; CAs to CO, 25 Oct. 1905, CO 525/10/38001; CO to CAs, 16 Mar. 1905, CO 525/10/38001; Harris note, 23 Feb. 1905, CO 525/10/3559; CAs to CO, 9 Mar. 1905, CO 525/10/7607. Use of the completed line was actually permitted by the contract.
[49] Crewe note, 11 June 1906, CO 525/15/20168; Just note, 20 May 1907, CO 525/20/16718.
[50] CAs to CO, 6 Dec. 1907, CO 525/20/42640.
[51] Harris note, 12 Dec. 1907, ibid.
[52] Just note, 13 Dec. 1907, ibid.
[53] Elgin note, n.d., ibid; Elgin to Rees, 15 Dec. 1907, ibid; CO to CAs, 17 Dec. 1907, ibid.
[54] Harris note, 31 Dec. 1907, CO 525/20/45056.
[55] PPR, q. 3500.

adopted an 'attitude of passive resistance', and failed to provide the consulting engineers with information or to take advice.[56] As a compromise, the Colonial Office allowed the colony to build itself, but required all particulars to be sent to the secretary of state, who could then, if necessary, obtain technical advice from a consulting engineer.[57] The colony agreed, but subsequently failed to provide the necessary information.[58] In Jamaica a catalogue of mistakes by the consulting engineer in charge of railway improvements led the Colonial Office to allow the colony to dismiss him and place the work in the hands of the railway manager.[59] In Natal the harbour board simply ignored all instructions from the Colonial Office and undertook works itself.[60] Elsewhere, numerous colonies campaigned for local construction.[61] It was variously argued that local staff had valuable local knowledge and, identifying with the colony and likely to be involved in the maintainance of the completed works, had a greater commitment to low cost and quality construction than consulting and resident engineers. Moreover, taking the work out of the hands of local engineers reduced morale and prevented them gaining the experience required for colonial construction.[62]

The Agents rejected all such requests, claiming that local staff lacked the necessary building experience and expertise and that the completed projects would therefore be expensive and poorly constructed. Local construction would also make it difficult to attribute responsibility for unsatisfactory works, particularly given the high turnover of public works department staff, and eminent engineering consultants would be reluctant to advise local departments of work, as they would thereby be nominally placed under the control of engineers inferior to themselves in both knowledge, experience and status.[63] The Agency was even reluctant to allow the Jamaica public works departments to undertake improvements to the Jamaica railways, or colonies to complete surveys without supervision by consulting engineer.[64] When, for example, in the 1890s Ceylon abandoned the supervision of preliminary surveys by engineering consultants, the Agents campaigned successfully for their reinstatement, warning that inadequate surveys would lead to higher costs and delay.[65]

---

[56] CAs to CO, 4 Aug. 1908, CO 273/342/28535; Stubbs note, 8 Sept. 1908, ibid.
[57] CO to Federated Malay States, 2 Oct. 1908, ibid.
[58] CO to Anderson, 17 June 1910, CO 273/364/16663.
[59] CO to Jamaica, 25 Apr. 1902, CO 137/631/7724.
[60] CO to Natal, 22 Feb. 1883, CO 179/149/2873.
[61] CAs to CO, 13 Aug. 1881, CO 137/502/14519; CAs to CO, 1 Nov. 1888, CO 54/580/21676; CAs to CO, 24 Apr. 1899, CO 273/253/10293.
[62] CAs to CO, 24 Apr. 1899, CO 273/253/10293; Straits to CO, 9 Nov. 1899, CO 279/249/33676; colonial secretary to CO, 28 Jan. 1905, CO 96/427/5543.
[63] CAs to CO, 2 July 1901, CO 273/276/22964; Lucas note, 3 Jan. 1901, CO 137/623/44147.
[64] Note, n.d., CO 137/623/3351.
[65] Lucas note, 18 May 1898, CO 54/650/10809; CO to Ceylon, 27 May 1898, ibid; CAs to

The first railway to be built locally was the twenty-two mile 2' 6" Zungeru line constructed by the Northern Nigerian governor Sir Frederick Lugard in 1901. Having obtained permission from the Colonial Office to move the colony's capital to Zungeru, Lugard then informed the secretary of state that he would require the line to transport supplies from the highest point of the Kaduna river to the new capital. The Colonial Office thus had little alternative but to authorise the project and, as it was needed urgently and the terrain was hostile, to allow colonial construction. The railway was built in six months and, lacking ballast and with few earthworks and stations, cost only £1,389 per mile.[66] The Agents and their engineers saw the railway as a threat. The new line, and river transport, would attract much of the export traffic of the region, reducing the need for a northward extension of the Lagos line, and any railways constructed by Lugard would probably be built locally. Such a situation could be avoided through the rapid construction of a bridge over the Niger, which would allow the Lagos line to be extended northwards. Lugard was unenthusiastic, but, if a bridge had to be built, favoured a site close to the colony's new capital, which would permit his line to be extended southwards. The Agents preferred Jebba, seventy-five miles from Zungeru, and, to ensure that this was chosen, instructed the surveyor to examine only locations that did not have rock river beds, which effectively ruled out the Zungeru region. Asked to explain their actions, after Lugard had complained to the Colonial Office, the Agents admitted that they had attempted to 'destroy' Lugard's line, though claimed that their motive was concern about the railway's narrow gauge rather than their own interests.[67]

Lugard's reaction was to propose another locally constructed line, from Baro to Kano.[68] Lack of funds meant that this project had to wait until 1906 when Winston Churchill, an arch-opponent of the Agents and the department system, became parliamentary under-secretary of state for the colonies, and proposed that the line should go ahead in order to allow local and department construction to be compared.[69] The Agents and their supporters criticised the line, Ommanney calling it a 'sheer waste of money'.[70] Their consulting engineers at first proposed a standard 3' 6" line, which they estimated at £5,679 per mile, but then submitted a counter proposal for a 20" railway, which they claimed could be built more cheaply than Lugard's 2' 6" line.[71] The efforts of the Agents and their engineers, however, were to no avail. On the appointment of Sir P. Girouard as high commissioner in

CO, 11 May 1909, CO 54/650/10594. See also CAs to CO, 17 Oct. 1908, CO 520/70/38072.

[66] Lugard to Chamberlain, 17 Feb. 1902, CO 446/22/10583.

[67] Lugard to Chamberlain, 14 Apr. 1902, CO 879/76/695, no. 13; CAs to CO, 15 Nov. 1902, CO 147/163/47616.

[68] Lugard to Chamberlain, 25 Feb. 1903, CO 446/30/15375.

[69] Churchill to CO, 14 July 1906, CO 446/58/26478.

[70] Ommanney note, n.d., ibid; CAs to CO, 19 Nov. 1905, CO 446/47/12976.

[71] Report, 28 Feb. 1905, CO 446/47/12976; CAs to CO, 14 Sept. 1906, CO 879/93/845.

Nigeria, the gauge of the proposed line was upgraded to 3' 6", the colony's estimate of construction increased to £3,000 per mile and the experiment was allowed to go ahead. In the event, the line, constructed by the public works department assisted by thirty-three officers of the Royal Engineers and fifty-one engineers and support staff from South Africa, was built for £3,915 per mile in a relatively short time, as compared to other West African railways, and to a standard that was praised by the inspection engineer appointed by the Colonial Office.[72] The success of the experiment led the Colonial Office to require that all future railways in the crown colonies be built locally and, at least in West Africa, to a far lower standard.[73]

Supervision of open lines

Not wishing to lose their commission on orders for rolling stock or for their consulting engineers to be deprived of their consulting fees, the Agents generally recommended government operation of newly completed lines. It was argued that the absence of data on cost and revenue would discourage contractors from bidding for them, and that those who did tender would submit excessively low offers that the colony would find difficult to judge. The government would also continue to bear its public responsibility as regards safety and services and would face high monitoring costs – contractor-operated railways in the United Kingdom being poorly managed.[74] As with construction, operation of lines by government was supervised by the Crown Agents' engineering consultants. In West Africa their involvement was relatively great. They provided advice on staffing and management structure, freight and passenger rates, rolling stock purchases and the maintenance of track and equipment; monitored the activities of the departments and selected their staff; and designed rolling stock and recommended the successful tenderer.[75] In the more developed colonies, they were less involved, and merely provided advice on request, recruited railway officers and organised the purchase of rolling stock. Their supervision allegedly ensured that railways were worked efficiently and economically, and reduced the Colonial Office's workload.[76] In return, Shelford received an annual salary plus expenses, which was progressively reduced as the open lines

---

[72] PP 1912–13, lviii (Cd 6007), 39; report, 19 Feb. 1912, CO 446/107/10210.
[73] By 1914 consulting engineers were employed only for electrical schemes, harbour works and water and drainage projects: Herbert to Fiddean, 4 Sept. 1923, CO 323/902/38790.
[74] CAs to CO, 21 Oct. 1864, CO 54/396/9656; CAs to CO, 30 Jan. 1863, CO 167/455/1084.
[75] CAs to CO, 13 Oct. 1900, CO 96/366/33577; CAs to CO, 5 May 1903, CO 96/412/16348. The recruitment of technical staff is discussed in chapter 10 below.
[76] Butler note, 22 Mar. 1907, CO 96/461/9405.

Table 16
Fees and salaries of open line consulting engineers, 1908–26

	West Africa		Ceylon	
	Shelford (1908–12)	Crown Agents (1920–6)	Messrs Gregory Eyles & Waring (1908–19)	Crown Agents (1920–6)
Average annual mileage supervised	1,300	1,727	946	1,747
Average annual remuneration per mile (£)	6.01	1.96	5.15	1.82

Source: memo, 6 Feb. 1928, CAOG 18/8; PP 1907, lvi (103).

departments became organised; consultants in other colonies received individual fees for each piece of work completed.[77]

As in other areas, consulting engineers succumbed to moral hazard, which, in their own interests, was accepted by the Crown Agents, but was increasingly opposed by governors, who began to criticise the engineers' open line role. It was firstly argued that their fees and salaries were 'out of all proportion' to the work involved, a claim that appears to be borne out by a comparison of the fees of consulting engineers with those charged by the Crown Agents when they later took over the supervision of lines (*see* table 16).[78] Such generosity no doubt was motivated by a desire to increase the cost of dismissal for opportunism, build trust and, in Shelford's case, help a relative or a colleague's relative. Second, in order to maximise their and by extension the Agency's income, they tended to be extravagant in their rolling stock and staff recommendations, and to discourage initiatives that could negatively affect their (and the Crown Agents') remuneration. In 1901 the Colonial Office had to remind Shelford that expenditure that was not strictly necessary should be avoided.[79] In 1907, meanwhile, both Shelford and the Agents strongly opposed a proposal that merchants should be allowed to use their own wagons on the Lagos line, arguing that this would lead to demands for heavy compensation for damage and demurrage.[80] In addition, to ensure that railways had sufficient funds to pay for the goods and services recommended,

[77] CAs to CO, 20 June 1906, CO 96/449/22251.

[78] Olivier note, 8 Nov. 1906, CO 96/449/44061.

[79] CAs to CO, 28 June 1901, CO 147/158/22311. Occasionally, the profligacy of the consulting engineers became so outrageous that Colonial Office staff were roused to anger. In 1901, for instance, the clerk G. E. A. Grindle, on receiving a recommendation for the employment of another person for the already overstaffed Lagos line, exclaimed 'this is too bad. Having screwed a general manager out of us, they try to screw an assistant by return of post': Grindle note, 25 Jan. 1899, CO 267/449/1979.

[80] CAs to CO, 11 Sept. 1907, CO 520/52/32579. It would also have reduced the purchasing income of consulting engineers and the CAs.

the engineers supported the setting of relatively high traffic rates, which slowed development. For instance, in 1902 and 1904 Shelford urged that Lagos rates be raised to an 'economic level' and in 1903 rejected demands that Gold Coast rates should be reduced.[81]

The consulting engineers' monitoring of open lines was also poor. They themselves accepted that it was not always possible for them 'to judge as to the necessity of proposed expenditure'.[82] Their knowledge of the operation of lines was based on correspondence with general managers, who could easily omit information, and annual reports on open lines, which by the time they reached the United Kingdom were often up to a year out of date.[83] Moreover, to ensure Colonial acceptance of their recommendations, they also advised against any interference by colonial goverments in the monitoring and management of lines, 'the control of which', if they were to be 'commercially successful', should 'as far as possible be placed in the hands of the general manager', who, selected by the consulting engineers, would be unlikely to oppose their advice.[84] As a result, many operating departments were inefficient and moral hazard was not unknown. The Gold Coast open lines department, for instance, was so ineffective that in 1906 the colony was forced to dismiss all its section heads with the exception of the chief accountant, and, in Sierra Leone, the Colonial Office sanctioned the appointment of a special officer to 'deal with the question of safeguarding railway revenue from fraud or neglect'.[85]

Disturbed by colonial criticism, the Agents first attempted to take over the consulting engineers' open line duties in 1904, but were repulsed by the Colonial Office, which was not convinced that they could perform the tasks involved satisfactorily.[86] In 1911, under colonial pressure, the Agents replaced Shelford's open line salary with special fees for each piece of work completed and, in the case of orders, a commission of 1 per cent. They also began to undertake some of the tasks themselves, overcoming further resistance from the Colonial Office, which held the duties to be 'rather foreign to the idea of an agent'.[87] To do the work, the Agency employed a locomotive draughtsman and assistant, expanded their engineering inspection department and introduced a sliding scale of fees, which ranged from ½ per cent to

[81] CAs to CO, 3 May 1902, CO 147/163/17564; Shelford to CAs, 12 Feb. 1904, CO 147/172/5748; CAs to CO, 14 Sept. 1903, CO 96/412/34414.
[82] Ezechiel note, 6 May 1902, CO 147/163/17509. A similar view is expressed in Shelford to Nathan, 19 Nov. 1903, Nathan papers, MS Nathan 313.
[83] Fiddian note, 11 Dec. 1907, CO 96/461/42349.
[84] CAs to CO, 12 Mar. 1902, CO 96/400/10216.
[85] Gold Coast to CO, 16 June 1906, CO 96/443/24376; CAs to CO, 30 Oct. 1906, CO 267/490/40090.
[86] CAs to CO, 14 Mar. 1907, CO 96/461/9405; Butler note, 22 Mar. 1907, ibid.
[87] Note, 26 July 1911, CO 323/577/20214; CAs to CO, 23 Mar. 1911, CO 446/101/9653.

1 per cent.[88] Their completion of the tasks was so successful that, by 1914, they had taken over the bulk of the consulting engineers' workload.[89]

In their supervision of projects undertaken by contractors and the private sector and of the operation of completed lines, the Agents sought to minimise adverse selection and moral hazard on the part of contractors, private constructors and open line departments. At the same time they cultivated their own institutional and personal interests through the promotion of Agency purchase of construction materials and the acceptance of the consulting engineers' benign post-construction opportunism. Their opposition to contractor and private sector displacement of the department system was again largely motivated by self-interest; the abandonment of department construction would reduce their purchasing income, influence, status and job satisfaction. However, their policy of sabotaging the Colonial Office's experiments with contractors and the private sector proved unsuccessful. Although they convinced the colonial secretary that these building methods were unsuitable, he turned not to the department system, but to construction by public works departments, which were relatively immune to sabotage by the Agency. The Agents' actions, furthermore, damaged their relationship with the Colonial Office and thus contributed to its determination to reform the Agency.

---

[88] CAs to CO, 17 May 1911, CO 323/577/16284; CAs to CO, 19 June 1911, CO 323/577/20214.
[89] The open line work of Messrs Gregory, Eyles & Waring for Ceylon, Trinidad and the Federated Malay States was taken over in 1919, and Messrs Hawkshaw & Dobson's work for Mauritius in 1923: CAs to CO, 8 Jan. 1923, CO 323/902/1521.

6

Public Loan Issue

The mechanics of imperial finance have been largely overlooked by historians, who have tended to investigate broad capital flows or the political machinations that led to the flotation of particular loans.[1] An investigation of the financial activities of the Crown Agents, who concentrated on the day-to-day supply and management of capital, will throw light not only on the funding of the crown colonies, but also on the techniques adopted by the City in financing all the countries of the empire. The duties of the Agents covered three main areas. First, they met those capital needs of their clients that could not be satisfied from local taxation. Funds were either raised on the London stock market, a process described in this chapter, or obtained from a variety of other sources, including bank loans, overdrafts and loan conversions, which will be discussed in chapter 7. In addition, they managed colonial investments in the United Kingdom and organised the transfer of money to and from the colonies, activities that are examined in chapter 8.

Colonies turned to the London stock market for the finance for infrastructure construction because of the sheer amount of capital required and the lack of alternative sources of funds. Few were sufficiently prosperous to capitalise the loans themselves and most lacked a business community wealthy and confident enough to finance construction. The Treasury, meanwhile, strong supporters of *laissez-faire* was unwilling to provide funds, fearing losses, and the United Kingdom private sector was discouraged from building self-financing railways by the cost of the work involved and the uncertainty of returns.

Unfortunately, many colonies faced bleak prospects on the stock market. Most found themselves in a catch 22 situation. Funds were required to build infrastructure, but the very lack of transportation networks and economic activity reduced the likelihood that they would be forthcoming at a price the colonies could afford. Unable to ascertain the profits likely to be earned from works envisaged, subscribers were only willing to invest in such loans if the

---

[1] See, for example, P. L. Cottrell, *British overseas investment in the nineteenth century*, London 1975; Youssef Cassis, *City bankers, 1890–1914*, Cambridge 1994; A. R. Hall (ed.), *The export of capital from Britain, 1870–1914*, London 1968; D. Kynaston, *The City of London: a world of its own, 1815–90*, London 1994; Dummett, 'Joseph Chamberlain', 287–321; Carland, *Colonial Office*. Only A. R. Hall discusses colonial finance in detail, but even he fails to delve into its more technical aspects and concentrates only on Australia's relationship with the City: *The London capital market and Australia, 1870–1914*, Canberra 1963.

Table 17
Crown colony loans issued by the Bank of England before 1860

Colony	Year	Amount (£)	Interest rate (%)	Yield (%)	Purchaser	Amount bought (£)
British Guiana	1851	70,000	4	3.81	J. F. Stanford	5,000
					Rock Life Assurance	65,000
	1852	50,000	4	3.65	Economic Life Assurance Corp.	50,000
	1853	80,000	4	3.65	Atlas Assurance Corp.	80,000
	1854	50,000	4	4.00	Ellis & Co	5,000
					Bank of England	45,000
Grenada	1858	7,000	4	–	Rock Life Assurance Corp.	7,000
Jamaica	1853	50,000	4	3.65	Atlas Assurance Corp.	50,000
	1855	433,000	4	3.95	J. F. Stanford	5,000
	1860	50,000	4	3.81	Guardian Assurance Corp.	50,000
St Lucia	–	13,000	4	3.81	Atlas Assurance Corp.	3,000
					Bank of England	10,000
	1860	5,000	4	3.86	Bank of England	5,000
Trinidad	1852	40,000	4	3.66	Economic Life Assurance Corp.	40,000
	1853	60,000	4	3.7	Atlas Assurance Corp.	60,000
	1854	25,000	4	4.00	Bank of England	25,000

Source: BE, M 1/21.

securities were sold at a low price or if there was to be a high rate of interest, and, in some cases, refused to invest at any price or rate. The use of the stock market also introduced the risk of self-seeking behaviour by officials in the colonies or by brokers. Under pressure from colonial business elites to build infrastructure, governors could be tempted to over-issue or float loans at excessively low prices, leading to repayment difficulties and account imbalances. Likewise, issuing houses and brokers could manipulate or 'rig' the market and reduce the price at which securities were sold. To overcome the low demand for stock and avoid moral hazard, all loans were therefore issued by the Crown Agents, who had the expertise required to maximise subscription and minimise rigging, and, on behalf of the Colonial Office, monitored all issues.

The crown colony loans floated by the Agents were part of the great increase in British overseas lending that began in the 1860s. Between 1865 and 1914 foreign governments and companies trading abroad issued securities in London worth £4.2 billion, 40 per cent of which went to the empire.[2] This

[2] R. C. Michie, *The City of London*, London 1992, 109; M Simon, 'The pattern of new

Table 18
Purposes of publicly-issued loans, 1860–1914 (%)

Purpose	1860–82	1883–1914
Harbour construction	15	–
Immigration	4	4
Internal finance	1	2
Military operations	3	–
Public works	14	20
Railway construction	33	10
Redemption/conversion	4	–
Combination of purposes including railway or harbour construction or public works	24	64
Combination of purposes excluding railway or harbour construction or public works	1	–

Source: GL and CAA, prospectuses.

Note: For a small number of loans no purpose is given.

outflow was the result of a combination of pull and push factors. Other countries required money for economic development and offered relatively high returns, even taking into account the greater risk of default.[3] At the same time, there was relatively little domestic demand for funds, as British manufacturers tended to draw capital from retained profits, savings and friends and relatives.

Early colonial government loans were issued through the Bank of England, which also paid investors their annual interest (*see* table 17). The Crown Agents merely received the money to meet these interest payments, which they passed on to the bank and, through their directorships in a range of financial institutions, perhaps acted as one of the bank's City monitors.[4] The Agents began to issue loans, pay the associated interest and, at the end of the life of each issue, repay investors their original investment from 1860. Of the loans floated, few were issued for purposes other than railway construction, and loans to make good deficiencies in ordinary revenue were particularly

British portfolio foreign investment, 1865–1914', in Hall, *The export of capital from Britain,* 24.
[3] M. Edelstein, 'Realised rates of return on United Kingdom home and overseas portfolio investment in the age of high imperialism', *Explorations in Economic History* xiii (1976), 302–6.
[4] See, for example, note, 12 June 1855, T 1/5972A/9438. Barnard was a director of the Bank of Australia, the London and Liverpool Insurance Co., the Australian Colonial and General Insurance Co. and the Fire Annihilator Co. Ltd. Baillie was a director of the Amicable Insurance Co.: CAs to CO, 4 May 1854, CO 323/241; *Who's who*, London 1849, 174.

Figure 9. Crown Agent and non-British empire issues, 1865–1914

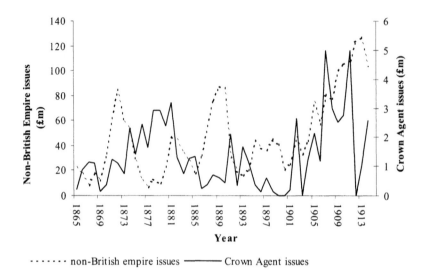

Source: GL and CAA, prospectuses; Hall, *Export of capital from Britain*, 41–2.

discouraged by the Agents (*see* table 18). The investing public believed that any government unwilling to raise taxes or cut expenditure in such circumstances would be unlikely to pay the interest on its debts.[5] Until the early 1900s most loans were floated when there were few non-empire issues (*see* fig. 9). During surges of investment in independent areas there was little demand for crown colony securities, which offered relatively low returns. Moreover, projects initiated at the height of such booms tended not to reach the construction stage until the independent area issue had exhausted itself. Thereafter, flotations generally occurred at the same time as non-empire issues, as the colonies needed capital so urgently that the Agency could not delay an issue until there was little competition for funds.

Issues can be split into two periods: from 1860 to 1882 and from 1883 to 1914. In the first period the Agents floated loans for both the crown colonies and a number of self-governing colonies that used the Agency in preference to those London and colonial banks which also issued securities. During these years, the Crown Agents floated ninety loans worth a total of £31.37m., twenty-four per cent of which was raised for the crown colonies (*see* appendix 3, table 1). In the 1870s, however, the Treasury began to have doubts about the wisdom of allowing the Agents to float self-governing colony loans. The Chancellor had 'not the slightest control' over the Agency

5 CAs to CO, 26 July 1867, CO 48/439/7227.

Table 19
Mean size of publicly issued loans, 1860–82 (£000s)

	All Crown Agent clients	Crown Agent Crown colony clients	Crown Agent responsible government clients	Australian responsible government colonies	Foreign governments
1860–70	0.18	0.13	0.23	2.23	–
1871–82	0.50	0.22	0.85	4.62	9.25
1860–82	0.35 (0.458)	0.18 (0.178)	0.52 (0.581)	3.64 (3.39)	9.253 (0.187) (1871–82)

Source: GL and CAA, prospectuses; Toshio Suzuki, *Japanese government loan issues on the London capital market, 1870–1913*, London 1994, 190–6.

Notes: Crown Agent responsible government clients = Cape, New Zealand, British Colombia, Vancouver. Responsible government colonies = Southern Australia, New South Wales, Victoria, Tasmania, Queensland, New Zealand (loans not issued through the CAs).
Standard deviation given in parenthesis.

and, if the Agents did behave dishonestly, the government 'would apparently be called upon to make good any default'.[6] Moreover, many investors believed that, as the Agents issued these loans, the imperial government must be guaranteeing repayment. Matters came to a head in 1879, when it appeared that a New Zealand loan was in danger of failing, leaving the Agents unable to repay the £1.1m. in short-term loans that they had borrowed on behalf of the colony from the Bank of England.[7] When it also emerged that the Agents' performance of their financial services had been criticised in the Cape legislature, the Treasury insisted that they cease to issue loans on behalf of self-governing colonies and, after some resistance, the Colonial Office complied.[8]

From 1883 to 1914, therefore, the Agency floated only crown colony securities, issuing fifty-four loans with a value of £41.58m. (*see* appendix 3, table 2). On average these issues were slightly smaller than those in the earlier period, and far smaller than those floated for self-governing colonies by the Bank of England and the London and Westminster Bank (*see* tables 19, 20). In the period 1899 to 1900, no loans were issued, and thereafter the Agents had problems selling securities (*see* chapter 8).

The stock and debentures issued by the Agents were sold for a set price and offered a given annual rate of interest. They were bought largely by stockbrokers, retailers of securities, who in the fullness of time sold them on to the

6 Note, 1 Nov. 1878, T 1/7710/17281.
7 BE, C 58/1; loan agents to New Zealand premier, 6 Dec. 1879, CAA, M 9; CAs to New Zealand premier, 6 Nov. 1879, ibid.
8 Cape to CAs, 12 Apr. 1880, CAOG 14/141.

Table 20
Mean sizes of publicly-issued loans, 1883–1912 (£000s)

	Crown colonies	Responsible government colonies	India	Foreign governments
1883–92	0.37	2.47	3.76	5.8
1893–1902	0.41	1.52	3.39	4.78
1903–12	2.07	1.84	3.82	3.35
1883–1912	0.76	1.91	3.68	4.66

Source: GL and CAA, prospectuses; Suzuki, *Japanese government loan issues*, 190–6.

Note: Responsible government colonies = Cape, New South Wales, New Zealand, Queensland, Tasmania, the Transvaal, Victoria, Western Australia (from 1892), Natal (from 1893).

public at a profit. After flotation the securities were quoted on the stock market and their post-issue price, which rose and fell according to demand and supply, was published each day in the Stock Exchange *Daily list*. As in other areas, the Agents' performance of their issue duties was determined by institutional self-interest. In this case, it was in their interest to minimise their costs, maximise loan subscription and the amount of securities sold at issue and to limit moral hazard on the part of brokers. The maximisation of subscription was important for a number of reasons. If all the securities of a loan were not sold, the colony would not obtain all the capital that it required and the Agents would receive less commission (commission was based on the value of the securities disposed of). Such commission, together with subsequent charges for the conversion and repayment of loans, was essential to the Agents, providing a large part of its income. A fully subscribed loan also increased their non-financial workload and receipts. The construction of infrastructure, financed by loans, generated considerable purchasing work, and, until it was required by the issuing colony, some of the money raised from a loan was usually lent to other colonies, enabling the recipients to finance further purchases in the United Kingdom and construction. Poorly subscribed flotations, moreover, would lead to damaging criticism in the colonies, weaken the credit of all crown colonies in the market and thus make it difficult to issue future loans, and leave the Agents with the problem of how to make up shortfalls.

To maximise the sale of securities, the Agents adopted four practices. First, they employed a number of strategies specifically designed to make the loans more attractive to brokers and investors. These measures occasionally benefited the Agents directly by reducing their costs and allowing them to earn additional fees. Secondly, they set low prices for loans, permitting investors to earn high yields, and used colonial investment funds to increase the quoted price of the existing securities of issuing colonies before an issue and to buy issued securities from brokers after a flotation had taken place. Thirdly, loans were informally, and, from the early 1900s, formally underwritten, that is agreements were made whereby brokers gave an undertaking to purchase either a given proportion of a loan or the securities left unsold. In addition, the Agents formed relationships of trust with their brokers and with other City institutions that not only facilitated sales, but also reduced the likelihood of dishonest practice by brokers. Inevitably, all these practices increased the cost of issues. The Agents, however, were unconcerned, confident that there would be little criticism from the colonies. Governors cared far less about cost than subscription, as they lacked the expertise and information to monitor yields and prices, and, whereas they themselves reaped the benefits to their reputations and careers of the financing and construction of infrastructure, the problems of repayment would be faced by their successors.

The issue of attractive loans

To increase the appeal of loan issues, the Agents made use of prestigious agents, closely monitored loan ordinances, and carefully timed and widely advertised issues, which were made in a form that was attractive to investors. As their brokers they employed Mullens Marshall & Co., whose senior partner acted as government broker, and Messrs J. and A. Scrimgeour.[9] It seems likely that Mullens were appointed purely for their prestige value and perhaps to allay Treasury doubts as to the Agents' competence. The bulk of the Agency's business was undertaken by Scrimgeours. Although, according to M. J. Mullens in 1908, the two firms discussed each issue before Scrimgeours advised the Agents, none of the surviving Crown Agent correspondence makes any reference to such discussions.[10] Furthermore, Mullens's client lists indicate that the Agents rarely dealt through the firm, which only purchased consols, and, on one occasion, Transvaal 3 per cent stock for the Agency.[11] Prestige was also acquired through the use, until 1893, of the Bank of England to receive investor payments for securities.[12] At first this service was performed free of charge, as the Agency kept a large non-interest-bearing current account with the bank. In 1878, however, the bank requested that it be paid a fee of £500 per £1m. of payments received, with a minimum fee of £500.[13] As this commission would have to be met out of their own charges, the Agents rejected the proposal and took over many of the bank's tasks

---

[9] David Wainwright, *Government broker: the story of an office and of Mullens & Co.*, London 1990, p. ix. The firm continued to operate commercially.
[10] PPE, q. 3713.
[11] Mullens Marshall papers, GL, MS 29104.
[12] Cape loan instalments were received by the Standard Bank of British South Africa: GL, prospectuses.
[13] CAs to CO, 2 July 1883, CO 323/354/11405.

themselves. The cost of that work, however, proved higher than expected, and the service provided was the subject of a number of complaints.[14] The Agents therefore reappointed the bank in 1883, largely on the terms demanded.

Once a colony had decided to issue a loan, the Agents received a copy of the loan ordinance, the legal document passed by the colony's legislative council that permitted flotation, which they checked to ensure that it conformed with the regulations of the Stock Exchange. A security that failed to be quoted could not be sold or bought easily after flotation. Its price would thus be 3 to 4 per cent lower than a quoted security, reducing the rate at which subsequent loans could be offered.[15] At the same time, they made sure that the ordinance conformed with the City's ethical norms. In 1871, for example, Antigua planned to issue a loan for hurricane relief on the basis of legislation that sanctioned issues for immigration purposes, a ploy that would have reduced the confidence of investors in the colony and lowered demand for future loans.[16] The Agents then drew up the loan proposal to be presented to investors. This contained full and accurate details of the issuing colony's revenue and expenditure, as it was believed that the 'slightest appearance of withholding [information]' damaged demand to a greater extent than the circulation of full details 'of the actual state of things – however bad'.[17]

Similar care was taken in the timing of issues. If market conditions were unfavourable, flotations would be delayed and work on the infrastructure project financed by sums borrowed through the Agents from other colonies and banks. Occasionally, a colony was allowed to finance an entire project in this way, raising a loan only after construction was at, or nearing, completion.[18] Investors were thus assured that the scheme would not be subject to escalating costs and that the revenues required to meet interest charges would start coming in soon after issue. Where possible, the actual issue occurred immediately before the payment of the interest on a previous loan of the issuing colony, when the price of the existing stock was high and the holders of the securities, anticipating interest, would be more likely to invest in more stock.[19]

After the decision to issue had been made, the senior Crown Agent and Scrimgeours rapidly determined the terms of the loan, seeking the advice of neither the Colonial Office nor the issuing colony. It was argued that discussions with either would lead to terms unacceptable to the market, result in delay, which could cause the Agency to miss an upturn in demand, and cause

[14] CAs to BE, 9 Aug. 1883, ibid.
[15] CAs to CO, 19 Mar. 1862, CO 54/382/2745.
[16] CO to Antigua, 9 Dec. 1871, CO 107/143/11548.
[17] CAs to CO, 3 Apr. 1867, CO 179/87/3313.
[18] Examples are the 1887 Hong Kong and Mauritius loans and the 1889 West Australian loan: GL, prospectuses.
[19] CAs to CO, 27 Dec. 1865, CO 167/483/1264.

a fall in City confidence in the Agency.[20] There was also the danger that the market might discover that an issue was imminent, and attempt, through sales of existing securities, to influence prices. Others, however, suspected that the Agents' failure to consult more widely led to mistakes and, from 1900, affected the success of issues. By comparison, the terms and timing of Indian loans were determined by the accountant-general of the India Office, representatives of the secretary of state and the finance committee of the India Council, the governor and other directors of the Bank of England, and the India Office's and the bank's brokers.[21]

Issues were advertised widely, partly to encourage the public to buy securities at issue, but also to increase post-issue demand and prevent a fall in prices, which would reduce broker profit and damage colonial credit and the terms of future issues.[22] In addition, from 1880 to 1886, and from 1893 to 1914, the Agents passed part of their issue fee on to brokers, the proportion paid depending on the number of applications for securities that came through broking firms. Each sale that resulted from a newspaper advertisement thus increased the Agency's earnings. The costs of advertisement, along with other miscellaneous expenses, for example printing and legal charges, were paid directly by the issuing colony, and amounted to between £750 for a £500,000 loan and £1,200 for an issue of £1m., comparable to the amounts spent by the Bank of England and the London and Westminster Bank.[23] Using their press agents, Messrs R. E. White, who had worked for the Agency since 1884 and also handled the accounts of the War Office, Admiralty and Inland Revenue, the Agents placed advertisements in all the major newspapers.[24] The Western Australian loan, for example, was advertised in *The Times* for four days, in four other national newspapers for two days and for one day in fifteen provincial, Scottish and Irish newspapers.[25] Prospectuses were also distributed to the leading banks and brokers, to sole holders of the issuing colony's previous stock and to other investors in crown colonies, who 'might be interested in the offer'.[26]

The form of the loans floated, the provision of a sinking fund and the size

[20] Antrobus to CO, 23 Dec. 1910, CAOG 9/36.
[21] PPE, q. 704. The date and terms of self-governing colony loans floated by the Bank of England were decided upon by the agents-general of the issuing colony, the governor of the bank, the chief cashier or deputy governor and the bank's brokers; the date and terms were then telegraphed to the colony for approval. See, for example, New South Wales to BE, 10 Sept. 1891, BE, AC 30/110; Queensland to BE, 13 Apr. 1897, AC 30/150.
[22] From 1900 underwriters also generally required that a certain sum be spent on publicity: CAA, memorandum on the procedures followed in connection with the issue of crown colony loans, 1919 (hereinafter cited as CAA, CCC memorandum), 21.
[23] Ibid.
[24] CAA, file 21.
[25] CAs to White, 17 July 1889, CAOG 9/21.
[26] CAs to Ceylon, 3 Mar. 1910, CAOG 9/94; memo, n.d., CAOG 9/14. Joint account stockholders were generally not contacted, as joint decisions to invest were difficult in the limited issue period: CAA, CCC, memorandum, 21.

of the issue were again designed to attract investors. There were two ways of floating loans. In the tender method, an issue was announced for sale at a minimum price of, say, £104 per security, but investors could offer to buy the security at any price above this minimum. Securities were then allocated to those applicants who had agreed to pay the highest prices. Under a subscription offer, on the other hand, loans could be bought only at one price, fixed by the issuer. The main advantage of tender issues was that they allowed the market to determine the price of securities within the limit set by the minimum price. Provided that the minimum price was not too high, they thus increased the likelihood that securities would be sold and absolved the Agents from responsibility for the price eventually obtained. Most loans, consequently, were raised by this method. In the 1860s and 1870s the minimum price was often concealed until offers to purchase were opened in the belief that, with no guide price, investors would increase the size of their bids. Later, when it was realised that the reverse often occurred and that concealed prices discouraged applications, the minimum price was always revealed at the start of an issue. Subscription issues, thought to be more attractive to ordinary investors, who disliked the riskiness of tenders, were generally only adopted for small loans and those likely to be unpopular with brokers.[27]

Loans could be issued as either debentures or inscribed stock. Debentures were securities payable to the bearer. They could thus be sold without reference to the issuing house and interest was paid on the presentation, by holders to the issuer, of coupons attached to the debenture certificate. Inscribed stock was so called because the name and address of the holder was inscribed or registered in the books of the issuing house. All changes of ownership therefore had to be registered with the issuer and interest was paid on proof of identity or sent to the investor's registered address. At the start of the period, most issues were floated as debentures. Incribed stock carried a higher stamp transfer duty, the government tax that had to be paid every time a security was sold to another party, and investors were reluctant to buy it, believing that it failed to appreciate rapidly in price. Gradually, however, the situation changed. The 1877 Colonial Stock Act allowed colonies to pay a one-off composition fee to the government on issue. This freed investors from stock transfer duty.[28] As more issuing houses adopted stock, it became more familiar to investors, and, more marketable, its quoted price no longer lagged behind that of debentures. The issuing public also became more aware of its advantages. Unlike debentures, which could only be sold in set amounts, for example £500 or £1,000, it could be disposed of in parcels of any value, and,

[27] CAs to CO, 1 May 1871, CO 267/313/4328.
[28] Later, when the number of transfers fell, the Agents set up a stamp duty fund for each loan on issue which contained an invested sum deposited by the issuing colony, from which the duty for each transfer was paid: CAs to Inland Revenue, 4 Nov. 1810, CAOG 9/36. Any surplus in the fund on redemption was returned to the colony.

since it was not a bearer security, it was not liable to theft or misappropria-tion.[29] Consequently, from the 1880s, the Agents began to issue convertible debenture loans, which permitted or requested investors to exchange the bonds bought for stock by a given date. Stock loans then began to be floated and, to cover the cost and facilitate the registration of the stock, the Agents' issue fee was raised and a City office established.

Ideally, the Agents would have preferred to issue guaranteed debentures and stock, the interest and repayment of which was guaranteed by the impe-rial government. Crown colony loans floated by the Bank of England prior to 1860, when the Agents took over its issuing duties, were guaranteed and had an average post-issue investor yield of 3.79 per cent, far lower than that subsequently provided by the Crown Agents.[30] Forty years later M. J. Mullens claimed that a guarantee would allow interest rates to be reduced by ½ per cent.[31] Unfortunately, all attempts by the Agents to persuade the Colonial Office to provide such security were blocked by the Treasury, which feared defaults.[32] To compensate, a number of governors proposed that colonies should guarantee each others' loans, or that stock should be issued by munici-palities and guaranteed by colonial governments.[33] The Agents rejected both proposals, pointing out that colonial guarantees would reduce City confi-dence and demand, and that municipal loans would be unacceptable to trusts.[34]

Each crown colony issue had a sinking fund, into which the issuing government paid a certain sum and which was used to repay the loan.[35] Prior to 1880, government contributions ranged from 1 per cent to 5.5 per cent of the loan value or involved the colony laying aside a given amount of money each year. Later, as the lifespan of issues lengthened and it was acknowledged that high sinking fund contributions could negatively affect demand for stock, they were generally set at 1 per cent.[36] If an issue produced a surplus, the Agents also occasionally placed all or a proportion of the excess proceeds in the fund.[37] Until the late 1880s funds were used annually or periodically to buy back a certain number of debentures, either on the market when prices were low, or more usually from investors. In the latter case, the debentures to be repaid were chosen by a draw, the investors paid £100 per security held

---

[29] CAA, CCC memorandum, 11; CAs to Gold Coast, 11 Dec. 1907, CAOG 9/76.
[30] BE, M/21.
[31] PPE, q. 3745.
[32] In 1895, for example, the Agents proposed that all colonial debt should be converted into one large guaranteed loan: Ommanney to Mercer, 29 Nov. 1895, CAOG 9/305.
[33] Anderson to Elgin, 3 Oct. 1906, CAOG 9/80; CAs to CO, 20 Mar. 1908, CAOG 9/94.
[34] CAs to CO, 20 Mar. 1908, CAOG 9/94; CAs to CO, 18 Oct. 1906, CAOG 9/80.
[35] The only two exceptions were the 1889 and 1891 Natal loans: GL, prospectuses.
[36] CAs to CO, 21 Nov. 1877, CO 273/92/14043. Many believed that high contributions to the sinking fund could threaten interest payments.
[37] CAs to colonial secretary, 26 Mar. 1895, CO 28/238/5423; CAs to CO, 27 Apr. 1895, CAOG 9/50.

Table 21
Average lifespans of loans, 1860–1914 (years)

	Crown Agent issues	Responsible government colony issues
1860–82	27	31
1883–1914	45	38

Source: GL and CAA, prospectuses.

Note: Calculation only includes loans for which redemption dates are given. In the case of convertible issues, the currency of the stock offered was taken.

plus any interest due, and the funds were known as drawing funds.[38] However, although such purchases reduced the number of securities on the market and thus increased their price and the credit of the issuing colony, they were disliked by both the Agents and their principals. The organisation involved increased the Agency's costs, while colonies had to meet the expense of a notary to monitor the draw and, since debentures were not registered, pay for advertisements that listed the bonds to be repaid.[39] It also became clear that potential investors were deterred by such repayments, as the amounts repaid were usually small and the costs of reinvestment therefore high, and repayment was often made at a time when reinvestment was not profitable. Furthermore, if the holders of the bonds drawn missed the announcement and failed to return them to the Agents for repayment, they ran the risk of losing up to half-a-years interest.[40]

With the introduction of stock in the early 1880s colonial government contributions were therefore allowed to accumulate and were invested by the Agents. At the end of a loan's lifespan, its fund's investments were then sold and the proceeds used to repay the issue. For the Agents, these funds, known as accumulated funds, were a source of income, as the Agency received a fee each time it bought or sold fund investments. It was also claimed that both drawing and accumulated funds, by minimising the risk of non-repayment, attracted subscribers and increased the likelihood that a loan would be a success and sold at a premium. The issuers of Indian and self-governing colony loans, however, disagreed, and made no use of sinking funds. Many in the City, meanwhile, believed that the opportunity cost of the capital tied up in accumulated funds far outweighed any price advantage gained.

The adoption of accumulated funds allowed the Agents, on issue, to set

38 CAs to CO, 21 Nov. 1883, CAOG 9/1.
39 CAs to CO, 29 Aug. 1863, CO 54/382/8527. The notary costs of the first, second and third drawings of the 1887 Mauritius loan were £5 5s., £4 4s. and £3 13s. 6d. respectively; the advertisement expenses were £2, £2 5s. 4d. and £2 10s respectively: drawings, 17 July 1891, 18 July 1895, 9 July 1903, CAOG 9/9.
40 CAA, CCC, memorandum, 11.

more accurate dates for repayment, which again supposedly increased the attractiveness of the stock.[41] Over the period, the lifespans of loans lengthened (see table 21). Issues became bigger and larger amounts of stock were bought by trusts, which had a minimum duration of thirty years and, due to the legal costs involved, were reluctant to disturb their original investments.[42] In the late 1880s the uniform lifespan adopted was fifty years, though the Agents usually retained the power to redeem on six to twelve month's notice after twenty to thirty years, which enabled them to take advantage of any improvement in a colony's credit and to issue a fresh loan at a lower rate of interest. Contributions to the sinking fund by a government usually commenced three years after issue, when the works financed by a flotation were remunerative, and it was calculated that a fund receiving contributions of 1 per cent *per annum*, with an estimated capital return of 3 per cent *per annum*, could provide the necessary sum for repayment in forty-seven years.[43] A fall in the yields of the securities in which they were authorised to invest, however, forced the Agents to extend lifespans to sixty years in 1898.[44] On the repayment of a loan the sinking fund was sold off and the proceeds used to buy back the debentures or stock. Where fund investments had been highly profitable, there was often a surplus, as loan ordinances generally prevented any part of a fund's contents being released before redemption.[45] When this occurred, the balance was generally transferred to the issuing colony's current account and, occasionally, to the sinking funds of its other loans.[46] Conversely, shortfalls were met by a further issue, from grants-in-aid, or loans from other colonies or banks.[47]

Finally, demand was increased by the flotation, wherever possible, of loans of at least £100,000, one large issue as opposed to several smaller issues over a period of time and loans with terms identical to those of previous issues. Flotations smaller than £100,000 were avoided as they were generally not quoted on the Stock Exchange. They were therefore difficult to trade, and the demand and the price of such issues was low.[48] One large loan was

---

[41] The governor of the Bank of England believed that the lack of fixed repayment dates was one of the main reasons for the fall in Indian loan prices after 1900: PP 1914, xix (Cd 7069), q. 3371.

[42] Ibid.

[43] CAA, CCC, memorandum, 12.

[44] CAs to CO, 7 Jan. 1898, CAOG 9/86.

[45] Conversely, when a fund was growing too rapidly, the Agents were allowed to reduce or temporarily halt government contributions or to exchange high-yielding investments for others with lower returns: CAs to CO, 16 Feb. 1900, CO 137/615/5176; Western Australia to CAs, 28 Mar. 1903, CO 323/492/42933; CA memo, 14 Mar. 1874, CO 209/233/3176.

[46] Ommanney note, 11 Jan. 1905, CO 323/492/42933; CAs to CO, 12 Dec. 1895, CO 323/400/22269.

[47] CAs to CO, 21 Nov. 1883, CAOG 9/1; CAs to Mauritius, 22 Mar. 1888, CAOG 9/9; Robinson note, 21 Sept. 1900, CO 323/453/29893; CAs to CO, 21 Aug. 1899, CAOG 9/71.

[48] CAs to CO, 3 Apr. 1867, CO 179/87/3313.

preferred to many smaller issues, as it attracted more publicity, and the greater volume of debentures or stock increased their marketability, allowing purchases to be immediately realisable and increasing the likelihood that the price would rise rapidly and to an appreciable extent.[49] In addition, if raised to finance public projects, large loans avoided the temporary and expensive cessation of work that would occur if, after a first small loan had been spent, a downturn in the market prevented a second issue.[50] The practice of issuing loans that were identical as regards interest rate and dividend and repayment dates to existing quoted stock encouraged holders of previous loans to tender. The security was familiar and holdings of old and new debentures or stock could be sold together, reducing selling fees.[51] The size of the resultant large block of stock again led to 'a freer market . . . in buying and selling', with all the attendant advantages.[52] Furthermore, the use of the same dividend payment dates and the ease with which transfers of stock could be registered etc minimised the Agents' management expenses, and a single sinking fund, if a drawing fund was adopted, reduced the colony's notary costs. The practice, however, was only adopted where the existing stock had been released relatively recently as the sinking funds of older loans, owing to their short remaining lifespans, could not generate the sums required for repayment. The only exception was the 1906 Hong Kong loan, which, to reduce the colony's interest costs, the Agents issued on terms identical to those of a loan issued twelve years previously and available for redemption in 1918.[53]

Loan terms

The terms on which loans were bought by investors comprised five elements: price, interest rate, accrued interest, free interest and full payment discount. Like other governments loans, all Crown Agent securities had a face or par value at which the debenture or stock was repaid. This was set at £100 per security. Ideally, the Agents would have issued all debentures or stock at or above their face value, as a minimum or fixed price below par led to a long-term loss when the securities were repaid. Such pricing, however, was not always feasible. If public demand for a loan was poor, a high minimum or fixed price would reduce subscription and there was a danger that much of the issue would be left unsold. When setting minimum or fixed prices the Agents

[49] CAs to CO, 24 Jan. 1905, CAOG 9/94.
[50] CAs to CO, 23 Aug. 1862, CO 167/444/8393.
[51] The Bank of England and the London and Westminster Bank also issued such stock: CAs to CO, 12 Feb. 1892, CO 137/552/2931.
[52] CAA, CCC, memorandum, 17.
[53] Blake to Nathan, 9 Feb. 1906, CAOG 9/25. The Colonial Office had 'doubts as to the propriety and expediency' of the issue, but nevertheless gave its authorisation: CO to CAs, 7 Feb. 1906, ibid.

consequently had to determine the price the public were prepared to pay for the securities to be sold. They thus referred to the price quoted on the stock market of debentures or stock previously floated by the issuing colony, which was usually identical in interest rate and form to the securities to be issued. Having ascertained the quoted price, they then set the minimum or fixed price some way below it. The bulk of debentures or stock were bought by brokers, who then sold their purchases on to the investing public at a price higher than that at which they were acquired. The resulting profit, the difference between the purchase and resale price, was known as the 'broker's turn' or premium. As brokers would only buy securities if they were assured a profit, the Agency therefore had little alternative but to set the minimum or fixed price of each new loan at below the quoted price of the issuing colony's existing securities, the price at which brokers could resell their allotments to investors.

How far beneath was dependent on the likely demand for the new securities, which, after 1880, could often be ascertained by the prices received and the subscription of recent self-governing colony loans. Brokers bought securities with borrowed funds, on which they had to pay interest. If demand was low, they would have to hold on to their purchases and pay interest on their loans for long periods before all the securities were sold.[54] This would discourage them from making purchases of crown colony debentures or stock in the future, and, inevitably, some would be tempted to cut their losses and dump their allotments on to the market. As a result, the price would fall even further, damaging the credit of the colony and forcing those who retained their acquisitions to hold them for an even longer period. When demand was likely to be poor, therefore, the Agents set the issue price far below the quoted price, allowing the brokers a large premium to compensate them for their higher interest payments. On the other hand, if demand was great and the brokers could dispose of their purchases rapidly, they would be allowed a relatively small premium and the issue price would be set far closer to the quoted price. Over the whole period the Crown Agents appear to have allowed their brokers a far larger premium than other issuing houses. Between 1860 and 1882, in the case of those loans for which a line of identical debentures or stock existed and prices were quoted, when setting the price of a new loan the Agents allowed their brokers an average premium 2.37 per cent greater than that offered by self-governing issuing houses. From 1883 to 1914 the additional premium fell to 0.34 per cent, no doubt because the Crown Agents' clients had become more familiar to investors, and hence securities were sold more rapidly (see table 22).[55]

---

[54] In the case of the 1888 Natal loan, Westgarth and Scrimgeours, who had bought 99% of the stock, still held 62% and 20% respectively of their purchases over a year after the issue: CAs to Natal, 26 July 1889, CAOG 9/12.

[55] For details of those loans for which no line of listed debenture or stock existed when

Table 22
Mean pre-issue and post-issue premiums on listed loans, 1863–1912 (%)

	Crown Agent premium		Responsible government premium	
	One week before issue	One week after issue	One week before issue	One week after issue
1863–70	13.92	3.49	8.19	–
1871–82	3.44	1.24	4.71	–
1863–82	7.84 (18.8)	2.19 (2.8)	5.47 (5.4)	–
1883–92	3.87	1.94	3.09	0.57
1893–1902	2.33	1.07	3.28	1.21
1903–1912	2.62	1.12	2.13	0.58
1883–1912	3.17 (1.154)	1.53 (1.066)	2.83 (1.508)	0.80 (0.934)

Source: *Daily list*, 1863–1912.

Notes: Premium week before issue = retail price one week before issue – minimum or fixed price. Premium week after issue = retail price one week after issue – fixed price or average allotment price. Standard deviation given in parenthesis. Responsible government average allotment prices are not available for the period 1863 to 1882.

To further maximise subscription and ensure profits for their brokers, the Agents also manipulated the quoted price of existing securities and recently issued loans before and after flotation respectively. Over time, they sought to limit the quantity of issued crown colony debentures or stock that could come on to the stock market in response to an increase in demand. The adoption of drawing sinking funds ensured that a number of securities from each loan was taken out of circulation annually, and each colony with accumulated sinking funds invested a proportion of the contents in securities issued by themselves, which were only sold when the funds loans were to be repaid. The Agents also encouraged trusts to buy crown colony debentures and stock, aware that trustees held acquisitions for long periods and, as will be discussed in chapter 8, bought large quantities of securities themselves for the other colonial investment funds that they managed.[56] These were set up for a variety of purposes, and, as with sinking funds, colonies annually contributed a given sum to each fund, which, along with the interest from existing fund investments, was invested by the Agents in securities that were held for relatively long periods. By 1913 such funds held £7.8m. in crown colony securities, 22 per cent of all the debentures and stock issued by the Agency.[57]

they were issued and which display similar results see David Sunderland, 'Agents and principals: the Crown Agents for the colonies, 1880–1914', unpubl. DPhil. diss. Oxford 1997, 139–41.
[56] PPE, q. 3737.
[57] CAOG 9/44, memo, 925, 7.

The result of these actions was that the quoted price of crown colony debentures and stock was highly sensitive to sudden increases in demand.[58] It was thus relatively easy for the Agents to 'rig' the quoted price of the existing securities of an about-to-issue colony upwards before a flotation. This allowed the Agents to set a relatively high fixed or minimum price for the new loan, and the public, aware of the rapid price rise, were more likely to buy the new securities. Between 1880 and 1913 the quoted price of the existing securities of 60 per cent of those loans with identical debentures or stock previously issued rose in the six months before the date of flotation.[59] The Agents did this by using colonial investment fund contributions to buy the issuing colony's existing debentures or stock in the months leading up to a new issue. As there was generally insufficient supply to meet the demand, the quoted price of the securities thus rose. Purchases were occasionally made by the Bank of England and the London and Westminster Bank too, perhaps in return for reciprocal acquisitions by the Agents prior to their issues, and both banks perhaps advised their customers to make similar purchases.[60]

If, after issue, demand was unexpectedly low and there was a possibility of price falls, the Agents would again rig prices by purchasing the issued securities with colonial investment fund contributions. Between 1880 and 1914 the quoted price of the existing securities of 53 per cent of those loans with previously issued identical debentures or stock either stayed constant or rose in the month following the day before issue.[61] Brokers thus avoided large losses and were not tempted to dump their holdings on to the market. Given their low price, the securities bought were also a good investment. As with pre-issue rigs, the Agents occasionally called upon the Bank of England and the London and Westminster Bank to make purchases (*see* table 23).[62] Both banks acquiesced, probably because if brokers failed to off-load their crown colony allotments rapidly they would be unable to purchase the banks' own new issues, and the dumping of securities on to the market would have a ripple effect on all colonial quoted prices. The Agents also made reciprocal purchases. In the five months after the Bank of England's Transvaal loan of 1904, which the bank had difficulty selling to the public, for example, the

---

[58] Scrimgeours to CAs, 16 Nov. 1911, CAOG 9/37.

[59] 17% fell.

[60] In the months before the 1881 Ceylon issue, for example, the Bank of England bought, in five purchases, £255,000 of the colony's debentures. Two months prior to the Jamaica 1882 flotation it bought £48,500 of that colony's securities; one month prior it bought a further £42,500 worth: BE, ADM 7/52/1075, 1072.

[61] Although new loans were only quoted some months after issue, price changes in the securities were reflected in the quoted prices of the issuing colony's existing identical debentures and stock.

[62] The Bank of England, for instance, after the 1880 Ceylon issue, bought £60,000 of the loan's securities, after the 1882 Ceylon flotation £48,000 of that loan's debentures, and after the 1882 Trinidad issue £83,000 of that loan's securities: BE, ADM 7/52/1075, 1072.

Table 23
Purchases of stock after issue by the Bank of England, 1872–1912

Year	Loan	Amount purchased (£)
1872	Jamaica 4 % guaranteed debentures	36,900
1874	New Zealand 4 % guaranteed debentures	194,500
1875	New Zealand 4 % guaranteed debentures	10,000
	Jamaica 4 % guaranteed debentures	111,600
1876	Mauritius 4.5 % debentures	44,300
1877	Mauritius 4.5 % debentures	1,500
	Ceylon 6 % debentures	2,500
	Mauritius 6 % debentures	5,000
1879	Straits 4.5 % debentures	20,000
1880	Ceylon 4 % debentures	110,000
1881	Ceylon 4% debentures	205,000
1882	Trinidad 4 % debentures	83,000
	Jamaica 4 % debentures	104,000
1887	British Guiana 4 % debentures	40,000
1911	Southern Nigeria 4 % (5 yr debentures)	100,000
	Southern Nigeria 4 % (4 yr debentures)	115,000
1912	Southern Nigeria 4 % (4 yr debentures)	10,000
	Southern Nigeria 4 % (5 yr debentures)	75,000

Source: BE, ADM 7/48; 7/52; 7/58.

Agents bought £263,945 of stock.[63] To further increase prices, the Agents also invested that part of the public works contractor fees, withheld until a project was satisfactorily completed, in the stock of the loan that financed those works.[64] This not only kept the price of stock high in the post-issue period, but also encouraged good performance on the part of the contractor, as rumours of poor quality work would cause the price of the stock to fall.

The Agents' rigging of prices before and after issue was not unusual. Before flotations underwriters of non-crown colony loans often engaged in a practice known as 'the premium dodge' that increased demand, and afterwards usually 'made a market' through fictitious purchases of the debentures or stock issued.[65] Similarly both the Bank of England and the London and Westmin-

[63] CO 323/504/1606, 15177, 24256, 37378. In the same period the bank bought £1.65m.: BE, ADM 7/56.
[64] See, for example, CAs to CO, 19 Jan. 1865, CO 54/408/675.
[65] Henry Lowenfeld, All about investment, London 1909, 177–9. The 'premium dodge' involved the manipulation by underwriters of an issue's 'grey market'. Before a loan was floated, a 'grey market' in its securities often developed within which brokers bought and sold as yet fictitious future acquisitions. To increase public demand between the release of

Figure 10. Crown Agent issues and annual average bank rate, 1860–1914

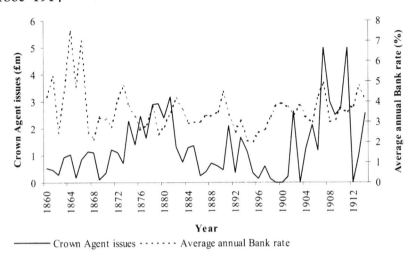

Source: GL and CAA, prospectuses; *Whitaker's almanac*, 1898, 1915.

ster Bank on occasion appear to have bought securities they themselves had issued.[66] The Agents' purchases seem to have increased over time, as the number and size of the managed colonial investment funds grew, and after 1900 securities bought after issue were often held for just one or two years until the price had risen.[67] The stock was then sold and the proceeds used to buy more securities in the pre- and post-issue periods. Aware of what was going on, the Colonial Office objected only once: in 1907 with regard to the Straits loan. Expecting demand to be low, prospective underwriters of the issue informed the Agents that they would provide support only if the Agency agreed to buy £500,000 of the securities from them if the price fell to a discount.[68] In the event, the price plummeted and the underwriters threatened to get rid of their allocations immediately unless the Agents bought a further £1m. of the stock.[69] The Colonial Office expressed its displeasure at

the prospectus and the allotment of the securities, underwriters would buy future purchases of the debentures or stock at a high price, causing the 'grey market' price to rise.

[66] The London and Westminster Bank bought £100,000 of the 1909 Western Australian loan six days after issue; in June 1910 it agreed to purchase £100,000 of the stock of that year's Western Australian issue on the market; and in 1914 it bought £23,000 of South African debentures two months after issue: NWB, 12915/212; 12915, 2 June 1910; 12917/220.

[67] CAs to FO, 1 Aug. 1905, CAOG 9/122; memo, 4 Mar. 1907, ibid.

[68] CAs to colonial secretary, 3 May 1907, CO 273/332/16226.

[69] CAs to colonial secretary, 3 Mar. 1907, ibid.

Figure 11. Crown Agent issues and mean accrued/free interest, 1860–1913

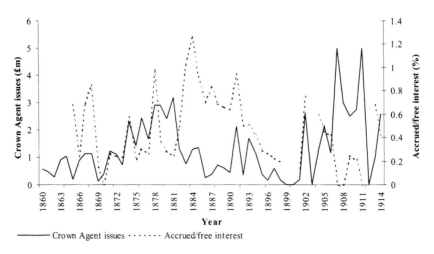

Source: GL and CAA, prospectuses.

the 'shifts and expedients for getting off the loan', regarding the £1m. investment as 'half way' to a 'bogus subscription'.[70]

After price, the next most important aspect of a loan was interest, the percentage of an issue's par value that was paid to investors every six months. The rate of interest was determined by the rates offered by other issuing houses and rarely changed, averaging 5.18 per cent between 1860 and 1882 and 3.7 per cent between 1883 and 1914. Movements in the base rate, the rate of interest set by the Bank of England that determined general interest rates, had little influence on the rates offered. Base rates, however, did help to determine the timing of issues. Prior to the early 1900s the Agents generally floated loans when base rates were low (see fig. 10). Issues during such periods increased broker purchase of debentures and stock and reduced the likelihood of a post-issue slump in prices. Brokers could borrow the funds used to finance their acquisitions relatively cheaply and were thus more eager to buy. Furthermore, they were less liable to dump their purchases at low prices in order to relieve themselves of their debt and the associated high interest payments.

At issue, the Agents also offered accrued and free interest. Both comprised unearned additional interest paid as part of the first six month's interest payment. Accrued interest was fictional backdated interest. If a loan was floated on 1 June and the first six month's interest payment was made on 31 August (ie. three months later), only three months of the interest paid would actually have been earned, and the remainder, accrued interest,

---

[70] Churchill note, 9 May 1907; Fiddes note, 8 May 1907, ibid.

Table 24
Mean accrued and free interest, 1860–82 (%)

	All Crown Agent clients	Crown Agent crown colony clients	Crown Agent responsible government clients	Responsible government colonies
1860–70	0.548	0.54	0.557	0.844
1871–82	0.347	0.303	0.508	0.659
1860–82	0.47 (0.408)	0.373 (0.375)	0.523 (0.546)	0.728 (0.81)

Source: GL and CAA, prospectuses.

Note: Standard deviation given in parenthesis.

Table 25
Mean accrued and free interest, 1883–1912 (%)

	Crown colonies	Responsible government colonies	India
1883–92	0.818	1.26	0.641
1893–1902	0.353	0.741	0.59
1903–12	0.241	0.893	0.516
1883–1912	0.498	0.964	0.577

Source: GL and CAA, prospectuses.

unearned. Such interest increased demand for securities from the public and encouraged brokers to hold on to their purchases, even if demand was poor. Free interest was given to those who opted to pay for securities in instalments spread over a number of months. Although during the first six months of ownership they had not fully paid for their purchases, they nevertheless obtained the full rate of interest when the first six month's payment was made. The interest, the difference between the amount of interest paid and the sum actually earned, increased demand for debentures or stock from those members of the public who bought at issue, but was largely aimed at brokers, encouraging them to hold their purchases during periods of poor demand. As would be expected, the amount of accrued or free interest offered was nega-tively related to flotations; high during periods when few loans were issued and demand was poor, and low when flotations were rising and demand greater (*see* fig. 11). Between 1860 and 1882, and between 1883 and 1914, the Agents relied far less on such inducements than other issuing houses (*see* tables 24 and 25). In the pre-1883 period, the highest accrued and free interest was offered to purchasers of loans issued by the Crown Agents' responsible government clients, who floated large amounts of stock, demand

Table 26
Mean accrued and free interest and mean yields at issue
of Crown Agent clients, 1860–1914 (%)

1860–82			1883–1914		
Crown colony	Mean yield	Accrued/free interest	Crown colony	Mean yield	Accrued/free interest
Sierra Leone	6.02	0.32	Bahamas	4.66	1.49
Antigua	6	–	Fiji	4.6	0.25
Gibraltar	6	–	Cape	4.43	0.31
British Colombia	5.89	0.37	St Lucia	4.3	0.72
Vancouver	5.71	–	Natal	4.21	0.82
Mauritius	5.59	0.21	Sierra Leone	4.13	0.63
Natal	5.43	0.58	Western Australia	4.09	0.68
New Zealand	5.18	0.41	Grenada	4.01	0.38
Ceylon	4.86	0.52	Antigua	3.93	0.46
Cape	4.75	0.61	Southern Nigeria	3.89	0.59
Straits	4.6	0.11	Gold Coast	3.89	0.53
Fiji	4.6	0.25	Jamaica	3.86	0.30
W. Australia	4.53	0.22	Straits	3.86	0.21
Trinidad	4.46	0.28	Trinidad	3.81	0.42
Jamaica	4.18	0.16	Hong Kong	3.75	0.62
			Mauritius	3.66	0.59
			Ceylon	3.65	0.63
			Barbados	3.55	0.29
			British Guiana	3.52	0.36

Source: GL and CAA, prospectuses.

Note: Yield = interest rate/price at issue (minimum or fixed price – accrued interest +/– free interest) x 100.

Table 27
Mean discounts, 1883–1912 (%)

	Crown colonies	Responsible government colonies	India
1883–92	2.95	2.72	2.29
1893–1902	1.68	1.89	1.87
1903–12	2.59	2.44	2.85
1883–1912	2.44	2.33	2.38

Source: GL and CAA, prospectuses.

Figure 12. Crown Agent issues and mean yields at issue, 1860–1913

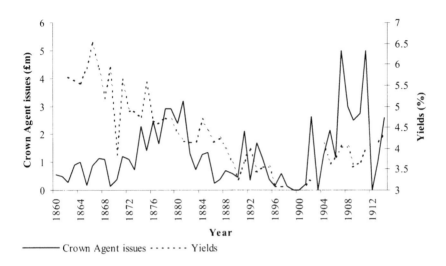

Source: GL and CAA, prospectuses.

for which often lagged behind supply (*see* table 26). Their loans were also relatively large and payment by instalment facilitated the collection of purchase money. In the second period, the greatest inducements were again associated with the loans of regular and large issuers, and with those of poorer, more debt-ridden colonies, whose stock was less well regarded by investors (*see* table 26).

Finally, most loan documents stipulated an interest charge on instalments paid in arrears, usually bank rate, to ensure that instalments were paid on time; and that those brokers and investors who paid for their purchases in full as opposed to in instalments obtained a discount on the amount paid. Discounts were first offered for the 1872 Cape loan, but were not universally adopted until the 1880s. They were slightly higher than those offered by the self-governing colonies, probably because crown colonies had a more urgent need for the proceeds of loans, due to their relative poverty and the tendency for capital to be raised only after infrastructure projects had been partly or wholly completed (*see* table 27). The number of purchasers who actually paid in full and obtained the discount varied. Of twenty-one loans issued between 1883 and 1892, whose applications were processed by the Bank of England, 43 per cent of the stock was paid for in full, the amount of each loan fully paid ranging from 9 per cent of the 1889 Western Australian loan to 80 per cent of that colony's 1864 issue.[71] The main determinants for immediate payment

[71] BE, C 16/1; C 16/2.

Table 28
Mean yields at issue, 1860–82 (%)

	Crown Agent clients	Crown Agent crown colony clients	Crown Agent responsible government clients	Responsible government colonies	Foreign governments	Consols
1860–70	5.77	5.72	5.86	5.99	–	3.26
1871–82	4.61	4.59	4.63	4.48	6.43	3.15
1860–82	5.04 (0.733)	5.05 (0.77)	5.03 (0.68)	4.88 (0.74)	6.43 (1.87)	3.2 (0.1)

Source and notes: For Crown Agent and responsible government colony yields see GL and CAA, prospectuses. Only the yields of loans for which price and interest rate are known were calculated. Yield = interest rate/price at issue (minimum or fixed price – accrued interest +/– free interest) x 100. For thirteen Crown Agent issues for which no loan proposal could be found yield = interest rate/minimum price or fixed price x 100.

For foreign government loans see Suzuki, *Japanese government loans issues*, 187–90. Yield = interest rate or fixed price x 100. The yields of seventy loans for twenty-nine governments were calculated.

For consols see Mitchell, *British historical statistics*, 678.

Standard deviations are given in parenthesis.

Table 29
Mean yields at issue, 1883–1912 (%)

	Crown colonies	Responsible government colonies	India	Foreign governments	Consols
1883–92	4.12	3.95	3.22	5.47	2.94
1893–1902	3.32	3.38	2.95	4.81	2.68
1903–12	3.85	3.66	3.45	5.0	2.97
1883–1912	3.78 (0.505)	3.65 (0.359)	3.22 (0.307)	5.14 (1.16)	2.86 (0.196)

Source and notes: For crown colony, responsible government colony and India yields see GL and CAA, prospectuses. Yield = Interest rate/price at issue (minimum or fixed price – accrued interest +/– 'free' interest) x 100. For the 1904 Sierra Leone, 1907 Straits, and 1908 and 1911 Southern Nigeria debenture loans, which were convertible to lower interest stock, the debenture yield has been calculated.

For foreign government loans see Suzuki, *Japanese government loans issues*, 190–6. Yield = interest rate / minimum or fixed price x 100. The yields of 178 loans of thirty-nine governments were calculated.

For consols see Mitchell, *British historical statistics*, 678.

Standard deviations are given in parenthesis.

appears to have been the discount, the free interest offered and the prevailing base rate. Brokers tended to opt for payment by instalment when the discount was low, free interest was available, interest rates were high and they wished to minimise the amount of capital borrowed at any one time.

If price, interest rate and accrued and free interest are combined, the yield or percentage return received by investors can be obtained. The average annual yields set by the Agents at the time of issue are again negatively related to flotations: high during periods when few loans were issued and there was little demand and *vice versa* (*see* fig. 12). During the whole period 1860–1914, they tended to be slightly higher than those of self-governing colonies floated by other issuing houses, rather than, as it would be reasonable to expect, much lower (*see* tables 28 and 29). Crown colony loans were arguably a less risky investment than their self-governing counterparts, and the Agents, if they had cared less about the dangers of undersubscription, could perhaps have offered the public lower yields. The investors assumed quite rightly that the Colonial Office would not allow crown colony governments to default on their debts, and the colonies, unlike responsible government colonies, never over-issued. On the other hand, that crown colony yields were below those of foreign government flotations and higher than those of Indian loans and consols, government consolidated stock, is less surprising. Foreign government issues involved considerable risk and the price carried a large premium to compensate for the greater possibility of default, whereas consols and Indian loans were regarded as completely safe and incorporated no risk premium. As with accrued and free interest, the higher yields were offered to poorer colonies and those that issued large quantities of securities (*see* table 26).

Underwriting and subscription

Underwriting

As some protection against undersubscription, the Agents' loans were informally underwritten, and, from the late 1890s, formally underwritten. Informal underwriting was a common practice in the City, though it was usually kept secret from the public who disapproved of the practice. Before a flotation, issuing houses recruited a group or syndicate of brokers who agreed to tender for a given proportion of a loan at the minimum price, or, in the case of fixed price issues, to purchase a certain amount of stock at a discounted price.[72] The Agents generally appear to have used only one underwriter, their own broker J. and A. Scrimgeours, who tendered for large blocks of debentures and stock at just above the minimum price (*see*

---

[72] Hall, *London capital market*, 77, 79; PP 1875, xi (367), qq. 137, 347, 352, 357, pp. xlvi, xlvii.

Table 30
Broker purchasers of loans with surviving allotment schedules, 1861–1906

Broker	Percentage of loans in which stock was bought	Percentage of loans in which broker was one of the three largest purchasers
J. and A. Scrimgeour	74	67
Linton Clarke	37	14
Sheppards Pelly	37	21
Mullens Marshall	21	14
Westgarths	21	14
W. P. Neville Horley	19	–
Ellis & Co.	19	12

Source: appendix 3, table 3.

appendix 3, table 3; table 30). The necessary finance appears to have come from Barings and the India Office, which lent companies on its surplus funds borrowers list a minimum of £50,000 between three and five, and occasionally, six weeks.[73] Between 1860 and 1891 Barings lent Scrimgeours, generally for between three and six months, almost £3m. in sums of up to £350,000.[74] In return the company paid bank rate interest and provided security, often unsold crown colony debentures and stock.[75] Similar sums were probably borrowed from the India Office too – between May 1912 and April 1914, the only period for which records survive, the firm obtained £1.05m. from this source.[76]

Despite its easy access to funds, Scrimgeours was unable to support all the loans issued, nor, in the case of large issues, to buy all the debentures and stock offered. It thus shared its underwriting duties with other brokers, particularly Linton Clarke and Sheppards Pelly. It was also unwilling to tender for flotations likely to prove unpopular, and, in the case of big issues, was often unable to garner sufficient underwriter applications for all the securities on sale. Consequently, from 1860 to 1882, 36.5 per cent of issues failed to be fully subscribed, and, from 1883 to 1914, 35 per cent went unsold. When this occurred, the Agents generally attempted to dispose of the unwanted securities to Scrimgeours and their fellow brokers immediately, though on at least two occasions balances were sold to financial institutions.[77] Depending on

---

73 PP 1914, xx (Cd 7071), 309.
74 Barings Brothers & Co., London, 101817, 101820, 101821.
75 See, for example, ibid. 101817.
76 India Office records, British Library, LAG 14/14/1, 131; LAG 14/14/2, 2.
77 CAs to CO, 30 Sept. 1865, CO 54/408/9548; CAs to CO, 7 July 1863, CO 167/455/6632; New Zealand to CAs, 2 Nov. 1864, CO 48/429/857. Credit Moblier bought the

the quantity of securities left unsold and the anticipated public demand, the debentures and stock were disposed off either at the minimum price, or at the minimum price plus an extra commission, or at a discount.[78] Occasionally, additional inducements had to be offered. In the case of the 1882 Natal 4 per cent loan, for example, the syndicate of eight brokers that agreed to buy £200,000 of the unsold balance at the minimum price of 94 obtained a loan from the Agents of £43,750, used partly to finance the purchase, and a pledge that the debentures would be converted to 4 per cent stock.[79] A similar arrangement was made with regard to the 1885 Jamaica 4 per cent loan. The Agents agreed to Scrimgeours' proposal that they and Westgarth purchase the debentures at the minimum price and in delayed instalments, and, in return, the brokers obtained a promise that the bonds would be converted free-of-charge to 4 per cent stock, and that holders of the colony's previous 4 per cent debenture loans would be given an option of conversion and would pay only half the associated stamp duty.[80] Where they found it impossible to organise a rescue operation or when the proceeds of the unsold securities were not urgently needed by the issuing colony, the Agents, through Scrimgeours, sold the debentures or stock privately over an extended period of time. The 1883 Ceylon loan was disposed of over seven months, brokers buying additional blocks of stock once they had passed their original purchases on to the public.[81] The Agents also occasionally purchased some of the unwanted stock themselves, sought sales in the issuing colony and, at least on one occasion, readvertised the issue.[82] If all else failed, the stock was withdrawn from the market and added to a later issue.[83]

For Scrimgeours, informal underwriting had a number of advantages. Its position as the Agents' brokers increased its reputation in the City and encouraged colonial banks and companies to make use of its services. Unlike most brokers, the firm was also assured of a regular income.[84] For each deben-

---

£960,000 balance of the New Zealand 1864 £1m. loan and the Bank of England acquired the whole of that colony's 1873 £200,000 issue.
[78] Purchasers of the unsold balances of the New Zealand 1874 £1.5m. and £500,000 loans bought at the minimum price plus extra commissions of respectively 1% and ½%. Credit Moblier obtained a discount of 10%.
[79] CAs to Natal, 30 Nov. 1882, CAOG 9/10; memo, 16 Dec. 1882, ibid; Sargeaunt to Blake, 14 Dec. 1882, ibid. The syndicate, in addition, agreed to consider the acquisition of the remaining £230,000 of debentures at 94, but eventually decided against this, despite the Agents reducing the price to 92.25 and then to 90.25: CAs to Scrimgeour, 21 Mar. 1883, ibid; CAs to Natal, 19 Apr. 1883, ibid.
[80] CAs to Jamaica, 27 Jan. 1885, CAOG 9/7; Sargeaunt to Scrimgeour, 25 Jan. 1885, ibid.
[81] Schedule, 31 Aug. 1867, CO 54/429/8596.
[82] CAs to CO, 30 Sept. 1865, CO 54/408/9548; CAs to Jamaica, 27 Jan. 1885, CAOG 9/7; CAs to Mauritius, 8 Mar. 1865, CO 167/483/2243.
[83] For instance, the remaining £230,000 of the 1882 Natal loan was added to the colony's 1884 issue.
[84] At no point between 1870 and 1914 did the firm make a loss: Scrimgeour papers (c/o Alexander Scrimgeur, Thorncombe House, Bramley, Surrey), profit figures. On the other

ture or stock it purchased from the Agents, it obtained a brokerage commission of ¼ per cent from the issuing colony, a selling commission of ¼ per cent from its clients and the premium on the securities sold.[85] Moreover, it possessed a strong relationship of trust with the Agents, the result of shared social backgrounds, many family and personal connections, constant and face-to-face contact over a long period of time (see appendix 1, table 5). The firm could thus be confident that, through the medium of setting minimum or fixed prices and the rigging of the market, the Agents would ensure that it prospered from its underwriting activities, any losses would be offset by later gains and favours would be reciprocated.

Scrimgeours's support for loans was similarly advantageous to the Crown Agents. If a tender loan failed to attract sufficient subscribers, informal underwriting created the illusion that it had been a success. After the 1892 £100,000 Trinidad issue, for example, the Agents informed the press that the loan had attracted £193,500-worth of subscriptions, failing to mention that £120,000-worth of applications had come from their own broker.[86] The Agency could thus issue future loans on similar terms and Scrimgeours could offload its purchases on to the public at a reasonable price and in a short period. The use of Scrimgeours also reduced the likelihood that loans would fail. The firm's trust relationship with the Agents meant that it could be relied upon to support a large proportion of colonial loans. If an issue failed, its membership of other syndicates and its strong family and professional connections with the City allowed it to organise a rescue operation easily (see appendix 1, table 6).[87] And, operating according to the social norms of the middle rank of brokers, of which it was a member, it was willing to resort to deals during rescues that its more elite counterparts would not consider.[88]

---

hand Foster and Braithwaite, a similar-sized firm, made no profits in 1903, between 1906 and 1907 and between 1913 and 1914, while Sheppards Pelly Scott & Co. made no profit in 1893: David Kynaston, 'The London Stock Exchange, 1870–1914: an institutional history', unpubl. PhD diss. London 1983, 118. On their deaths in 1937 and 1955 respectively, the partners Walter Scrimgeour and Harry Blunt left £205,586 and £112,000: SH, probate records.

[85] W. G. Cordingley, Cordingley's guide to the Stock Exchange, London 1893, 20.

[86] Schedule, 7 June 1892, CAOG 9/8. See also schedule, 7 Apr. 1892, CAOG 9/18; CAs to Western Australia, 26 July 1889, CAOG 9/21; press release, 23 July 1889, ibid.

[87] New Zealand parliamentary debates, xxxii. 377. The firm, for example, applied for stock in both the 1859 and the 1862 Victoria loans and led the syndicate that supported the 1872 Japanese loan: GL, loan and company prospectuses, press clippings; Suzuki, Japanese government loan issues, 62.

[88] Occasionally the firm's activities bordered on the illegal. In 1860 it was suspended from the Stock Exchange for nine months when it was discovered that it had broken Exchange rules and bought stock on behalf of a clerk. The clerk in question was the chief cashier of the Union Bank of London, who had paid for his purchases with part of the £263,070 he had embezzled from the bank: NWB, Union Bank report, 11 July 1860, 2. Six years later the firm acted as broker to Charles Lafitte & Co., which fraudulently passed itself off as the subsidiary of the Parisian bankers, Lafitte & Co.: PP 1878, xix, qq. 6602, 6597. Some time

Formal underwriting involved an issuing house entering into a legal contract with brokers whereby they agreed to buy all of the unpurchased stock of a particular loan at a given price in return for a commission. The formal underwriting of crown colony loans began in 1901, although the first issue underwritten was the 1892 Grenada loan, £14,450 of which was required for debt repayment.[89] By 1900 underwriting was universal in the City, as informal support arrangements broke down at times of financial crisis and brokers wished for guaranteed remuneration for their activities. The Agents initially opposed the practice, which increased costs and further discouraged subscription by a public that preferred to buy during the post-issue discount period.[90] Since underwriters purchased unsold stock after the issue rather than entering tenders, underwriting also revealed the low demand for crown colony loans, which further reduced the colonies' credit-worthiness. Attempts to hide low subscriptions, through announce-ments that loans had been 'fully covered', were defeated by the press, which took delight in revealing the subterfuge.[91]

The Agents, nevertheless, had little option but to accept formal under-writing eventually, as 'the Stock Exchange have it in their power to kill any loan by leaving it severely alone'.[92] The only alternative was for the Agents to underwrite crown colony loans themselves using colonial investment funds. This mechanism was rejected by the Agency. The fact that self-under-writing could result in a profit without the allocation of stock meant that most loan ordinances precluded the use of sinking fund contributions for this purpose.[93] The Agents usually lacked sufficient fund contributions to under-write a whole loan, regarded the practice as speculative and believed that the support of some loans would only increase the cost of normal underwriting, as underwriters would suspect that they only covered popular issues.[94] They also feared that the purchase of a loan by its issuer would contravene Stock Exchange regulations and preclude quotation.

Underwriting was again arranged by J. and A. Scrimgeours, for which they were paid a fee of ¼ per cent, the same as that received by Indian railway

later Panmure Gordon, a Scrimgeour partner, was broker to a fraudulent Lisbon tramway venture, insisting, when the scheme was revealed as a sham, that 'the swindle must proceed' to avoid the loss of his and other brokers' commission: Kynaston, *The City of London: a world of its own*, 279–80.

[89] CAs to colonial secretary, 19 May 1892, CO 321/144/10204.

[90] CAs to Ceylon, 24 Jan. 1902, CAOG 9/4; CAs to Lagos, 3 Mar. 1905, CO 147/177/6936.

[91] In the case of the 1906 Hong Kong issue, for example, *The Times* commented that the statement that the loan was 'fully covered' was 'of course not inconsistent with the fact that the underwriters have taken 70%': *The Times*, 21 Feb. 1906, in CO 129/336/6544. See also *Daily Graphic*, 23 Feb. 1906, ibid.

[92] Blake to Hong Kong, 23 Feb. 1906, CAOG 9/29. Only India Office sterling loans were not underwritten: PPE, q. 713.

[93] Memo, 27 June 1922, CAOG 9/101.

[94] CAs to CO, 20 July 1911, CO 273/376/23857.

brokers.[95] The actual underwriters obtained 1 per cent, the market average, though for the 1902 Gold Coast and Ceylon loans commissions of respectively 1¼ per cent and 1½ per cent were paid.[96] In addition, if a loan were fully subscribed and the underwriters required a portion of the stock, the amount underwritten would occasionally be added to the amount publicly subscribed and the stock distributed *pro rata*.[97] A large number of the loans were underwritten by Scrimgeours, who continued to charge their 'arrangement' fee.[98] Moreover, the firm claimed commission on the whole of the loan, even when the Agents reserved a portion of the stock for themselves, arguing that this was a recognised custom of the City.[99] Other underwriters used include the Bank of British West Africa, which underwrote many West African loans, and the London and Westminster Bank, which covered at least six issues.[100] In addition, in 1906 and 1907 the Agents directed Scrimgeours to offer a portion of underwriting the Hong Kong and Straits loans respectively to certain local trading companies and banks in order to 'enlist their sympathies'.[101] Unfortunately for the Agents, this initiative proved a failure. The Bank of India, Australia and China asked for their allotment of Hong Kong securities to be taken off their hands.[102] In the case of the Straits loan, meanwhile, the Hong Kong and Shanghai Bank informed the Straits governor that it believed that the price of the loan had been set excessively low, and another underwriter was suspected of beginning a rumour that the loan would be a failure.[103] Thereafter the Agents left the choice of underwriters to Scrimgeours.

95 PPE, q. 719.
96 F. Lavington, *The English capital market*, London 1929, 197; CAs to Gold Coast, Mar. 1902, CAOG 9/86; CAs to Ceylon, 24 Jan. 1902, CAOG 9/4. Foreign governments paid far more. In 1904 and 1905, for example, Japan paid commissions of 3½% and 2½% respectively: Suzuki, *Japanese government loan issues*, 19.
97 CAA, CCC, memorandum, 34.
98 The firm, for example, purchased 92% and 88% respectively of the 1905 and 1906 Mauritius and Hong Kong loans.
99 Antrobus to CO, 9 Mar. 1914, CAOG 9/105; CAs to Blunt, 13 May 1907, CAOG 9/80.
100 Couper to Scrimgeours, 14 May 1909, CAOG 9/76. The London and Westminster Bank underwrote £50,000 of the 1907 Straits loan, the 1908 Southern Nigerian loan, the 1910 Straits loan and the 1911 Southern Nigerian loan, and £25,000 of the 1909 Gold Coast and Ceylon loans; NWB, 12914/339; 12915/94; 12915/208; 12915/270; 12916/182, 12916/33.
101 CAs to colonial secretary, 3 May 1907, CO 273/332/16226; Blake to Nathan, 23 Feb. 1906, CAOG 9/25. The Agents may have had more personal motives for encouraging the use of these firms. John Finlayson, the head of Messrs E. Boustead, was 'a great friend' of the CA Sir Maurice Cameron; Sir George Murray, the manager of the Mercantile Bank of India, was another friend; and Thomas Shelford, the managing director of Messrs Patersons Simons & Co., was the uncle of Frederick Shelford, Sir Montague Ommanney's son-in-law, and another of Cameron's friends: Cameron memoirs, 88, 89.
102 CAs to CO, 2 Apr. 1906, CO 273/322/11688.
103 CAs to colonial secretary, 3 May 1907, CO 273/332/16226; CAs to Hong Kong & Shanghai Bank, 18 Apr. 1907, ibid.

Subscription

The number of applications for debentures and stock was generally small, averaging in the case of loans for which details are available, ninety-five per issue in the period 1860–82 and 175 per issue in 1883–1914, as compared to 675 per issue for the period 1883–1914 for the slightly larger loans floated by the London and Westminster Bank for the self-governing colonies. The number of applications that were allocated debentures or stock was even lower, averaging twenty-two per loan for the issues floated between 1860 and 1880 for which allotment schedules survive, and sixty-two for the loans with allotment schedules issued from 1880 to 1914 (*see* appendix 3, table 3).[104] Partly as a result of informal and formal underwriting, the bulk of securities were bought by stockbrokers. Few banks or other financial institutions made purchases. Of those that did the largest buyers were the Bank of England and the London and Westminster Bank which acquired debentures and stock, often whole loans, at relatively high prices for their official reserves (*see* table 31).[105] As regards loans for which allotment schedules survive, only eight other banks and eight insurance companies bought securities. Demand from non-financial institutions, and from the Crown Agents, at least prior to 1900, was even smaller.[106] Only two organisations, the Transvaal & Estate Development Co. and the Post Office Employers Association bought securities in the surviving schedule issues and, between 1860 and 1900, the Agents made only four successful applications for securities.[107]

Public subscription was similarly poor and involved the purchase of relatively small amounts of debentures and stock. Most private investors preferred to buy securities after an issue was over, as the tendering process was complex, required a decision to invest to be made relatively rapidly and, for those with little knowledge of market prices, carried a high level of risk. Applications could fail to receive an allocation of securities, or could discover they they had bought debentures or stock at excessive prices. According to Sir Ernest Blake, a large proportion of public applicants were 'small people and clerks, . . . who form the fringe of the Stock Exchange and City business'.[108] These generally 'stagged' the loans, making a large number of

---

[104] In many cases applicants made more than one successful application.
[105] The Agents believed that if the Bank of England had not taken the 1881 Trinidad loan, which it bought at 101.75, the average price would have been only 100.17: CAs to CO, 14 July 1881, CO 295/292/12578. The bank's price, 101.05, for the 1882 Trinidad issue was thought to be 'very satisfactory': CAs to CO, 4 May 1882, CO 295/295/8016.
[106] Acquisitions by the CAs after 1900 are discussed in chapter 8 below.
[107] In 1865 the Office obtained £19,100 of the Ceylon £100,000 loan, £112,000 of the 1865 £300,000 Mauritius issue, £42,000 of the 1888 Mauritius £209,800 loan and £6,600 of the 1883 Ceylon £491,000 loan: schedule, 30 Sept. 1865, CO 54/408/9848; schedule, 8 Mar. 1865, CO 167/483/2243; schedule, CAOG 9/9; note, Nov. 1883, CAOG 9/3.
[108] Blake to Hong Kong, 23 Feb. 1906, CAOG 9/25.

Table 31
Purchases at issue by the London and Westminster Bank
and Bank of England, 1860–1900

Year	Loan/size (£)	Bank	Amount purchased (£)
1870	Jamaica, 367,600	Bank of England	20,000
1876	Ceylon, 100,000	Bank of England	100,000
	Cape, 650,000	Bank of England	250,000
1880	Ceylon, 700,000	London and Westminster	99,900
1881	Ceylon , 575,000	London and Westminster	319,900
	Ceylon , 575,000	Bank of England	100,000
	Trinidad, 100,000	Bank of England	100,000
1882	Trinidad, 100,000	Bank of England	100,000
	Jamaica, 509,000	Bank of England	300,000
1894	Ceylon, 500,000	Bank of England	125,000
1905	Lagos, 2m.	Bank of England	150,000
1908	Southern Nigeria, 5m.	Bank of England	500,000
1911	Southern Nigeria, 5m.	Bank of England	250,000

Source: NWB,12908/441; 12909/117; NAN, NT 164/5529/1893; NT 164/1824/1884; BE, ADM 7/48/791; 7/48/797; 7/48/895; 7/52/1071; 7/52/1074; 7/52/1075; 7/54/914; 7/5/56/1228; 7/58/1216; 7/58/1234; CAOG 9/77; 9/10; 9/4.

applications and selling any allotments immediately for the premium.[109] Amongst their number were members of the staff of the Crown Agents and Scrimgeours, who generally purchased £100 blocks of stock, and, in modern-day parlance, were insider trading, using their private knowledge of bids to make applications for debentures or stock at the lowest price at which the securities would be allocated. Louis Adams, the Agency's chief cashier, took part in at least four flotations; E. G. Antrobus, chief clerk and accountant, and Samuel Stephens, assistant head of shipping, each participated in at least two, and William Hodgson, head of the correspondence branch, and Horace Martin, head of appointments, in one.[110] There were no office rules preventing such purchases, which had little impact on the size of colonial proceeds from loans, and, by increasing the cost of dismissal, helped to ensure good performance and honesty.

At first, brokers largely sold their allotments to London-based banks and other financial institutions seeking secure investments. In 1864, for example,

[109] William Chapman and Albert Gearing, for example, obtained allotments in six loans and a Miss Anne Gilbert received allotments in three issues.
[110] WASA, ACC 527/1326, 2834; NAN, NT 164/1824; CAOG 9/120, 9/4, 9/7, 9/65, 9/11. Curtis Francis and Alexander Thomson, clerks at Scrimgeours, invested in two loans each: ibid; CAOG 9/14, 9/10; NAN, NT 164/1824. W. P. Wrinkley, the Agents' shipping agent, invested in at least one issue: schedule, 30 June 1863, CO 167/955/8111.

Table 32
Large bank holdings of three 1860s loans

Ceylon 1861 £100,000		Ceylon 1863 £250,000		Mauritius 1862 £200,000	
Bank	% of stock held	Bank	% of stock held	Bank	% of stock held
Samuel & Montagu	26.5	Union Bank of London	16	London Joint Stock Bank	14.6
William Deacon Labouchere Thornton & Co.	25.7	Messrs Drummond	10	Union Bank of London	14.05
Oriental Bank	15.2	Agro & Masterman's Bank	10	Bank of London	6.35

Source: CAs to CO, 19 Jan.1865, CO 54/408/675; schedule, 30 June 1863, CO 167/455/8111.

90 per cent of the debentures of the Ceylon 1861 £100,000 loan and 68 per cent of the colony's 1863 £250,000 issues were held by seventeen and twenty-three banks respectively (*see* table 32).[111] As already discussed, Crown Agent, Bank of England and London and Westminster Bank purchases were specifically undertaken to raise the quoted price of securities before and after issue. The public began to buy from brokers in large numbers from the 1880s. Most of the investors were males living in London or the home counties, and either *rentiers*, dependent on investment returns for their incomes, or members of the professions, beneficiaries of the relatively rapid growth in middle-class salaries. Of those who purchased the British Guiana (Demerera Railways) 4 per cent loan, for instance, 10 per cent were gentlemen and almost a quarter employed in the armed forces, medicine, the law, the Church and finance (*see* table 33). Some, again, had connections with the Crown Agents. The Agency's shipping agent, Freelands, bought at least £2,000-worth of Cape 4.5 per cent and New Zealand 6 per cent bonds, its Birmingham agent purchased £1,000-worth of the 1883 Fiji loan, and the Crown Agent Sir Penrose Julyan acquired £1,000-worth of the Mauritius 1863 issue.[112]

The main attraction of crown colony stock appears to have been its relative safety. It was thought unlikely that the imperial government would allow colonial administrations to default on the payments of dividends or capital as

[111] CAs to CO, 19 Jan. 1865, CO 54/408/675. In the case of the Mauritius 1862 £200,000 loan 83% of the stock was held by 26 banks: schedule, 30 June 1863, CO 167/455/8111.
[112] BE, C 62/10/70; C 58/1/277; schedule, CO 83/28/7032; schedule, CO 167/455/8111.

Table 33
Retail purchasers of British Guiana (Demerara railway) 4 per cent stock

Characteristics		Percentage of holders
Sex	Male	72
	Female	28
Place of abode	London, south-east and Midlands	83
	North, Scotland and Ireland	15.5
	Overseas	1.5
Occupation	None given	31
	Spinster	13
	Gentleman	10
	Law and Church	9
	Widow	8
	Married women	7
	Finance and medical	7
	Armed Forces	6.5
	Miscellaneous	8.5

Source: CAA, British Guiana (Demerara Railway) 4% loan stock register.

this would destroy the Agents' ability to raise further loans and damage the legitimacy of the empire. The Agents also ensured that yields were competitive and the loans were attractive to investors. The market price of the securities, furthermore, was relatively free from fluctuations or 'shocks'. Colonies were secure from external and internal aggression, largely due to the might of the British army and navy, and the high ethical standard of colonial administration made it unlikely that loan proceeds would be subject to fraud. There was also perhaps a patriotic element. Thanks to the Crown Agents, the materials used in the construction of the public works financed by issues were purchased in the United Kingdom and the completed infrastructure ultimately increased British exports and reduced the cost of primary imports.

Broker moral hazard

Unfortunately for the colonies, the quoted prices of crown colony loans could be rigged by brokers as well as by the Agents. Brokers rigged the market by holding back a proportion of their purchases of a particular colony's debentures or stock until a further issue was imminent. Their holdings were then dumped on to the market, forcing the quoted price of the securities to fall and the issuing house to set a low minimum or fixed price for the new loan. The broker then purchased large amounts of the new debentures or stock and rigged the price of both the old and new securities upwards through further purchases. The resultant price rise stimulated public purchase and caused the price to increase even further, at which point the brokers sold both their issue and post-issue purchases at a profit.[113] Rigging took place for two reasons. Some brokers simply wished to make excess profits. Others however merely wanted to avoid losses and only rigged when a colony, after issuing a loan, floated another one before brokers had sold their purchases of the first issue on to the public. If this occurred, they would have to hold these purchases and pay the interest on the money borrowed to finance them for a longer period than originally envisaged. Moreover, the new issues would cause the quoted price of the securities to fall, reducing their expected premium. They consequently rigged the new loan, using the profits to offset the losses that would result from its flotation.

The rigging of loans was common practice in the City and both the Agents and Scrimgeours were aware of the 'opportunities for plunder'.[114] Indeed, Scrimgeours itself had occasionally taken part in rigging. The Cape agent-general believed that, together with Barings, the colony's issuing house, Scrimgours rigged its 1882 loan. In the weeks leading up to the issue, the market price of Cape securities mysteriously fell and the debentures were floated at a relatively low price of 94.[115] That Scrimgeours and Barings attempted to rig the colony's next loan, there can be little doubt; both sold a total of £2m. of the new securities at very low prices on the issue's 'grey' market. Fortunately for the colony, their machinations became known to the issuing house, the London and Westminster Bank, which set the price at a relatively high 98, and, with the help of other City institutions, successfully defeated the rig.[116]

---

[113] A. Porter, 'Britain, the Cape Colony and Natal, 1870–1915: capital, shipping and the imperial connection', *Economic History Review* xxxiiii (1981), 562–3; A. J. Purkis, 'The politics, capital and labour of railway building in the Cape Colony, 1870–85', unpubl. DPhil. diss. Oxford 1978, 293. A second, more complex and less used rig involved brokers forcing an issuing house to set a low price for a loan through the manipulation of the issue's 'grey market'. Brokers who wished to rig a loan before the prospectus was released, sold future purchases in the grey market at a low price. This caused the grey market price to fall, which forced the issuing house to set a low minimum fixed price and reduced demand for the securities. During the flotation, large blocks of the new loan were purchased, some of which were used to fulfil 'grey' market sales agreements. Then, after the issue, further purchases were made, causing prices to rise, demand to be stimulated and further price increases to occur, at which point the broker's holdings were sold at a profit.
[114] CAs to CO, 20 Mar. 1908, CAOG 9/94. See also CAs to CO, 11 Feb. 1908, CO 520/69/5174.
[115] Porter, 'Britain, the Cape Colony and Natal', 562–3.
[116] The bank employed the former CA Sir Penrose Julyan and the Standard Bank of South Africa to use their influence to persuade City institutions to buy the debentures: Julyan to Mills, 3 Nov. 1883, NWB, 1597; account, 19 Jan. 1884, ibid; Scanlon to Mills, 5 Jan. 1884, ibid. The result of their efforts was that the loan was fully subscribed and Barings and Scrimgeours were forced to 'pay dearly to obtain . . . [securities] to exercise their engagements' in the grey market: Mills to Cape, 24 Dec. 1883, ibid.

Given their small size, their solid reputation among investors, who con-tinued to make purchases even if the price occasionally dipped, and the Agents' efforts to restrict the supply of securities to the market, crown colony loans were particularly susceptible to broker moral hazard. Rigging for profit was partly avoided by the Agents' underwriting practices: large portions of loans were bought by Scrimgeours and a small number of other brokers, who sold their purchases on to genuine investors and the Crown Agents. Potential riggers thus had little opportunity to acquire large blocks of securities. At the same time Scrimgeours, along with Mullens, the Bank of England and the London and Westminster Bank, no doubt used its City connections to monitor the activities of the broking community, informing the Agents when a rig was planned. Informal underwriting, however, merely passed the oppor-tunity for rigging on to Scrimgeours and its syndicate. As has been seen, the firm was not immune from temptation, and would have found the rigging of crown colony loans relatively simple.

In fact, little rigging appears to have occurred. In the case of the ninety-one issues that added to an existing line of securities over the period, the quoted price of the existing debentures or stock of only five fell in the week before their flotation announcement.[117] There were also suspicions that an unsuccessful attempt had been made to rig the 1867 Ceylon loan, and in 1882 the Agents were forced to postpone a Natal issue for five months when the quoted price suddenly fell in the week before the original flotation date.[118] The relative absence of moral hazard can be attributed to a number of factors. The Agents' strong bonds with Scrimgeours discouraged rigging for profit. Rigs to avoid losses, meanwhile, were made unnecessary by the Agents' determination to avoid the issue of debentures and stock before previously floated securities had been sold on to the public. Colonial and Colonial Office proposals to issue by instalment were strongly opposed, and colonies that had recently issued but required further funds were given temporary loans from other colonies or banks.[119] Scrimgeours was also no doubt aware that the Agents monitored its activities closely through their strong family and social links with the City (see appendix 1, table 5), and that the long-term cost of any rigging that was discovered would offset any short-term gains from it. If any manipulation of the market were uncovered, the firm would almost certainly have been dismissed and would thus have lost the income earned from the underwriting and stagging of loans and the other services it performed for the Agency. Indeed, the loss of the Agents' business could even threaten the firm's survival. According to Sir George Aylwen, a

---

[117] None of the falls were accompanied by declines in other CA issued stock. The loans rigged were the 1865 £300,000 Mauritius issue, the £300,000 Cape issue, the 1880 £535,000 Cape issue, the 1909 £1.5m. Ceylon issue and the 1910 £2.75m. Straits issue.
[118] CAs to Ceylon, 13 Dec. 1867, CO 54/429/11968; Natal to CAs, 26 June 1882, CAOG 9/10.
[119] CAs to CO, 31 Mar. 1908, CAOG 9/94.

Figure 13. J. and A. Scrimgeour profits, 1870–1914

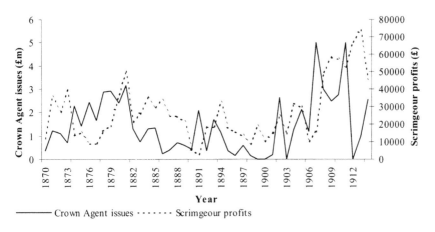

Source: GL and CAA, prospectuses; Scrimgeour papers, profit figures

partner, 'no great effort was made . . . to collect business', and the company's profits appear to have largely been derived from its sales of Crown Agent stock (*see* fig. 13).[120]

In issuing loans, the Crown Agents met both their own and their principals' interests. The issue of securities in an attractive form, the setting of relatively low minimum or fixed prices and the provision of high yields, and the arrangement of informal and formal underwriting ensured that most debentures and stock were eventually sold. The colonies thus obtained the capital required for infrastructure projects, and the Agents maximised their finance and purchase commissions. The relatively high cost of the issues was regarded by the colonies as unimportant. Governors cared only about subscription, and, as will be seen in chapter 8, only began to criticise the Agents when loans began to fail.

If they were to serve their own and their principals' interests, the Crown Agents had to act duplicitly towards the public, who to some extent were as much their principals as the colonies. Prices were rigged both before and after issue, and, until 1900, loans were informally underwritten. But again neither the colonies, the Agents, nor the Colonial Office were concerned about such practice. The public was unaware of the Agents' activities, as indeed were the colonies, and, even if this had not been the case, any public complaint would have been far less damaging to the Agency than colonial criticism resulting from the failure of loans. In the event, somewhat ironically, the investing public appears to have gradually developed a strong trust in the

---

[120] Reminiscences of Sir George Aylwen, Scrimgeour papers.

Agents. Investors began to place their savings in Crown Agent rather than crown colony loans, permitting colonies with little or no credit of their own to make issues at prices far higher than would otherwise have been possible.

It was also in the interests of both the Agency and the colonies for which it acted that the Agents were integrated into the City's network of trust relationships. These developed out of shared backgrounds, prolonged and face-to-face contact, long relationships, and, most important, self-interest. By supporting crown colony loans through market purchases, the Bank of England and the London and Westminster Bank ensured that the Agents would reciprocate and, in the case of post-issue purchases, increased the probable success of their own forthcoming loans. The Agents would also be more likely to co-operate in the timing of issues, important as both crown colony and self-governing colony securities appealed to the same investors, and continue to lodge colonial government funds in current accounts with the Bank of England, which paid no interest. The Agents' relationship with Scrimgeours was merely an extension of this trust network. They made sure that the firm benefited from the relationship, and, in return, Scrimgeours supported poor quality loans and acted honestly.

7

The External Finance Safety Net:
Monitoring the Crown Agents

In the provision of external finance to colonies, the Agents walked a dangerous path beset on either side by a range of expenses and unforeseen events that could damage both their own and colonial prosperity. The failure of a loan, its sale at too low a price, escalation in the cost of infrastructure construction or sudden trade depressions could all lead to a shortfall of funds. Money might be needed to finance very small infrastructure projects, to meet the expenses of an issue or to repay previous loans. Exchange rate movements, meanwhile, could make the transfer of funds to the United Kingdom overly expensive. With no access to imperial finance, the Agents met these contingencies with a safety net of stratagems and alternative sources of funds that included private issues, loan conversions, overdrafts and advances, and bank and local loans (*see* table 34). The first part of this chapter examines the operation of each of these stratagems in turn.

For the colonies, the provision of loans and other such services incorporated a danger of Agent dishonesty. Neither the colonies nor the Colonial Office had much knowledge of the intricacies of the financial world and the Agents could easily have acted fraudulently. On a number of occasions the Agency was also accused of charging excessive fees. The second part of this chapter considers the procedures adopted to monitor the Agency and their effectiveness, and compares charges levied by the Crown Agents with those set by the Bank of England.

The placing and conversion of loans

The placing of loans involved the direct sale of debentures or stock to individuals and institutions without the benefit of a public issue. Between 1860 and 1914 the Crown Agents placed sixty-two loans worth £1.66m., and with an average size of £19,985 up to 1882 and £20,394 between 1883 and 1914. Some of the securities placed were unsold debentures or stock of previous public issues. Others were sold to raise funds to finance small infrastructure projects, repay previous loans, or to meet public issue and conversion expenses. The Crown Agents were generally reluctant to use placing. They received no issue commission, the prices obtained were relatively low and debenture and stock were generally bought by a small number of investors, increasing the likelihood of market manipulation and limiting dealings in the

Table 34
Sources of external finance other than public loan, 1880–1914

Source	Amount (£ million)
Colonial current account/fund advances	approx. 33
Loan conversions	22.4
Bank advances	15.6
Treasury loans	1.5
Placed loans	1.7

Source: See appendix 3, tables 4–7; CO 323 correspondence.

Notes: The total for colonial current account and fund advances was calculated from figures in colonial Blue Books, CA correspondence and the surviving monthly overdraft and advance schedules, and is almost certainly a gross underestimate. Conversion total includes amounts converted, and, where this was not given, the amount available for conversion. For some conversions, neither figure has survived.

securities and subsequent market price rises.[1] They relented when the size of the sum to be raised failed to justify the cost of public flotation, the poor state of the market made a successful issue unlikely, or they wished to avoid further depreciation of a colony's credit.[2] Knowledge of the placing of unquoted stock was likely to be restricted to the buyers, and the public, unaware of the increase in the colony's debts, would thus retain their confidence that it could meet repayments. The debentures and stock were generally sold by Scrimgeours, though the two 1903 Mauritius loans were disposed off by the Agents themselves.[3] In return, the firm obtained its usual brokerage fee, unlike the Bank of England's brokers, who received half their usual commission.[4] The firm either approached potential investors directly or through an advertisement in *The Times*, and were either given a minimum price by the Agents, asked to discover the price potential investors were prepared to pay, or allowed to sell the stock at the best price available.[5] Purchasers appear to have been investors rather than brokers, and included the Bank of England, the Economic Life Assurance Co., the Agents themselves (who bought £9,000 of the 1896 St Lucia loan) and private firms with an interest in the issuing colony.[6] In addition, on at least two occasions, stock was purchased by

[1] CAs to Mauritius, 26 Jan. 1861, CO 54/364/3077.
[2] CAs to Scrimgeours, 2 July 1890, CAOG 9/5; CAs to CO, 21 July 1883, CO 179/149/12426.
[3] CAs to colonial secretary, 20 Mar. 1903, CO 167/764/11471.
[4] BE to Transvaal, 31 Mar. 1910, BE, AC 30/290; Scrimgeours to CAs, 2 Aug. 1889, CAOG 9/6.
[5] CAs to Scrimgeours, 30 July 1889, CAOG 9/6; CAs to Scrimgeours, 13 Feb. 1896, CAOG 9/64.
[6] CAs to CO, 26 Feb. 1896, CO 321/168/4311; Scrimgeours to CAs, 3 Apr. 1895, CAOG 9/62; BE, ADM 7/52.

Table 35
Issued yields of placed crown colony loans, 1860–1912 (%)

	Mean yield
1860–70	6.6
1871–82	5.3
1860–82	6
1883–92	3.91
1893–1902	3.66
1903–12	3.89
1883–1912	3.79 (0.506)

Source: CAOG 9; CO 323 files.

Notes: Yield = interest rate/price x 100. Standard deviation is given in parenthesis. The 1903–12 yield represents just four loans.

Table 36
Mean issue premiums of placed crown colony loans (%)

	Mean premium (%)
1883–92	0.51
1893–1902	1.04
1903–12	3
1883–1912	0.827 (0.68)

Source: *Daily list*, 1883–1912.

Notes: Premium = Listed price on day of issue – fixed price. The standard deviation is given in parenthesis. The 1903–12 premium represents just one loan.

relatives of the Crown Agents. A cousin of Sir Montague Ommanney bought, 'on the recommendation of . . . Sir Montague', £2,000-worth of the 1892 St Kitts and 1894 Montserrat loans, and, in 1932, £400-worth of the Montserrat stock was held by Miss E. M. and Miss A. J. Blyth, cousins of the wife of Sir Ernest Blake, and in the case of Miss E. M. Blyth a Crown Agent clerk.[7]

The yields of placed loans were similar to those of public issues (*see* table 35), and, as brokers did not have to be compensated for holding the stock until its sale to ordinary investors, the mean premium was half that of public loans (*see* table 36). Often there was little demand for the issues, owing to their small size and, in some cases, short lifespans and unquoted status, a depressed market or the poor state of the issuing colony's finances. In 1897

---

[7] Metcalfe to CAs, 18 Apr. 1915, CAOG 9/56; CAs to Metcalfe, 20 Apr. 1915, ibid; schedule, 8 Oct. 1932, ibid; *Colonial Office list*, 1895–1910.

the Agents also pointed out that the tendency of some colonies to name such loans Treasury debentures, which suggested that they were analogous to Treasury bills, short-term securities, also affected their marketability.[8] Occasionally, demand was so poor that the loans had to be sold in small blocks, and Scrimgeours had great difficulty disposing of stock. For example, in 1892 the company was unable to find any buyer for the £23,500 St Kitts loan, forcing the Agents to reduce the price, and, in 1887/8, the firm took more than seven months to dispose of £25,000 of Grenada stock.[9] At times the Agents expressed disappointment at the prices obtained, and sometimes had reason to doubt Scrimgeours' honesty. In the case of the 1894 Bahamas 4 per cent loan, for instance, the company claimed that it had sold £10,000 of bonds at 103.5, because only one investor was willing to purchase.[10] In fact, the Agents had been informed by the London and Westminster Bank on the day of the sale that 'friends in Nassau' were keen to take up the debentures, an offer that Scrimgeours, for its own reasons, perhaps deliberately ignored.[11] Generally, however, the company appears to have made great efforts to obtain the best price available and thus maximise its own commission. In 1896, for example, the firm postponed the sale of Trinidad stock until after the stagnant Christmas period and in January 1897 informed the Agents that they had rejected a 114 offer for the stock and were 'holding out for more', as it was 'worth a better price'.[12]

Both publicly and privately issued loans, as well as those raised in the colonies, could be converted. Conversion involved the exchange, with the investors' permission, of existing debentures or stock, generally with less than half of its lifespan yet to run, for new debentures or stock identical to securities recently issued and with a full lifespan of fifty or sixty years.[13] During the period 1872–1914 fifty-nine loans were converted in 117 operations (see appendix 3, table 4). Between 1868 and 1882 the conversions largely involved the exchange of existing debentures for new debentures which paid a lower interest rate. Thereafter, debentures were generally swapped for stock paying the same or lower dividends (see table 37). The first stage in the conversion process was for the Agents and Scrimgeours to decide whether a loan should be converted. Conversion was particularly likely to go ahead when interest rates were low, capital abundant and investors unlikely to be resistant to an exchange of securities; when unquoted debentures were to be

[8]   CAs to CO, 19 Feb. 1897, CO 152/226/3807. The term was dropped.
[9]   Scrimgeours to CAs, 5 Feb. 1892, CAOG 9/55; CAs to Scrimgeours, 28 July 1887, CAOG 9/6; Scrimgeours to CAs, 12 Mar. 1888, ibid.
[10] Scrimgeours to CAs, 27 June 1894, CAOG 9/57. St Lucia and Grenada 4% stock stood at, respectively, 108 and 109: CAs to CO, 1 Sept. 1894, ibid.
[11] London and Westminster Bank to CAs, 26 June 1894, ibid.
[12] Scrimgeours to CAs, 21 Dec. 1896, CAOG 9/68; Scrimgeours to CAs, 27 Jan. 1897, ibid.
[13] In 1867 the New Zealand government also converted £159,900 Treasury bills to debentures: CAA, CA M 5.

Table 37
Types of debenture to stock conversion, 1868–1914 (%)

Type of conversion	1868–82	1883–1914
Debentures to stock with the same interest rate	0	50
Debentures to stock with a lower interest rate	0	48.5
Debentures to debentures with the same interest rate	2	0
Debentures to debentures with a lower interest rate	98	0
Stock to stock with the same interest rate	0	1.5

Source: appendix 3, table 4.

exchanged for more marketable quoted securities; and, in the case of debentures with drawing sinking funds, when the bonds had been in existence for sufficient time for investors to fully appreciate 'the superior attraction of stock' and its concomitant accumulated sinking funds.[14] The Agents then set the terms of conversion, taking into account unpaid accrued interest, the quoted price of the new debentures or stock and the costs that investors would incur if they undertook the conversion process themselves.[15] The period of conversion was determined, advertisements placed in a range of national and provincial newspapers and, in the case of at least one loan, application forms sent to each security holder. Where debentures were to be exchanged for a line of securities that had not previously been issued and was therefore not quoted on the Stock Exchange and the colony invested fund contributions in its own loans, the Agency would also immediately convert £100,000 of the colony's own holdings of the debentures or stock. The new securities would thus receive a quote, and, marketable, would be more attractive to investors.[16] If, after the conversion closed, investor response had been poor, a further conversion would be arranged, usually a few years later, or the public might be invited to apply privately for conversion on terms set by the Agents and 'governed by the market price of stock at the time'.[17]

For investors there were a number of benefits to conversion. They obtained a security with a longer lifespan, allowing them to postpone the decision of where to reinvest repaid funds, received a rate of exchange superior to that which could be obtained in the market and generally avoided market transaction costs, though, in 1885, holders of Ceylon, Western Australian and Jamaican debentures respectively were required to pay a portion of stamp duty.[18] In addition, in the case of the 1881 and 1888 Mauritius conversions, they were given respectively a cash payment of £4 to £16 per

14 CAs to colonial secretary, 26 Feb. 1894, CO 321/156/4028.
15 CAs to colonial secretary, 28 July 1896, CAOG 9/68.
16 CAs to CO, 3 May 1880, CO 167/591/4599.
17 CAs to colonial secretary, 12 Dec. 1894, CAOG 9/50.
18 Advert, 27 June 1885, CAOG 9/3.

Table 38
Conversion terms, 1868–1914 (%)

Terms	1868–82	1883–1914
Conversion of same interest debentures/stock at 100	2	36.5
Conversion of same interest debentures/stock at less than 100	0	10.5
Conversion of same interest debentures/stock at over 100	0	3
Conversion of debentures/stock to lower interest debentures/stock at 100	2	4.5
Conversion of debentures/stock to lower interest debentures/stock at less than 100	0	6
Conversion of debentures/stock to lower interest debentures/stock at over 100	96	36
Terms privately agreed	0	3

Source: appendix 3, table 4.

debenture, and an extra 2½ months interest on the new stock.[19] Where debentures were exchanged for stock, they also received a more secure holding and, when debentures with drawing sinking funds were swapped for debentures or stock with accumulated sinking funds, they no longer ran the risk that the bonds would be drawn and repaid at par, and their new holdings were more likely to rise in price.[20]

For the Agents, conversion increased Agency income. They obtained a commission for conversion, the consolidation of colonial debts led to administrative savings, and, where debentures with drawing sinking funds were converted, they no longer had to incur the cost of arranging draws. In addition, they postponed the fall in colonial quoted prices that occurred when a large loan with an accumulated sinking fund was redeemed and the fund's crown colony investments were sold. If a loan were about to be issued, such price falls could force them to set its minimum or fixed price at a relatively low level.

The practice was, similarly, lucrative for colonies. Colonial governments avoided loan repayments and, if securities with an accumulated sinking fund were converted, they could sell the fund's investments and use the proceeds for other purposes. Where debentures with drawing sinking funds were exchanged for debentures or stock with accumulated funds, they no longer had to meet notary costs, and the price of the new security was likely to rise more rapidly and to a greater extent than the drawing sinking fund debentures, increasing the credit of the colony and the price of future loans. They

[19] CAs to CO, 17 Jan. 1881, CO 167/598/814; CAs to Mauritius, 22 Mar. 1888, CAOG 9/9.
[20] CAs to colonial secretary, 17 Oct. 1888, CAOG 9/7.

could also make a profit from the transactions (*see* table 38). Between 1868 and 1882, 96 per cent of debentures were exchanged for securities earning a lower interest rate at a price of over £100 each. Since repayment was at £100, the colonies made a loss as regards price, but this was often offset over the longer term by interest savings. For example, the £32,300 increase in Mauritius's nominal debt that arose from the colony's 1881 conversion, was outweighed by the £78,531 saved, from 1883 to 1895, in annual interest payments.[21] Between 1883 and 1914 36 per cent of conversions were made on these terms. In the case of 21 per cent of the conversions, however, the colonies made a clear profit, giving investors in 6 per cent of cases lower interest securities at a price of less than £100, in 10.5 per cent of cases same interest debentures or stock but at a price below £100, and in 4.5 per cent of conversions lower interest securities at a price of £100.

Overdrafts and advances

A further method of meeting colonies' financial demands was through the provision of overdrafts and advances.

Overdrafts

All colonies were allowed overdrafts on their current accounts. Lodged in United Kingdom banks, the contents of these accounts paid for the colonies' transactions in the United Kingdom and comprised money sent to the Agents by each colonial government and the unspent proceeds of loans. Overdrafts were generally small, rarely exceeded £100, and were usually repaid within the month. In return the borrowers paid 5 per cent interest until 1887, and, thereafter, bank rate with a minimum of 3 per cent, though no interest was charged if the debt was due to events outside the colony's control.[22] The interest which for all crown colonies amounted to £879 in 1902, was kept by the Agency, which, not surprisingly, did little to discourage these debts. Many smaller colonies, such as Bermuda and Heliogoland, thus got into 'a habit' of not remitting sufficient funds to the Agents and had almost a continuous overdraft.[23] Others had difficulty repaying their debts and on occasion were forced to obtain the necessary funds from grants-in-aid, the disposal of investments or the sale of Treasury bills.[24]

Advances

The Agents secondly provided colonies with short-term loans, known as advances. These were obtained from current account surpluses, from banks,

[21] CAs to CO, 11 July 1881, CO 167/598/12385.
[22] See, for example, CAs to CO, 4 Nov. 1880, CO 147/43/17208; PRO, AO 25/25, 1870.
[23] Note, 15 Feb. 1888, AO 25/25, 1870.
[24] For example, CO 323/453/36822; CAs to CO, 11 Oct. 1890, CO 323/453/33441; CO 323/415/7841.

Table 39
Colonies with the largest and smallest total overdrafts/advances,
Aug. 1870–Nov.1873; Oct.1897–Nov. 1900

Aug. 1870–Nov. 1873			Oct. 1897–Nov. 1900		
Colony	Total amount lent (£)	Number of monthly overdrafts/ advances	Colony	Total amount lent (£)	Number of monthly overdrafts/ advances
Largest total overdrafts/advances					
St Helena	122,333	36	Seychelles	177,479	26
Lagos	112,533	37	British East Africa	147,595	19
Trinidad	50,558	11	St Helena	133,794	36
Mauritius	48,025	8	Gold Coast	96,255	13
Sierra Leone	44,819	20	Jamaica	86,809	7
Smallest total overdrafts/advances					
Canada	87	1	Leeward Islands	2,191	10
Nova Scotia	84	6	Ceylon	1,021	1
Ionian Islands	30	10	Basutoland	966	36
New Brunswick	7	7	Bahamas	327	2
New South Wales	4	2	Bermuda	211	2

Source: CO 323/299; 323/304; 323/308; 323/416; 323/428; 323/429; 323/441; 323/442; 323/452; 323/453.

and, on at least one occasion, from the Agents' own brokers. Surviving records show that between 1870 and 1873 the average sums lent from current accounts, inclusive of overdrafts, amounted to £17,383 per month, and, between 1897 and 1900, to £40,572 per month, with the smaller poorer colonies borrowing the largest amounts (*see* table 39). The actual loans varied in size, ranging from £4,700 lent to Grenada in 1889 to the £1.1m obtained by Hong Kong in 1905.[25] Many were renewed and all carried the same interest rates as those charged for overdrafts, though the interest paid was passed to the lending colonies.[26]

Advances were provided largely to allow colonies to postpone issues when the market was depressed or their credit poor, occasionally, if the exchange rate was unfavourable, to enable them to avoid the remittance of funds to the United Kingdom and, in one or two cases, for political purposes.[27] The £1.1m. advance to Hong Kong in 1905, for instance, was lent to the Chinese

[25] CAs to colonial secretary, 16 Aug. 1889, CAOG 9/6; CO to CAs, 30 June 1905, CAOG 9/25.
[26] CAs to CO, 2 Apr. 1886, CO 323/364/5663.
[27] See, for example, Ommanney note, 18 June 1894, CO 323/396/9862.

government in return for an agreement to allow British concessionaires to extend the Canton–Haukau railway to the colony.[28] The provision of such advances was not unusual. Both the Bank of England and the London and Westminster Bank made similar short-term loans to self-governing colonies that used their issue facilities.[29] Moreover, they tended to lend larger amounts and charge lower interest than the Agents. For example in 1883 and 1893 respectively the Bank of England advanced £1m. and £250,000 to India at ½ per cent below bank rate, and, in 1891 and 1912 the London and Westminster Bank lent the Cape and Western Australia £500,000 for twelve and four months respectively, again at below bank rate.[30]

Theoretically, advances were made only if a colony could supply security 10 per cent greater than the amount advanced, in the form of investments or an ordinance permitting the future issue of a loan for the same purpose as the advance. In reality, to ensure colonial liquidity, the Agents often succumbed to moral hazard and paid little attention to the provision of collateral. Occasionally, no security was provided. Between 1910 and 1912, for instance, the Agents advanced Trinidad £85,000 for the purchase of a local estate in 'anticipation of the passing of legislation for the raising of £100,000 for this purpose'.[31] In August 1905 the Agency continued to lend Mauritius £92,000, even though the investments that acted as collateral had been sold.[32] Similarly, some of the security put forward was far from adequate. Between 1899 and 1900, neither loan ordinances nor investments were a creditable form of collateral, given that most loans could only have been issued at a large discount and the market price of investments was often lower than their cost price on which their collateral value had been based.[33] The Agents also sometimes used advances, obtained on the security of a loan ordinance, for purposes other than those for which the loan was to be raised. In 1892, for instance, they used advances provided on the security of the Antigua Stock Act to place St Kitts, Dominica, the Virgin Islands and the Leeward Islands federal account in funds.[34]

To the Agents and the colonies such advances were beneficial. They allowed colonies in need of funds to continue to purchase United Kingdom goods and to construct infrastructure, and maintained colonial demand for Crown Agent services. Lending colonies received a return at bank rate rather than at the lower deposit rate that they would have earned if the funds had

[28] CO to CAs, 30 June 1905, CAOG 9/25; *The Standard*, 10 Oct. 1905.
[29] Colonies that did not issue through the banks were refused advances: BE to Cape, 23 Aug. 1883, BE, G 23/67/1; NWB, 12911/123.
[30] BE, G 23/67/94; G 23/68/162–3. See also G 23/67/264, G 23/66/249, G 23/67/33; NWB, 12911/164, 12916/284, 12909/290, 12912/31.
[31] CO to CAs, 24 Feb. 1912, CAOG 9/81.
[32] CAs to CO, 28 Aug. 1905, CO 167/773/31121.
[33] See, for example, Blake to CO, 30 Mar. 1906, CAOG 9/222.
[34] CAs to CO, 9 Nov. 1892, CO 152/185/21834; memo, 26 July 1893, CAOG 9/54. The Colonial Office regarded the practice as 'rather questionable' and an 'irregularity': Winfield note, 11 Nov. 1892, CO 152/185/21834; Harris note, 6 Nov. 1893, CO 152/188/18432.

remained in the Crown Agents' bank account. The borrower obtained cheap funds, bank rate being lower than the borrowing rate or the rate of exchange, and were able to issue loans or remit funds on better terms when the market or the rate of exchange improved.[35] Furthermore, the interest paid was kept by the colonies or the Agency, rather than being lost to the banking system. The Colonial Office, however, viewed advances with suspicion, fearing that their use could get out of hand. In 1875 current accounts became so denuded of funds that, to avoid the suspension of payments, the Agents had to borrow £30,000 from the City.[36] There was also concern about the absence of any colonial legislative authority for such loans, the Agents' failure to seek permission to borrow from the lending colony and the source of liability if a borrower defaulted.[37] In addition, it was believed that advances were essentially speculative, and that for the sake of ½ per cent or 1 per cent lower interest or exchange rate for a few months, a colony ran the risk of far greater losses if the market or rate of exchange had worsened by the time the loan was issued or funds remitted.[38]

Bank loans were resorted to only when the Agents were unable to finance a colony themselves and were obtained from the London and Westminster Bank and the Bank of England (see appendix 3, tables 5 and 6). Both banks were on good terms with the Agents and could be relied upon to keep advances secret from those in the City who would seek to rig the issue that often followed them. The first London and Westminster Bank advances were made in the late 1870s after the Crown Agent Sir Penrose Julyan became a director of the bank and a member of its daily committee, which determined day-to-day loan policy.[39] Ad hoc Bank of England advances were made in the 1860s, but the bank only agreed to provide loans on a regular basis in 1871 when the Crown Agents made a commitment that all colonial government accounts would be lodged interest-free at the bank.[40] Generally the advances were granted for periods of between one and six months, though on occasion they were rolled over for up to a year.[41] In return, colonies paid interest at

35 Ommanney note, 23 June 1888, CO 323/371/2922.
36 CAs to CO, 23 Dec. 1875, CO 323/322/13976. In an attempt to prevent a repeat of this incident, the Colonial Office continually drew governors' attention to overdrafts. In 1888, for instance, all the West Indian colonies were sent a letter critical of their debts, and, in 1896, the overdrawn Leeward Islands received a 'sharp lecture by mail': ibid; Olivier note, 14 Oct. 1896, CO 323/406/21074.
37 PPE, q. 1741; Round note, 17 June 1893, CO 323/393/9871. Borrowed sums appeared in the lending colonies accounts only as 'loans to the CAs', presumably to prevent inter-colonial jealousies: Ommanney note, 23 June 1893, ibid. In 1897 Round concluded that liability ultimately rested with the secretary of state: Round note, 15 Mar. 1897, CO 323/415/5301.
38 Antrobus note, 17 Apr. 1897, CO 323/415/7841, marginal note.
39 A number of CA applications for advances in the 1860s had been unsuccessful. See, for example, NWB, 12903/275; 12904/223.
40 BE, G 8/41/117.
41 Ibid. G 4/94/21.

bank rate, with the exception of Zanzibar, Barbados and St Vincent in 1899 and the Transvaal in 1903, which obtained loans from the Bank of England at respectively 1 per cent and ½ per cent below this rate. A Bank of England offer of a loan to Natal in 1883, at 1 per cent above bank rate, was rejected by the Agents, who obtained the advance from the London and Westminster Bank.[42]

In theory colonies additionally provided collateral in the form of promissory notes, bills in the process of discounting, investments or an ordinance for a forthcoming loan; the Bank of England agreeing to accept such security, 'an exception to the ordinary regulations', as part of its 1871 agreement with the Agency.[43] In reality the attitude of the bank to collateral varied according to the perceived credit-worthiness of the borrower. The Bank of England required no security for the 1899 loans to St Vincent, Barbados and Zanzibar, nor for those to the East Africa protectorate and the Federated Malay States in 1914. On the other hand, in 1879 it refused to extend a loan to Griqualand on the grounds that the ordinances provided were only 'permissive'.[44] Where an ordinance was regarded as unacceptable, however, the Bank of England was occasionally willing to circumvent its own rules and provide an advance via the purchase of part of the loan prior to its issue. In 1861, for example, it rejected a Ceylon ordinance as collateral, but agreed to buy £300,000 of the loan at par in advance of its flotation.[45] When security was insisted upon and such circumventions were not possible, the Agents again at times resorted to moral hazard and arranged for the borrowing colony to create an ordinance specifically to act as collateral, or gave the banks loan ordinances that had been created for purposes different from the intended use of the advance. In 1898, for instance, they presented the Bank of England with a Gold Coast railway ordinance for an advance that was to be used to pay off the colony's overdraft, an act the assistant under-secretary, F. Graham, believed to be 'very unpleasant'.[46]

Not all of the Agents' requests for assistance were met. The banks were particularly reluctant to tie up their resources during periods of high interest rate, when they could obtain greater profits elsewhere.[47] For example, in September 1890 the London and Westminster Bank refused to provide further advances for 'the current year', and in 1906 both banks warned the

---

[42] CAs to BE, 16 Mar. 1883, CAOG 9/213.
[43] BE, G 8/41/117.
[44] BE to CAs, 4 Sept. 1879, BE, G 23/66/18–9.
[45] BE to CAs, 31 May 1861, CO 54/364/5123; CAs to CO, 19 Aug. 1861, CO 54/364/ 1484. The purchase was made on the understanding that, after the issue, it would receive a 5% commission from the Agents or that they would buy back the securities at the reigning price plus interest. See also BE, G 8/43/21; G 8/43/37.
[46] Graham note, 22 Sept. 1898, CO 96/321/20985. See also CAs to CO, 28 June 1910, CAOG 9/25.
[47] CAs to Colonial Secretary, 3 May 1907, CO 273/332/16226.

Agents to keep their 'requirements . . . within the lowest possible limits'.[48] None the less, there is evidence that the banks' reluctance to lend could be overcome with the assistance of the Treasury. In 1903 the Chancellor, on rejecting a request for further Treasury aid for Sierra Leone, stated that he would 'be disposed to support' an application to the Bank of England for advances to the colony, and later advised Ommanney that there would be 'no difficulty in giving the Agents the desired assistance'.[49]

The Agents and the Colonial Office were reluctant to publicise advances. In the 1908 enquiry, when asked about the Jamaican governor's claim that a short-term loan had been obtained from the London and Westminster Bank, Blake insisted that he could not remember such a loan and suggested that the governor had been mistaken.[50] Both the Crown Agents and the Colonial Office were no doubt aware that public knowledge of the use of advances could have a negative effect on colonial credit, and may have had doubts about the legality of the loans and feared criticism of the payment of bank interest.[51] They may also have been uncomfortable with the influence the banks had on policy. In 1889 the Bank of England only agreed to lend £250,000 to Ceylon on the understanding that the colony would issue a loan within twelve months.[52] Ten years later it provided advances to Zanzibar in the expectation that the Agents would issue a loan by early 1900 and, when this failed to occur, demanded an explanation.[53]

Finally, on at least one occasion the Agency obtained an advance from its brokers. In 1868 the Bank of England, the London and Westminster Bank and the joint stock banks all refused to provide Mauritius with loans except on the deposit of investments readily convertible on the market. Although the colony's currency commissioners held such securities, the Treasury would not allow the trustees to relinquish them.[54] Unable to provide the funds themselves, the Agents were thus forced to turn to their brokers, who advanced them £40,000 for three months on the security of promissory notes at the relatively high interest rate of 4.5 per cent per annum.[55]

---

[48] NWB, 12895/266; Blake to Hong Kong, 23 Feb. 1906, CAOG 9/25. See also BE, G 8/39/57.

[49] Ommanney notes, 27 Feb., 2 May 1903, CO 96/412/4505. In the event, the Agents financed the colony from the proceeds of the Transvaal loan: Blake note, 16 May 1903, ibid.

[50] PPE, qq. 1313–14.

[51] In 1883 the Bank of England questioned whether it had authority to make such advances, pointing out that it was precluded from making government loans except under an act of parliament: BE to CO, Mar. 1883, CAOG 9/213. The Colonial Office replied that the Agents acted as representatives of the crown colonies rather than on their own behalf: CO to BE, 9 Apr. 1883, ibid.

[52] BE to CAs, 1 Aug. 1889, CAOG 9/4.

[53] CAs to BE, 11 May 1900, CAOG 9/122. See also CAs to London and Westminster Bank, 15 Jan. 1900, CAOG 9/71.

[54] CAs to CO, 8 Oct. 1868, CO 167/511/11050.

[55] CAs to CO, 7 Nov. 1868, CO 167/511/12303. It is not clear whether it was Mullens or

Local loans

The amount of stock issued in the colonies was, when compared to the sums raised in London, minuscule, probably amounting to no more than £2.2m.[56] The Agents, receiving no remuneration from their flotation, usually advised against such loans, claiming that the low demand for stock within the colonies and colonial governments' lack of financial experience and expertise led to low prices.[57] There were exceptions to this policy, however. Local loans were encouraged where there was no alternative source of funds, when it was believed that a show of confidence by colonists in their own government stock would increase the colony's London credit and where it was advisable to stay away from the City to allow previous loans to be absorbed by the public.[58] The Agents also preferred very small loans to be raised locally, as they were difficult to sell in Britain and the Agency's remuneration often failed to cover the associated administration costs.[59] If an issue went ahead, the Agents, when requested, drew up an ordinance, arranged for the printing of the debenture or stock certificates, brought the loan to the attention of Scrimgeours and other stockbrokers, and gave general advice.[60] Occasionally they would also manage the loan's sinking fund, organise the payment of interest, and, from 1909, arrange redemption, charging their usual fees.[61]

Monitoring of the Agents' services

In their provision of colonial finance, the Agents had great scope for personal moral hazard. Monitoring of their activities by the secretary of state was poor.[62] The Colonial Office authorised all the Agents' actions, checked all loan ordinances drawn up by them and sanctioned any subsequent alterations. It also received a short report on issues, a monthly schedule of overdrafts and advances that listed borrowers and the amounts lent during the previous four weeks, and the Agents' half yearly accounts, which contained details of the income earned from their financial role. Ommanney apart, however, Colonial Office staff had little knowledge or interest in financial

Scrimgeours that provided the money or whether 'the brokers' provided it themselves or obtained it from a third party.
[56] Figure calculated from references to local loans in colonial correspondence.
[57] CAs to CO, 16 Nov. 1908, CAOG 9/100.
[58] CAs to Natal, 22 Jan. 1885, CAOG 9/11.
[59] CAs to CO, 21 June 1871, CO 107/143/6154.
[60] For example CO to CAs, 1 July 1892, CAOG 9/39; Scrimgeours to CAs, 4 May 1893, ibid; CAs to colonial secretary, 27 Jan. 1886, CAOG 9/17; weeded files, CAA, a307, a316, a376, a460.
[61] Memo, 19 Feb. 1895, CAOG 9/49; memo, 25 Oct. 1909, CAOG 9/42; CAA, weeded files, a230.
[62] Their actions may also have been monitored by the Treasury through the Bank of England and Mullens, though there is no evidence of such supervision.

matters, and never seem to have checked the validity of the Agents' actions with an external expert.[63] The Agents could easily encourage authorisation through the provision of biased advice, or simply circumvent the Colonial Office entirely.[64] In the case of the overdraft and advance schedules, if a colony had not borrowed during the previous month, its total debts failed to be listed, an anomaly that, according to the principal clerk, G. W. Johnson, made the return 'useless'.[65] There was also no distinction between current account overdrafts and advances, and, from approximately 1902, advances in anticipation of loans or for which security had been lodged were excluded from the returns as the loans were 'the sole concern of the Agents'.[66] The office accounts, meanwhile, recorded only total receipts from each charge. Consequently when, in 1879, the Agency received a fee of only $1/8$ per cent for the issue of the New Zealand loan, the other $1/8$ per cent being paid to the former Senior Crown Agent, neither the Colonial Office nor the Audit Office noticed the irregularity.[67]

Given the poor standards of monitoring, it is suprising that there were only three incidences of impropriety. In 1871 Sir Penrose Julyan was asked by the New Zealand government to act in his private capacity as its loan agent, a post that merely required the holder to choose who would issue each loan and then liaise between the issuer and the government.[68] As New Zealand loans were floated through the Crown Agents, the Colonial Office, assuming that the position was largely honorary and unpaid, gave Julyan permission to accept the offer.[69] Four years later Julyan (and Sargeaunt, who had also become a loan agent), entered into a long-running dispute with Julius Vogel, the New Zealand agent-general over the colony's forthcoming loan. Vogel insisted that one large £4m. issue, rather than two small loans, should be

[63] In 1908, on accepting the Agents' advice on a Southern Nigerian prospectus, Butler concluded that 'it would be a serious responsibility to overrule the CAs and their brokers . . . I, at any rate, do not feel equal to criticising their belief that the statement suggested would prejudice . . . the loan': Butler note, 22 Apr. 1908, CO 520/69/14128.

[64] In 1908 the Agency, wishing the secretary of state to authorise the issue of a loan for Southern Nigeria, supplied him with details of the cost of raising such a loan, but not, as requested, that of obtaining a Treasury loan: CAs to CO, 5 Feb. 1908, CO 520/69/4195. The Colonial Office had to obtain that information from the Treasury: CO to Treasury, 26 Feb. 1908, ibid. Although the Agents obtained permission to charge a ¼% conversion fee for the 1887 Natal conversion from the Natal department of the Colonial Office, they failed to request authorisation to charge this fee for all subsequent conversions, either from 'the general department (who are supposed to deal with CA charges) or, by the way, any other department in the Office from that day to this': Round note, 10 Oct. 1900, CO 137/615/14855. See also Blake to Nathan, 10 Nov. 1905, CAOG 9/25; CAs to Ceylon, 8 Nov. 1907, CAOG 9/94.

[65] Johnson note, 18 Oct. 1897, CO 323/416/21917.

[66] Round note, 21 Oct. 1905, CO 323/504/36392; Blake note, 7 Nov. 1905, ibid.

[67] Ebden note, 16 Mar. 1881, CO 537/218. A proposal by Meade that the accounts should be rendered in greater detail was not put into effect: Meade note, 16 Mar. 1881, ibid.

[68] Julyan to CO, 11 Apr. 1871, CO 209/224/3326.

[69] Note, June 1871, ibid.

floated and that the issuer should be Rothschilds. No doubt concerned at the loss of the Agency's commission, Julyan and Sargeaunt objected, pointing out that the bank charged a relatively high issue fee and that one large loan would flood the market with stock and damage the colony's future credit.[70] Their protests were ignored.

Fearing the loss of future issues, Julyan and Sargeaunt decided to inform the New Zealand government that they would no longer work with Vogel, whom they found 'impossible', on future issues.[71] Vogel, seeking to engineer the removal of the Agents out of 'personal malice' and to protect his own position, then complained to the Colonial Office that between 1871 and 1875 Julyan and Sargeaunt had insisted upon and had been paid by the New Zealand government fees amounting to £6,000.[72] At first Sargeaunt denied that any payments had been made. Julyan accepted that they had been remunerated, but argued that the commissions were quite unrelated to their positions at the Agency and that, as loan agent, he had placed a great deal of issuing business in the hands of the Crown Agents.[73] He also implied that he had a moral right to take such commissions. As he later wrote, his acceptance of the post of Senior Agent had been on the understanding that his efforts in making the Agency 'prosperous' would be reciprocated by his 'position' being 'improved according to results'.[74] 'Never for a moment doubting that both sides would comply' with the agreement, his trust in the Colonial Office had been shattered by its refusal to grant him large pay increases.[75] Unconvinced, the Colonial Office fined the two Agents £1,000, and instructed them never to act for any colony in any capacity other than collectively as Crown Agents. In addition, it increased their salaries, though by far less than demanded by Julyan, and employed a third Agent to lighten their duties.[76]

The Colonial Office's actions failed to act as a deterrent to further fraudulent behaviour. In 1879 New Zealand asked Julyan and Sargeaunt to act as loan agents for the colony's forthcoming issue, which was to be floated by the Agency. The Colonial Office, given 'the difficulties of the past', were loath to agree, but eventually relented on the understanding that the Crown Agents

[70] Raewyn Dalziel, *Julius Vogel: business politician*, Oxford 1986, 198. The bank charged a commission of 2%: Rothschilds Bank, xi (109/118).

[71] In the event, the government sided with Vogel and took the letter to mean that Julyan and Sargeaunt no longer wished to work for the colony in their official capacities: New Zealand to CO, 26 June 1876, CO 209/235/10087. It thus sought to withdraw the management of its previous loans from the Agency, 'sweep[ing] the whole . . . business to Vogel': memo, 28 Oct. 1876, CO 54/349/10087. It was instructed that such an act would be illegal: CAs to CO, 7 Dec. 1876, CO 209/235/14556.

[72] Herbert to Canaervon, 9 Jan. 1876, CO 209/235/14556; Julyan to Herbert, 17 Feb. 1876, CO 537/157.

[73] Julyan and Sargeaunt to CO, 17 Feb. 1876, CO 209/235/14556; Julyan to Herbert, 23 May 1876, ibid.

[74] Julyan to CO, 14 July 1879, CO 323/339/18599.

[75] Ibid.

[76] Ebden note, 22 Feb. 1881, CO 537/217.

would not obtain personal remuneration.[77] The loan was duly issued, but the Agency only received a commission of ¹/₈ per cent, half its usual fee. The other ¹/₈ per cent, £6,250, was paid to Julyan, who had retired four days before the loan was issued, supposedly for his work as a private individual after his retirement.[78] In reality, as Ommanney later admitted, Julyan had given the New Zealand government an ultimatum on his retirement to the effect that unless he received a commission he would cease to represent them, which would have a detrimental effect on investor confidence.[79] The Colonial Office remained unaware of the payment until 1881, when Vogel, who had requested but failed to obtain a similar 'special' fee from the New Zealand government and no doubt jealous of Julyan's payment, told them about it.[80] Enraged, the secretary of state wrote a strong letter to Sargeaunt and Ommanney criticising them for their failure to inform the secretary of state of Julyan's actions.[81] An attempt was also made to persuade Julyan to pay the honorarium into the Crown Agents' office reserve fund. Julyan refused, arguing that the timing of the loan and his retirement were wholly fortuitous, and that the fee was genuinely paid for work performed and recompensed him for the remuneration denied him by the Colonial Office.[82] After a further exchange of letters, the secretary of state accepted defeat and decided 'not to pursue the matter'.[83]

The Agents succumbed to personal moral hazard for a third time in the early 1880s, when they performed a 'flagrant job' on the Cape.[84] After their financial duties had been handed over to the agent-general, a Captain Charles Mills, they advised the colony to employ Barings as its new issuing house. Given that Barings had never floated a colonial issue and Scrimgeours, Baring's broker, held a large proportion of the colony's previous loans and could easily rig its future issues, this was remarkably poor advice.[85] It nevertheless served the Agents' interests, permitting them to revenge themselves on the colony for its earlier criticism of their financial duties and strengthening their relationship with Scrimgeours. Mills took their advice and appointed Barings for a period of ten years, only to see the colony's first loan rigged and sold at an excessively low price. Determined to ditch the bank, he asked the Agents to negotiate a new issuing contract with the Bank of

77 Notes, 2, 3 Feb. 1878, CO 209/237/1334.
78 Ebden note, 2 May 1881, CO 537/218.
79 Ibid.
80 Raewyn Blackstock, 'Sir Julius Vogel, 1876–80: from politics to business', New Zealand Journal of History v (1971), 67.
81 CO to Ommanney and Sargeaunt, 2 June 1881, CO 537/218.
82 Julyan to CO, 25 June 1881, CO 537/219.
83 CO to Julyan, 14 Oct. 1881, CO 537/220.
84 Cape Argus (weekly edition), 15 Aug. 1882, 10–11; 2 Dec. 1883, 14.
85 Purkis, 'Railway building in the Cape Colony', 307. Barings also charged the colony excessive issue and management fees: Cape Argus (weekly edition), 13 Dec. 1883, 12–13.

England on his behalf.[86] But, yet again, the Agents appear to have behaved dishonourably, appointing the ex-Crown Agent Sir Penrose Julyan as their negotiator. As they must surely have known, Julyan, by now a director of the London and Westminster Bank, which wished to establish itself as a major issuing house, had little incentive to ensure the success of the negotiations. Inevitably the talks broke down and Julyan advised the colony to turn to the London and Westminster Bank.[87] The Agents, eager to help a former colleague and to cement good relations with that bank, concurred, and the colony, now with little alternative, placed its issuing activities in its hands.[88]

The cost of the Crown Agents' services

The Agents' charges for the issue, conversion, management and repayment of loans were high, though not so excessive as to discourage the issue of loans or to lead to calls to abandon the Agency in favour of the private sector. Issue costs were covered either by including the estimated amount in the loan, or selling the required amount of stock after flotation. The latter method could only be used in stock issues, as debentures were numbered, but was generally preferred. Post-flotation sales removed the danger that expenses would be greater than the amount reserved, and allowed colonies to avoid the payment of interest on the securities in the period before they were issued on the stock, and, from 1900, underwriting charges on the stock. Between 1860 and 1863 there was no set fee for the issue of loans. Fees were negotiated for each issue separately and, in an arrangement 'practically recognised' by the Colonial Office, these were paid to the Agents, adding 'very considerably to their salaries'.[89] In 1863, however, Julyan introduced a compulsory fixed charge of ½ per cent, which incorporated an Agency issue fee and the ¼ per cent paid to brokers for applications made through them (*see* table 40). As not all subscriptions came through brokers, the Office's actual charge was slightly over ¼ per cent.[90] This combined fee continued to be charged until 1886 when, concerned at the fall in the Agency's income after the loss of the self-governing colony business, the Colonial Office decided that the brokerage commission should be paid separately by colonies and the Agency issue fee raised to ½ per cent. The result was a rise in Crown Agent earnings and, in 1893, the Colonial Office instructed that the Agents' fee should again

---

86 Mills to Barings, 7 Nov. 1883, Baring Brothers, HC 15.2.1.
87 Mills to Treasurer, 24 Dec. 1883, NWB, 1597.
88 The bank later rigged at least one of the colony's loans: Purkis, 'Railway building in the Cape Colony', 317.
89 CAs to CO, 3 Mar. 1870, CO 323/299/2437; Julyan to Herbert, 23 May 1876, CO 537/157.
90 CAs to CO, 23 Mar. 1912, CO 323/591/9213.

Table 40
Crown Agent and Bank of England issue charges, 1863–1914

Crown Agents	Bank of England
1863–86: £2,500 per million, excluding brokerage	*Self-governing colonies* 1880–1908: £5,000 per million, excluding brokerage
1886–93: £5,000 per million, excluding brokerage	1908–14: £2,500 per million, excluding brokerage
1893–1914: £2,500 per million, excluding brokerage	*India* 1880–1914: £1,250 per million (fixed price loans) and £625 per million (tender loans), excluding brokerage

Source: CAs to CO, 2 Apr. 1886, CO 323/364/5665; CAs to CO, 13 July 1903, CO 323/393/11909; Antrobus to CO, 23 Mar. 1912, CAOG 9/40, 12; memo, 12 Aug. 1908, BE, AC 14/14.

incorporate brokerage. The charge from 1880 to 1886 and from 1893 to 1908 was therefore half, and, for the rest of the period, equivalent to that set by the Bank of England for the issue of self-governing colony loans. On the other hand it was up to eight times the bank's rate for the flotation of India Office issues, and in the late 1870s there were complaints from the Cape and New Zealand that the Agents' were making excessive profits.[91] Although acknowledging that the size of Indian issues allowed the bank to make economies of scale, the 1908 enquiry came to a similar conclusion and recommended a reduction in the fee.[92]

The Agents' management charge varied considerably. It was originally set in 1863 at ½ per cent of all interest payments made. The economies of scale arising from the increase in the total amount of interest paid then allowed it to be reduced to ¼ per cent in 1867.[93] It returned to its original level in 1886 in response to the fall during the previous ten years in crown colony loan interest rates, which had reduced receipts, to the loss of responsible government income and to the introduction of inscribed stock, which increased the labour involved in the payment of dividends (*see* table 41).[94] The increase, however, led to an unreasonable rise in Crown Agent income and in 1893 the charge was again set at ¼ per cent. These fees were then lower than those charged by the Bank of England to both India and the self-governing colonies, even though the bank benefited from economies of scale.[95]

91 *New Zealand parliamentary debates*, xxxii. 377; Porter, 'Britain, the Cape Colony and Natal', 561.
92 PPR, p. xix. This failed to occur.
93 CAs to CO, 5 Dec. 1867, CO 323/286/12013.
94 CAs to CO, 2 Apr. 1886, CO 323/364/5665.
95 In 1913 the bank managed £66m. of New Zealand debenture and stock alone and £167m. of Indian sterling stock loans: memo, 20 Apr. 1914, BE, AC 14/17. Although

Table 41
Crown Agent and Bank of England management charges, 1863–1914

Crown Agent (half yearly dividends)

1863–7: ½%, equivalent to:
* £300 per million *p.a* for 5% loans
* £400 per million *p.a* for 6% loans

1868–6: ¼%, equivalent to:
* £100 per million *p.a* for 4% loans
* £112 per million *p.a.* for 4½% loans
* £124 per million *p.a* for 5% loans
* £148 per million *p.a* for 6% loans

1886–93: ½%, equivalent to:
* £150 per million *p.a* for 3% loans
* £175 per million *p.a* for 3½% loans
* £200 per million *p.a* for 4% loans
* £250 per million *p.a* for 4½% loans

1893–1912: ¼%, equivalent to:
* £75 per million *p.a* for 3% loans
* £87/10/– per million *p.a* for 3½% loans
* £100 per million *p.a* for 4% loans
1912–14: £100 per million *p.a*

Bank of England
Self-governing colonies (half yearly dividends)

1880–85: £600 per million *p.a* up to £10m, thereafter £550 per million

1885–95: £600 per million *p.a* up to £10m, £550 per million *p.a* up to £15 million, £500 per million *p.a* thereafter

1895–98: £500 per million *p.a* up to £10 million, £450 per million *p.a* up to £15 million, £400 per million *p.a* thereafter

1898–1908: £200 per million *p.a*

1908–14: £350 per million *p.a* (stock), £200 per million *p.a* (debentures)

India (quarterly dividends)

1880–88: £300 per million *p.a*, £450 per million *p.a* if debt fell below £400 million

1888–96: £360 per million *p.a*

1896–1905: £360 per million *p.a* for first £100 million, and £100 per million *p.a* for amounts over £100 million

1905–14: £300 per million *p.a,* if debt over £125 million. If debt below £125 million, £360 per million *p.a* for first £100 million and £60 per million *p.a* for amounts over £100 million

Source: CAs to CO, 2 Apr. 1886, CO 323/364/5665; CAs to CO, 13 July 1903, CO 323/393/11909; Antrobus to CO, 23 Mar. 1912, 12, CAOG 9/40; BE to NSW/Queensland, 9 May 1898, BE, G 23/70/61–2; BE to New Zealand, 12 June 1885, G 23/67/127–8; BE to New Zealand, 11 Apr. 1895, G 23/69/293; BE to New Zealand, 6 May 1898, G 23/70/59–60; BE to India Office, 19 Aug. 1887, G 23/67/355; BE to India Office, 24 Jan. 1888, G 23/68/76; BE to India Office, 12 Feb. 1896, G 23/68/322; memo, 20 Apr. 1914, AC 14/17.

The Agents' commissions on conversion and redemption were far higher than those charged by the Bank of England, and were the subject of a number of complaints from the colonies (*see* table 42). In 1900, for instance, Jamaica criticised the Agency's proposed commission for the conversion of £1.5m. of

Indian dividends were paid quarterly, the extra work does not appear to have doubled costs, with from 1886 to 1896 the bank charging the India Office £300 per £1m. *per annum* for the management of half-yearly dividend issues.

Table 42
Crown Agent and Bank of England conversion
and redemption charges, 1880–1914

	Crown Agents	Bank of England
Conversion	1880–87: £5,000 per million	1880–1908: £1,000 per million
	1887–1912: £2,500 per million	1908–14: £600 per million
	1912–14: £1,000 per million	
Redemption	1880–1912: £5,000 per million	1880–1914: £1,000 per million
	1912–14: £1,000 per million	

Source: CAs to CO, 2 Apr. 1886, CO 323/364/5665; CAs to CO, 13 July 1903, CO 323/393/11909; Antrobus to CO, 23 Mar. 1912, CAOG 9/40,12; memo, 12 Aug. 1908, BE, AC 14/14; memo, 20 Apr. 1914, ibid..

railway debentures, suggesting that the work be undertaken in the colony.[96] The Agents' defence was that the charges offset the losses made in the management of loans brought about by the adoption from the mid-1890s of 3 per cent interest rates, and partly subsidised the provision of miscellaneous services, the cost of which was not wholly covered by the annual contributions made by the colonies, and other duties for which they received no fee.[97] In the case of Jamaica, the Agency obtained an annual contribution of only £150 *per annum* for miscellaneous services involving, it asserted, £78,000-worth of business *per annum*.[98] Moreover, it was argued that they rarely received the full redemption commission because of conversion, the reluctance of many self-governing colonies to pay the full remuneration, and the decision not to charge the whole fee for loans with a short lifespan, few holders or not issued by themselves.[99] In 1905, for example, the Agents charged a fee of only £625 per £m. for the redemption of £12.9m. of loans issued by the former South African government and, in 1912, the New Zealand high commissioner refused to pay more than £1,000 per £m. for the redemption of loans issued by the Agents in the 1870s.[100] In addition, in the case of conversion, no charge was made for short-dated bonds convertible to stock and, in 1904, the Agents discovered that, due to an oversight, they had failed since 1883 to collect commission on the conversion of £1,258,800 worth of Natal debentures.[101] Despite these extenuating circumstances the

96 Hemming to CO, 10 Apr. 1900, CAOG 9/74. The colony claimed that, as the conversion was the result of a court case and the Agents had not arranged the terms, no advantage had been gained from their 'position and credit': ibid.
97 PPE, qq. 1249, 4181; CAs to CO, 11 May 1900, CO 137/615/14855.
98 CAs to CO, 11 May 1900, CO 137/615/14855.
99 Antrobus to CO, 16 Aug. 1912, CAOG 9/40; AO 25/25, 1870.
100 Antrobus to CO, 16 Aug. 1912, CAOG 9/40; CAs to CO, 6 Dec. 1905, CO 291/89/43316.
101 Weeding document, CAOG 9/48; memo, 4 Mar. 1904, CAOG 9/13. Staff had

1908 enquiry none the less concluded that the Agents' redemption commission was excessive, and proposed that the fee should be reduced or a consolidated charge that covered issue, management and redemption costs be set.[102] The Agency decided to cut the redemption and conversion charges, and slightly increase its management commission.[103] The proposal for a consolidated fee was rejected, as no other issuing house charged in this way, and comparisons of costs would therefore be difficult.[104]

As regards the provision of overdrafts and advances, the cost of the former was recouped from the interest paid by borrowing colonies, and the latter from the annual contributions from the colonies.[105] The size of the annual charges, however, failed to keep pace with the workload involved and by the late 1890s the cost was partly supplemented by the Agents' purchase, conversion and redemption commissions. An attempt by the Agent to reduce its workload in 1905 through the introduction of a single account to contain all moneys, which would have eliminated the need to debit or credit the current accounts of the borrower or lender each time a loan was made, was blocked by the Colonial Office.[106]

In the provision of fiscal safety nets, the Agents avoided, at least until 1900, colonial financial embarrassments that would have been against both their own and their principals' interests. Such mishaps would not only have unbalanced colonial accounts, but would have slowed economic growth and damaged the stock market credibility of the crown colonies and their ability to issue further loans. The Agents were in a unique position to provide such safety nets. They possessed the necessary financial experience and expertise, had close trust relationships with other City institutions, and were able to act as an external Treasury and transform the colonies into a financial co-operative. The current account surpluses of prosperous colonies could thus be used to meet the deficits of the less fortunate and each loan could help to finance a multitude of projects.

Given their complexity, it is hardly surprising that these and the Agency's

---

assumed that the decision not to make a charge in 1883, because the 1882 loan was convertible to stock, applied to all Natal conversions. Although the unpaid commission amounted to £3,141, it was decided that no attempt would be made to reclaim the sum from the colony, though unpaid stamp duty was recovered: memos, 19 Apr., 11 Nov. 1904, CAOG 9/13.

[102] PPR, p. xix.

[103] Ibid. The new charges did not apply to loans issued within colonies, by self-governing colonies, to those redeemed by periodical drawings or to the 1901 Zanzibar 3% loan: ibid.

[104] Antrobus to CO, 23 Mar. 1912, CAOG 9/40.

[105] Circular, 12 May 1886, CAOG 17/24. The contributions, paid by seventeen of the larger colonies, ranged in 1908 from £30 to £650 per annum and totalled £3,100: PPE, appendix 3.

[106] Memo, 10 Oct. 1905, CAOG 9/234. The account, termed the joint colonial fund, was eventually established in 1929: Abbott, Short history of the Crown Agents, 40.

loan duties were poorly monitored. Similarly, there is little surprise that so few Agents took advantage of their positions. On the one hand those Agents who wished to make large amounts of money could easily and legally do so by using insider knowledge in their own security dealings.[107] On the other, the very nature of the services provided by the Agents meant that any fraud would have involved very large sums and discovery would therefore have resulted in instant dismissal, social disgrace and even imprisonment. The personal dishonesty that did occur was minor, in the case of Julyan partly the result of the Colonial Office's own duplicity and therefore avoidable, and, no doubt, appeared to involve little risk of criticism. The Cape in 1880 was no longer a client of the Crown Agents and his, and his colleagues' advice to the colony was easily defended. The Colonial Office, meanwhile, only found out about Julyan's questionable dealings because Julius Vogel, pursuing his own personal agenda, informed the secretary of state. The Agents were also guilty of some institutional moral hazard, in that they provided themselves and banks with inadequate collateral for advances and set relatively high fees. The latter increased Agency income and deposits in its reserve fund, and allowed them to perform new duties from which they derived much work satisfaction and the ability to influence policy. The overcharging, though, was slight and benign, in that the colonies benefited from the services subsidised.

[107] Although Blake left only £23,173, he appears to have lived in a luxurious manner after his retirement and two years before his death gave very large sums to his three children. It seems likely that this money was earned from his dealings in colonial securities: personal communication from Rowena Berry, 2 Nov. 1993.

8

External Finance, the Remittance of Funds and Colonial Investments after 1899

The first part of this chapter discusses how, in the early 1900s, the Agents slipped from the tightrope that constituted their provision of external finance and failed to be saved by their safety net. By the late 1890s both the colonies and the Agents were close to bankruptcy. Owing to a decision by Chamberlain to halt all loan issues, the subsequent collapse of the loan market, the Agents' rejection of treasury funds and the escalation of construction costs, the Agency found itself unable to provide the funds necessary to finance the railways being built in the colonies. At the same time the cut in their fees, the extra cost of organising railway construction and various other duties, and the loss of their loan commission income meant that the Agency itself was suffering losses. As the abandonment of infrastructure projects would have led to criticism, drastically reduced their purchasing income and damaged the likelihood of successful loan issues in the future, the Agents were forced to borrow money from colonial investment funds and adopt other suspect methods of finance. Later, when the market improved, requiring funds to repay these loans and to finance escalating construction costs and in need of commission income, they sold issues at excessively low prices, and, in doing so, severely weakened their reputation for fiscal competence.

The second part of the chapter discusses the Agents' other financial services: the transfer of funds and the management of colonial investments. As the colonies developed and their dealings with the Agency multiplied, an increasing amount of money had to be sent from colonial governments to London and *vice versa*. To ensure the safe movement of these sums, the Agents had to adopt new techniques of monetary transfer or remittance. Economic growth, similarly, greatly increased the pool of money that was needed for investment by the colonies. Only a small proportion of loan proceeds was immediately spent, and, by the 1880s, most issues had invested sinking funds. Likewise, the establishment of stable banking systems and currencies necessitated the creation of savings bank funds and currency funds, and the expansion of administration resulted in the setting up of widows and pension funds. To ensure that colonies obtained the highest possible returns, it was important that sums were placed in high-yielding investments, but that these were secure and that the money was available when needed. Investment management was thus undertaken by the Agents, who had the required expertise and City connections. Fearful of the criticism that would result from the loss of funds, they placed sums in a small number of trusted British banks, a narrow range of quality stocks or lent them to other crown colonies. Use of the Agency for these purposes again raised the spectre of dishonesty on the part of Agents and their activities were therefore closely monitored by the Colonial Office.

Post-1900

The Agents' difficulties in providing colonies with finance were partly due to changes in the economic environment. In the late 1890s the Treasury agreed to finance Chamberlain's railway construction programme through advances from a colonial development fund.[1] In anticipation of the fund's low interest long-term loans, the Agents were ordered to halt all loan issues and to meet colonial needs from current account surpluses and bank advances. Unfortunately, the passage of the empowering legislation through parliament was delayed, and the Treasury then had second thoughts about the entire scheme. It was strongly suspected that most of the projects to be financed were unlikely to generate sufficient revenue for repayment. The bill, consequently, was scrapped and replaced by the Colonial Loans Act, which provided imperial government advances only for those schemes that had been connected to the proposed fund.

The Agency was reluctant to make use of the act. The loans firstly constituted a first charge on the revenue and assets of a borrowing colony; if its government defaulted on its debts, any revenues or assets available would be used to repay these loans before any others. The Agents would therefore have to set a low price on the colony's future issues, as potential investors would be discouraged from buying securities, both by the charge itself and because the Treasury, in making such a stipulation implied that it had little confidence in the colony's ability to repay its debts.[2] Secondly, the need for funds to finance the South African War caused the Treasury in August 1899 to increase the interest rates to be charged on the loans from 2¾ per cent to 3¾ per cent. Many of the advances made were also insufficient for the designated projects, the cost of which rose constantly, and there was little likelihood that further Treasury help would be forthcoming. A request, made by the Colonial Office in 1903 for the borrowing powers of Sierra Leone to be extended through a further bill was rejected by the Treasury.[3]

[1] Carland, *Colonial Office*, 154–69; Kubicek, *The administration of imperialism*, 80–8. The fund was financed by Post Office savings accounts that contained more money than could profitably be invested in the United Kingdom.
[2] CAs to Trinidad, 22 Jan. 1901, CAOG 9/66; CAs to CO, 11 Feb. 1908, CO 520/69/5174.
[3] Ommanney note, 27 Feb. 1903, CO 96/412/4505.

The Agents decided to use the loans only to pay off a number of the current account and bank advances made during 1898–9 and to finance small projects in colonies that were unlikely to require further funds (*see* appendix 3, table 7). But, having made this decision, they found that changes in market conditions prevented them from raising the money needed through the public issue of loans. The onset of the South African War and large-scale high-yield government borrowing, together with the Treasury's abandonment of the colonial development fund, had almost eliminated market demand for crown colony stock. Moreover, shortfalls could not continue to be met from advances. Current accounts, no longer swollen by the unspent proceeds of loans, contained relatively small surpluses, most of which had already been advanced. Banks, meanwhile, able to obtain greater returns elsewhere, were reluctant to lend further sums and were beginning to demand repayment.

It would be wrong, however, to clear the Agents of all responsibility for their predicament, which was at least partly the result of their determination to maximise their income. This had led to the adoption of the department system of construction, for which greatly increased funds were needed, and which, by encouraging the construction of uneconomic railways, contributed to the Treasury's decision to abandon the colonial development fund and the market's reluctance to invest in colonial loans. Similarly, the need for income played a part in the Agents' rejection of the Colonial Loans Act. The acceptance of Treasury loans would have lost them the commission that they would otherwise have earned from public issues and they would have had to receive, pay the interest on and redeem the loans for no fee. The act also raised the spectre of Treasury intervention in future financial operations, and, more importantly, Treasury pressure for infrastructure projects to be reduced in scope or undertaken by contractors rather than the department system, which assured the purchase of construction materials.

To avoid financial crisis the Agents began to use colonial contributions to colonial investment funds as advances, to sell fund securities and, in West Africa, to raise capital from private sources.[4] They first requested Colonial Office permission to use fund contributions in March 1900 (*see* table 43).[5] It was proposed that they be allowed to advance only annual contributions to sinking funds, and that only those colonies empowered to borrow from the Treasury would obtain the loans. In return, each fund would receive interest at bank rate and the scrip, certificates representing securities yet to be issued, of the borrowing colony's intended loan up to the value of the advance as security.[6] Repayment would be either in the stock of the loan when it was issued, which would help to ensure its success, or, if a Treasury loan was obtained, in cash. The Agents argued that, given the ability of borrowers to

4 The 10% margin between the size of advances and the value of the supporting collateral was also abandoned: CAs to British Guiana, 17 Apr. 1900, CAOG 9/71.
5 CAs to CO, 23 Mar. 1900, CO 323/452/9313.
6 CAs to British Guiana, 17 Apr. 1900, CAOG 9/71.

Table 43
Fund contributions invested in loan scrip, 1903–4

Year	Colony	Amount (£)
1903	Gold Coast	84,777
	Lagos	154,098
	Sierra Leone	233,133
	Trinidad	5,390
1904	Gold Coast	59,566
	Lagos	63,113
	Mauritius	16,149
	Trinidad	13,111
1908	Gold Coast	214,065

Source: CO 323/483/40333; CO 323/504/5969.

Note: Incomplete. No full record of these investments, which continued to be made after 1908, appears to have survived.

obtain a Treasury loan 'at any time', the scheme was safe, and the return 'somewhat more favourable' than that from ordinary investments.[7] The Colonial Office was dubious. It was pointed out that the Treasury 'if approached . . . too long after the present time' might be unable to provide loans, that the price of the scrip would be fixed by the Agents rather than the market and that bank rate varied and was determined not by 'the credit of the lender, but by the general state of the money market'.[8] Nevertheless, aware of their 'urgent need of money', the secretary of state gave the Agents permission to go ahead with the scheme.[9]

In April the Agents asked for authority to advance contributions to colonial surplus funds, which contained government income that was not immediately required. Sinking fund contributions had failed to cover all the demands for capital, and the banks had required the repayment of £100,000 of advances.[10] The Colonial Office was again doubtful. The contents of surplus funds might be required at short notice, and it was therefore not desirable that they should be locked up in unissued scrip that could 'not be realised for the present or possibly for some time to come'.[11] There was also a feeling

[7] Ibid.
[8] Round note, 14 Nov. 1901, CO 323/463/40022; Antrobus note, 24 Mar. 1900, CO 323/452/9313; Hamilton note, 6 Apr. 1900, ibid.
[9] CO to CAs, 29 Mar. 1900, CO 323/452/9313. In its authorisation the Colonial Office failed to reiterate that contributions should only be advanced to colonies named in the 1900 Colonial Loans Act, with the result that the Agents continued to lend to Lagos long after it had exhausted its power to obtain Treasury loans: Round note, 13 Nov. 1903, CO 323/483/40333.
[10] CAs to CO, 25 Apr. 1900, CO 323/452/12697.
[11] Round note, 26 Apr. 1900, ibid.

that, if the Agents were unable to provide advances in the normal manner, either expenditure should be halted 'until somebody will lend the colonies money on terms that are acceptable', or the Agents should be instructed to issue loans on the market whatever the price.[12] Such views, however, were strongly opposed by both Antrobus and Ommanney, who argued that West African railway expenditure was 'practically impossible to stop', and that Chamberlain 'would not contemplate either stopping the railway or other works, which are in the course of construction, or limiting the full discretion, which has hitherto been given to the Agents, as to when they should place loans on the market'.[13]

Before a decision could be reached, the Agents, believing that surplus fund contributions would also prove inadequate, asked permission to advance contributions to the larger saving bank funds too.[14] These contained sums equal to some proportion of a bank's deposits, which would be used to meet early demands for the repayment of deposits in any banking crisis.[15] Ommanney and his colleagues were willing to consider the proposal which, if it covered only the larger funds would be relatively safe. Chamberlain, on the other hand, believed that all such funds stood 'in an exceptional position' and rejected the scheme, though the advance of surplus fund contributions was permitted.[16] The Agents refused to accept the decision, and in June 1901 proposed that sinking, surplus and also savings bank fund contributions be advanced to the protectorate of Zanzibar, which had Foreign Office authority to issue a guaranteed loan.[17] F. R. Round strongly opposed the proposal, drawing attention to the fact that the protectorate could not, if the market fell, borrow from the Treasury under the Colonial Loans Act, and that the Agency envisaged the use of contributions to all rather than, as before, only the larger saving bank funds. He also objected to the use of crown colony fund contributions to support a protectorate, and argued that in the longer term the money would obtain a higher rate of return if immediately invested in 3½ per cent colonial stock which, unlike Zanzibar securities, would rise rapidly when the market improved.[18] Ommanney, on the other hand, believed that the imperial guarantee of the proposed loan made the use of savings bank fund contributions acceptable, provided that no more than $^1/_{10}$th of any Fund was so invested.[19] Chamberlain agreed, and the Agents

12 Evans note, 21 June 1900, ibid; Round note, 26 Apr. 1900, CO 323/452/9313.

13 Antrobus note, 2 May 1900, CO 323/452/12697; Ommanney note, 22 June 1900, CO 323/452/17204.

14 CAs to CO, 31 May 1900, CO 323/452/17204.

15 Such repayments would stop depositors panicking and prevent a run on the bank.

16 CO to CAs, 28 June 1900, CO 323/452/17204.

17 CAs to CO, 8 June 1901, CO 323/463/19745.

18 Round note, 11 June 1901, ibid. The Zanzibar government had also been the author of its own misfortunes, getting 'into difficulties partly through it having ... acquired powers to borrow on terms on which no one is willing to lend': ibid.

19 Ommanney note, ibid.

were allowed to put the proposal into action.[20] During November 1901 the Colonial Office again permitted the Agency to advance savings bank fund contributions to Ceylon, though it specified that no more than $^1/_{10}$th of each fund could be advanced and only funds worth more than £10,000 and spread over a number of securities could contribute.[21]

In the event Round's misgivings about the use of fund contributions proved to be well founded. In 1902 the Straits complained that the Gold Coast and Zanzibar stock in which its contributions had been repaid was of poor quality and subject to price falls.[22] A year later British Guiana criticised the policy's bias towards borrowers.[23] During the period contributions were advanced, funds suffered losses equal to the difference between the bank rate that they received and the rewards available from permanent investment, which, because money was in short supply, were relatively high. Whereas, when the market improved and the funds were repaid, they experienced a loss equal to the difference between the return that they could have earned, if contributions had been immediately invested, and, because of the plentiful supply of money, the lower return earned from the stock with which they were repaid or they purchased.[24]

Capital, secondly, was raised through the sale of securities held by colonial funds.[25] Although colonies generally pressed for such sales, the Agents were less enthusiastic. Disposals reduced a colony's potential collateral for current account and bank advances, could lead to problems if the contents of the fund were required at short notice and, owing to the fall in the market, could result in capital losses. When a colony was in need of money, therefore, the Agents preferred to provide advances. Fund sales were only resorted to when these were no longer available or when the bank interest rate charged for the advances was higher than the interest earned by the securities that the colony wished to be sold. A drawback of this policy was that if the Agents were ultimately forced to sell a colony's holdings and the price of the securities had fallen since the decision to provide advances, the delay in selling could lead to a capital loss that exceeded the interest gain from the provision of the advances. Such a situation occurred on a number of occasions. In August 1898, for example, Mauritius, with the approval of the Colonial Office, asked the Agents to sell savings bank fund investments.[26] Instead the Agency provided advances, generating, between August to October, a profit of £30 for the colony, bank rate being lower than the interest rate on the securities.

---

20 CO to CAs, 17 June 1901, ibid.
21 CO to CAs, 19 Nov. 1901, CO 323/463/40022.
22 Swettenham to CO, 17 July 1902, CAOG 9/2.
23 Swettenham to CO, 16 Oct. 1903, CO 323/483/40333.
24 The Colonial Office reluctantly accepted that this analysis was correct: Round note, n.d. CO 101/539/45969; Bourne note, 29 Dec. 1903, ibid.
25 Round note, 8 July 1897, CO 323/416/14660; CAs to CO, 21 June 1899, CAOG 9/71. See also CO 323/504/29442.
26 Round note, n.d., CO 323/429/25604.

Unfortunately for the Agents, when, in late October, the bank rate rose and the securities were sold, the price had fallen to such an extent that the colony obtained £527 less than could have been raised two months previously. The loss led G. W. Johnson to propose, unsuccessfully, that the secretary of state should 'instruct the Agents more definitely as to the time at which they should realise'.[27]

In West Africa infrastructure projects were partly financed from surplus revenues, inter-colony advances and private capital. Between 1901 and 1914 the Gold Coast and Sierra Leone invested £3.1m. and £167,146 respectively of their surplus funds in the construction of public works.[28] Likewise the Northern Nigerian Baro–Kano line was financed by Southern Nigerian advances lent at 3¾ per cent.[29] In the Gold Coast, the Agents made use of private capital. In 1900 the Ashanti Goldfields Corporation agreed to cover half the annual interest and sinking fund charges on loans raised for the Tarkwa–Kumassi line, and to make up the net earnings of the railway to £30,000 per annum for twenty years if they fell below this figure.[30] In return, the company obtained 1/5th of all profits, if earnings exceeded 4.5 per cent of capital expenditure, a guaranteed transport rate of of 1s. 6d. per ton mile for imports and 1s. for exports and an efficient means of transportation to its mines. Similarly, in 1902, the Osinu–Apadua road was partly financed by Goldfields of Akiu Ltd and other interested companies, who agreed to put up two-thirds of the capital.[31] Attempts to obtain private finance for the Tarkwa–Prestea and Princisu lines proved more difficult. In 1903 a number of mining companies agreed to advance up to £150,000 at 5 per cent for the construction of the Prestea line, and another mining company, backed by the Bank of British West Africa, offered to provide £70,000 at 3 per cent for the Princisu branch.[32] Unfortunately support for both schemes later collapsed. The organiser of the Prestea Syndicate died, and the Bank of British West Africa, on discovering that the Princisu loan would be repaid in Gold Coast

---

[27] Johnson note, 4 Feb. 1898, ibid. A similar situation occurred in 1905. In September of that year the Agency disposed of Straits securities for $66,490 less than could have been obtained eight months previously, and the colony demanded that it be reimbursed: Anderson to Elgin, 12 Sept. 1907, CAOG 9/222. Believing the claim 'childish', Blake refused, pointing out that the actual loss was only £241, as the majority of the securities had been sold to the Straits' Commissioner of Currency Fund, and, that since the proceeds were to be spent in the United Kingdom, they were unaffected by the appreciation of the sterling – dollar rate of exchange between February and September: Blake to Fiddes, 14 Nov. 1907, ibid; Blake to CO, 24 Oct. 1907, ibid. The Colonial Office agreed, believing that the colony had made the complaint because it 'could not resist the temptation of having a fling at the CAs': Hopwood note, 29 Oct. 1907, CO 273/332/37623.
[28] Tsey, 'Gold Coast railways', 183, table 4; PP 1913, lviii (287), 31.
[29] CAs to CO, 24 Mar. 1908, CO 520/69/10585.
[30] CAs to CO, 9 Mar. 1900, CO 96/365/7707.
[31] CO to Goldfields of Akiu Ltd, 14 Feb. 1902, CO 96/400/2661.
[32] Tarbutt to CAs, 21 Apr. 1903, CO 96/412/18397; CAs to CO, 22 May 1903, CO 96/412/19242.

stock, pulled out of the project.[33] In 1906, however, in the case of the Prestea branch-line, the Fanti Consolidated Mines Ltd, supported by the Union of London and Smiths Bank, agreed after some negotiation to provide up to £122,000 at 3 per cent to be repaid in cash or stock towards the construction of the railway, and to make good annual receipts if they fell below 3.5 per cent of capital expenditure.[34] On completion of the line, the company further agreed to finance the extension to Broomassie on similar terms.[35]

Finally, the Agents adopted a number of miscellaneous methods of financing colonies. In 1906 they avoided the issue of a £500,000 loan for the construction of the Kowloon–Canton railway through the creative use of the annual repayments on the £1.1m. loan the colony had made to the viceroy of Wuchang.[36] That loan had been financed by another slightly longer term issue floated by the colony in London, and the repayment should have been placed in a sinking fund and eventually used to repay this issue. Instead the Agents directed the repayments into a special fund, from which they were re-lent to the colony. The Agency also allowed Tanjong Pagar Dock Board shareholders to take money owed to them by the Straits government in the form of stock in the colony's 1907 loan; between 1903 and 1905, to finance the Sekondi–Kumassi line, it created £63,000 of 3 per cent Gold Coast stock, which it purchased itself on behalf of various colonial funds; and in 1899 it proposed that Ceylon should raise finance through the issue of treasury bills, short- term high-yield securities issued by a colony's treasury on the security of the receipt of its annual income.[37] In addition, there is evidence to suggest that the Agents may have begun to issue loans to credit-worthy colonies earlier than necessary, and used the proceeds as advances until they were required. In 1908, on receiving authority to issue a loan for Southern Nigeria, Blake informed the principal clerk, G. W. Fiddes, that 'there is no longer any object in pushing the Ceylon issue'.[38] And, in 1914, the Agents lamented a fall in the market, as 'in ordinary circumstances we would have chosen a favourable moment for the issue of either a Ceylon or a Straits loan and the proceeds would have enabled us to provide for all the requirements we should have to meet'.[39]

In 1901 the Agents re-entered the stock market and issued a number of

[33] CAs to CO, 11 Aug. 1904, CO 96/423/28192; CAs to CO, 22 Apr. 1904, CO 96/423/14326.
[34] Butler note, 23 Aug. 1906, CO 96/449/28594; note, 21 Jan. 1908, CO 96/474/2064.
[35] CAs to CO, 15 May 1908, CO 96/474/17414.
[36] CO to CAs, 7 Feb. 1906, CAOG 9/25; CO to CAs, 24 Aug. 1906, ibid.
[37] CAs to CO, 13 Sept. 1906, CAOG 9/80; memo, 26 Jan. 1903, CAOG 9/76; memo, 23 Jan. 1903, ibid; CAs to Ceylon, 6 Oct. 1899, CAOG 9/4; CAs to British Guiana, 19 Mar. 1900, CAOG 9/71. Of the 1907 Straits loan £460,500 (9%) was taken by shareholders: Fiddes note, 8 May 1907, CO 273/332/16226.
[38] Blake to Fiddes, 16 Apr. 1908, CAOG 9/94.
[39] CAs to CO, 21 Dec. 1914, CO 323/631/50952.

significant loans that eased finances.[40] The sale of crown colony stock, none the less, remained difficult, and to maintain subscription the Agents were forced to adopt a number of new strategies. First they set excessively generous terms. Although they claimed the contrary, the average yield at issue of crown colony loans from 1903 to 1912 was 0.2 per cent higher than that of self-governing colony loans (see table 29). Secondly, they began to issue fixed price loans and, for particularly difficult flotations, debentures with short lifespans that could be converted into fifty-year stock at the option of holders. Fixed price issues slightly reduced the Agents' administration costs and ensured that loans always had 'the appearance of a great success'.[41] They were therefore popular with underwriters, who often pressed for them. In the case of the 1902 Ceylon loan, for example, the fixed price 'was pressed upon us most strongly and made in effect a sine que non'.[42] A further advantage for brokers was that the issues were closed as soon as sufficient applications had been received.[43] The amount of stock obtained by the public was thus reduced, which increased post-issue demand and prices, and the late stagging of successful loans and the resultant post-issue fall in prices – when those who had stagged sold – was prevented.

The great advantage of convertible debentures, known in the City as 'floaters', was that their high dividends, short lifespans, and usefulness as collateral made them attractive to brokers.[44] Their principal drawback was the danger that at the end of the debenture's lifespan investors would redeem their holdings rather than convert them into stock, forcing the colony to return to the market and issue a further loan.[45] Such an outcome was prevented through the promise of preferential allotments to applicants who gave an undertaking to convert; the provision of a relatively large first dividend if conversion occurred by a specified date; the adoption of drawing sinking funds for the debentures (though not for the stock), with all their attendant drawbacks for investors; and, most important, highly favourable conversion terms, which became less advantageous as the debentures matured (see table 44).

The Colonial Office strongly opposed the use of these debentures, which they believed to be an 'antiquated system of borrowing' that did little to improve demand, and incorporated, in their dependence on investor conver-

---

[40] In 1903 the Agency also took charge of the proceeds of the £30m. Transvaal loan issued by the Bank of England, a portion of which it lent out to colonies in need of finance: CO 291/74/26286.

[41] CAs to Ceylon, 24 Jan. 1902, CAOG 9/4. In tender issues, the failure of the minimum price to be bidded up was often regarded negatively.

[42] Blake to Ridgeway, 9 Oct. 1902, ibid.

[43] The 1902 Ceylon loan, for example, opened at 12 p.m. and closed at 1.20 p.m.: memo, 29 Jan. 1902, CO 323/474/3803.

[44] CAA, CCC, memorandum, 10; Blake to CO, 13 Dec. 1905, CAOG 9/25.

[45] CAs to CO, 19 July 1905, CAOG 9/76.

Table 44
Percentage gain from immediate conversion to stock, 1904–11

Year	Issuing colony	Percentage gain
1904	Sierra Leone	7
1907	Straits	6
1908	Southern Nigeria	5
1909	Gold Coast	4
1911	Southern Nigeria	4.5

Source: GL, prospectuses.

Notes: Percentage gain = (100 – conversion rate) + (100 – fixed price). Except for the 1909 Gold Coast loan, the percentage conversion gain would be offset, over the lifetime of the debenture, by the lower stock dividends.

sion, a dangerous 'element of speculation'.[46] They were often further outraged by the high conversion terms offered. G. W. Fiddes, for example, believed that the terms of the 1909 Gold Coast loan were 'not a very splendid bargain' for the colony, and that the rates offered in the 1904 Sierra Leone issue indicated that the Agents were prepared to obtain money 'at any price'.[47] The Colonial Office also objected to the Agents' tendency, in their issue of such debentures, blatantly to ignore colonial ordinances. In the case of the 1907 Sierra Leone loan, the Crown Agents failed to abide by a regulation that required government contributions to the debentures' sinking fund to be made half-yearly.[48] Since the bi-annual determination of the amount of bonds that remained unconverted would greatly increase their costs, the Agents made only annual contributions to the fund. As this was 'the second recent occasion in which . . . [they] . . . have ignored the law', the Colonial Office sent the Agency a strong letter of condemnation.[49] Three years later the Agents, when issuing the Gold Coast loan, ignored a general loan ordinance, specifically a ruling that permitted conversion of debenture to stock only when the debentures had a higher rate of interest than the stock. Fiddes believed that it was 'a very serious business to find that they are capable of breaching the law in this way', adding that 'if they can do this they can do

[46] Ommanney note, 21 Oct. 1905, CO 129/330/36884; Fiddes note, 15 Dec. 1905, CO 129/330/44106.
[47] Fiddes note, 1 Feb. 1910, CO 323/564/2287; Fiddes note, 15 Dec. 1905, CO 129/330/44106.
[48] CAs to colonial secretary, 29 Nov. 1907, CO 267/527/30679.
[49] Fiddes note, 23 Dec. 1907, ibid. This proved ineffective, and by 1909 the Agents had reverted to their former practice, claiming, when discovered, that the requirements of the ordinance and of the prospectus were incompatible: CAs to colonial secretary, 12 July 1910, CAOG 9/156.

Table 45
Crown Agent and Bank of England purchases of stock, 1901–14

Year	Loan/Amount (£)	Purchaser	Amount Purchased (£)
1901	British Guiana 100,000	Crown Agents	73,300
1902	Gold Coast 1.035m.	Crown Agents	160,000
	Trinidad 200,000	Crown Agents	80,400
1905	Lagos 2m.	Crown Agents	100,000
		Bank of England	150,000
1907	Straits 5m.	Crown Agents	1.7m
1908	Southern Nigeria 3m.	Crown Agents	100,000
		Bank of England	500,000
1909	Gold Coast 1m.	Crown Agents	100,000
1910	Straits 2.75m.	Crown Agents	not known
1911	Southern Nigeria 5m.	Bank of England	425,000
1914	Trinidad 550,000	Crown Agents	500,000

Source: CAOG 9/36; CAOG 9/66; CAOG 9/70; CAOG 9/76; CAOG 9/81; CAOG 9/86; CAOG 9/105; CO 520/69/16505. BE, ADM 7/56/1228; ADM 7/58/1216; ADM 7/58/1234.

anything'.[50] His colleagues agreed, and the Agents were again warned not to act illegally.[51]

Demand was further increased by purchase of debenture or stock by the Bank of England and Crown Agents, the removal of Treasury first charges and the 1900 passage of the Colonial Stocks Act. Between 1905 and 1911 the Bank of England bought at issue £1.075m. of stock at or below the minimum price, no doubt in response to Agency requests (see table 45). Similarly the Agency began to buy at issue. A change in stock market rules permitted them to reserve rather than tender for the securities they required, and purchases reduced the amount of stock that had to be offloaded on to the public and encouraged and minimised the cost of underwriting.[52] Consequently, between 1901 and 1914 the Agency bought £2.8m. of securities in nine issues (see table 45). Among other issuing houses, such purchases were not unusual. Both the Bank of England and the London and Westminster Bank tendered, usually at the minimum price, for portions of loans they were in the process of issuing. The Bank of England, for example, agreed to tender for £250,000 of the 1897 New Zealand, and £200,000 of the 1893 Queensland issues,[53] and

---

[50] Fiddes note, 1 Feb. 1910, CO 323/564/2287.
[51] CO to CAs, 17 Feb. 1910, ibid.
[52] Reserved stock could not be listed.
[53] BE to New Zealand, 23 July 1897, BE, AC 30/8; BE to Queensland, 11 Jan. 1893, AC 30/117.

the London and Westminster Bank applied for £274,400 of the 1906 New South Wales loan, and £250,000 of the 1890 Cape issue.[54]

First charges on Jamaica and Southern Nigeria were removed by the early repayment of their treasury loans, and in the case of Southern Nigeria by the issue of a further loan on the market.[55] In 1899 Chamberlain likewise persuaded the Treasury to convert a Gold Coast War Office debt, which had acted as a first charge, into a special grant-in-aid.[56] In 1900 the Agents also successfully lobbied for the inclusion of crown colony issues in the Colonial Stock Act, which allowed trustees to invest in colonial stock even when they were not otherwise permitted to do so by the terms of their trust deeds.[57] The act supposedly increased demand for colonial issues, and enabled many colonies, which had previously been debarred from the market, to issue on reasonable terms.[58] In fact, although the exclusion of the crown colonies from the act would have made their loans less competitive than those of self-governing colonies and greatly reduced subscription, it seems unlikely that their inclusion significantly increased demand. Even before the act many trust deeds permitted the purchase of colonial stock, and a large number continued to exclude colonial investments after its passage.[59] Furthermore, few trusts made fresh investments after their initial formation, the act did not cover protectorates and, in order to comply with its requirements, colonies had to pass costly fresh legislation to ensure interest payments and prevent default.[60]

The adoption of the strategies described above and the upturn in the market from approximately 1904 had little effect on subscription. From 1904 to 1914, 71 per cent of the loans floated were undersubscribed. Crown colony issues found it difficult to compete with foreign issues, which offered relatively high rates of return, and, because of the unexpectedly high cost of railway construction and the Agents' reluctance and inability to float loans earlier, issues were far larger than market demand. In addition, many of the issuing colonies were practically unknown to the general public and, in the City, some were regarded as poor risks; the credit-worthiness of the Gold Coast, for instance, was affected by the Ashanti wars and the gold-mining boom. By 1904 investors were also beginning to suspect, through press reports and parliamentary questions, that many of the West African railways were not commercially viable, and some institutional investors, who had previously subscribed, began to take stock on underwriting terms.[61] Moreover the Agents were often forced to issue at unpropitious times, owing to urgent

---

54 NWB, 12914/229; 12911/32. See also 12909/378; 12910/201; 12911/168.
55 Weeded file, CAA, a144.
56 Kubicek, The administration of imperialism, 314-15.
57 CAs to CO, 13 June 1900, CO 323/453/18747.
58 Kesner, Economic control and colonial development, 82, 87-9.
59 David Jessop, 'The Colonial Stock Act of 1901: a symptom of new imperialism', Journal of Imperial and Commonwealth History iv (1976), 154-63.
60 CO to CAs, 21 Aug. 1903, CAOG 9/88; CO to CAs, 29 Mar. 1901, ibid.
61 CAs to CO, 31 July 1902, CAOG 9/86; CAs to Straits, 21 Oct. 1910, CAOG 9/36.

colonial needs for finance or Colonial Office interference. The 1905 Lagos loan, for example, was delayed by a Colonial Office request for advice on whether it should be issued on the combined revenues of Lagos and Nigeria, and the 1908 Southern Nigerian issue by the secretary of state's deliberations on whether a Treasury loan should be obtained.[62] On both occasions the delays caused the Agents to miss upturns in the market. Sometimes the Agency was also the victim of unforeseen events, while Blake suggested that some issues were deliberately sabotaged.[63] The failure of the Straits loan, for instance, was partly blamed on 'the enemies of the colony and of the Office', who had begun rumours that the issue would be undersubscribed.[64]

Many, however, suspected that a number of the failures were the result of the Agency's incompetence. City issuing houses, that, after unsuccessful Crown Agent flotations, had to postpone their own issues until underwriters had relieved themselves of unsold stock, expressed their views through the press. In 1905 the *Daily Graphic* reported that financiers believed that the Agents did 'not understand their business', and, in 1903, the *Westminster Gazette* advised the Agency to take 'a lesson . . . from the Bank of England'.[65] Similar criticism came from the colonies and from the Colonial Office. Discontent in the Straits reached such a pitch in 1906 that the legislative council proposed that the colony should abandon the Agency for the forth-coming £5m. loan.[66] Antrobus, meanwhile, believed that the Crown Agents' report on the 1905 Lagos loan was not 'very convincing', the Colonial Office clerk A. J. Harding dismissed the reasons put forward for the failure of the Mauritius issue as an 'apologia' and Fiddes regarded the Agency's explana-tions for poor response to the 1906 Hong Kong loan as 'more ingenious than convincing'.[67]

---

[62] CAs to colonial secretary, 3 Mar. 1905, CO 147/177/6936; CAs to CO, 8 May 1908, CO 520/69/16505. The 1905 Mauritius loan was floated because the Office could no longer obtain advances for the colony, and the timing of the 1907 Straits issue, partly raised to pay compensation to Tanjong Pagar dock shareholders when the dock was taken over by the government, was dictated by the court that awarded the compensation: CAs to Mauritius, 21 Dec. 1905, CAOG 9/77; CO to colonial secretary, 3 May 1907, CO 273/332/16226.

[63] The 1906 Hong Kong and the 1908 Southern Nigerian loans, for example, were affected by sudden falls in demand caused respectively by the conference of Algeciras and 'bad news from India': ibid; Blake to Hong Kong, 23 Feb. 1906, CO 129/336/6544.

[64] CO to Straits, 3 May 1907, CO 273/332/16226.

[65] *Daily Graphic*, 23 Feb. 1906, CO 129/336/6544; *Westminster Gazette*, 19 Dec. 1905, CO 167/773/45066. The Agents dismissed such comments, arguing that they emanated from 'enemies, whose constant aim is to destroy our business and to get it into the hands of the City': Blake to Fiddes, 8 May 1907, CO 273/332/16226.

[66] CAs to CO, 2 Apr. 1906, CO 273/322/11688. In response, Blake pointed out that the leading critic, G. S. Murray, was the manager of 'one of the local banks', and that 'the reasons for his remarks would therefore appear to be apparent'. Lucas, though, reported that both the present and previous governors of the colony 'have spoken to us in high terms of Mr Murray. Sir S. Anderson would like him to be knighted': Lucas note, 4 Apr. 1906, ibid.

[67] Antrobus note, 21 Mar. 1905, CO 147/177/6936; Harding note, 23 Dec. 1905, CO 167/773/45066; Fiddes note, 27 Feb. 1906, CO 129/336/6544.

Concerned at the Agency's performance, the secretary of state increasingly began to intervene in the issuing process. In 1905 the Colonial Office opposed the Agency on four separate occasions. In May it insisted that the Lagos loan be issued as stock rather than in the form of debentures as proposed. The Agents, themselves doubtful as to the suitability of bonds, acquiesced, though Blake later complained, when the issue proved only 'a qualified success', that 'the Colonial Office did not accept . . . responsibility'.[68] Later in the year the Colonial Office strongly pressed the Agents to issue a Gold Coast loan. After a number of letters to this effect, Blake informed the secretary of state 'that it is usual to leave such matters to our discretion'.[69] The colonial secretary then rejected the Agents' proposal to convert an earlier Mauritius debenture loan to lower interest stock. Although 'financially worthwhile', it was argued that a conversion was politically undesirable as the proceeds of the loan had been advanced to planters, who would demand lower interest rates and the extension of repayment periods.[70]

Relations between the Crown Agents and the Colonial Office broke down at the end of the year, when the secretary of state expressed his reservations as regards the Agents' intention to issue the forthcoming Hong Kong loan in the form of convertible debentures. Although the Colonial Office agreed to instruct the colony to pass an amendment to its loan ordinance that would allow the sum required to be raised as either debentures or stock, Blake was warned that 'very cogent reasons' would be required before the use of debentures was sanctioned.[71] Blake's reaction was to write personally to Fiddes, drawing attention to the fact that 'it has always been held in the past that the Agents ought to have a free hand in such matters, and that the Colonial Office should confine themselves to expressing an opinion on our actions'.[72] A letter was also despatched to Ommanney, in which he was informed that the Agents believed that the warning 'implied' that they did not 'know their business' and that 'the secretary of state has to teach us'. To avoid 'sharp opposition', he was asked to arrange for the offending words to be withdrawn.[73] In addition, Blake, believing the Colonial Office's alteration of the ordinance to be inadequate, directly instructed the colony to pass his own amendment.[74]

In his reply, Ommanney adopted a conciliatory approach, claiming that the Office had been 'anxious to show the utmost deference to your opinion', but refused to withdraw the warning. Feeling that he had no alternative, Blake wrote an official letter of complaint, which, significantly, received no

68 Blake to Ommanney, 21 Nov. 1905, CAOG 9/25.
69 Blake to CO, 21 Aug. 1905, CAOG 9/76.
70 Harding note, 12 May 1905, CO 167/773/15872.
71 CO to CAs, 3 Nov. 1905, CAOG 9/25.
72 Blake to Fiddes, 7 Nov. 1905, ibid.
73 Blake to Ommanney, 21 Nov. 1905, ibid.
74 Blake to Nathan, 10 Nov. 1905, ibid.

reply.[75] On discovering a few weeks later that his own amendment to the ordinance had arrived in the colony too late to replace the Colonial Office's version, he informed the secretary of state that the new amendment was inadequate. Not only did it contain an inaccurate reference to the loan ordinance, but its inappropriate wording could lead to repayment difficulties.[76] The Colonial Office was unconvinced. It was discovered that Blake's first point was based on the reading of an out-of-date ordinance, Fiddes was 'unable to see' his second argument, and Ommanney believed that there was no 'real foundation to . . . Blake's difficulty'.[77] In their investigation of the criticisms, however, a real fault was discovered in the amendment, which was scrapped as there was insufficient time before the issue to pass a replacement.[78]

Emboldened by their stand against the Agents, the Colonial Office stepped up its interventions, and by 1908 was beginning to play a part in the issue of loans, albeit in the face of fierce resistance from Blake.[79] After the enquiry and Blake's 'retirement', this opposition ceased and the Agency accepted the Colonial Office's new role. This continued to grow, so that, by 1914, loan flotation was a combined operation conducted not only by the Agents and their brokers, but also by the Colonial Office and the issuing colonies, which had final approval of the terms and timing of flotations and of the loan prospectus.[80]

Other financial services

As well as supplying external funds, the Agents provided colonial governments with two other important financial services. First, they organised the movement of money into and out of London and the colonies; and second, they managed the investment of balances on colonies' current accounts and their contributions to investment funds.

---

[75] Blake to CO, 13 Dec. 1905, ibid.
[76] CAs to CO, 26 Jan. 1906, CO 129/336/2919.
[77] Fiddes to Blake, 31 Jan. 1906, ibid; Ommanney note, 3 Feb. 1906, ibid. When given the opportunity to withdraw his first point, Blake refused, claiming that it was the later edition of the ordinance rather than him that was wrong: Blake to Fiddes, 1 Feb. 1906, ibid.
[78] Ibid; CO to CAs, 7 Feb. 1906, ibid.
[79] See Cox note, 12 Mar. 1906, CO 273/322/7309; Lucas note, 30 Mar. 1906, CO 273/322/10776; CO to CAs, 28 Aug. 1906, CO 273/322/30972; Fiddes note, 24 Aug. 1906, ibid; CO to CAs, 19 Nov. 1907, CAOG 9/94; Blake to Lucas, 20 Nov. 1907, ibid; Blake to CO, 6 Dec. 1907, ibid.
[80] See Cox note, 20 Oct. 1910, CO 273/364/32074; Winfield note, 6 Feb. 1914, CO 295/494/4546; CO to CAs, 21 Feb. 1914, CAOG 9/23; CAs to CO, 17 Feb. 1914, CO 54/775/6200; CAs to CO, 9 Mar. 1914, CO 54/775/10373; CAs to CO, 31 Mar. 1914, CO 54/775/11907; CAs to CO, 1 Apr. 1914, CO 54/775/12043.

The remittance of funds

Throughout the period 1883–1914 there was a continuous transfer of money between the Crown Agents and their clients. Colonial governments sent sums to the Crown Agents to pay for their purchases in the United Kingdom, to meet other commitments and to be invested in London. The Agents, meanwhile, transferred to the colonies the proceeds of loans and investment funds that were to be spent locally. These transfers or remittances could be completed in a number of ways. In the 1860s and 1870s the Agents often arranged for the transport of gold to and from colonies or entered into private arrangements with merchant banks with colonial connections.[81] In 1862, for instance, it was agreed with Messrs Burnett Hoare & Co that the bank would receive £30,000 per month from the Agents in London and would arrange for the Bank of Mauritius, with which it was closely linked, to make the same sum available to the railway authorities in Mauritius.[82] Colonies also occasionally transferred money to the UK in the form of surplus or worn coin, subsequently sold for its metallic value, and the Agents sometimes arranged for remittances to be made via book-keeping entries.[83] In 1863 the Ceylon government paid the sums required to meet its debts in England into its railway department's account held at a local bank. The department had funds on deposit in London, and the Agents therefore then moved a corresponding amount from this deposit account into the colony's general account, from where the debts were paid.[84]

All of these methods of transfer had drawbacks. Gold could be lost through theft or accident, accounting transfers were often not possible and were highly dubious, and private arrangements with banks were subject to misunderstanding and deceit. The arrangement with Messrs Burnett Hoare & Co broke down when the company decided that it had the right to make a monthly charge of £810 for its work.[85] The Agents, therefore, usually transferred money by the purchase or sale of bills of exchange. These were similar to cheques, except that their value was only payable at a specified future date, usually 30 or 90 days from the date of issue. Using bills, colonies could remit funds to the Agents in one of two ways. First, they could buy a bill in the colony from a local bank, which would charge a selling commission, and then place it on a ship sailing to London. In the 1860s and 1870s such purchases

---

[81] See, for example, CAs to CO, 23 Aug. 1862, CO 167/444/8393.

[82] Ibid. In return, the Bank of Mauritius was promised funds for railway construction which would enable it to make large profits from the difference between its 2% deposit interest rate and the 12% that it could charge borrowers: CAs to CO, 2 Jan. 1863, CO 167/455/56.

[83] For example, CAs to CO, 26 Jan. 1878, CO 884/3/32, no. 75; Gambia to CO, 4 July 1899, CO 879/59/592, no. 38.

[84] CAs to CO, 9 June 1863, CO 54/382/5645. A similar procedure was adopted by Mauritius and the Straits: CAs to Mauritius, 27 July 1863, CO 167/455/7371; Straits to CO, 8 July 1908, CO 882/9/108, no. 262.

[85] CAs to CO, 23 July 1863, CO 167/455/825.

generally occurred after the main primary crop had been exported, when the demand for money was great and banks sold the bills at a discount.[86] Later, purchases and remittances were made on a more regular basis, generally every month or three months.

How the Agents obtained the bill's value on its arrival depended on the time taken to transport it to London. If the bill's maturation date was imminent, it would be allowed to mature and then passed to a bank, which would pay the Agents its full value which would eventually be recouped from the issuing bank. On the other hand, if it would not fall due for some days, the Agents would immediately sell it to a bank at a discount of its value. Bills were sold by the Crown Agents bill brokers, Messrs R. W. Carter, who worked for the Agents continuously from 1861 and charged a small fee for their services.[87] The largest purchaser appears to have been the Colonial Bank, which in 1885 and 1895 respectively bought 59 per cent and 39 per cent of the Agents' bills, though a wide variety of other banks and discount houses were also used.[88] The advantage of this method of remittance was that bills could be purchased on relatively good terms, as the selling bank had use of the money paid for the bill at no interest for the whole of its life. On the other hand, local banks in the colonies generally charged a high selling commission of ½ per cent and the colonial government suffered an opportunity loss, in that during the life of the bill it obtained no interest on the money used to buy it. As the bills were bought in one currency and the money received in sterling, the colony could also suffer losses due to unfavourable exchange rates.

The second method of remittance involved the Agents selling a bill drawn on the colonial government to a London bank. The bill was sold at a discount of its value and the bank charged a selling commission. The Agents received the money immediately and the bank mailed the bill to an agent in the colony, who received its value from the colonial government. These bills too were sold by Messrs R. W. Carter, whose employees visited all banks with an interest in the colony to discover the discount each would demand to pay the whole or more generally a portion of the value of the bill.[89] If an offer was obtained for a portion of the value, this was used 'as a lever wherewith to obtain from the others an increase in their original quotation'.[90] No preference was given to the larger colonial banks as, if this were to occur, there was a danger that the UK banks would form themselves into a ring 'and agree among themselves a (discount) rate which would be mutually satisfactory'.[91] When the quotations of colonial banks were equal to those of the UK banks,

---

[86] CAs to CO, 27 Aug. 1867, CO 54/429/8501.
[87] CAs to CO, 19 Oct. 1903, CO 111/539/38390.
[88] BE, C 23/6/72.
[89] Carter to CAs, 12 Sept. 1905, CO 129/330/35163.
[90] Ibid.
[91] CAs to CO, 2 Oct. 1905, ibid.

however, the former obtained a larger proportion of the amount offered. This method of remittance, again, had advantages and drawbacks. Colonies benefited from the London banks' relatively low selling commissions (of 1/16 per cent) and acquired an opportunity gain equal to the interest on the money obtained for the life of the bill. Conversely, to cover the risk that the debt would not be met and their opportunity loss, the London banks bought bills on relatively poor terms. Since the bills were sold in sterling and the colony paid the money in the local currency, losses could also again occur through unfavourable exchange rates.

Over the period there was much discussion over which method of remittance was preferable.[92] An experiment which took place in 1903 found that the difference in cost was slight.[93] However, after 1884, when the Oriental Bank collapsed and a number of colonies lost funds which were in the process of remittance, the Agents and the Colonial Office generally encouraged colonial governments to adopt the second method of fund transfer.[94] Not only were London banks less likely to experience financial difficulties but, as the Agents were relatively more aware of colonial United Kingdom needs, less money had to be remitted and the opportunity cost of keeping large sums in the UK was reduced. None the less, a number of colonies, including British Guiana, Trinidad and Jamaica, continued to purchase and despatch bills to England.[95]

The management of colonial investments
The Agents managed the colonies' current account balances and their investment funds.

Current account balances
The contents of the colonies' current accounts met their transactions in the United Kingdom and consisted of funds remitted to the Agents and the unspent proceeds of loans. At any one time, the accounts contained a surplus balance, the size of which was largely determined by the number and size of recent loans and the rate at which the issuing colonies had been spending the money raised.[96] Unlike the India Office, which monitored its current account on a day-to-day basis, the Agency reviewed its balances only every fortnight until 1912, with the result that a lot of money lay idle for relatively long

[92] Funds were remitted from the Agents to the colonies using the same methods, but in reverse. Either the colonial government sold bills drawn on the Agents to a bank in the colony or the Agency bought bills in London and despatched them to the colony.
[93] CAs to CO, 19 Oct. 1903, CO 111/539/38390; CAs to CO, 28 Aug. 1903, CO 111/539/32258.
[94] CAA, O/Sec 12/3, 19. Colonial remittance was only recommended when the London market in bills that could be sold in a colony was restricted: CAs to CO, 26 Aug. 1908, CAOG 9/216.
[95] Bourne note, 29 Dec 1903, CO 111/539/45969.
[96] Memo, Mar. 1924, CAOG 9/234; CAOG 9/276, table 1.

periods.[97] The balances held by each colony were also kept distinct and invested separately, which greatly reduced possible returns.[98]

A small proportion of the money held, £74,687 (10 per cent of the total) at the end of 1908, was kept in the Agents' Bank of England general account to meet anticipated colonial requirements in the United Kingdom.[99] This account, like the others kept there by the Crown Agents, paid no interest, though the bank provided various services for no charge, and, as has been seen, helped the Agency in other ways. The remaining balances were advanced to colonies in need of finance, or, if there was insufficient colonial demand, placed on deposit with joint stock banks or invested in securities. The surplus balances placed on deposit were at first invested in the joint stock bank that offered the highest return. Sums were generally lent at 7 to 10 days call, and the interest determined at the end of each week.[100] Banks regularly used included the London and Westminster Bank, the London Joint Stock Bank, the City Bank and the Union.[101] As time passed and the Agents became more sensitive to criticism, they increasingly began to use the London and Westminster Bank, which they regarded as the most secure, and which in September 1908 held £1.03m. (27.5 per cent of total balances).[102] This bank was also prepared to provide a variety of free services and offered highly competitive interest rates. During the 1908 enquiry, for instance, it emerged that in 1907, when bank rate was 7 per cent, the Agents obtained '7 per cent on some occasions and 6 per cent continuously', whereas the joint stock bank used by the India Office only paid 6 per cent interest.[103]

The other possible repositories of deposit funds, the Bank of England and colonial banks, were rejected by the Agents. The former refused to pay deposit interest rates and charged its self-governing colony clients a commission of ¼ per cent for the investment of loan proceeds.[104] It was therefore only used for a portion of the 1903 Transvaal loan, the deposit of which helped it to maintain bank rate.[105] The Agents' suspicion of colonial banks, unsurprisingly, was strongly opposed by the colonies. It was claimed that such banks paid relatively high deposit rates and that local investments would promote economic growth and reduce the cost of remitting money from

97   CAs to CO, 23 Mar. 1912, CO 323/591/9213.
98   Colonial balances were pooled in 1928: circular, 26 July 1928, CO 323/1019/8.
99   CAs to CO, 1 Sept. 1909, CO 323/553/11325.
100 PPE, qq. 1207, 1210. See, for example, CAs to CO, 23 Apr. 1869, CO 247/111/4604.
101 CAs to Cape, 21 Sept. 1867, CO 48/439/9353; CAs to CO, 23 Apr. 1869, CO 247/111/4604.
102 Ommanney note, 17 Jan. 1895, CO 28/238/825; CAs to CO, 1 Sept. 1909, CO 323/553/11325. The bank held £1,826,000 in September 1909, and £930,300 in October 1914: CAs to London and Westminster Bank, 19 Sept. 1905, CAOG 9/24; CAs to CO, 13 Oct. 1914, CO 323/631/39645.
103 PPE, qq. 732, 1208.
104 PPE, q. 1193; Queensland to BE, 7 Sept. 1897, BE, AC 30/150.
105 R. S. Sayers, Bank of England operations, 1890–1914, London 1936, 39.

London.[106] At first their appeals fell on deaf ears. The Agents believed that all colonial financial institutions were inherently unsafe and that local investment would have little effect on development. They thus strongly opposed demands for local investment. In 1905, for instance, Barbados was forced to withdraw part of the proceeds of its 1896 loan from a local bank despite the fact that the rate offered was 1 per cent higher than that current in London.[107] Later, when colonial finances were tighter and their banks more secure, the Agents were prepared to look more favourably at colonial investment. In 1908 a Southern Nigerian request for £25,000 of the proceeds of the 1907 issue to be placed with the Bank of British West Africa was strongly supported. The bank offered an interest rate of 3½ per cent, as opposed to the London and Westminster Bank's 1 per cent, and had authorised capital of more than £1m.[108] Persuaded by the Agents' arguments, the Colonial Office allowed the deposit, which was followed in January 1909 by a further investment of £25,000; in November 1911, despite Colonial Office suspicion that the bank took 'exceptional risks', by a £50,000–£100,000 deposit; and, in 1913, by a deposit of £100,000.[109]

Securities were used as a refuge for balances between the 1860s and 1880s. Investment occurred when bank deposit rates were low and, after 1867, when the current account surpluses of a colony exceeded £100,000, the Treasury in that year making this sum the maximum that a colonial government could keep on deposit.[110] At first balances could only be placed in exchequer bills, short-term government securities.[111] These were then used only for sums likely to be required in the near future, and amounts that would be needed six to twelve months hence were placed in consols or imperial securities, depending on the state of the market.[112] Until 1863 all securities were bought and sold by the Bank of England, which passed the relevant instruction on to their brokers, Mullens, with whom they shared the commission. Thereafter the Crown Agents instructed Mullens directly, thus reducing the cost of the transactions.[113] In order to obtain the most advantageous price, the broker was given discretion both as to when the purchase or sale was to be made and at what rate.[114]

[106] New Zealand parliamentary debates, 1875, xc. 561.
[107] CAs to CO, 18 Nov. 1895, CO 28/238/20574.
[108] CAs to CO, 13 Nov. 1908, CO 520/70/41598.
[109] CAs to CO, 8 Jan. 1909, CO 520/84/897; CAs to CO, 16 Nov. 1911, CO 520/109/37005; Anderson note, 17 Nov. 1911, CO 520/109/37005; CAs to CO, 6 Oct. 1913, CO 520/129/34784.
[110] Note, 12 Feb. 1867, CO 179/87/1336.
[111] CAs to CO, 17 Feb. 1859, CO 323/254/1471.
[112] CAs to CO, 27 Nov. 1862, CO 179/66/11563.
[113] CAs to CO, 6 Aug. 1863, CO 167/455/7689; CAs to CO, 19 Aug. 1863, CO 167/455/8228.
[114] CAs to Mullens, 13 July 1863, CO 167/455/7689.

Investment in securities, however, was short-lived, declining from the 1880s when the Treasury's 1867 ruling fell into disuse, bank deposit rates became more competitive and colonial securities were more difficult to obtain.[115] Such investment also had a number of drawbacks. Purchase and sale commissions increased costs, an urgent need for money could force sales before the payment of the dividend and price fluctuations could lead to losses.[116] Wishing to avoid the associated 'good deal of trouble', the Agency therefore abandoned colonial securities until the end of the century, when they began to purchase new two- or five-year bonds, the price of which was unlikely to fall drastically.[117]

Investment funds

Colonies created investment funds for a variety of reasons. As well as sinking funds, saving bank funds and surplus funds, which have already been discussed, there were also pension and bank note funds. Pension funds and the related widows and orphans funds held investments that produced sufficient returns to pay the pensions of former colonial government officers and their dependants. Bank note funds, meanwhile, contained invested sums equal to some proportion of the value of the notes in circulation and were used to meet any demands from the public for the exchange of notes for currency.

At first many self-governing colonies managed their own funds.[118] As regards other colonies' funds, the Agency merely received the money that governments wished to invest in a particular fund, which it passed on to the Bank of England. All investments were made by the bank through Mullens Marshall and under the direction of the Treasury.[119] The Agency merely invested the resultant dividends in the same securities as the original investment.[120] Crown Agent management began in the 1860s. By 1870 there was a total of six funds under its management, containing investments worth £257,051.[121] The amount supervised then rose rapidly to £3m. in 1879, £4.16m. in 1887 (when there were 116 funds), £11m. in 1905 (in 231 funds)

[115] Owing to their security and high return relative to consols, colonial debentures and stocks were held increasingly on a long-term basis by banks as part of their reserve funds: CAs to CO, 9 Feb. 1869, CO 54/449/1507.

[116] CAs to CO, 7 July 1863, CO 167/455/6632. In 1865, for example, the Agents sold debentures bought on behalf of Ceylon at a loss of £6,000: CAs to CO, 11 Oct. 1865, CO 54/408/9871.

[117] PPE, q. 1194. In 1912 £1m. of the £2m. Southern Nigerian loan was used to purchase New Zealand two year bonds: CAs to CO, 14 June 1912, CO 520/118/18477.

[118] PP 1823, xiv, 22; memo, 1955, CAA, M 68.

[119] Note, Dec. 1855, T 1/5872a/20027; note, 7 July 1855, T 1/59727/1175.

[120] Note, 9 Jan. 1855, T 1/5972a/509.

[121] CAs to CO, 26 Feb. 1870, CO 323/299/1423.

and £22m. in 1912 (230 funds).[122] As 'the opening of numerous small accounts . . . imposes much labour and expense upon us, for which we are not paid', the Office generally attempted to minimise the number of funds in existence.[123] In 1906, for example, British Guiana, which proposed the creation of a reserve savings bank fund, was advised to earmark a portion of the existing savings bank fund as a reserve.[124]

The Agents' management duties included the investment of fund contributions and dividends, the sale of securities when necessary and ensuring that any stipulations in fund constitutions as to the amount and type of securities to be held, were followed.[125] In return for these services, they received a ¼ per cent brokerage fee on every investment bought or sold that they passed on to Scrimgeours, who undertook the transactions, and a further ¼ per cent commission on purchases and sales that they kept for themselves. The latter commission continued to be charged even after 1900 when investments were transferred between funds rather than bought or sold on the open market. The Agents could invest only in securities approved by the Colonial Office. In the 1860s these were consols, Exchequer and Treasury bills, metropolitan board of works loans, guaranteed colonial government issues, the government debentures of Canada, the Cape, Ceylon, Mauritius, New South Wales, Western Australia and Victoria, Indian 4 per cent stock and Indian railway 5 per cent stock.[126] With the introduction of stock, the Agents' scope for investment was restricted by the regulations of some leading stock issues that disallowed purchases by official bodies.[127] At the same time, the high price of approved securities reduced their yields to a level below that prescribed by the constitutions of some funds, and at which it was unlikely that sinking funds would generate sufficient sums for loan repayment.[128] In 1888 the Agency consequently requested and obtained permission to hold the trusteeship of funds in their personal rather than their official capacities.[129] It also successfully lobbied the Colonial Office to be allowed to purchase cheaper

122 Julyan to CO, 13 Apr. 1880, CO 323/343/5381; CO 323/393/11909; Blake to CO, 2 June 1905, CAOG 9/210; CAs to CO, 17 Dec. 1912, ibid.
123 CAs to CO, 23 Feb. 1906, CO 111/553/6545.
124 Ibid. See also CAs to CO, 1 June 1908, CO 54/720/20128.
125 In the case of the Mauritius savings bank fund half of the investments had to be held in Indian government 6% rupee paper, 25% in United Kingdom government securities and the remainder in first-class colonial securities other than those of Mauritius: CO to CAs, 18 Apr. 1888, CAOG 9/147.
126 CAs to CO, 20 Nov. 1869, CO 323/294/12843; CAs to CO, 26 Jan. 1880, CO 323/343/1211. In the 1850s the Bank of England was instructed by the Treasury to invest in 3% consols: note, 4 Sept. 1857, T 1/6111/14085.
127 CAs to CO, 4 June 1888, CO 323/371/11143.
128 CAs to CO, 14 Mar. 1889, CO 323/375B/5332.
129 Since 1885 the under-secretary of state had used his own name when trustee on the insistence of the Treasury, which feared that the use of an official title would give the impression that the British government had a 'pecuniary interest' in the funds: Round note, 18 Apr. 1900, CO 323/452/9228.

securities including Indian 3½ per cent loans and government stock of any British colony quoted at a price that was equivalent to 105 for a 4 per cent stock.[130]

In the event, the additions to the list proved to be too limited. Security prices continued their inexorable rise and the self-imposed restriction on colonial purchases, which had been chosen because 'it had been adopted by a Parliamentary committee and seemed likely to be approved', was found to be 'very inconvenient and anomalous'.[131] In 1892 the Agents were therefore permitted to buy any quoted colonial government debenture or stock and the securities named in the 1889 Trust Amendment Act, which included the stocks of the leading English railway companies and county councils. Thereafter the Agents made no attempt to extend the list, though they occasionally requested permission to invest funds in non-colonial government securities not included in the Trust Act. In 1911, for example, the Colonial Office authorised investments in 3½ per cent guaranteed first mortgage stock of the Ontario railway company, which was supposedly as secure as Canadian government stock, but 7 per cent cheaper.[132]

On receiving fund contributions, the Agents in the 1860s placed the sums in their general account at the Bank of England and from 1867, to avoid confusion, separate fund accounts, where they remained until a favourable investment opportunity arose.[133] Before 1880 contributions often stayed in these accounts, earning no interest, for up to three months, with the interest lost often offsetting any gain from the eventual investment.[134] There was also the possibility that the market, rather than improving during the pre-investment period, would actually worsen. The Agents, after a complaint from the Colonial Office, therefore began to ensure that the state of the balances accumulating for investment were brought to the attention of the Senior Crown Agent at least once a month.[135] The type of security in which fund contributions were invested varied according to the nature of the fund. Sinking fund contributions were generally placed in securities that would mature at or as near as possible to the date on which the loan was due for redemption.[136] Since securities were repaid at par, the value of even the most unsuccessful investment at the time of repayment would therefore be close to £100 per debenture or stock. Surplus funds and other funds, the contents of which could be required urgently, were invested in consols and annuities. Funds with no definite realisation date were placed in securities with a spread of

---

[130] CAs to CO, 14 Mar. 1889, CO 323/375B/5332; Anderson note, 16 Mar. 1889, ibid.
[131] CAs to CO, 10 Nov. 1892, CO 323/388/21970.
[132] CAs to CO, 18 Dec. 1911, CO 273/376/40643. See also CAs to CO, 18 Mar. 1922, CO 323/888/13204.
[133] CAs to CO, 9 Oct. 1867, CO 323/286/9921.
[134] CAs to CO, 20 Nov. 1880, CO 323/343/18004.
[135] Note, 26 Nov. 1880, ibid.
[136] Memo, 1955, CAA, CA M 68.

Table 46
Fund investments, 1870–1908 (%)

	Colonial securities	Consols	Indian securities
1870	79	21	0
1879	71	12	7
1908	84	7	1.2

Source: CAs to CO, 26 July 1870, CO 323/299/1423; Julyan to CO, 13 Apr. 1880, CO 323/343/5381; CO 323/553/11325.

Notes: No figures are available for the period 1879–1907. In 1908 45.9% of investments were in self-governing colony securities, 37.8% in crown colony debentures/stock, 0.42% in annuities and 0.76% in miscellaneous securities including war bonds, Bank of England stock, local loans, Greek debentures and Egyptian irrigation certificates. The remainder of the funds was invested in own currency Indian, Belgium, Danish, German and Prussian securities.

maturities, so as to provide for unexpected calls on their contents at times when prices were low.[137]

The range of securities bought changed little over the period (*see* table 46). Most funds were invested in colonial securities, 38 per cent of which were issued in the crown colonies in 1908. As discussed in chapter 6, purchases of crown colony securities were often used to increase the price of an issuing colony's existing securities in the months before issue and, after flotation, to maintain the price of recently issued debentures or stock. In many cases a proportion of a particular colony's funds were invested in securities issued by the colony, a practice that increased both the price and the colony's credit as regards future issues. In 1880 a Mauritius sinking fund contained £14,700 of Mauritius debentures; in 1896 the Trinidad savings bank fund held £12,500 of Trinidad 4 per cent debentures; and in 1906 one third of the British Guiana savings bank fund was invested in British Guiana stock.[138] The Colonial Office, needless to say, had doubts about self-investment and occasionally refused to authorise schemes. In 1903, for instance, it rejected a proposal to replace securities in the Western Australian 4 per cent sinking fund with other Western Australian stock.[139] It was argued that the sale of the funds' existing colonial securities would depress colonial stock prices, and that the disposal of the Western Australian stock at the maturity of the loan would cause the price to fall dramatically and lead to redemption difficulties.[140] Likewise, in 1908, the office disallowed a Crown Agent request

[137] Ibid.
[138] CAs to CO, 3 May 1880, CO 167/591/4599; Trinidad to CAs, 29 Sept. 1896, CAOG 9/68; CAs to CO, 26 Nov. 1908, CO 273/342/43329.
[139] West Australia to CO, 23 Oct. 1903, CO 323/483/38916.
[140] Note, 21 Oct. 1903, ibid.

for a proportion of the Straits savings bank fund to be invested in Straits stock, as it was feared that in an emergency the stock price would fall, and the government would be unable to release its holdings and deal with the crisis except at a large discount.[141]

During market falls, capital losses were avoided through the sale of fund securities either to other funds that belonged to the selling colony, or, if this was not possible, a fund held by another colony. For example, in 1907, £61,190 of the Straits general fund was sold to the colony's commissioner of currency fund, and, in 1901, £20,028 of the Western Australian 6 per cent sinking fund was disposed off to fourteen other funds held by a variety of colonies.[142] Stock was transferred at the market price of the day, except where this was precluded by fund constitutions, as a cost price would have been unfair to one or other of the funds concerned.[143] In addition, the Agents occasionally avoided sales through the provision of short-term loans advanced to funds on the security of their investments.[144] In the case of the Western Australian 4 per cent debentures sinking fund, meanwhile, they attempted to transfer the fund's securities, which could only be sold at a loss, to the colony's 4 per cent stock sinking fund, an equivalent amount of whose securities, which carried a higher market price, would be sold in place of the 4 per cent debenture fund's investments.[145] The Colonial Office, however, believed it 'almost incredible' that none of the debenture sinking fund securities could not be sold at an advantage, and suspected that it was illegal for fund investments to be sold for the repayment of a different loan.[146] The Agents disagreed but, finding their arguments 'very far fetched if not fallacious', the Colonial Office refused to alter its decision.[147]

Monitoring colonial investments

As with the supervision of the Agents' issuing duties, the monitoring of their investment activities was not completely satisfactory. Nevertheless, there is no evidence that they abused their position for the advancement of their own or the Agency's interests. Until 1902 the Agents sent colonies investment valuations, and thereafter, when required, copies of the Stock Exchange *Daily list*.[148] The Colonial Office received monthly returns, which recorded the investments held by each colonial fund, and, from the Agents' bankers, a list

[141] CO to Straits, 8 Dec. 1908, CO 273/342/43329.
[142] CAs to Straits, 18 July 1907, CAOG 9/222; CAs to CO, 9 Jan. 1901, CO 323/463/1131.
[143] CAs to CO, 3 Sept. 1900, CO 137/615/28948; CO to CAs, 31 Oct. 1900, ibid.
[144] The use of advances was sometimes precluded by fund regulations. See CO to CAs, 14 June 1902, CO 54/678/23609.
[145] CAs to CO, 12 Jan. 1905, CO 323/504/1206.
[146] Round note, 14 Jan. 1905, ibid.
[147] CAs to CO, 26 Jan. 1905, CO 323/504/2750; Round note, 27 Jan. 1905, ibid.
[148] CAs to CO, 6 June 1902, CO 323/474/22769; weeded file, CAA, a832.

of all the fund stock certificates in their possession. The two returns were then compared and the former passed to the colony. By 1905, however, the 'considerable delay' in comparing the returns had 'sacrificed the object of the system' and the task was taken over by the auditor-general.[149] The Agents also sent the Office a quarterly return that listed fund investments and current account balances, and, from 1905, an annual statement that showed the position of all accounts and funds under Agency management.[150]

As a further check, most of the funds theoretically had three trustees appointed by the secretary of state, two of whom were Crown Agents, and the third, until 1880, the permanent under-secretary for the Treasury and there-after the colonial under-secretary.[151] The Agents, when buying and selling fund investments, thus had to obtain the agreement of the under-secretary, who, before sanctioning the transaction, checked, in the case of sales, that the stock belonged to the fund and that its disposal did not breach any clause in the fund's constitution.[152] In reality, the under-secretary often failed to question the Agents' actions. In 1896, for example, Round sanctioned the sale of £26,000 of Sierra Leone sinking fund securities to redeem £25,000 of the colony's debentures, merely commenting that 'doubtless the Crown Agents have good reason for selling out more than is apparently necessary'.[153] Similarly, until 1896, the Agents were able to sell or transfer stock between funds without permission from the Colonial Office, and, as purchases were not recorded, when recently purchased securities were sold, the under-secretary did not know in which fund they were held.[154]

More importantly, by 1888 only thirty-four (46 per cent) of the funds with trustees appointed by the Colonial Office had a third trustee.[155] The remainder, largely sinking funds, had the Agents as sole trustees. Wishing to end the practice altogether, the Agency, on the death of Sargeaunt, proposed that they be made the sole trustee of all existing and future funds. It was argued that fund safety was safeguarded by the provision of monthly and quar-terly accounts by the Agents, which provided 'a real and effective check' and were far superior to the half-yearly returns supplied by other institutions that managed trusts.[156] Given that there had never been a single criticism of their work, there was also little need for further security, and an external trustee, dependent on information supplied by them, was in any case unable to main-

---

[149] CO to CAs, 1 May, 21 June 1905, CAOG 9/210.

[150] CAs to CO, 1 Apr. 1909, CO 323/553/11325.

[151] Treasury to CO, 11 Apr. 1881, PP 1881, lxiv (C 3075). In 1888 the trustees of twelve funds were appointed by the holding colonies: CAs to CO, 4 June 1888, CO 323/371/ 11143; Treasury to CO, 11 Apr. 1881, PP 1881, lxiv (C 3075).

[152] CAs to CO, 28 Jan. 1898, CO 323/428/2083.

[153] CAs to CO, 12 May 1896, CO 323/406/10278.

[154] Round note, 13 May 1896, ibid; CAs to CO, 20 Aug. 1896, CO 323/406/17705.

[155] CAs to CO, 4 June 1888, CO 323/371/11143.

[156] Ibid.

tain an independent opinion. Moreover, an additional trustee increased the Agency's workload and costs and the likelihood of mistakes, and gave the impression that the imperial government took some responsibility for crown colony issues. The Colonial Office was not convinced, but to reduce confusion and the Agents' workload agreed that all existing and future funds should have the same external representative, the under-secretary of state for the colonies.[157] Unfortunately, this decision, which was made by the general department, failed to be circulated to the geographical departments, and the Agents continued to be appointed sole trustees of sinking funds and by 1900, ninety-two of them (84 per cent) still had no third trustee.[158]

The situation in which the Agents found themselves at the end of the century was partly due to changes in the economic environment in which they operated, but was also partly the result of their own self-interested behaviour. Their use of the department system of construction increased the financial needs of the colonies and their rejection of treasury loans threw away what might have been at least a partial solution to the colonies' problems. The rescue package they adopted was in their own and in the constructing colonies' interests. The abandonment of infrastructure projects would have damaged colonial economies and plunged the Agency into a financial crisis that, along with the criticism likely to have been heaped upon it, would almost certainly have led to its disappearance. Alternatively, the package was against the interests of non-constructing colonies, whose support of a colonial financial co-operative evaporated when it started to cost them money. Similarly, it was not in the long-term interests of the Colonial Office: high-cost loans raised the probability of many years of unbalanced accounts. The Agents' moral hazard in their failure to comply with ordinance regulations also clearly demonstrated to the colonial secretary that he lacked control over their activities and helped to shatter his trust relationship with them.

In their remittance of money to and from the colonies and their management of colonial investments, the Agents were more successful. Remittance costs were reasonable and, although safety was paramount, investments appear to have reaped an adequate return. Moreover, by using debenture and stock purchases to manipulate prices before and after flotations, the Agents

---

[157] CO to CAs, 21 July 1888, ibid.
[158] Round note, 18 Apr. 1900, CO 323/452/9228. An attempt by the Agents in 1900 to persuade the Colonial Office to abandon the external trustee was again unsuccessful. The Colonial Office argued that to allow the Agents to become sole trustees would 'recognise to some extent their inadmissible contention that they have some authority and control over the Funds . . . independent of the Colonial Office', an acknowledgement that 'Parliament . . . [would] . . . not tolerate': Herbert note, 31 May 1900, ibid.

contributed to the success of crown colony public loan issues, and, by investing in their securities, extended the co-operative nature of colonial external finance, making the colonies partly self-financing.[159] Monitoring of investments was again inevitably poor, though there is no evidence that the Agents took advantage of the situation.

[159] It would be interesting to discover whether the Agents' investments in securities issued by self-governing colonies were reciprocated. If responsible government colonies did invest their United Kingdom funds in their own and crown colony debentures and stock, it is possible that the whole empire was partly self-financing.

9

Concessions, Currency and Stamps

The Colonial Office promoted economic development not only through the construction of infrastructure, but also through the sale of government-owned concessions – largely land and mineral rights – and the establishment of secure and stable banking systems, strong currencies and efficient postal networks. The Crown Agents played a crucial role in all these areas, largely seeking to eliminate self-interest that could slow economic activity and increase colonial expenditure. As concessions were the seed corn of economic growth and a valuable source of revenue to colonial administrations, it was crucial that they were awarded to those who would exploit them most successfully. To prevent opportunistic behaviour in the colonies and misrepresentation by applicants, all potential lessees were therefore vetted by the Agents to ensure that they possessed the necessary capital and expertise, intended to work the concession rather than use it to extract money from investors fraudulently, and were British subjects and that their efforts would benefit only the mother country. Similarly, they investigated those who wished to open banks in the colonies, and their supply of coins, notes and stamps allowed them to guard against printer, mint and bullion broker moral hazard, and to monitor (and the Colonial Office to control) colonial issue. As with other goods, in their supply of these articles they exhibited a bias towards high quality products, caring little about cost.

The award of concessions

Concessions were offered to Europeans because the Colonial Office had become disenchanted with royal charters, which had given recipients economic and administrative control over whole territories, and because local governments and business communities lacked the capital and technical knowledge necessary to exploit resources successfully. The decision to award land or mineral rights was made by the Colonial Office, the Agents checked the backgrounds of applicants, negotiated agreements and created the necessary legal documents. In addition, they employed their consulting engineers to undertake surveys of works connected with concessions, dealt with extensions of agreements and the subleasing and sale by lessees of the whole or part of their concessions and, if required, received rents and

Table 47
Samples of links between colonial governors,
Colonial Office and concessionaires

Concession	Concessionaire
Brunei petroleum concession	British Brunei Petroleum syndicate. Directors included Sir John Anderson, ex-Colonial Office principal clerk, and Sir William Hood Treacher, former acting consul-general of Brunei and resident-general of the Federated Malay States.
Guano monopoly, Fiji	Awarded to an ex-high commissioner of the colony.
Labuan coal mines	The Central Borneo Co. Sir Evelyn Ashley, former under-secretary of state for the colonies, was a director.
Pearl fisheries, Ceylon	Gulf Syndicate. Sir West Ridgeway, ex-governor of Ceylon, was managing director and owner of 1,000 ordinary shares and 1,600 deferred shares.
Trinidad asphalt concession	The Trinidad Asphalt Lake Co. Directors included Sir William Robinson, former governor of Trinidad, and Sir Neville Lubbock, president of the West India Committee.

Source and notes: *Hansard* 1906, 4th ser. xlviii. 1133; 1906 cxl.216; 1907 clxxi..554–5, 1492. It was Ridgeway, whilst governor, who had decided that the fisheries should be operated by the private sector. The terms of the concession were excessively generous. *Hansard*, 4th ser. 1907 clxxi.554–5; CAs to CO, 4 Jun. 1894, CAOG 14/7; Trinidad Lake Asphalt CO to CAs, 21 Feb. 1899, CAOG 14/165; Central Borneo Co. prospectus, 7 May 1889, CAOG 14/162.

royalties.[1] This work was performed by the Agency, rather than by colonial governments, because it had access to legal and technical advice and in theory was less subject to moral hazard.[2] In fact, aware that their continued existence was dependent on the support of the colonies and the Colonial Office, the Agents were more than willing to award concessions to former governors and former Colonial Office officials, who, moreover were less likely to succumb to misrepresentation and fraud (*see* table 47). Its control of

[1] See, for example, CO to CAs, 19 Sept. 1908, CO 879/99/914, no. 298; CAs to CO, 26 Apr. 1911, CO 879/107/965, no. 147; CO to CAs, 20 July 1910, CO 879/104/951, no. 283; CAs to CO, 4 Jan. 1912, CO 879/110/985, no. 2. Afraid that their findings could be used by the concessionaires against the colonial administrations for whom they usually worked, consulting engineers were reluctant to perform such surveys: Coode to CAs, 16 May 1896, CO 879/46/513, no. 100.
[2] In 1901 Sir F. A. Swettenham, governor of the Federated Malay States, obtained 25,000 acres alongside the proposed Johore–Negeri–Sembilan railway: H. S. Barlow, *Swettenham*, Kuala Lumpur 1995, 597. Barlow argues (p. 597) that the concession was granted in return for a promise by Swettenham that he would use his position to keep Johore out of the federation and prevent the appointment of a British resident. In the same year native chiefs in Sierra Leone gave a 4,000 square mile rubber concession to Sir Frederick Cardew, former governor of the colony: *Hansard* 1906 clxv. 386; 1907 clxxi. 554–5.

patronage, together with the resulting expansion of the Agency, was doubt-less one of the reasons why the Agents took on the role, which was unpaid and involved a great deal of work. The tasks were also intellectually satis-fying, prestigious and carried social rewards, and the successful working of concessions contributed to the growth of colonial economies and the demand for the services of the Crown Agents.

Applicants for concessions were either individuals or syndicates, who intended to work the concession themselves, or company promoters, who once they had obtained the concession raised the capital required to exploit it through the flotation of a new company. With both types of applicant there was the danger that they lacked, or would be unable to raise, the requisite capital, that they sought the concession for monopolistic purposes or that they represented a foreign power, which would thus gain from the exploita-tion of British assets.[3] In the case of company promoters, whom the Agents greatly distrusted, there was also the possibility that the prospectus of the company formed would misrepresent the value of the concession in order to attract subscribers.[4] Shareholders' returns would therefore be less than expected, discouraging further investment in similar operations and in colo-nial government loans.[5] Finally, the Agents were concerned lest promoters, once they had floated the company, would lose interest in the undertaking, which would then be poorly worked, thus 'postpon[ing] . . . the development of the country's resources'.[6]

To prevent misrepresentation, the Agents checked the financial and commercial background and nationality of all potential lessees. In order to determine their financial resources, they asked applicants for bank references, and for the prospectus of any company to be formed to work the concession, and to determine the likely success of a flotation, contacted their brokers, J. and A. Scrimgeours. Commercial reputations were discovered through enqui-ries directed through Scrimgeours and organisations such as the London Chamber of Commerce.[7] As the Agents themselves accepted, however, such enquiries 'seldom are or can be satisfactory'.[8] Applicants were unlikely to give as their referees institutions that would supply negative appraisals, and banks, indirect beneficiaries of the award of a concession, would be loath to risk the loss of a client. It was also unlikely that the Agents' advisors would be fully aware of the activities and reputations of all applicants. The results of the

---

3   In 1887 the Colonial Office instructed the CAs to satisfy themselves that the grant of a coal concession to the Central Borneo Co. would not allow one of the directors of the company, the local colliery owner, Mr Cowie, 'power to control the output of coal in Labuan': CO to CAs, 23 Feb. 1888, CAOG 14/162.
4   CAs to CO, 7 June 1905, CO 879/87/772, no. 82.
5   CAs to CO, 12 July 1910, CO 879/104/951, no. 259.
6   Scrimgeours to CAs, 17 Dec. 1910, CAOG 14/168.
7   London Chamber of Commerce to CAs, 13 Sept. 1913, CAOG 14/144; CAs to Cadman, 16 Dec. 1910, CAOG 14/168.
8   Antrobus to Le Haure, 4 July 1910, CAOG 14/166.

Agents' investigations therefore proved inaccurate on occasion. In 1911, for example, they reported that there was no reason why the Trinidad United Oilfields Co. should not obtain an oil-drilling lease, only to discover from the Trinidad inspector of mines that its chairman was a bankrupt and that it had failed to make full use of a previous prospecting lease.[9] Moreover, when there was only one applicant for a concession, the Agents often recommended acceptance, even if it were possible that his means would provide inadequate.[10]

The British nationality of applicants was regarded as particularly important when oil concessions were being considered. The construction of oil-powered submarines and destroyers from the early 1900s and the decision to convert the fleet to oil in 1911 led to fears that the oil industry would be dominated by a small number of companies, a danger in time of war.[11] All model prospectuses and mining licences, consequently, required lessees to be and to remain British subjects, or to be British companies registered and with their main place of business in Britain or a British colony and with a chairman, managing director and a majority of other directors who were British subjects.[12] This clause, however, often made it difficult for potential lessees to raise capital and exposed them to exploitation. In 1913 the British Borneo Co. found that the only source of capital available that could be regarded as British was Shell, who informed their chairman that 'he had no choice but to accept such terms as they chose to give him or to drop out of the oil business altogether'.[13] Despite the Agents' best efforts, therefore, many companies attempted to circumvent the clause. In 1911 the British and Foreign Oil and Rubber Trust Ltd formed a secret alliance with the foreign-owned Shell Transport and Trading Co., and two years later it was discovered that some concession holders deliberately failed to pay dividends to shareholders to encourage them to sell their shares to foreign-dominated trusts.[14] If there was little demand for a concession, however, the Agents and the Colonial Office were themselves willing to stretch the ruling. The British Brunei Petroleum Co., for example, was allowed to receive backing from the Royal Dutch Co. provided that the directors nominated by the company were British subjects and agreed to act independently.[15]

---

9 CAs to CO, 3 July 1911, CAOG 14/169; Trinidad to CAs, 1 Mar. 1912, CAOG 14/169. See also CO to CAs, 29 Apr. 1886, CAOG 14/162.
10 For example, National Provincial Bank to CAs, 10 Dec. 1885, CAOG 14/162; CO to CAs, 29 Apr. 1886, ibid.
11 Marshall to CAs, 27 Jan. 1911, CAOG 14/168; G. C. Higgins, A history of Trinidad oil, Port of Spain 1996, 68.
12 Model licence, CAOG 14/7, 13.
13 Memo, 30 Oct. 1913, ibid.
14 Marshall to CAs, 27 Jan. 1911, CAOG 14/168; CO to Trinidad, 10 Mar. 1913, CAOG 14/166.
15 Memo, 5 Jan. 1914, CAOG 14/7. See also CO 884/12/194.

To protect shareholders and future investment, the Agents received in draft the prospectus and all other public notices issued by any company formed to work a concession. They then checked that the material did not contain any false or misleading statements, demanding changes if it did.[16] Promoters who failed to submit material were threatened with penalties. In 1910, for instance, East African Estates Ltd, which had issued a pamphlet that gave 'an unduly favourable impression of local conditions', was forced to withdraw the notice and warned that, if any further misinformation was published, permission to sublet its lease, from which it derived most of its profits, would be withdrawn.[17] Fearing that involvement in the drafting of prospectuses could give the impression that the government supported the flotations, the Colonial Office strongly suggested in 1910 that the monitoring should cease. The Crown Agents, however, successfully opposed the proposal, pointing out that all prospectuses carried a disclaimer of government responsibility, and that monitoring not only reduced loss to investors but also prevented 'irregularities' from appearing in a company's memorandum and articles of association, where they would be 'difficult and embarrassing for the government to correct'.[18]

To enable them to determine the accuracy of prospectuses the Agents, similarly, strongly recommended that colonial governments collect information relating to concessions. In 1911, for instance, they proposed that oil prospecting licences for Trinidad should contain a clause requiring those lessees who wished to obtain a mining permit to provide the authorities with geological maps and reports on the work performed.[19] They also discouraged promoters from raising more capital than was required to work the concession, for this could lead to poor dividends and discontented investors, and queried the names chosen for companies.[20] Grandiose titles were rejected and more accurate ones suggested. The British Somaliland Co., for example, was asked in 1915 to change its name to the British Somaliland Fibre Co.[21]

Finally, the abandonment of leases by concessionaires once the working company had been formed was discouraged by the deposit of securities and by requirements on capital investment. The Agents generally asked concessionaires for substantial securities. In 1891, for example, the Trinidad Asphalt Co. had to give the Agency a sum of £10,000.[22] Securities were invested, and forfeited if the concession were abandoned or the company failed to pay the required rent. Lessees, similarly, were required to invest a given amount of money in the concession over a fixed period of time, to earmark a sum for

---

16 CAs to CO, 8 Mar. 1910, CO 879/104/951, no. 52.
17 CAs to CO, 21 Sept. 1910, ibid. no. 374.
18 CAs to CO, 8 Mar. 1910, ibid. no. 52.
19 CAs to Trinidad, 13 Mar. 1911, CAOG 14/168.
20 CAs to CO, 12 July 1910, CO 879/104/951, no. 259.
21 CAs to CO, 16 Nov. 1915, CO 879/87/772, no. 233.
22 CO to CAs, 7 July 1891, CAOG 14/65.

capital investment purposes in the working company's memorandum of association or to lodge capital with the Crown Agents, who would release it on receipt of evidence that it would be spent on the concession.[23]

The Crown Agents' involvement in the negotiation of leases grew over time. Colonial development increased the number of concessions offered, only a small proportion of which could be dealt with by the Colonial Office. Negotiations proceeded through meetings and voluminous correspondence. The Agents invariably started by setting high terms, 'in order that there may be a margin for purposes of negotiation', obtained legal and technical advice from their solicitors and expert consultants, and kept the relevant colony and the Colonial Office notified of progress.[24] The main issues to be determined were the period of the lease, the size of the concession and the value and form of government remuneration. The latter was often highly complex. In the case of oil-drilling licences, for example, concessionaire payments took the form of annual surface rents, the size and life of which was dependent on the costs of drilling, and royalties, which could include an allowance for the oil lost between well-head and storage tank.[25] The royalties were either *ad valorem*, a percentage of output that the colony then sold; a flat rate, an agreed cash payment per ton, which involved the determination of the likely quality of the oil to be recovered; or both, the government reserving the right to vary the method of payment according to circumstances.[26]

Inevitably, the agreements negotiated by the Agents were the subject of criticism. In 1913 their decision to give the United British West India Petroleum Syndicate the right to build a shared pipeline led to strong protests from other concessionaires and from the Trinidad legislative council.[27] It was claimed that the company would set excessive rates and use its right to refuse to take small quantities of oil to force small producers to sell their output to it at low prices. In fact, the company had given the Crown Agents its assurance that it would not misuse its pipe monopoly and none of the anticipated problems actually arose.[28] Concessionaires also occasionally attempted to exploit supposed loopholes in their agreements or challenged the terms in the courts.

[23] CAs to CO, 12 Oct. 1905, CO 879/87/772, no. 205; CAs to CO, 12 Aug. 1907, CO 879/95/869, no. 372; CO to CAs, 30 Jan. 1907, ibid. no. 42.

[24] CO to CAs, 27 July 1914, CAOG 14/7. The CAs' oil consultants were John Cadman, Professor of Mining and Technology at Birmingham University and president of the Institution of Petroleum Technologists, and Sir Boverton Redwood, advisor on petroleum to the Admiralty, Home Office, India Office and Corporation of London: *Who was whom* (CD-ROM).

[25] British Brunei Petroleum Syndicate to CAs, 27 Aug. 1914, CAOG 14/7; Higgins, *Trinidad oil*, 101.

[26] British Brunei Petroleum Syndicate to CAs, 14 July 1913, CAOG 14/7; Cadman to CAs, 1 Sept. 1913, ibid.

[27] *The Financier*, 30 May 1913, in CAOG 14/167; *Daily Chronicle*, 24 June 1913, ibid.

[28] Benjamin to CAs, 14 July 1913, CAOG 14/167. The monopoly was partly awarded to prevent refining falling into the hands of the American Standard Oil Co.: CO 884/12/194.

In 1902, for instance, the Christmas Island Phosphate Co., which were allowed to deduct transport costs from their royalty payments, included wear and tear of roads and rolling stock as deductibles.[29] The Crown Agents closely monitored the implementation of agreements, forcing concessionaires to abide strictly by their terms and, through their solicitors, fought and invariably won all legal challenges.[30]

Currency

In order to ensure the maintenance of uniform and stable currencies it was important that steps be taken to prevent dishonest practice on the part of the colony itself, suppliers or bullion brokers. The minting of poor quality coins could lead to forgery and suppliers could easily mint and sell excess coins on their own behalf. Bullion dealers could manipulate the price at which bullion was bought and sold, and colonial governments could be tempted to over-issue. The tender value of coins was generally higher than the metallic and minting cost and, in the case of silver coins, freight and insurance were paid by the Royal Mint.[31] To prevent such problems, all government orders for coinage were passed to the Crown Agents, who, on behalf of the Colonial Office, monitored issues, passed requisitions on to mints, bought the requisite bullion and organised the sale of surplus and other coin repatriated to the United Kingdom.

Not all colonial currency was supplied by the Crown Agents. Most colonies had local currencies, for example brass rods and cowries in West Africa, and a variety of foreign coins that arrived through foreign trade. In West Africa, prior to the 1890s, merchants were often allowed to import silver specie from the Mint, and thereafter these coins were supplied by the Bank of British West Africa and later the West African Currency Board. In Ceylon, the main circulating coinage was the silver rupee obtained by the banks from India.[32] The early colonial agents ordered their currency from the private sector. The Ceylon agent William Huskisson, for instance, bought copper coin from Boultons.[33] From the middle of the nineteenth century, however, coin were largely supplied by the Royal Mint (see appendix 4, tables 1 and 2), though the Calcutta and Bombay Mints struck much of the coinage for

29 CAs to CO, 15 Jan. 1902, CO 273/285/2141.
30 For example, CAs to CO, 10 Apr. 1904, CAOG 14/165.
31 CAs to CO, 19 Nov. 1897, CO 129/278/27371. A rare exception to the profitability of coin issue occurred in 1909 when an increase in the price of nickel-bronze caused the metallic value of Southern Nigerian nickel-bronze coins to rise above their tender value: Treasury to CO, 23 Feb. 1909, CO 520/86/1649. See also PRO, Mint 26/2, 1873, 11.
32 H. A. De S. Gunasekera, *From dependent currency to central banking in Ceylon: an analysis of monetary experience, 1825–1957*, London 1962, 9.
33 CO to Huskisson, 28 Sept. 1803, CO 324/115, 51; CO to Huskisson, 5 Apr. 1806, ibid. 146.

Ceylon and the Straits, and between 1864 and 1868 Hong Kong's own mint was responsible for that colony's currency.[34] The Royal Mint either manufactured the coins itself, or, if it were busy, passed the order either to James Watt & Co., or, from the 1870s, to Messrs Ralph Heaton & Sons, known as the Birmingham Mint, which produced coins under its supervision (see appendix 4, table 2).[35] If both the Royal Mint and Heatons were fully occupied, the order was postponed.[36] In the case of urgently required sterling currency, the Mint also occasionally obtained coin from Bank of England stocks, undertaking to strike replacements by a given date.[37]

When colonial coins were to be struck, the Agents bought the necessary bullion on the open market through its brokers. Like the Bank of England, the India Office and the Royal Mint, they at first used the broking firm of Mocatta Goldsmid.[38] In the 1880s, however, dissatisfied with the company's performance and perhaps wishing to improve their relationship with the Bank of England, they appointed Pixley Abell & Blake, the Bank's bullion broker which had been established in 1852 by the son of its bullion office manager and a former employee of its cashiers' office.[39] To avoid sellers, particularly of silver, holding back supplies in an attempt to raise prices, and banks increasing the bill exchange rate of colonial purchasers, the decision to buy was concealed.[40] Little bullion was bought in advance of need if prices were low, as it was believed that such purchases were speculative and would lead to much criticism from the colonies if prices subsequently fell.

The Agents' relationship with the Royal Mint was poor. The Mint gave priority to orders from self-governing colonies. These were relatively large and lucrative and there was a fear that failure to fulfil them on time would result in the loss of the work to local mints. Crown colony orders, therefore, were subject to delays, which could damage colonial economies.[41] The cost of production was also excessive. For colonial coins the Mint charged a commission of between 3 and 10 per cent and for imperial silver currency seignorage, the difference between the nominal value of the coin paid by the colonies and the far lower cost of the bullion.[42] Over the period, as silver prices fell, seignorage increased, and although the Mint paid the packing, freight and insurance charge of shipping coin to the colonies, it increasingly made 'enor-

---

34 Mint 26/2, 1873, 1905, 1906.
35 Mint 28/2, 1875. Use of Heatons was temporarily suspended in 1873 when it was discovered that the company had bribed Mint officials in return for orders: CO to CAs, 13 Mar. 1873, CO 431/30/2027.
36 Mint to Treasury, 29 Oct. 1853, T 1/5825b/21282; note, 5 Nov. 1853, ibid.
37 CO 879/109/980, q. 2468.
38 C. Walton, 'Broker to the Bank of England', Goldsmiths Review ix (1988/9), 10.
39 Memo, 23 Apr. 1923, CAOG 17/64; Walton, 'Broker', 14.
40 CAs to CO, 23 Apr. 1903, CO 129/320/15064.
41 CAs to CO, 24 Jan. 1900, CO 87/161/2710.
42 Memo, 21 Oct. 1913, Mint 20/538.

mous profits'.[43] Between 1881 and 1890, for instance, net profits on the supply of West Indian silver coin amounted to 87 per cent.[44] The Agents, however, were reluctant to use alternative, and perhaps less honest, mints. Whereas they received few complaints regarding the cost of coinage, the supply of poor quality coins or unauthorised issue would lead to severe criticism from the colonies. Moreover, no single firm could handle the crown colonies' large orders, which would have had to be divided between suppliers, creating problems of uniformity, and the coinage legislation of a number of colonies specified that coins could only be struck at the Royal Mint.[45]

Demand for coin rose during the demonetisation of foreign coins and their replacement by colonial or British currency. In Malta, the replacement of the Sicilian dollar and half-dollar by sterling was prompted by the Italian government's decision in 1885 to demonetise these coins. To avoid a financial crisis in the period before the arrival of British currency, the government gave holders of Sicilian coins currency bonds that circulated freely in the colony. In addition, bond-holders were allowed to buy bills of exchange drawn on the Crown Agents in London at five days notice. Holders of bonds could thus obtain the value of their dollars in Britain before the date of conversion and the colony reduced the amount of coin it needed to import and thus its freight and insurance costs. None the less, despite these preparations, the colony still experienced a dearth of coin and withdrawals from the government-owned savings bank began to exceed deposits. The administration therefore had to ask the Agents for funds. Unable to sell bills on the Crown Agents in the colony without alerting the local commercial community to its difficulties, the governor obtained the money from a retired merchant who sold bills of exchange on Barings, who were then reimbursed by the Agents.[46]

In the West Indies, West Africa and the Straits, demonetisation was necessitated by changes in the price of silver. The fall in silver prices in the 1870s caused the bullion value of Spanish, Mexican and Colombian dollars in the West Indies and Mexican dollars in West Africa to fall below the fixed rate of 4s. 2d. Merchants thus began to buy dollars in London at 3s. 8d. and 3s. 9d. and to ship them to these colonies, making a profit of between 4d. and 7d. per dollar less freight costs.[47] To avoid inflation, British Guiana in 1876, the Gold Coast in 1879, Sierra Leone and Lagos in 1880 and a number of other West Indian colonies replaced their coins with British currency.[48]

---

[43] CAs to CO, 23 Apr. 1906, British Museum, London, M/Coins; regulation, 12 Feb. 1879, Mint 4/86.

[44] Mint 13/52.

[45] CAs to CO, 29 Mar. 1911, CO 520/109/1027; CAs to CO, 19 May 1905, CO 520/32/17001.

[46] Malta to Stanley, 29 Nov. 1885, CO 883/4/24, no. 22; CAs to CO, 7 Dec. 1885, ibid. no. 26.

[47] Langden to CO, 24 May 1876, CO 884/3/27, no. 4.

[48] British Guiana to CAs, 25 Sept. 1876, CO 884/3/32, no. 36; CO to Treasury, 1 Nov. 1879, CO 879/18/239, no. 10; Sierra Leone to CO, 10 Apr. 1880, ibid. no. 51.

Demonetisation by the Straits in 1906 was the result of rising silver prices, which caused the bullion value of the silver dollar to rise above the exchange rate.[49] The colony therefore replaced its dollars with new coins with a lower silver content, importing between 1906 and 1909 $19m.-worth of coin.[50]

Demonetised and worn coin was disposed off through the Agents' broker, the Agency charging a commission of ^{1}/16th per cent for its services.[51] 'Clean' demonetised coins were sold for recirculation. Many of the foreign dollars replaced by the West Indies in the 1870s, for example, were bought by Chinese merchants.[52] Worn coin was disposed off for its metal value, generally in small amounts over a period of time to avoid disruption of the market, with 'great stress . . . [laid] . . . on keeping the sales quiet, as it is clearly an advantage to the banks to know that there are large quantities of dollars on the market'.[53] A suggestion made by the Crown Agents in 1908 to the effect that, during periods of low prices, coin should be retained and the selling colonies provided with advances until prices recovered was rejected by the Colonial Office, which regarded the proposal as 'a pure gamble'.[54]

Given the falling price of silver, losses were inevitable and the Agents' sales were the subject of a number of colonial complaints.[55] Criticism reached its peak in 1906 when the Straits sold $2m. of its demonetised silver dollars to the Hong Kong and Shanghai Bank. In their official protest to the Colonial Office, the Agents argued that the sale had resulted in a financial loss to the colony. The bank, whose actions were motivated by 'self-interest', had sold the coin on to the Indian government for a large profit and had informed other brokers of the Straits' future coin sales, allowing them to rig the market.[56] The Colonial Office supported the Agency, but ruled that the Straits should be allowed to set a minimum price for sales.[57]

Finally, in addition to organising the supply of coin, the Agents on a number of occasions became involved in the creation of colonial currency policy. In 1871, at the request of the Colonial Office, Sir Penrose Julyan prepared a long memo on the currency of Mauritius, whose governor wished to introduce the Indian rupee as sole legal tender.[58] After investigating the various alternatives, Julyan recommended the retention of the *status quo*,

[49] CO to CAs, 10 Nov. 1906, CO 882/9/108, no. 170.
[50] CAs to CO, 5 Mar. 1909, ibid. no. 281.
[51] CAs to Straits, 23 Aug. 1907, ibid. no. 221.
[52] CAs to CO, 1 Dec. 1876, CO 884/3/32, no. 42.
[53] Pixley & Abel to CAs, 15 Aug. 1907, CO 882/9/108, no. 221.
[54] CAs to CO, 1 June 1908, CO 129/350/20045; note, 11 June 1908, ibid.
[55] In 1880 Lagos dollars with a nominal value of £16,440 were sold for £14,422, and Gold Coast dollars worth £10,524 were sold for £9,935: CAs to CO, 9 Dec. 1880, CO 879/18/239, no. 88.
[56] CAs to CO, 1 Sept. 1908, CO 882/9/108, no. 268; CAs to Straits, 16 July 1907, ibid. no. 220; CAs to Straits, 23 Aug. 1907, ibid. no. 221.
[57] CAs to CO, 1 Sept. 1908, ibid. no. 268.
[58] CO 882/2, no. 4.

pointing out that the island was not geographically close to India, that half of its trade was with Europe and that the relatively low exchange rate between London and India that encouraged bills of exchange to Mauritius to go via India was likely to be a temporary phenomenon. Impressed by the report, the Colonial Office sent Julyan to Malta two years later to examine the periodic scarcity of silver coin and the high value of the Sicilian silver dollar in comparison with the British gold coin in which British subjects were paid.[59] Julyan's proposals regarding the dollar's high exchange rate were that the Sicilian currency should either be replaced or devalued. The scarcity of coin was found to be related to the high cost of high denomination gold currency, which encouraged merchants to remove goods from customs in small quantities and thus pay the associated duty in low cost, low denomination silver coin, a problem that could be solved by increasing the minimum quantity of goods that could be taken out of customs.[60] In the event, neither of these proposals was implemented. The colony believed that a change in currency would damage business confidence and the merchant contingent in the local legislature blocked any alteration in customs procedure.[61]

Bank notes and banks

The Agents' role in the issue of bank notes and the establishment of colonial banks again involved the avoidance of adverse selection and moral hazard. At first bank notes were issued only by private banks. The Colonial Office and the Treasury discouraged government issue, as the distribution of notes was time-consuming and banks were more than willing to take on the role as it increased their customer base. To prevent the pursuit of self-interest by banks, all issues had to be secured by depreciation funds, one-third of which had to be in specie or bullion stored in the colony and the remainder held in first-class securities deposited with the Crown Agents. Each time a bank's note issue was increased, it had to lodge with the colony and the Agents the appropriate amount of cash and securities, and, from 1895, the Agents made an annual valuation of these holdings, valuing bonds and stock at the current market price.[62] In reality, however, these rules were not always rigidly adhered to. Not wishing to discourage the issue of notes, the Crown Agents often allowed banks to lodge less than first class securities. In 1896 the Chartered Bank's Straits reserve fund contained $266,667 of Chinese Imperial 7 per cent stock and $237,500 of 5 per cent Japanese stock that was only market-

---

[59] J. C. Sammut, *From scudo to sterling: money in Malta, 1798–1887*, Malta 1992, 119.
[60] Ibid. 121.
[61] Ibid. 122, 127.
[62] Treasury to CO, 4 Mar. 1897, T 1/9163a/10620/1969; CO to CAs, 8 Jan. 1895, T 1/9163a/10620/477.

able in Japan.[63] The Treasury, similarly, was willing to disregard the rules if it was in its interests to do so. In 1900, for instance, to avoid direct imperial involvement, the Treasury asked the Hong Kong & Shanghai Bank to make a £75,000 advance to the viceroy of Wuchang, allowing the bank to hold the non-marketable loan as security for its Hong Kong note issue.[64]

The first colony allowed to issue government notes was Mauritius, which in 1849, two years after the failure of one of its two note-issuing banks, began to distribute rupee notes.[65] No other colony was permitted to follow its lead until 1884 when the collapse of the Oriental Bank and Ceylon's decision to guarantee its notes highlighted the drawbacks of relying on the private sector. To prevent the dubious practice of printing notes to generate revenue, colonies were required to obtain notes from the Agents, who passed orders on to the printing firm De La Rue, and to secure all issues against a bank note fund. Between half and two-thirds of the fund had to be in bullion or specie lodged in the colony, though from 1907 the gold reserve of the Straits, the only colony on the gold standard, was stored in London.[66] The remainder was again held in first-class securities, which were managed by the Crown Agents. If the bullion or specie reserve fell below the set limit, as a result of note holders demanding coin, the Agents sold securities and despatched coin to the colony and, when the reserve rose above its permitted level, the excess was sent to London and invested. An exception to this procedure occurred in the case of Ceylon, which held part of its securities reserve in the colony in the form of rupee investments. It could thus make any adjustment to its specie reserve itself relatively rapidly and cheaply by selling or buying the securities in the Indian market.[67]

The Crown Agents involvement in the establishment of banks was greatest in West Africa, which until the 1890s was without banking facilities and had little western currency, apart from sterling silver coins. Silver coinage was imported by governments and merchants. Governments obtained their coin from the Royal Mint via the Agents free of freight expenses and, to cover its distribution and repatriation costs, were permitted to charge a 1 per cent issue fee. Merchants, after gaining Crown Agent permission to import, had to pay the freight costs and also lost interest on their payments for coin, which had to be made in advance.[68] They nevertheless preferred to import coin themselves rather than obtain supplies from the government as there was a

---

63 CAs to CO, 8 Mar. 1897, T 1/9163a/10620/4517. On discovering the existence of these securities, the Treasury permitted the bank to keep the stock, though required it to lodge better-quality investments in the future: Treasury to CO, 2 Apr. 1897, ibid.

64 Foreign Office memo, 10 Aug. 1900, T 1/9590b/14138; T 1/9590b/15361.

65 Gunasekera, Dependent currency, 75.

66 CO to CAs, 19 Oct. 1909, CO 882/9/113. The gold was kept at the Bank of England, which charged a fee of $1/32\%$ per annum for the service: CAs to CO, 4 Dec. 1909, ibid. no. 29.

67 Gunasekera, Dependent currency, 83.

68 Their costs were estimated by the Agents at 1.5%.

demand for new unworn coin from native traders. Merchant imports, however, proved expensive for colonial administrations, which had to bear the cost of returning worn and surplus coin to the United Kingdom.[69] A solution to this problem appeared in 1891 when the African Banking Corporation offered to establish a branch in Lagos and to pay for the repatriation of coin provided that it obtained the government account, its free import monopoly and the right to charge a 1 per cent issue fee. Although the bank would organise its own imports and they would thus lose their management commission, the Agents recommended acceptance of the proposal. The establishment of the bank would relieve the colony of its repatriation expenditure, which was likely to rise as the economy grew, and would promote development.[70] The income earned from their commission in Lagos was also relatively small and the rise in government receipts would increase the Agents' business with the colony.

The bank opened for business in January 1892, but was almost immediately the object of criticism from the colony's merchant community. Situated in premises owned by Elder Dempster and managed by the Lagos agent of Sir Alfred Jones, it was accused of being 'a trading company under another name'.[71] Criticism increased in the following year when Elder Dempster officially took over the branch. Although they fully shared the critics' disquiet, the Agents were unwilling to disrupt their reciprocal trust relationship with the Colonial Office, which favoured Jones.[72] They therefore asked him to establish the bank as a separate company, informing the Colonial Office that 'our position will be stronger if we can point to the articles of the bank as authorising nothing but genuine banking business'.[73] After a period of resistance, during which the Agents took over the import of silver coin, Jones acceded to their demands and set up the Bank of British West Africa, 72 per cent of which was owned by him and his fellow Elder Dempster directors.[74] The bank subsequently opened branches and obtained the free import monopoly in the Gold Coast (1896), Sierra Leone (1898) and Gambia.

As a result of the import monopoly, the bank prospered. It increased its customer base, made large profits from the difference between the tender and metallic value of the coins imported and expended little of its 1 per cent issue

[69] A. G. Hopkins, 'The creation of a colonial monetary system: the origins of the West African Currency Board', *International Journal of African Historical Studies* iii (1970), 107; CAs to CO, 4 Mar. 1898, CO 96/325/5012.
[70] CAs to CO, 2 Sept. 1908, CO 520/70/32246.
[71] Ommanney note, 1 Feb. 1894, CO 147/97/1318.
[72] CAs to CO, 5 Apr. 1893, CO 147/92/5624; CAs to CO, 19 June 1893, CO 147/92/10284.
[73] Ommanney note, n.d., CO 147/93/6569; Ommanney note, 1 Feb. 1894, CO 147/97/1318.
[74] Richard Fry, *Bankers in British West Africa: the story of the Bank of British West Africa Ltd*, London 1976, 26.

fee, as intended, on the export of excess and new coin.[75] Colonial development and the bank's avoidance of repatriation meant that between 1896 and
1907, although it imported £1.4m.-worth of silver coins into West Africa, it
returned only £270,228-worth.[76] The bank also succumbed to dishonesty.
Allowed from 1896 to charge its normal banking fees for transactions that
involved the import of silver coinage (e.g. loans paid in coin), the bank began
routinely to add a banking charge of between ¼ per cent and ½ per cent to its
issue fee and to charge this commission when it reissued coin returned from
circulation.[77] Likewise, it used its position to support Sir Alfred Jones's other
business interests. Competitors allegedly experienced delays in the supply of
silver and were only granted loans if they agreed to use the Elder Dempster
shipping line.[78] Native businessmen, meanwhile, were denied advances
altogether.

Despite their belief that the bank 'ought from the beginning . . . [to] have
been . . . independent' and that it 'had been very detrimental to the trade
generally of colonies', the Agents continued publicly to support the Colonial
Office's pro-bank policy.[79] Change did not come until 1907 when their relationship with the Colonial Office finally broke down. In that year they
recommended that Jones should be forced to resign his chairmanship of the
bank and reduce his shareholding.[80] The Colonial Office, believing it to be
'too childish for serious consideration', rejected the proposal.[81] Unbowed,
Blake suggested a year later that the control of silver currency into and out of
West Africa should revert to the South Nigerian government.[82] Accepting
that 'the favours shown to Sir Alfred Jones' bank can hardly be defended',
senior Colonial Office officials agreed.[83] Once informed of this decision,
however, Jones contacted the secretary of state, Lord Crewe, who a month
later overruled his officials and allowed the Bank of British West Africa to
retain its monopoly.[84]

In the event, the bank's victory proved short-lived. On the death of Jones
in 1909 and the appointment of a new secretary of state, a committee was set

[75] Ibid. 24; PPS, q. 5433.
[76] CAs to CO, 2 Sept. 1908, CO 520/70/32246. Coin was transferred to other West
African colonies: Fry, *Bankers*, 35. In 1898 and 1899 the bank unsuccessfully tried to refuse
to repatriate gold sovereigns: CAs to CO, 6 June 1898, CO 96/325/12678; CAs to CO,
12 Apr. 1899, CO 96/347/9091.
[77] CAs to CO, 8 May 1894, CO 147/96/7974; Fry, *Bankers*, 28. In 1907 the bank charged
an issue fee of 1.25% for most of the year: PP 1909, xlvii, q. 5433.
[78] *West African Mail*, 8 Sept. 1907, 1180; 11 Apr. 1907, 56; Davies, *Trade makers*, 120; PPS,
q. 4407.
[79] CAs to CO, 28 Jan. 1901, CO 520/10/3684; CAs to CO, 2 Sept. 1908, CO 520/
70/32246.
[80] Blake to CO, 2 June 1907, CO 96/461/20929.
[81] Strachy note, 22 June 1907, ibid.
[82] CAs to CO, 2 Sept. 1908, CO 520/70/32241.
[83] Antrobus note, 2 Feb. 1908, CO 520/50.
[84] Hopkins, 'A colonial monetary system', 101–32.

up to investigate the whole issue of West African currency.[85] Its report recommended the introduction of a new silver currency to be managed and issued
by a currency board, proposals put into effect in 1912. The resultant board
bought bullion, ordered the coining of the new currency from the Mint,
arranged its shipment and issue, and was largely an extension of the Crown
Agents. It made use of the Agents' office and clerks; one of the board
members, Sir William Mercer, was a Crown Agent; and its one full-time
employee, its secretary, was also drawn from Crown Agent staff.[86] Although
the board spent much of 1913 in dispute with the Treasury over the control of
the repatriation of coin, by 1914 it had exported £883,000 of the new coinage
to West Africa, which was distributed through the Bank of British West
Africa.[87]

Stamps

Crown colony postage and duty stamps were supplied by the Agency's stamp
department, which charged a commission of one per cent and, regarded as a
separate establishment, managed the printing of stamps for a number of
self-governing colonies.[88] At first orders were placed with Messrs Perkins
Bacon. Dissatisfied with the quality of its work, the Agents then moved to
Messrs De La Rue. The company had a good reputation for the printing of
stamps for the Inland Revenue and India, and its owner, William 'Colonel
Billy' De La Rue, had, like Penrose Julyan, strong connections with the
militia, which no doubt encouraged the development of a trust relationship.[89]
The Agency also had personal experience of the firm's work. In 1857 Perkins
Bacon had subcontracted an order for stamped envelopes to the company,
which possessed the necessary machinery.[90] The envelopes had been rapidly
and well produced, and the Agents subsequently gave the firm a number of
stamp orders that were equally satisfactorily completed.[91]

As well as crown colony stamps, the firm also printed postal orders, first
used by the Straits in 1884, bank notes, headed writing paper, debenture and

[85] J. B. de Loynes, *A history of the West African Currency Board*, London 1974, 11. One of its
members was the CA Sir William Mercer.
[86] Fry, *Bankers*, 75.
[87] J. M. Carland, 'The Colonial Office and the first West African note issue', *International
Journal of African Historical Studies* xxiii (1990), 497; Fry, *Bankers*, 77.
[88] Although no record of the number of stamps supplied has been kept, some indication of
the volume is given by the fact that between 1871 and 1880 duty stamps to the value of
£12.5m. were purchased by Ceylon alone: De La Rue to CAs, 23 Feb. 1881, De La Rue
papers, National Postal Museum, London, vol. 6; CAs to CO, 1 July 1913, CO 323/648/
22741.
[89] J. P. Bunt, *The De La Rue definitives of the Falkland Islands, 1901–29*, Truro 1986, 11.
[90] Perkins Bacon to CAs, 10 Mar. 1857, CO 54/331/2258.
[91] A. G. Rigo de Righi, *Postage stamps of De La Rue*, London 1970, 6.

stock certificates, envelopes and stamp duty paper (sheets incorporating an embossed stamp that obviated the use of a postage or revenue stamp).[92] Where stamps were produced within colonies, it also supplied printing presses and embossing machines.[93] Although, not wishing to lose lucrative contracts, it generally discouraged colonial printing and embossing. In 1881, for example, it strongly advised Cyprus to abandon a proposal to purchase a public stamp-embossing machine. The colony was warned that to prevent operator fraud it would require a press that recorded the number of stamps embossed, that as such machines could not distinguish between stamp type, a separate machine for each stamp duty would have to be acquired, and that a monitoring officer and an engineer would have to be employed to take payments and machine readings and perform daily maintenance – both of whom could act fraudulently.[94]

The Agents stayed with De La Rue until long after 1914, partly because the company retained ownership of those plates and dies that it provided for no charge, but largely to ensure the supply of good quality stamps. Their long association with the company led to the development of a trust relationship, and the permanent use of just one supplier eased the inspection of stamps. By the 1860s the Agents had inspectors at the mills that produced their water-marked paper and, at De La Rue's printing plant, employed a chief inspector of stamps, generally a former Crown Agent clerk, six male examiners and approximately a dozen female assistants.[95] The firm also possessed patents for processes that reduced the likelihood of criminal behavious by customers i.e. the forgery of bank notes and the reissue of stamps through the removal of franking marks. Bank notes had watermarks, deckled edges, green underprints and microscopic printing, and stamps were produced with fugitive and double fugitive inks, both of which were soluble if solvents were used on them.[96]

Like the Agents' other supplies, stamps were expensive and, from turn of the century, the subject of a number of complaints. In 1901, for instance, the Falkland Islands claimed that De La Rue's charge for the engraving of dies was twice that quoted by its previous supplier.[97] In response, the Agents argued that high prices were inevitable given the quality of the stamps produced, and pointed out that when they had held open competitions for orders the

[92] CAs to De La Rue, 15 July 1884, De La Rue papers, vols 12/4.
[93] Straits to CAs, 30 Dec. 1882, ibid. vols 8/9.
[94] De La Rue memo, Apr. 1881, ibid. vol. 6; De La Rue to CAs, 20 Apr. 1881, ibid. Not surprisingly, the plan was abandoned.
[95] CAs to De La Rue, 26 Oct. 1872, ibid. vol. 1; memo, 10 Apr. 1904, British Museum, philately collection, G/1736a.
[96] CAs to De La Rue, 17 Sept. 1884, De La Rue papers, vols 12/14; De La Rue to CAs, 9 Feb. 1881, vols 17/29; De La Rue to CAs, 6 Jan. 1910, vols 51/4. See also De La Rue to CAs, 4 Apr. 1882, vols 8/9.
[97] Bunt, The De La Rue definitives, 27–8. Prior to this date, the Falklands had insisted on using their own supplier.

company had always undercut the bids of its competitors.[98] In fact the firm was indeed overcharging. In 1924 it emerged that, from the 1880s to 1901, it had paid Waterlows and other competitors £20,000 in compensation for not tendering seriously for government contracts.[99] Thereafter, only Waterlows received this bribe, with the result that, when the Inland Revenue's contract with De La Rue came to an end in 1910 and it requested fresh tenders, it received a bid from Messrs Harrisons and Sons that was far lower than that submitted by its former supplier. Having discovered that De La Rue's fugitive inks could easily be replicated, the Inland Revenue decided to accept the tender.[100] The Agents, wishing to maintain a quality supply, declined to follow their lead, preferring to place pressure on De La Rue to reduce its prices.[101]

From 1906, as well as supplying stamps to the colonies, the Agents also began to sell them to collectors and dealers. In the early days, stamp retailers obtained their stocks by writing to the postmaster-general of the relevant colony, who sold them the stamps required. This arrangement, however, created a great deal of work in the colonies, particularly once stamp collecting became a popular hobby, and encouraged dishonesty. In 1894, it was discovered that the Lagos collector of customs had sold, on his own behalf, large quantities of unused stamps that should have been destroyed.[102] The Colonial Office wanted to ban all sales to dealers, but was afraid that such action would lead to 'more scandals than under the present system' and that retailers would create an 'outcry to the press and parliament'.[103] Wishing to avoid such difficulties, it therefore asked the Agents to create a store of stamps that they could sell to collectors and dealers. Unwilling to cover the cost of this, estimated at £1,000, or to carry the risk of theft from it, the Agents rejected the proposal, but in 1905 agreed to obtain from the colonies and to sell to dealers obsolete stamps, and, in 1906, all stamps, charging a commission for the service of 1 per cent and from 1906 ¼ per cent.[104]

The Agents' handling of concessions, currency and stamps benefited both them and the colonies. Through their actions, they prevented self-interested behaviour in the colonies in the form of concession fraud and stamp and

[98] De La Rue to CAs, 23 July 1894, De La Rue papers, vols 26/9; De La Rue to CAs, 29 Sept. 1902, vols 41/3.
[99] *The Times*, 27 June 1924, in PRO, IR 79/34. From 1901 Waterlows received compensation of £500 *per annum*: ibid.
[100] CAs to CO, 23 July 1910, CO 323/564/22534; note, 12 Sept. 1910, CO 323/573/28242.
[101] De La Rue to CAs, 18 May 1910, De La Rue papers, vols 51/4; De La Rue memo, 6 Mar. 1911, vols 55/7.
[102] CAs to CO, 15 June 1894, CO 147/96/10424.
[103] CO memo, 27 May 1910, CO 323/564/12496.
[104] Ibid; CO to CAs, 12 May 1905, CAOG 17/129; CO circular, 19 Jan. 1906, CAA, CA M 202.

currency over-issue, and minimised the opportunism of service providers and, by restricting forgery, colonial residents. Dubious practices on the part of the Royal Mint and De La Rue as regards pricing and the duplicity of the Bank of British West Africa were accepted, as they ensured respectively the provision of a quality product and the maintenance of mutual trust between the Agents and the Colonial Office. The adoption of these particular duties also increased the status and indispensability of the Agency, the satisfaction the Agents derived from their work and, by promoting economic growth, colonial demand for Crown Agent services. Conversely, many of the tasks were time-consuming and unpaid and therefore contributed to the Agency's financial problems.

10

The Crown Agents and Personnel

One outcome of colonial development was the need for skilled men to operate completed infrastructure, officers to staff enlarged administrations and, in the West Indies, coolies to work the plantations. Unlike their responsible government counterparts, the crown colonies had no local settled European population from which to recruit administrative and technical personnel and therefore had to obtain staff from the United Kingdom. Administrators were appointed by the Colonial Office and technical officers by the Crown Agents and their consulting engineers, who possessed the necessary knowledge to judge the expertise and experience of candidates and thus identify any misrepresentation by them. To counter deception by claimants, the Agents also arranged for the payment in Britain of pensions and some salaries, and settled the estates of all those colonial officers who died in the colonies. Coolies were recruited by skilled officers based in India. From 1878, however, the Crown Agents organised their transportation, devising a number of strategies to counter bad practice by shippers, whose cost-reducing inhumane treatment of their human cargo could reduce its later productivity and damage the reputation and legitimacy of the empire.

Recruitment

Until 1902 notification of any full-time technical and specialist appointment that was not to be filled by promotion was sent to the Colonial Office for approval, and then passed to the Crown Agents.[1] Thereafter, in order to reduce delay, only posts with salaries in excess of £250 *per annum* or that were additional to the authorised establishment were deemed to require Colonial Office endorsement. In theory, candidates were selected by the Crown Agents. In reality, to minimise adverse selection and to relieve the Agents of the mundane tasks associated with recruitment, when technical qualifications or experience were required, the vacancy was passed to the consulting engineer who worked in the recruiting colony and specialised in the technical area of the appointment.[2] The Agents thus dealt only with those vacancies, 26 per cent of the total between 1908 and 1910, that required little

---

[1] Fiddes note, 21 Oct. 1912, CO 554/7/32031; circular, 14 Apr. 1902, CAOG 13/310.
[2] Memo, 27 May 1910, CAOG 17/25.

technical expertise or that demanded specialist skills outside the remit of their engineering consultants (*see* table 48). As far as the remaining 74 per cent was concerned, on receiving notice of the vacancy, the engineer referred to the register each maintained of men wishing to work in the colonies, and, if there were few suitable candidates, would make personal enquiries.[3] If still unsuccessful, either he or the Agents would advertise the post.[4] The consulting engineers generally preferred qualified men, who had some practical experience and were under 35 years of age, older men being 'not . . . so well suited to colonial life'.[5] The candidates were then interviewed and a report and a recommendation sent to the Agents who, after adding their own comments, passed them to the Colonial Office. The Agents and Colonial Office invariably accepted the consultants' recommendations, even though they had seen neither the candidate nor the letter of application or references. The Agency's own recruitment process was similar to that of their engineers, except that, in the case of specialist vacancies, they sought advice and recommendations from experts in the field.[6]

The service provided was much criticised. First, it was regarded as overly expensive. Although the Agents were not remunerated, their consultant engineers were paid a fee of five guineas for each man selected, and half of this for each candidate recommended by them who withdrew or was rejected for medical or other reasons beyond their control.[7] As a 'large proportion of the men at first selected . . . [fell] . . . through in this manner', the consulting engineers average per candidate total fee was far higher than five guineas.[8] In 1909, for example, Messrs Middleton, Hunter & Duff were paid £21 for the recruitment of just two officers.[9] Although the consultants' costs are not known, it seems likely that their profits for the service were indeed high and were intended to increase the cost of moral hazard. When the Agents took over the work of two of the consulting engineers in 1911, they charged a fee of only two guineas per appointment filled, which covered the cost of both

---

3   CAs to CO, 13 Jan. 1913, CO 323/648/1521.
4   For example, CAs to CO, 29 June 1908, CO 129/350/23550; Pownall to CAs, 7 Oct. 1901, CO 96/386/35306.
5   CAs to CO, 2 Sept. 1914, CO 323/631/33386.
6   The Office obtained recommendations for technical school teachers from the City and Guilds of London Institute, for mining inspectors from the Royal College of Science and for ships' engineers from the Admiralty: CAs to Institute, 14 Aug. 1897, City and Guilds' London Institute papers, GL, MS 21899; note, 1 Mar. 1902, CO 273/285/12219; CAs to CO, 14 May 1873, CO 287/323/4731.
7   Memos, 20 Oct. 1910, and 20 Feb. 1914, CAOG 17/25. Remuneration for the selection of railway operating staff was included in the consulting engineers' open line salary at a similar rate.
8   Ibid.
9   Fiddian note, 16 Feb. 1909, CO 96/488/3152.

Table 48
Technical recruitment, 1908–10

	West Africa	Other colonies
Number of candidates employed by the CAs	64 (21%)	46 (38%)
Number of candidates employed by their consulting engineers for a fee	54 (18%)	26 (21%)
Number of candidates employed by their consulting engineers for a salary	187 (61%)	50 (41%)
Total	305	122

Source: memo, 16 Feb. 1911, CAOG 17/25.

their new and their old work and of finding replacements for those who failed to take up appointments, though this was raised to four guineas in 1914.[10]

Secondly, the recruitment process was slow and the men employed often unsuitable. Many candidates were subsequently found to lack the qualifications or experience that they claimed to possess, or were incompetent or slothful.[11] Others were alcoholics; 19 per cent of the men employed by the West African colonies in 1898/9, for example, were subsequently dismissed for drunkenness.[12] The Agents and consulting engineers blamed delays in recruitment on the high medical failure rate and the tendency of men to withdraw from appointments at the last minute, and the poor quality of candidates on the general shortage of skilled technicians, due to the world-wide expansion of infrastructure construction.[13] They also believed that the colonies expected far too much of new appointees, who were not used to the different nature and isolation of colonial work and often sought solace in drink.[14] In addition, recruitment was made difficult by specifications laid down by the colonies. Many colonial governments would employ only unmarried men,[15] or would not take on trade unionists.[16] Uganda preferred district officers who were 'of the public school type' and could work in

[10] CAs to CO, 18 Mar. 1911, CAOG 17/25; memo, 20 Feb. 1914, ibid.
[11] For example, CAs to CO, 9 Oct. 1905, CO 129/330/36062; CAs to CO, 24 Oct. 1900, CO 96/366/34783; CAs to CO, 16 Sept. 1902, CO 273/285/38747; CAs to CO, 7 June 1912, CO 96/524/17570. According to Hemming, the maxim of Sierra Leone officials was to 'sit tight and do as little as possible': Hemming note, 26 May 1888, CO 96/191.
[12] CAs to CO, 21 Nov. 1899, CO 96/347/32341.
[13] CAs to CO, 17 Aug. 1901, CO 54/672/28956.
[14] Shelford to CAs, 25 Oct. 1901, CO 267/460/38251; CAs to CO, 30 May 1901, CO 323/463/18750; Cameron note, 9 Apr. 1900, CO 96/347/32341.
[15] Gregory to CAs, 2 Dec. 1902, CO 273/285/50537; CAs to CO, 27 Oct. 1901, CO 129/308/37041.
[16] Note, 31 June 1909, CO 54/704/33012.

harmony with district and medical officers in outstations.[17] Others asked for highly qualified candidates and, occasionally, demanded combinations of skills that it would be 'difficult if not impossible' to find in one person.[18] In 1901, for instance, Ceylon asked the Agents to fill the newly created post of electrical and gas adviser and chemical analyst.[19]

A further factor was the reluctance of technicians to work in the crown colonies, because the relatively low salaries offered failed to offset the various costs of colonial employment. In 1907 Jamaica offered a salary for a railway inspector that was the same as that paid in the United Kingdom.[20] The costs of colonial employment were high. Candidates for first-class appointments had to meet the expense of travelling to the interview and the subsequent medical examination.[21] If appointed, they were advised to purchase special clothing and equipment. Although they were given an advance on salaries for the purpose, the cost, £24 8s. in the case of West Africa in 1895, caused many to be 'taken aback'.[22] Until 1897, to prevent moral hazard, the cost of passage was also deducted from future salaries and officers were not reimbursed until their first home leave.[23] From that year, deductions were retained until the termination of the engagement, though the practice was abandoned for those who had served in a colony for three years. Officers who were dismissed lost this money altogether, and had to find their own return passage to the United Kingdom.[24] Similarly, few colonies provided candidates with full pay on the voyage out.[25] Instead, officers were given an advance, which was again deducted from their salaries. Given the deductions for outfit and passage, and the tendency for married men to pass salary advances to their families and single men to squander them on the journey to the colony, many officers lived in penury on arrival.[26] In 1905, in an attempt to ease the problem, the Colonial Office, on the advice of the Agents, extended the advance repayment period from four to six months, and converted the outfit advance to an allowance.[27] Men, however, continued to find their first six months of service difficult.

---

17 Uganda to CO, 17 Aug. 1912, CO 536/51/29310.
18 CAs to CO, 16 Apr. 1903, CO 54/685/13969; CAs to CO, 20 Nov. 1901, CO 54/672/40865.
19 CAs to CO, 20 Nov. 1901, CO 54/672/40865.
20 CAs to CO, 7 May 1901, CO 137/623/15932. See also CAs to CO, 5 Mar. 1901, CO 267/460/8430; CAs to CO, 30 Mar. 1903, CO 96/412/12074; CAs to CO, 24 Oct. 1901, CO 273/276/37219.
21 CAA, weeded files, m/sa 1055/1. If a candidate were rejected on medical grounds, the one guinea examination fee was refunded: CAs to CO, 20 May 1869, CO 54/449/5802.
22 CO to CAs, 9 Feb. 1895, CAOG 13/323; memo, 17 Jan. 1905, ibid.
23 CAs to CO, 3 Feb. 1897, CO 96/301/2773; Meade note, 10 Feb. 1897, ibid.
24 Meade note, 10 Feb. 1897, ibid.
25 CAA, weeded files, m/sa 908/1.
26 Ellis note, 1 Mar. 1911, CO 554/2/5664.
27 CO to CAs, 11 May 1906, CO 96/448/14310.

Colonial employment had other drawbacks. To prevent officers obtaining more lucrative employment when they arrived in the West African colonies, new recruits could not resign until they had served for three months, and then had to give three months notice or pay the colonial government one month's salary, lost their outward passage money and had to pay their own return passage. Furthermore, to encourage satisfactory work, appointments were initially for only one tour of duty, in West Africa two tours. Candidates only obtained permanent pensionable positions if they performed their duties well.[28] Moreover many governments refused to allow wives to accompany appointed officers, as they were reluctant to pay the cost of the extra passage, and believed that women hampered movement and were more prone to illness, which distracted men from their work.[29] Officers therefore had to maintain two households, and often had difficulty fending for themselves when they arrived in the colony, a problem partly solved in Southern Nigeria in 1911 by the establishment of a co-operative mess.[30] There was also a distinct possibility that officers would die or become seriously ill during their tour of duty; the European mortality rate in the Gold Coast, for example, was 7.5 per cent, and in Lagos 5.3 per cent.[31] While, on their return to Britain, they often found it difficult to obtain fresh employment, as their colonial experience was often 'practically useless in any other country'; during their time away, they had lost valuable business contacts; and in the case of West Africa, time spent in the colonies raised doubts about their general state of health.[32]

A further reason for the employment of unsuitable people and the delay in filling vacancies, however, was the system of recruitment adopted, and the general ineffectiveness of the Agents and their consultants.[33] The use of a number of engineering consultants, each with their own employment register, restricted the choice of candidates and increased costs, advertisements issued by them attracted fewer and poorer quality candidates than those that originated from the Agency, and correspondence between the Agents and their consultants led to delay.[34] In addition, the engineers had a monetary incentive to select men who would break their contract before they set sail, or would prove unacceptable to the colony and thus force the employment of a replacement. Both the Agents and their engineers were also inefficient. The Agents, who were unwilling to commit resources to the

---

[28] C. Jeffries, *The colonial empire and its civil service*, Cambridge 1938, 107.
[29] Darnley note, 8 Mar. 1904, CO 96/423/5870.
[30] Ellis note, 1 Mar. 1911, CO 554/2/5664.
[31] CAs to CO, 29 Nov. 1902, CO 96/400/49546.
[32] CAs to CO, 18 Jan. 1902, CO 273/285/2317; note, 1 Mar. 1902, CO 273/285/12219.
[33] In 1910 the Gold Coast railway manager claimed that, of the twenty-three Europeans whose services he had dispensed with between 1907 and 1910, he would not have chosen fourteen 'had they been put before me in London': Smythe to colonial secretary, 10 Oct. 1910, CAOG 17/25.
[34] Memo, 20 Oct. 1910, ibid; Lagos Government Railway to CO, 27 Sept. 1910, ibid.

provision of a service for which they were not paid, monitored qualifications and references in 'a very perfunctory' manner, and, even where checks were made, the findings were often ignored.[35] In 1899, for example, the Agents employed a foreman, even though they had been informed that he had previously been dismissed from the colonial service for drunkenness.[36] The consulting engineers were even more ineffective. In the case of Messrs Shelford & Son, recruitment was undertaken by a single clerk, and neither Shelford nor his various 'partners' had any involvement in the selection process.[37] Both the Colonial Office and Agents expressed dissatisfaction with the work of the consultants. F. R. Round had 'never much believed' in their use, and argued that they 'probably had little knowledge of the general experience required in particular colonies'.[38] The Agents later accepted that the engineers did not go 'about the matter [of recruitment] in the right way', that they took too long to select candidates and that, at least Messrs Gregory, Eyles and Waring, did their work 'very badly'.[39]

In 1908 it was discovered that the engineer Osbert Chadwick had failed to investigate the references and qualifications of a Hong Kong drainage engineer, who was subsequently dismissed. Although Chadwick was not paid and was told that he would not be used again, the Colonial Office demanded that the selection process be tightened up. The Agents therefore asked the consulting engineers to ensure that all candidates completed application forms, and to enclose, with their recommendation, the application form and references of the selected candidate.[40] Complaints, none the less, continued, and in 1909 Andrew Fiddean called for a reappraisal of the use of consulting engineers. In 1911, after further criticism, the Colonial Office asked the Agents to take over the work.[41] Lacking staff and office space, the Agents at first assumed only the responsibilities of the engineers Frederic Shelford and Duncan Elliot, but, by 1918, had taken over the tasks of all the consultants.[42] On the advice of West African governors, they also established informal links with English railway officials, began to obtain advice from colonial officials on leave in the United Kingdom and started to issue general advertisements. Those who responded were placed on their register of poten-

---

35 Antrobus note, 31 Oct. 1900, CO 96/366/34783.

36 CO to CAs, 24 Feb. 1899, CO 96/347/3318; Harris note, 10 Mar. 1899, CO 96/347/5954.

37 Memo, 7 Dec. 1910, CAOG 17/25.

38 Round note, 1 June 1901, CO 323/463/18750.

39 Memo, 20 Oct. 1910, CAOG 17/25; memo, 30 Jan. 1914. ibid ; Ellis note, 1 Mar. 1911, CO 554/2/5664.

40 CAs to CO, 15 Aug. 1908, CO 129/350/29987.

41 Fiddian note, 16 Feb. 1909, CO 96/488/3152; CAs to CO, 18 Mar. 1911, CO 554/2/5664; CO to CAs, 16 June 1910, CAOG 17/25.

42 CAs to CO, 18 Mar. 1911, CO 323/577/9051; CO to Ceylon, 28 Feb. 1918, CAOG 13/318.

tial candidates.[43] Suggestions that they set up an examinations board composed of retired officers, or obtain men through an English railway company were rejected, as retired officers' knowledge of local conditions would be out of date, and the use of a railway company could have a negative effect on the quality of candidates employed (in that the company might recommend men whom it wished to relieve itself of).

The difficulty of recruiting Europeans, their unsuitability and high cost in terms of salary, allowances, leave and time spent ill, caused many colonies to propose that the Agents employ other nationalities.[44] In 1903 the governor of Lagos suggested the recruitment of East Indian railway fitters and drivers, who could be employed on low salaries, and, able to withstand the climate better than Europeans, would be less prone to sickness.[45] The Agents opposed this, arguing that they would be unable to adjust to the West African climate, and that under the 1883 Indian Emigration Act, they would be classed as emigrants and would need sanction from the Indian government to leave India. This could take time to secure, be refused or involve employment conditions that would reduce the economic benefit of employing them.[46] On the advice of their consulting engineers, they instead recommended the recruitment of West Indians, who were better suited to the climate and whose passage to the colony would be cheaper.[47] On contacting the Jamaican administration, however, it was found that no Jamaican wished to take up the colony's offer, owing to the high demand for workers from the Jamaican and Central and South American railways, which paid relatively high salaries. Undeterred, the Gold Coast in 1905 proposed the recruitment of black Americans. Asked to comment, Shelford pointed out that salaries in the United States were ten to twelve times higher than those paid in West Africa, that passage costs would be high and that it was unlikely that men would be willing to leave the United States for as long as twelve months, the colony's proposed tour of duty.[48] The colony consequently, in 1907, again sought to employ West Indians and managed to obtain five men from Trinidad.[49] In the same year Sierra Leone also recruited two West Indian locomotive drivers, and Northern Nigeria began to employ East Indians as clerks and artisans.[50] The latter experiment, however, proved a failure – 'isolated, detesting and detested by the natives' and ostracised by the Europeans, the Indians spent 'all their spare time grumbling and composing petitions about their grievances'.[51]

43 CAs to CO, 18 Feb. 1911, CO 554/2/5664.
44 Gold Coast to CO, 6 Feb. 1907, CAOG 13/283.
45 CO to CAs, 5 June 1903, ibid.
46 CAs to CO, 19 Sept. 1904, ibid.
47 Shelford to CAs, 15 June 1903, ibid.
48 Shelford to CAs, 4 July 1905, ibid.
49 CO to Trinidad, 11 Nov. 1907, ibid.
50 CAs to CO, 4 Dec. 1907, CO 267/499/42475.
51 Note, 8 Sept. 1909, CO 96/488/27512.

Some governors began to favour the recruitment and training of indigenous workers for lower ranking technical jobs. In 1897 the governor of
Ceylon proposed that those natives of the island who had freshly graduated
from the Royal Engineering College should be given preference when vacancies in the colony's public works department occurred.[52] The Agents rejected
the proposal, insisting that candidates needed a three-year pupillage with a
member of the Institution of Civil Engineers, and between eighteen months
and two years construction experience. Their consulting engineers, however,
seem not to have been informed of the Agents' views and gave preference to
Ceylonese graduates of the Royal Engineering College until 1904 when, on
the instructions of the then governor, the practice was abandoned.[53] In West
Africa, attempts to employ indigenous labour were less successful. Those in
authority tended to have a low opinion of the West African, who allegedly
'did not take kindly to mechanical or any work requiring sustained effort', and
European workers, wishing to protect their own jobs, were reluctant to train
them.[54]

Other personnel duties

The Agents' other duties connected with personnel included the payment of
some colonial service salaries and pensions, the provision of insurance
company bonds for those officers appointed to positions of responsibility, the
administration (in the United Kingdom) of the estates of those who died in
the colonies, the supervision of colonials attending colleges in Britain and
Europe and the arrangement of transport.[55] By 1913 the Agents paid 5,708
salaries and pensions, for which they received no remuneration.[56] The salaries paid included the full wages of those officers serving in Southern and
Northern Nigeria who chose not to be paid in the colonies, any portion of an
officer's salary that he wished to be paid to a relative in Britain, the half salaries of officials on leave, and salary advances and outfit allowances to those
entering the colonial service.[57] To prevent dishonesty, payments were made
only on the receipt of the relevant colonial instructions and, from 1877, officers wishing part of their pay to go to relatives in the United Kingdom were
furnished with a draft to be given to their relations, which was drawn on the
Crown Agents for the amount that they wanted to remit.[58]

[52] CAs to CO, 8 Feb. 1897, CAOG 13/288.
[53] CO to Ceylon, 3 June 1904, ibid; Ceylon to CO, 13 July 1904, ibid.
[54] Glaster to colonial secretary, 19 Dec. 1902, CAOG 13/283; CO to CAs, 5 June 1903,
ibid.
[55] CAA, security bond file.
[56] Memo, 16 June 1914, CAOG 16/1.
[57] CAs to CO, 23 Feb. 1910, CO 520/97/5580.
[58] Treasury instructions, 1860, CO 323/337/16885; CAs to CO, 14 Mar. 1877, CO 323/
331/3064.

The Agents' pension work largely involved the pensions of widows and orphans of colonial officers and the management of the associated invest-ment funds.[59] To prevent adverse selection, the Agents required newly-appointed officers to provide evidence of their particulars in the form of marriage and birth certificates.[60] Officers then paid a minimum contribution equal to approximately 4 per cent of their salary; non-payment being allowed only if contributions were being made to another scheme.[61] Pensions were calculated at the current rate of exchange and, to save costs, were paid quar-terly and had to be collected by the recipients or their representatives from the Agents' office.[62] Only children born in wedlock were eligible for benefit, and pensions ceased on the death, remarriage or bankruptcy of the widows, and, in the case of child allowances, when male children reached the age of eighteen and girls married or attained the age of twenty-one. Fraud was coun-tered by requiring widows to inform Crown Agents within three months of any change in their circumstances; delay carried a fine of £2, and non-disclo-sure the forfeiture of the entire pension.[63]

On the death of a colonial officer, or, in East Africa any British subject, a local administrator was appointed, who sold the deceased's large possessions and, to avoid remittance costs, paid the proceeds together with any outstanding officer's salary into the colony's general account and sent smaller items to London.[64] The Agents then contacted the deceased's known rela-tives or the beneficiaries under his will to whom they passed the small articles and the money, which was paid from the colony's current account.[65] Decep-tion was avoided by requiring relations or beneficiaries of estates of a greater value than £100 to provide the Agency with letters of administration or a proved will, and others to complete a form of declaration and supply evidence of death in the form of a death certificate or bill for funeral expenses.[66] Although the Agents performed their duties efficiently, local administrators were the subject of numerous complaints. It was claimed that the time taken to settle estates, a minimum of nine months, was excessive, that known possessions disappeared after death, that goods were sold before relatives' wishes were known and that the prices obtained were poor. In response, colo-

---

[59] Some early funds were managed locally. See, for example, CAOG 15/365, memo.
[60] Memo, 19 Jan. 1914, CAOG 15/274.
[61] Trinidad to CAs, 30 May 1890, CAOG 15/365; CO to CAs, 6 July 1914, CAOG 15/260.
[62] CO to CAs, 28 Oct. 1886, CAOG 15/364; memo, 29 Dec. 1881, CAOG 15/365; declaration form, ibid.
[63] Memo, CAOG 15/304.
[64] CO to CAs, 28 July 1910, CAOG 15/158; administrator-general to Mombassa, 29 Nov. 1904, CAOG 15/161; memo, 20 Jan. 1898, CAOG 15/121.
[65] Note, 5 Jan. 1905, CAOG 15/161. In the case of deceased officers of the King's African Rifles, War Office regulations required that unpaid salaries be sent to the United Kingdom by draft: CO to CAs, 28 Oct. 1905, CAOG 15/162.
[66] Memo, 9 Feb. 1898, CAOG 15/121.

nies argued that delays were unavoidable and that possessions had to be sold immediately to prevent price depreciation. Theft were blamed on servants, and it was claimed that the proceeds of sales were low because goods were often sold in remote places, where there was little demand and that locals were reluctant to buy the clothing of the dead.[67]

The Agency's supervision of colonials studying in Europe can be traced back to 1822 when the Maltese agent was given responsibility for five youths – two in England and three in Rome.[68] The Agents acted as 'a sort of good angel' to the students, providing them with advice, in some cases paying them their government grants, closely monitoring their performance and requiring their places of study to supply confirmation of results and termly certificates of attendance.[69] Sir William Mercer, who at the end of the century was responsible for the Office's miscellaneous duties, saw the students 'privately and socially' and built up 'special' trust relationships that no doubt benefited the Agency when their *protegées* attained positions of authority in their home colonies.[70]

The Agency's role in providing transport included the arrangement of passages for colonial officers and troops leaving or returning to the colonies and the management of colonial emigration. The emigration work was inherited from the Colonial Land and Emigration Commission. By the mid-1870s most self-governing colonies had their own emigration agents and the commission was no longer cost-effective.[71] In 1876, on the retirement of one of the two remaining commissioners, its financial and some miscellaneous duties were passed to the Agents and, two years later, on the retirement of the second commissioner, the commission was abolished and all its work transferred to the Agency.[72] The Crown Agents thus became responsible for the granting of guano licences, the arrangement of passages to Western Australia and Tasmania for the families of former convicts, the supervision of emigration to Natal and the Falkland Islands and the management of the transport of Indians to the West Indies and Fiji.[73] The newly-won Natal and Australian duties disappeared when they were taken over by the colonies concerned in

67 CAOG 15/158.
68 PP 1824, xvi. 10, 14.
69 PPE, q. 2255. See, for example, CAs to CO, 25 June 1867, CO 54/429/6098.
70 PPE, qq. 2255–6.
71 F. H. Hitchens, *The Colonial Land and Emigration Commission*, London 1931, 311.
72 Ibid; Walcott to CAs, 30 Mar. 1878, CO 384/121/3867.
73 With regard to their Australian and Tasmanian work, the Agents corresponded with those nominated by the colonies' governors to discover when they wished to travel and then arranged their passages. The transport of Natal emigrants was arranged by the colony's own agent: the CAs merely negotiated the contracts with the shipping company used, the Union Steamship Co., and monitored the Natal agent. The passage of emigrants to the Falklands was organised by the CAs and financed by money deposited with the Agency by the Falkland Islands Co. for the purchase of land in the colony: Walcott to CAs, 30 Mar. 1878, CO 384/121/3867.

1880, and few people emigrated to the Falklands. The organisation of the shipment of coolies to the West Indies, however, continued to take up a considerable amount of the Agency's time.[74]

In this the Agents acted as intermediaries between the receiving colonies and the emigration agents, who, based in India, recruited the emigrants. They chartered the necessary vessels and appointed for each voyage a surgeon superintendent, who provided the emigrants with medical assistance and ensured their general well-being. At first the Agents worked without fee. In 1883, however, they proposed that the colonies be charged 2s. per emigrant and that the proceeds be paid to them personally as they rather than the Agency, did the extra work.[75] The Colonial Office, 'only imperfectly' aware of the amount involved, agreed but, wishing to protect West Indian finances which had been damaged by the depression in the sugar industry, requested that the sum be paid from the Agency's Reserve Fund.[76] The payments, which from 1889 to 1892 averaged £1,233 per annum, continued to be made until 1896, when the Colonial Office, believing that they were not 'free from objection', halted the arrangement.[77] Thereafter, neither the Agents nor the Agency were compensated for the service, with a 1912 Crown Agent appeal for the introduction of a charge of 6d. per emigrant being rejected by the Colonial Office.[78]

The shipping contracts negotiated by the Agents generally ran for one, three or five years. Approximately half were filled by open competition, which prevented 'adverse criticism' of the Agency.[79] Advertisements were placed in the press, displayed in the London, Liverpool and Glasgow Shipping Exchanges, and, on occasion, sent direct to firms likely to be interested.[80] Generally, only a few tenders were received and the contracts were won by the same firms.[81] As colonies preferred the use of sailing ships and required emigrants to be transported during a three-month 'season', only companies with large fleets of passenger steamers were able to tender.[82] In addition, from the early 1890s, James Nourse and Messrs Sandbach Tinne &

---

[74] CAs to CO, 29 Oct. 1883, CO 384/147/18524. Between 1878 and 1883 the Agents chartered ninety-eight ships that transported 41,457 emigrants: ibid. Between 1899 and 1907 they arranged the passages of 69,258 emigrants: PP 1910, xxvii (Cd 5194), no. 26e.
[75] CAs to CO, 29 Oct. 1883, CO 384/147/18524.
[76] CO to CAs, 4 Feb. 1883, CO 323/499/23361; Round note, 5 July 1904, ibid.
[77] CAA, M 38.
[78] CAs to CO, 18 May 1912, CO 323/591/15603.
[79] CAs to CO, 20 Apr. 1893, CO 384/188/6554.
[80] CAs to CO, 25 Feb. 1881, CO 384/136/3486; CAs to CO, 2 Dec. 1892, CO 384/185/23446.
[81] From the late 1880s the successful contractor was usually James Nourse, but Messrs Sandbach Tinne & Co., Messrs Tyser & Co. and the British India Steamship Co. were also used.
[82] CAs to CO, 20 Apr. 1893, CO 384/188/6554. It was thought that emigrants transported by sailing ship were landed in 'better condition' than those shipped by steamer, owing to the superior ventilation and the longer duration of the voyage during which their general

Co. entered into an arrangement whereby Nourse bid for contracts, and, if successful, shared them with Sandbach.[83] Before 1886 contracts also failed to incorporate all the requirements of the Indian government, and companies new to the trade therefore often unknowingly contravened regulations, were fined and hence discouraged from tendering in the future.[84]

The remaining contracts were renewed without competition or given to James Nourse. It was argued that Nourse offered lower rates when there was no competition, as he was aware that if his offer was considered excessive a tender would be held and he might lose the contract.[85] Moreover, by dispensing with competition, the Agents saved the cost of organising the tender and reaped the benefits of the use of one trusted contractor. The colonies and Nourse's competitors, however, strongly criticised the lack of competition. In 1891, for example, the unofficial members of the Trinidad legislative council objected to the extension of a Nourse contract by one year and in 1887 Messrs Sandbach Tinne & Co. complained about a further extension of a contract, claiming that they would have undertaken the work for a lower fee.[86]

The Agents further minimised contractor moral hazard through performance-related remuneration, bonds and monitoring. The contractors' payment took the form of a passage fee for each emigrant landed. No fee was received for healthy emigrants who died at sea and, for those who died and were deemed by the surgeon superintendents to be invalids, a fee was paid in proportion to that part of the trip completed at the time of death.[87] Contractors, consequently, had a strong incentive to ensure that their passengers survived the voyage. Moreover, on accepting a contract, the contractor and two third parties had to provide a surety of between £2,000 and £3,000, from which fines would be deducted for contravention of the provisions of the contract.[88] To ensure that any breaches were discovered, contractors were closely monitored. Vessels transporting emigrants from India to the colonies, which always sailed from England, were subject to a three-day inspection by the Board of Trade and a further examination when they arrived in India.[89] During the voyage, the surgeon superintendents kept a close eye on the

state of health improved. Steamers were used occasionally in the 1880s: Basil Lubbock, *Coolie ships and oil sailors*, Glasgow 1955, 81.

83 CAs to CO, 20 Apr. 1893, CO 384/188/6554.

84 CAs to CO, 3 Aug. 1886, CO 384/162/13863.

85 CAs to CO, 20 Apr. 1893, CO 384/188/6554. This view is supported by the 1893 Trinidad and British Guiana tenders that were won by Nourse at rates respectively 10s. and 15s. above his pre-tender offer: CAs to CO, 30 Nov. 1893, CO 384/188/20237.

86 CAs to CO, 20 Mar. 1891, CO 384/182/5787; Sandbach to British Guiana, 29 Mar. 1887, CO 384/166/8984.

87 Contract, CO 384/190/9599.

88 CAs to CO, 3 Aug. 1886, CO 384/162/13863; contract, CO 384/190/9599.

89 CAs to CO, 12 Mar. 1884, CO 384/152/3067. Ships sailing from the colonies to return emigrants to India were inspected at the port of departure.

contractors' treatment of the emigrants and reported any unacceptable behaviour to the Agents.

The Crown Agents minimised unscrupulous behaviour by surgeon superintendents by means of short-term contracts, long-term relationships and
high performance-related salaries. Surgeons were employed for single jour-
neys only, with re-employment 'subject to their good behaviour'.[90] Those,
however, who performed their duties effectively, worked for the Agents
continuously; by 1892 some had done so for thirty years.[91] Their pay again
took the form of a passage fee for each emigrant landed, the size of which
increased with each voyage completed up to the eleventh passage.[92] Surgeons
were thus encouraged to perform their work adequately, and experienced men
discouraged from leaving the profession. A single fee would have attracted
candidates who regarded the work 'only in the nature of casual employment'.[93]

To increase the cost of dismissal, the fees paid to surgeons were relatively
high and were again the subject of a number of complaints. Criticism came to
a head in 1892 when Trinidad, concerned at average earnings of £740 per
voyage, proposed that the surgeons be replaced by officers of the island's
medical department.[94] The Agents strongly opposed this initiative, claiming
that the island's officers lacked sufficient experience, and that, given the
onerous, responsible and temporary nature of the work and their inability to
obtain employment between voyages, the surgeons were not overpaid.[95] The
Colonial Office, however, agreed with the colony, pointing out that since the
rates were introduced the carrying capacity of ships had increased, surgeons
were able to make two rather than a single voyage per year and there was no
longer a shortage of medical personnel.[96] They consequently required the
Agents to submit a reduced pay scale, which was eventually introduced in
1895.[97]

In their performance of their role in the supply of personnel, which had been
taken on to increase the status and job-satisfaction of their work, the Agents
achieved mixed success. The recruitment of technical officers no doubt
reduced the likelihood of criticism of their activities by the men employed,

[90] CAs to CO, 26 Apr. 1892, CO 384/185/8372.
[91] Note, 16 June 1892, ibid.
[92] CAs to CO, 8 Aug. 1894, CO 384/190/14019.
[93] Ibid.
[94] CAs to CO, 26 Apr. 1892, CO 384/185/8372. In comparison, it should be noted that
doctors employed on passenger steamers earned £120 per passage as well as fees from
passengers: note, 16 June 1892. ibid.
[95] CAs to CO, 26 Apr. 1892, ibid; CAs to CO, 8 Aug. 1894, CO 384/190/14019.
[96] Note, 16 June 1892, CO 384/185/8372.
[97] Under the new scale, surgeons obtained the usual passage fee for the first 500 emigrants
on a voyage, and half that sum for each additional emigrant: CAs to CO, 8 Aug. 1894,
CO 384/190/14019.

but, unremunerated, it increased the Agents' costs and took up valuable time. It also led to colonial criticism. Despite the delegation of most of the selection process to consulting engineers who, to ensure good conduct, were paid high fees, many of the men employed were of poor quality. The consultants devoted few resources to recruitment and it could be argued that it was in their interest to employ men unacceptable to colonies. Moreover, the costs and conditions of colonial employment, partly designed to prevent moral hazard by recruits on arrival in the colonies, discouraged applications from well-qualified candidates. In their responsibilities for the payment of salaries and pensions and the transportation of coolies, the Agents were more successful. There is no evidence of fraud by claimants, and, although transportation costs were high, most coolies arrived at their destinations in good condition.

11

The Enquiries of 1901 and 1908

By 1900 the Agents' maximisation of their income and the resultant high cost of stores, infrastructure and loans, the failure of issues and poor quality railways had begun to damage their relationship with both the colonies and the Colonial Office. Trust was further undermined by their increasing involvement in policy-making and the corresponding reduction in power of local administrations, by the relocation of the Agency from Downing Street to Whitehall Gardens in 1902, which reduced face-to-face and social interaction with officials of the Colonial Office, and by the promotion, in 1901, to the post of Senior Agent of the Crown Agent Sir Ernest Blake.

The son of a rector, one of eleven children, and educated at Norwich Grammar School, Blake's social origins were far humbler than those of his Colonial Office and colonial counterparts, who thus trusted him less, and of his predecessors, which weakened Crown Agent staff trust and respect. Furthermore, he seems to have been a man of lax private norms and an aggressive and autocratic character. The Colonial Office was aware of these characteristics when it appointed him and perhaps believed that they would prove advantageous in helping to return the Agency to profitability. It appears, however, not to have suspected the effect his new-found power would have on his personality. On the assumption of his new position, he began to act in an arrogant and aggressive manner, no doubt believing that this action was in his own and the Agency's best interests, but perhaps, on occasion, obtaining personal pleasure from his behaviour, regardless of its long-term consequences. Faced with criticism of the Agency's actions, he withdrew its acceptance of Colonial Office moral hazard, threatening in his evidence to the Royal Commission of Shipping Rings to 'say that I do not agree in several cases with the policy pursued' with regard to Sir Alfred Jones's shipping and banking monopolies.[1] To weaken the validity of complaints, he began to mock officials' lack of commercial knowledge and repeatedly sought to undermine the reputation of colonial governors with the secretary of state.

---

[1] In 1907 Blake complained that the secretary of state allowed Jones to 'pose as a great philanthropist and benefactor', but ignored the fact that his wealth had been 'sweated out of the trade of West Africa': Blake to CO, 29 Apr. 1907, CO 323/527/15468. After an interview with the under-secretary, Sir Francis Hopwood, he agreed to refuse to reply to any of the enquiry's questions on policy: Green note, 6 May 1907, ibid.

Favours went unreciprocated and his staff were treated poorly, no doubt prompting them to reduce the quality of their work in retaliation.[2]

As their faith in the Agency weakened, and the size and therefore the influence of local business elites grew, colonial governors were increasingly moved to criticise the Agents to the Colonial Office through unofficial channels. This complaint by diluting the Agency's trust relationship with governors no doubt reduced still further its desire to act in the colonial interest. The Colonial Office was in a quandary as to how it should respond to the criticism. By the end of the nineteenth century it was becoming clear that there had been a sea change in society's moral norms. In response, in the absence of class politics, political parties, seeking the support of the newly enlarged electorate, began to adopt the politics of scandal and governments were forced to cleanse aspects of official life that could be susceptible to criticism.[3] Official committees of enquiry were established, for example into the War Office and shipping conferences, and the powers of those non-state bodies that had succumbed to dishonest practice were returned to state control.[4] The Colonial Office, however, was reluctant to take action where the Crown Agents were concerned. As the Agency was a quasi-independent body, the Colonial Office already had some control over its activities; both the Agents' personal and institutional moral hazard had been benign for many years; and a state takeover of their functions was unlikely to be in the Office's interests. Colonial governments would campaign strongly for imperial financing of the services, thus increasing Treasury intervention in its policy-making procedures, and it would lose the ability to use the Agency as a conduit for its own moral hazard. For a long period it therefore turned a deaf ear to complaints, only taking action when it believed its relationships with governors and local elites, and its own reputation as an effective government office, were at risk.

The enquiry of 1901

The first enquiry into the Agency occurred in 1901, and took the form of a circular despatch that was sent to all forty-nine crown colonies, requesting detailed critiques of the Agents' performance. The investigation was initiated by a complaint from Sidney Olivier, a trusted Colonial Office official, who had served in three West Indian colonies and in 1900 was appointed colonial secretary of Jamaica. Olivier informed Chamberlain that in all the colonies in which he had served, 'the universal opinion, not only among uninterested unofficial members of councils and the public, but amongst governors,

2   Green note, 1 May 1907, ibid. The Crown Agents' clerks were 'brimming over with discontent': *Pall Mall Gazette*, 20 Aug. 1904, 4.
3   G. R. Searle, *Corruption in British politics, 1895–1930*, Oxford 1987, 44.
4   Martin Daunton, 'Payment and participation: welfare and state formation in Britain, 1900–1951', *Past and Present* cl (1996), 170.

colonial secretaries, and other high placed officials' was that the service provided by the Agency was unsatisfactory.[5] Although he did not himself believe that 'the colonies as a whole are ill-served or expensively served', he had come across cases in which it had been 'a disadvantage to do business' with the Agency. Consequently, he proposed the establishment of a commission of enquiry composed of past and present governors and other critics, including a commercial representative, whose findings would 'dispel colonial prejudice' and improve the efficiency of the Agency.[6]

In Chamberlain, Olivier found a receptive audience for his criticisms. The secretary of state had long been concerned about the high cost of West African railway construction and, two months previously, had been perturbed by the discovery that the Agency had supplied Lagos with a locomotive twice as expensive as that ordered and, because of its excess weight, totally unusable.[7] He was also, owing to the revelations emerging from the Select Committee on War Office Contracts, more aware than usual of the susceptibility of the Agents to corruption, and, as he and a colleague had been the subject of accusations of sleaze earlier in the year, was keen to protect the Colonial Office from further scandal.[8] Having 'a shrewd suspicion that the mercantile side (not the financial) of the Crown Agents' office did require a little looking up' and feeling that an enquiry would ward off 'a serious attack' from parliament, he consequently asked Olivier to supply 'specific charges'.[9] Olivier declined 'on private and public grounds', but repeated that there was great colonial disquiet about the Agency. Unwilling to let the matter drop, particularly after it emerged that the Agents had again ordered expensive and unusable rolling stock for Jamaica, Chamberlain decided that colonial governors should be asked for their opinions of the Agency.[10]

Replies to the circular were passed to the Crown Agents for comment and then returned to the Colonial Office. In his 1904 despatch on the findings, Chamberlain reported that the investigation had been searching and exhaustive, and that only a small number of complaints had been received, few were

[5] Olivier to Chamberlain, 18 July 1900, CO 137/611/25176.
[6] Ibid. At the Colonial Office, Olivier was regarded as 'indiscreet and intolerant of others' inadequacies': Kubicek, *The administration of imperialism*, 19.
[7] CAs to CO, 9 May 1900, CO 147/152/14525. Chamberlain believed that the locomotive order was 'a very important case', reflecting the Agents' failure to follow the normal course of business: Chamberlain note, 24 July 1900, ibid.
[8] The War Office committee met from 4 May to 1 August 1900: PP 1900, ix (313). In 1899 it was discovered that the parliamentary under-secretary, the earl of Selborne, was a director of P. & O. Ltd, which did a great deal of business with the Colonial Office. During 1899 – 1900, Chamberlain was found to hold £3,000 in Royal Niger Co. shares (compensation for the revocation of that company's charter was currently being discussed by the Colonial Office), and his immediate family to part-own and operate four firms that supplied goods on government contracts: Searle, *Corruption*, 38–9, 47–8, 52–6.
[9] Chamberlain note, 12 Aug. 1900, CO 137/611/25176.
[10] CAs to CO, 9 Nov. 1900, CO 137/615/36622.

important and most had proved groundless.[11] Nevertheless, to improve the efficiency of the Agency, he put forward a number of recommendations, primarily designed to reduce delays in supply, all of which were adopted subsequently. In fact, some of the complaints had been serious, and the Colonial Office had found a number of the Agents' rebuttals dubious. For example, the Federated Malay States complained about the supply of two defective locomotives and £11,000-worth of poor quality rails, and J. F. N. Green felt that a price list supplied by Waterlow & Sons, which allegedly showed that the company charged the Agents relatively low prices, involved some 'economy of the truth'.[12]

As regards the number of complaints, only twenty-eight colonies replied to the circular (twenty-six if the Transvaal and the Orange River, colonies which had no experience of the Agency are discounted), and ten claimed to be perfectly satisfied with the service provided. However, some colonies sent in large numbers of criticisms – Jamaica, for example, forwarded thirty-one; many administrations, not wishing to overload their despatches, had supplied only examples of their grievances; and five of the satisfied colonies had government revenues below £50,000 and therefore had little to do with the Agency.[13] As C. P. Lucas acknowledged, it also seems likely that in their replies to the circular governors 'preferred to speak well rather than ill of the Crown Agents', fearing the consequences that criticism could have on their careers.[14] Most governors realised that 'whilst the colonial governments are nearer the requirements of the colonies, the ground floor of Downing Street ... [the Agents' office] ... is nearer the secretary of state' and that the Colonial Office used the Agency to monitor their activities.[15] Some may also have had personal experience of Sir Ernest Blake's ruthless and vindictive personality or may have been unwilling to antagonise an organisation, the goodwill of which could prove useful to them in their private capacities.[16]

It seems unlikely that Chamberlain's report on the enquiry would have been written and circulated to the colonies had there been little further criticism of the Agency. In the event, from 1901 the number of complaints increased and became progressively more public. The distinguished jour-

11 PP 1904, lix (Cd 1944).

12 CAOG 17/24, misc. 142, no. 26; Green note, 12 Sept. 1902, CO 885/8/151.

13 Green note, 12 Sept. 1902, CO 885/8/151; CAOG 9/24, misc. 142, no. 20; Hemming to Chamberlain, 8 Oct. 1901, ibid.

14 Lucas note, 21 Nov. 1906, CO 323/524/41857. Both the former governor, Sir A. W. L. Hemming, and *Sells Commercial Intelligence* made similar points: *Empire Review* xi (1906), 508; *Sells Commercial Intelligence*, 25 May 1904, 13.

15 Olivier note, 11 Sept. 1900, CO 137/613/31708.

16 The benefits of good relations with the CAs with regard to the award of concessions was discussed in chapter 9 above. In 1907 Sidney Olivier instructed the Agents to employ, as architects for the replacement for public buildings destroyed in the 1906 earthquake, a firm in which his brother-in-law was a partner: CAs to CO, 16 July 1907, CO 137/660/ 25319. See also CAs to CO, 12 June 1911, CO 446/101/19481.

nalist, E. D. Morel, made a number of charges against the Agency that Blake and the Colonial Office believed were 'outrageous' and 'disgraceful and libellous'.[17] In a speech to the Manchester Chamber of Commerce, governor of the Gold Coast, Sir William MacGregor was highly critical of the Agents' work on that colony's railway.[18] The following year Sir Harry Johnson, another former governor attacked the extravagant cost of departmentally built railways in a Royal Society of Arts speech and claimed that consulting engineers were chosen for their work 'because they were people who somebody wanted to provide for'.[19] From 1902 criticism began to spread to the press and parliament. Damning articles appeared in the *Daily Mail*, the *British Trade Journal*, and *Sells Commercial Intelligence*, and *The Times* published a lengthy correspondence on the Agency.[20] Even more vehement accusations were made in colonial newspapers. The *Straits Times*, for example, variously described the Agents as 'licensed pickpockets', 'objectionable parasites', 'vultures', 'a blight', and 'a cancer on the community'.[21] In the House of Commons, the Colonial Office faced a series of questions on every aspect of the Agents' work and in a House of Lords debate on the office in June 1904, the earl of Portsmouth called for the appointment of a select committee 'to enquire into the system by which the Crown Agents are paid and their methods of transacting their duties'.[22]

The strategies adopted by the Agents to deflect this onslaught were many and varied. They refused to accept responsibility for even the most minor complaints, were reluctant to disclose details of their operations even to parliament, which only strengthened the suspicion that they had something to hide, and constantly stressed the altruistic nature of their work.[23] In order to undermine and avoid criticism they also trivialised incidents and deliberately misunderstood the nature of complaints or concentrated on those

[17] Morel, *Affairs of Africa*, 17, 30–3; Blake note, 6 June 1904, CO 323/492/6877; Antrobus note, 16 Mar. 1904, CO 147/168/8585.
[18] CAs to CO, 4 Mar. 1903, CO 147/168/8385. MacGregor was reprimanded by the Colonial Office, a fact which no doubt discouraged other governors from publicly criticising the Agents: R. B. Joyce, *Sir William MacGregor*, Oxford 1971.
[19] *Journal of the Royal Society of Arts*, 8 Apr. 1904, 450.
[20] See, for example, *Daily Mail*, 22 Apr. 1904, 4; 23 Apr. 1904, 4; 26 Apr. 1904, 4; *British Trade Journal*, 1 Apr. 1902, 128; *Sells Commercial Intelligence*, 9 Mar. 1904, 7; 16 Mar. 1904, 7; 23 Mar. 1904, 15; *The Times*, 16 Aug. 1904, 5; 23 Aug. 1904, 6; 30 Aug. 1904, 10.
[21] *Straits Times*, 6 Nov. 1906, 5; 7 Nov. 1906, 4; 13 Nov. 1906, 5.
[22] *Hansard*, 4th ser. 1904, cxxxv. 1328–62. See, for example ibid. cxxxiv. 1375; cxxxvi. 361; cxxxviii. 950.
[23] CAs to CO, 13 Feb. 1903, CO 323/483/6134; CAs to CO, 15 Sept. 1904, CO 323/492/32297. The Colonial Office believed that the CAs 'erred in never admitting the rare mistakes they inevitably make' and that 'from their point of view . . . the largest amount of publicity is desirable': Harris note, 10 Feb. 1908, CO 323/538/4590; Green note, 16 Feb. 1903, CO 323/483/6134. See also PPE, q. 1005. Blake claimed that the Agency was 'a vast benevolent institution run in the interests of the colonies': Blake to Anderson, 27 Dec. 1905, CAOG 14/66.

aspects that they could easily refute.[24] Press criticism was blamed on the failure of the Colonial Office to defend them rigorously, which they attributed to their quasi-government status and the fact that the secretary of state did not 'feel that the attack was on himself'.[25] Blake, meanwhile, declared that the Agency was the victim of an organised campaign of vilification set in motion by merchants, firms that had been denied access to their suppliers lists, and City issuing houses, all of whom would gain if the Agency was closed down.[26] It was pointed out that Sir Harry Johnson was a director of the Shire Highlands Co., with which the Agency had recently come into conflict, that Lord Grey, a House of Lords critic, was the director of a shipping company that had failed to receive the Agents' support on the South African freight question and that Lord Rothschild, another critic, was the head of a bank that undertook a large amount of loan issue work.[27] Such claims, however, appear to be more a reflection of Blake's growing paranoia than of the true situation. From approximately 1902 he became increasingly convinced that 'everybody is trying to get his knife into us', and by 1908, believing that Colonial Office staff were intent on creating 'difficulties', had begun to correspond on all matters exclusively with the under-secretary of state.[28]

At first the Colonial Office dismissed criticism of the Agency. But as the complaints mounted and became more public, it was decided that action would have to be taken. Unfortunately the Office was divided as to how to proceed. J. F. N. Green's suggestion that an inter-departmental investigative committee, composed of Treasury, Foreign and Colonial Office representatives and ex-colonial governors, should be established was rejected as being too extensive.[29] The proposal made by the secretary of state, Alfred Lyttelton, that the evidence of the 1901 enquiry be presented to parliament, was similarly discounted. Publication of the full evidence, with its derogatory

---

[24] In 1903 the Colonial Office noted that the Southern Nigerian governor, when making a complaint, 'cannot have meant what the CAs suppose', and in 1900 with regard to another criticism, that the Agents 'ignore the fact that the whole difficulty arose from their action in ordering goods in enormous excess': Strachy note, 26 Nov. 1903, CO 520/21/39973; CAs to CO, 23 May 1900, CO 147/152/16137. See also Antrobus note, 20 June 1896, CO 147/108/12759; CO to CAs, 31 Dec. 1903, CO 520/21/39973.

[25] PPE, q. 1167; Blake note, 3 Feb. 1908, CO 323/538/3706.

[26] Blake note, 6 June 1904, CO 323/492/6877.

[27] Ibid. The Agents could have added that most colonial newspapers were owned or supported by merchants, that E. D. Morel was the mouthpiece of Sir Alfred Jones and that the MPs Austin Taylor and Herbert Samuel, the Agents' most persistent parliamentary critics, were supporters of the French Congo campaign organised by the West African merchant John Holt, a hardened opponent of the Agency: memo, n.d., John Holt papers, MS Afr. s. 1525, 18/2; Holt to Morel, 18 Dec. 1902, and 20 July 1903, ibid. 18/14.

[28] PPE, q. 122; Blake to Hopwood, 22 May 1908, CAOG 17/22. See also CAs to CO, 11 June 1909, CO 323/553/5185; PPE, q. 282; Blake to Hopwood, 6 Feb. 1908, CAOG 17/22. Blake's mental state may have been associated with his wife's death in 1902.

[29] Green note, 3 June 1904, CO 323/492/6877; Lucas note, n.d., ibid.

comments against the Agents and descriptions of the nefarious activities of suppliers, would be detrimental to the colonies, while the presentation of an edited version would only fuel suspicions.[30] A further suggestion put forward by Lyttelton, for the formation of a two-man commission to investigate all recent complaints was also strongly opposed. Blake pointed out that the Agency had been completely vindicated by the 1901 enquiry, and that a further investigation would add another burden to its already heavy workload. After more discussion, a compromise was reached. Chamberlain's report on the 1901 enquiry was presented to parliament. The Colonial Office, at the end of the Lords debate, agreed to investigate all further complaints and publish their findings, and, to refute claims made in the *Sells Commercial Intelligence* that the Agency had bought excessively expensive metal files for Ceylon, it was arranged for 'a friendly question' to be asked in parliament.[31]

The ensuing respite in attacks on the Agents was brief. By 1906 parliament had again begun to question their conduct and there was renewed press complaint.[32] The most damaging article appeared in the *Empire Review*, written by the former governor Sir Augustus Hemming, who sent a copy to the new parliamentary under-secretary, Winston Churchill.[33] The Colonial Office disparaged both the article and its author. Hemming was 'not a man of first rate judgement or of first rate tact', he had a personal animosity towards Blake, who had severely criticised him when he was governor of Jamaica, and at one time had been 'anxious to be appointed a Crown Agent' himself.[34] On the other hand Churchill supported both the article and Hemming's call for an enquiry. New to his post, he was unencumbered by any prior relationship with the Agents and, through his connections with the Transvaal, which from 1902 to 1904 had successfully beaten off a Colonial Office attempt to enforce the monopoly regulation upon it, was well aware of the depth of feeling against the Agency that existed in the colonies. Furthermore, possessing strong private moral norms, he was not himself 'a great admirer' of the Agency. He particularly objected to its methods of recruitment by 'favour unadorned', to the office reserve fund, which he believed to be 'objectionable and I think indefensible', and to the inability of parliament to investigate its activities.[35] Seizing his opportunity to act, Churchill therefore declared himself unable to undertake 'a sustained parliamentary defence' of the Agency without 'a full enquiry'.[36] As on most topics, however, his feelings

[30] Lucas, note, n.d., ibid; Blake note, 6 June 1904, ibid.
[31] *Hansard*, 4th ser. 1904, cxxxv. 1356–7, 1361; Lucas note, 6 July 1904, CO 323/499/20711.
[32] See, for example, *Hansard*, 4th ser. 1906, clxii. 700; clxv. 384; clxvi. 290; clxvii. 657, 1507; *Jamaica Daily Telegraph*, 1 Sept. 1906, 10.
[33] *Empire Review* xi (1906), 507–10; Hemming to Churchill, 6 Nov. 1906, CO 323/524/41857.
[34] Lucas note, 21 Nov. 1906, CO 323/524/41857.
[35] Churchill note, 25 Nov. 1906, ibid; Churchill note, 4 Nov. 1906, CO 111/554/40273.
[36] Churchill note, 25 Nov. 1906, CO 323/524/41857.

were not shared by the earl of Elgin, the new secretary of state. Wishing to avoid rash decisions in his first months in Office, and probably unwilling to fall in with the demands of his junior minister so early in their relationship, he rejected all calls for an enquiry.[37]

In February 1908 Churchill returned to the fray. He rejected a proposed answer to a parliamentary question on the Agents' recruitment of staff, stating that he was unable to 'associate . . . [himself] . . . with this whitewashing'.[38] On the same day, with regard to a further parliamentary question, he expressed the view that 'the system cannot be defended if it is severely attacked', adding 'I entirely disapprove of it'.[39] A few days later, he proposed that the secretary of state should agree to a parliamentary demand for an enquiry.[40] The Colonial Office was again divided. J. F. N. Green believed an enquiry was 'to be desired'.[41] C. Harris rejected the proposal, unable to 'see . . . what we should gain that we do not now know'.[42] Inevitably, Blake opposed an investigation, as no *prima facie* case had been made against the Agency, and 'the committee would feel itself almost bound to make recommendations' that could 'prove embarrassing to both the secretary of state and ourselves'.[43]

The enquiry of 1908

After much debate, it was decided that an enquiry should indeed take place. Precisely why this decision was reached is not recorded. It seems likely that the Colonial Office had begun to realise that its failure to act was damaging its relationships with governors and local elites and governor-elite collaboration and thus threatened to weaken its ability to push forward development, tackle colonial moral hazard, and minimise colonial administration costs. It also perhaps feared for its own reputation. In 1906 C. P. Lucas pointed out to his colleagues that a parliamentary accusation that the Agents' consulting engineers encouraged the construction of uneconomical railways for their own gain inferred that 'successive Secretaries of State have connived at abuses'.[44] Other contributory factors probably included Churchill's visit to East Africa in the autumn of 1907 when he heard further criticism of the Agency, as well as the constant press and parliamentary attacks on the supposed immorality of the Liberal government, and the retirement in

---

37 Elgin note, 26 Jan. 1907, ibid.
38 Churchill note, 4 Feb. 1908, CO 323/538/3706.
39 Churchill note, 4 Feb. 1908, CO 323/538/3707.
40 Churchill note, 6 Feb. 1908, CO 323/538/4106.
41 Green note, 5 Feb. 1908, ibid.
42 Harris note, n.d., ibid.
43 Blake to Hopwood, 6 Feb. 1908, CAOG 17/22.
44 Lucas note, 15 Dec. 1906, CO 323/516/46090.

January 1907 of Sir Montague Ommanney, who would have argued strongly against an enquiry.[45] The presence as secretary of state of Lord Elgin, who, as a former viceroy of India, had first-hand knowledge of the efficiency of the India Office purchasing department and had 'a Gladstonian belief in the seriousness of public office', similarly no doubt played a part.[46]

The purpose of the enquiry was to give the Agency a clean bill of health, and to 'enable the secretary of state to get the necessary reforms carried out'.[47] To achieve this the Colonial Office first restricted the terms of the enquiry to such an extent that the Agents were bound to 'emerge triumphant'.[48] The committee was required only to discover 'the best method of selecting clerical and technical employees' and to consider the 'conditions of service, the scale of payment of salaries and pensions, and how far arrangements can be brought into harmony with the principles covering the civil service'.[49] The narrowness of the terms, however, led to parliamentary and press criticism and the Colonial Office, wishing to avoid an official extension of the enquiry, allowed the committee itself to determine the scope of its duties, no doubt confident that committee members would be reluctant to increase their workload.[50] In the event, the committee decided to examine the Agents' performance of their various tasks only 'with a view to arriving at the questions laid before them', and to form a subcommittee to investigate the Agency's shipping and packing arrangements.[51]

Secondly, the Colonial Office ensured that only those likely to be sympathetic to the Agency were appointed to the committee or called as witnesses. All committee members were past or present government officials and none, apart from Sir Ralph Moor, had business experience.[52] Because Churchill, who was to have chaired the enquiry, was moved to the Board of Trade in April 1908, the committee chairman was Sir John Seely, the new parliamentary under-secretary of state, who had no knowledge or experience of the Agency. Similarly, of the thirty-six witnesses interviewed by the

---

[45] Searle, *Corruption*, 123–71; CO 323/524/46167. During his trip Churchill met the manager of the Uganda railway, the director of the East African public works department and a number of other engineers: Churchill to Grey, 29 Dec. 1907, FO 881/9125.

[46] R. Hyam, *Elgin and Churchill at the Colonial Office*, London 1968, 349–56, 484.

[47] Antrobus note, 31 Dec. 1908, CO 323/538/45740.

[48] Note, 10 Feb. 1908, CO 323/538/4590.

[49] *Hansard*, 4th ser. 1908, clxxxviii. 46.

[50] Ibid. 418.

[51] PPR, p. iv.

[52] The committee comprised a former governor, the comptroller of the Stationery Office, the second civil service commissioner, the assistant comptroller and auditor-general, the permanent secretary to the Treasury and C. A. Harris, principal clerk at the Colonial Office: *Hansard*, 4th ser. 1908, clxxxviii. 417. A former governor, Sir Ralph Moor, had on retirement become a director of the African Steamship Co.: *Directory of directors*, London 1904. An attempt to recruit a businessman, after press criticism, proved unsuccessful: *British and South African Export Gazette*, June 1908, 518; note, 1 June 1908, CO 323/546/22118; note, n.d., ibid.

committee, five were past or serving governors, two were colonial officials, five were members of the Colonial Office and sixteen were connected with the Crown Agents.[53] Only the representatives of the War Office, Admiralty, India Office, Canadian High Commission, and the Army and Navy Co-operative Society shipping department, the builder, Sir J. D. Rees, and the engineer of the Nyasaland railway, were independent of the Colonial Office.[54] In the case of witnesses from the Agency, the evidence given appears to have been restricted even further by the Agents. Owing to an 'epidemic of illness at the Office', neither the head of the general stores department, his deputy, nor the head of the works department was able to appear before the committee.[55] Likewise, details of the Agency's financial activities were given by the senior partner in Mullens Marshall & Co., who, as he himself acknowledged, did little work for the Agency.[56]

Much of the enquiry was devoted to an examination of staff conditions of employment. Of the small amount of evidence presented on the Agents' commercial activities, most was complimentary and uncritical. Only the ex-governor of the Straits, Sir J. Anderson, and Sir J. D. Rees and Sir B. Leslie of the Shire Highlands Railway Co. criticised the Agency. The evidence of the latter was dismissed on the grounds that they represented interests that would benefit from its closure.[57] The committee concluded that colonial discontent was

> due either to a want of touch between . . . [the Agents] . . . and the Colonial Office, to some want of elasticity on the part of officials, . . . or to personal considerations, but not any failure in the work of the Office, which appears to be on the whole well done and to be clear of all suspicion of corruption.[58]

An earlier conclusion that was 'a complete eulogism' of the Agents was abandoned when 'the oldest and most experienced member of the committee', presumably Sir Ralph Moor, refused to commit himself to it.[59] Despite the lack of any 'proof of misconduct . . . or even of incompetency', however, the committee recommended widescale reorganisation.[60]

Not surprisingly, Blake strongly opposed the committee's conclusions. In a twenty-nine-page letter, which he demanded be published with the report, he rejected the mildly critical evidence presented to the enquiry, and claimed that its support of the Agency was too 'lukewarm', that the phrase 'appears on

53 PPR, pp. iii–iv.
54 Rees, and presumably his consulting engineer, felt 'some delicacy in criticising the Crown Agents . . . as the chairman of a company which has an extremely large contract with those gentlemen': PPE, q. 496.
55 Harding to Blake and Blake to Harding, 28 Oct. 1908, CAOG 17/22.
56 PPE, q. 3705.
57 Harris note, 14 Feb. 1909, CO 323/553/5185.
58 PPR, p. iv.
59 Harris note, 14 Feb. 1909, CO 323/553/5185.
60 Crewe note, 8 Jan. 1909, CO 323/538/45740.

the whole to be well done' suggested 'some reservation or exception' and that the proposed changes were unnecessary.[61] His pleas fell on deaf ears. The Colonial Office, believing the letter to be 'highly irregular and indeed improper' and that the Agents wanted 'a grievance and have made the very uppermost of every statement that can be considered disparaging' in order to oppose changes, published the report as it stood.[62] In response, Blake, angered both by the 'unjust statements and insinuations made by the committee' and by the reorganisation of the Agency 'for some reason which has not been avowed', decided that he 'could no longer with satisfaction continue to occupy . . . [his] . . . present position'.[63] This view was wholly endorsed by the Colonial Office, who felt that, as he had been 'in opposition to many of the views of successive Secretaries of State, . . . it was well that he should retire'.[64]

Blake was replaced by Sir Reginald Antrobus, who proceeded to implement the committee's various recommendations.[65] Staff began to be recruited through the civil service exam and paid according to civil service salary scales, the life insurance scheme became less generous, poundage payments were eliminated and the Agents took over the work of their shipping and packing agents. In addition, Antrobus introduced further reforms. The Agency established a drawing office, introduced greater competition in the purchase of goods, made less use of retailers and set up a marine insurance fund and a colonial information bureau. It also took over from its consulting engineers much of the recruitment, railway construction and open line management, leaving only those services that it would be too expensive to undertake in-house in the private sector.

At first the Colonial Office strongly supported Antrobus' reforms. After a short time, however, they began to suspect that some were designed to avoid the implementation of the committee's recommendation that surplus receipts and income from the reserve fund be redistributed to the colonies in the form of lower charges. The 20 per cent increase in staff from 1908 to 1911 was claimed by Harris to be an attempt to 'use up surplus funds'.[66] The Agents' proposal that the income of the reserve fund be transferred to the insurance fund was dismissed as a way of 'piling up . . . the reserve fund under another name'.[67] The Agents' decision in 1910 to exclude issue income from annual receipts, as the fee partly covered the cost of managing loans over their lifetime, meanwhile, was again believed to be an attempt to 'absorb the surplus'.[68]

61 Blake to CO, 11 Feb. 1909, CO 323/553/5185.
62 Seely note and Crewe note, 17 Feb. 1909, ibid.
63 Blake to CO, 7 Apr. 1909, CO 323/562/12428.
64 Harris note, 13 May 1910, ibid.
65 In the enquiry, Blake had proposed Sir Maurice Cameron as his successor: PPE, q. 1279.
66 Harris note, 12 Oct. 1911, CO 323/577/32800.
67 Harris note, 26 Mar. 1910, CO 323/564/5727.
68 Green note, 4 Feb. 1911, CO 323/577/3364.

In 1912, after much delay, the Agents finally agreed to reduce their loan charges, but at the same time recommended that the reserve fund be allowed to grow through the receipt of the Agency's loan issue and redemption income and fund dividends.[69] It was argued that the fund would be considerably reduced when, owing to compulsory purchase of their existing offices by the Board of Works, they were obliged to relocate. Apparently unable to find suitable Whitehall premises, the Agents had decided to construct a new office at Millbank, which they estimated would cost up to £260,000.[70] Moreover, an actuarial investigation that they had commissioned from the Equitable Life Assurance Co. suggested that, even at its present level, the fund would be unable, ten years hence, to cover staff pension costs in the event of the closure of the Agency.[71] The Colonial Office had little faith in that report's findings, which they believed were based on the fallacy that the Agency would be abolished at 'one fell stroke'.[72] In reality, it was likely to be wound down over a number of years, and many members of staff would be transferred to the regular civil service. In addition, the majority of the Agents' staff served under the 1909 Superannuation Act and would therefore have no claim whatsoever to pensions from the fund. Nevertheless, after much consideration, the secretary of state decided to authorise the lower charges and to allow fund dividends, though not issue and redemption income, to be transferred to the fund.[73]

The reorganisation of the Crown Agents was undertaken with great reluctance. Colonial Office officials were well aware of its possible consequences and after the abandonment of the department system, their seizure of greater control over the issuing procedure and the gradual recovery in the Agency's income, probably believed that the worse was over. Their policy of *laissez-faire*, however, was not to be. Their failure to act began to damage their relationships with governors and local elites and collaboration between elites and governors. At the same time, press and parliamentary criticism threatened their own reputation, and Churchill, unlikely to be affected by the fall-out from reorganisation, began to campaign for an enquiry. In the event, Churchill's victory was short-lived. On his transfer, the Colonial Office wasted little time in ensuring that the enquiry's conclusions would be anodyne. The resultant reform was thus minor and merely involved putting a stop to the Agents' personal moral hazard, which, once exposed to public view, had become an embarrassment to the Office.

69 CAs to CO, 23 Mar. 1912, CO 323/591/9213.
70 Note, 17 Sept. 1912, CO 323/591/25949.
71 Report, May 1911, CAOG 17/26.
72 Just note, 30 Apr. 1912, CO 323/591/9213.
73 CO to CAs, 27 Sept. 1912, CO 323/591/25949.

Conclusion

The Crown Agents acted as actual and trust intermediators, linking the network of principal–agent, trust and family and social relationships that constituted colonial rule to similar financial and manufacturing networks through which the resources and services required for development were obtained. Each member of each network was self-interested, and, as an agent, was prone to personal and/or institutional moral hazard, and, as a principal, would accept a level of benign moral hazard only if, in return for his tolerance, the other party helped to fulfil his primary objectives. The goal of the Colonial Office was to reduce the cost of colonial administration and to limit the benefits of imperial development to the mother country. To achieve this aim it needed to minimise excessive self-interested behaviour on the part of colonies, suppliers and service providers and thus turned to the Crown Agents. The Agency monitored colonial expenditure and borrowing, could be relied upon to source goods, services and capital in the United Kingdom, and possessed the necessary expertise and experience to counter dishonesty on the part of suppliers and service providers. Its use, however, raised the prospect of Crown Agent personal and institutional moral hazard, and, to counter this, the Colonial Office maximised the cost of opportunism and built trust relationships with the Agents through careful recruitment, sureties, high salaries and perks. It also monitored their activities through the colonies and, to discourage major fraud, permitted some minor benign personal moral hazard.

Like the Colonial Office, the Crown Agents and colonial governors also had their own goals, respectively to ensure the survival and growth of the Agency and to serve the best interests of their colonies and local business elites. To meet these aims, the Agents firstly minimised corruption among its staff through monitoring, sureties, the development of trust relationships and the acceptance of benign moral hazard. More importantly, aware of the colonies' monitoring role, they attempted to fulfil those colonial needs that governors regarded as important and could easily monitor and that produced a monetary gain for the Agency. They thus provided colonies with high quality goods and services and fully subscribed loans. The concomitant additional cost was accepted by the colonies and the Colonial Office as it was less than the opportunity cost of the provision of defective articles and the failure of issues. In addition, both had difficulty monitoring costs, and the Agents reciprocally accepted their own moral hazard – the purchase of local goods and favouritism towards Sir Alfred Jones.

To ensure the provision of high quality supplies and services and fully subscribed loans, the Crown Agents sought to minimise self-interest on the

281

part of subagents which might affect quality. They thus sought to increase the cost of dishonesty and to establish trust through the restriction of competition, long relationships, the employment of friends and relatives, the payment of high fees and the tolerance of benign price moral hazard on costing. Subagents, again, were monitored, both formally by themselves and paid inspectors, and informally, through other subagents and trust and social and family networks. Where the possibility of discovery or the utility loss was relatively slight, the Agency was also willing to act duplicitly towards its other principals. Quoted stock prices were rigged, false securities given to banks that provided advances and colonial regulations ignored. In extreme circumstances, help was sought from other organisations with whom it had good relations, such as the Bank of England, which, by assisting the Agency, ensured reciprocity and benefited in other ways.

Inevitably, these strategies occasionally failed and subagents succumbed to self-interested behaviour. Nevertheless, the Agents generally succeeded in providing colonies with both high quality goods and the requisite funds and received little criticism of their services. This situation changed in the 1890s, when their moral hazard became malign. The expansion of empire caused the Colonial Office to change the way in which it achieved its goals. Its policy of colonial development, along with the cut in the Agents' fees, in turn forced the Agency to alter its goal achievement strategy and to seek to maximise its income. The resultant restriction of competition increased the cost of supplies, the adoption of the department system led to the construction of expensive, unprofitable and poor quality railways, and the refusal to accept Treasury finance contributed to the poor subscription of loans and the provision of high yields. No longer trusting the Agents, colonies increasingly began to criticise their performance, prompting the Colonial Office to establish the 1908 enquiry.

The changes introduced by the enquiry, however, were designed to benefit the Colonial Office rather than the colonies. Although they reduced the costs of supplies and the likelihood of future personal moral hazard and political embarrassment, the Agents' incentive to provide expensive quality goods and services remained. Colonial criticism of the Agency's performance therefore continued. In 1934 calls were made for the secretary of state to include the Agency in his enquiry into colonial administration.[1] Five years later the colonial press demanded a parliamentary investigation of the Agency, and the Federation of the Chambers of Commerce of the British empire asked the government to reconsider the Agents' purchase monopoly.[2] After the war, delays in the supply of equipment to the Nigerian railway finally prompted the Select Committee on Estimates to question the Agents and to ask the

---

[1] *Crown Colonist* ci (1934), 511.
[2] *West Africa*, 15, 22, 29 July 1939.

organisation and methods division of the Treasury to investigate the Agency. The resulting report, though, merely recommended routine procedural changes and failed to tackle the root principal–agent dilemma.

Of the possible solutions to the problem, a number were probably unworkable. It seems likely that if colonial governments had themselves provided the services carried out by the Agents there would have been over-expenditure and more corruption. Supplies would have been highly expensive and of poor quality as would have been infrastructure projects. With the Colonial Office unable to monitor their activities, the colonies would have acted in their own interests and purchased/built an excessive amount of goods/works financed by long- and short-term loans that they had little hope of repaying. At a distance from Britain, they would also have been unable to control the dishonesty of their agents, who would have over-charged and supplied substandard materials and services. Fraud, both in the colonies and in the United Kingdom, would have been rife.

Equally, changes in the Agency's form of remuneration, such as the replacement of the fixed commission with a set fee or a flexible commission, would have had little effect on its performance. The major drawback of fixed commissions was that they gave the Agency an incentive to ensure quality through the acquisition of expensive goods and services, which increased its returns, rather than through monitoring, the cost of which (except in the case of the inspection of supplies) came out of its own income and thus reduced its profits. Moreover, such commissions caused the amount of monitoring that occurred to fall over time. Owing to the Agents' reluctance to request rate rises for fear of loosing their reputation for fiscal competence, commissions failed to keep pace with the Agency's workload, which rose as its tasks became more complex and it took on more duties. A progressively smaller proportion of the Agency's income was thus available for supervision, the cost of which again rose as the work of service providers became more complex.

With a set fee, although the Agents' income incentive to purchase expensive goods and services would have disappeared, the quality incentive would have remained, and the cost of monitoring would still have reduced their profits. Furthermore, the failure of the Agency's income to rise with the actual work undertaken would have caused the amount of supervision to fall even more quickly over time and, from the Colonial Office's point of view, reduced the Agents' incentive to ensure that all colonial goods and loans were purchased and issued through them and monitored.

In theory, a better performance could have been obtained with a commission that was adjusted upwards or downwards each year according to whether the Agents failed to reach or exceeded a target rate of return based on a study of their costs. Although the Agency would still have had the quality incentive to purchase expensive goods and services, the fact that higher costs would be recouped through higher rates would have increased monitoring, which would have remained high over time. In reality, such a commission would have had little effect on the service offered and would not have been in the interests of the Colonial Office. Unable to maximise their income through the acquisition of expensive goods and services, the Agents would have increased their costs artificially, which the Colonial Office, unable to discover their level of effort and quality enhancement and exogenous cost parameters, had difficulty monitoring. More easily identified than high service and good prices, the high costs would have resulted in greater Treasury and parliamentary criticism of the Agency and the Colonial Office. In addition, unless a target rate of return had been carefully set, the commission would have reduced the Agents' incentive to ensure that all goods or loans were purchased or issued through them and monitored.

Ultimately, the Agents high costs could only have been reduced through government provision of its services. With their security of employment, civil servants would have had no need to maximise income or service quality. This did not occur because the removal of the Agency's independence, although in the interests of the colonies, was against those of the Colonial Office. The takeover of the Crown Agents would have reduced the autonomy of the Colonial Office, increased its workload, destroyed its good relations with governors and colonial business elites and governor–elite collaboration, and caused it to lose its immunity from commercial scandal.

'Own account' activities after 1960

In the event, the problem was solved by political factors. The dissolution of the empire and the Crown Agents' loss of their monopoly caused many clients to abandon the Agency, although some returned later having experienced supplier duplicity at first hand. It was widely believed that, as they were no longer of use to the government, which had 'washed its hands of them', the Crown Agents would wither away and eventually vanish.[3] That assumption, however, did not take account of the organisation's 'remarkable will to live'.[4] 'Unwilling to face the prospect of redundancy', the Agents began to offer a more diverse, efficient and cost-effective service, and in 1967 moved into private banking. Borrowing from the City and increasingly using their principals' funds, they began to trade in gilts, equities and commodities both at home and abroad, to acquire shares in subsidiary and associated companies, and invest in property and exchange movements. By December 1967 the Agency had borrowed and invested £47m. in these activities and by 1970 their 'own account dealings' were worth more than £180m. Although

---

[3] PP 1977–8, viii. 4. The government denied that it had abandoned the Agency.
[4] Ibid.

initially successful, the Agents' private banking business ran into difficulties in the early 1970s. In 1974, on discovering that a number of the loans made were irrecoverable, the new Senior Agent, John Cuckney, requested financial assistance from the government. The consequent uproar led to the establishment of the Fay Committee to investigate the reasons behind the Agency's financial problems, and, in 1978, to a further tribunal of enquiry.

The collapse of the business again appears to have sprung from principal–agent problems and a breakdown of trust. The Agents, the finance directorate and a number of the Agents' clients were guilty of moral hazard – the Agency through its use of its principal's funds, the finance department through its 'rash lending' and alleged personal corruption, and some of the borrowers through their fraudulent activities.[5] 'Nobody', however, 'took the lead' in 'grappl[ing] with the problem'.[6] Supervision of the Agents by the Ministry of Overseas Development and the Bank of England was minimal. The Bank of England stood to gain from the disappearance of the Crown Agents. The ministry felt 'ill-equipped to assess or control . . . financial activities' and, obtaining no benefit from the Agency, 'kept the Crown Agents at arm's length'.[7] Sir Claude Hayes, the Senior Agent, in turn, 'was secretive toward the Ministry', and, lacking 'the necessary experience' of financial affairs, failed to monitor the finance directorate.[8] Given an 'open invitation to build up his own empire', Mr Challis, the director of finance, 'was secretive towards Hayes' and appears to have inadequately supervised his staff and clients.[9]

As in 1908, there also appears to have been a breakdown in the trust between the Senior Agent and both the Ministry of Overseas Development officials and Crown Agent staff. Like Blake, Hayes came from a more humble background than his government counterparts and his personal morality was suspect.[10] His predecessor, Stephen Luke, had an 'informal working relationship' with the permanent secretary at the Ministry of Overseas Development, seeking 'his formal approval when this seemed necessary' and consulting 'him informally on questions of policy'.[11] Hayes, on the other hand, distrusted the ministry and 'adopted a defensively belligerent attitude that made co-operation difficult'.[12] His behaviour was reciprocated. Officials denied him access to important information and 'wrote rude minutes [about him] in official files'.[13] To his staff, Hayes was 'unapproachable', 'hierarchical and cool'

---

5 PP 1982, 522. An official of the department, a Mr Wheatley, died of a heart attack the day before his trial for fraud was to open.
6 Ibid. 523.
7 Ibid; Hayes to Butler, Aug. 1973, Hayes papers, 5.
8 PP 1982, 522.
9 Ibid. 364, 521, 522.
10 Hayes's father was an estate carpenter: Hayes papers.
11 PP 1982, 364, 522.
12 Ibid.
13 Hayes to Butler, Aug. 1973, Hayes papers, 5.

and 'had no capacity for readily establishing good relations'.[14] Morale was therefore low and those who had doubts about the activities of the finance directorate did not express them.

The nineteenth-century Agents and their present-day counterparts

Concentrating on its core procurement work, the Agency eventually weathered the storms of the 1970s. In 1980 it became a statutory corporation, and in 1977 a private limited company owned by the Crown Agents Foundation and answerable to a board of directors composed of representatives of its major clients. Today it purchases goods worldwide to the value of $400m. and provides a range of other financial and miscellaneous services for a variety of multilateral and bilateral development agencies.[15] Similarities with its nineteenth-century forbear, however, remain, particularly in its work for the Overseas Development Administration. A study of the Agency's procurement business in the United Kingdom in the mid-1980s, for example, found that orders predominantly went to large firms and to a limited number of companies.[16] Seventy-five per cent of indents worth over £5,000 were passed to less than 5 per cent of the firms used by the Agency, and in eleven of the twenty industries from which it purchased materials over 50 per cent of orders went to just two companies.[17] It was also discovered that the Agents favoured certain regions, and that, even when the geographical concentration of industries producing materials for aid countries was taken into account, Yorkshire, Humberside and the East Midlands still received a greater proportion of indents than other parts of the country.[18]

Similarities between Blake's agency and organisations such as the World Bank and the International Monetary Fund are even more pronounced. As in the nineteenth century, the primary goal of western investment in the third world is to develop primary production and foster new markets.[19] Aid organisations ensure that both bilateral and multilateral assistance is spent on

14 Ibid. 8; PP 1982, 364, 522.
15 The Agency provides project management, shipping, training, computer and legal advisory services, debt and investment management and trade finance and advance facilities. Its clients include the Overseas Development Administration, the European Commission, the World Bank, the United Nations and Japan's national aid agency.
16 Almost two-thirds of orders went to companies employing 1,000 workers or more: R. S. May, D. Schumacher and M. H. Malek, *Overseas aid: the impact on Britain and Germany*, London 1989, 225.
17 Ibid. 160, 225.
18 Ibid. 224.
19 It could be argued that the west, lacking the direct control exercised by imperial Britain and faced with more informed populations, also uses aid as a political weapon to force recipients to toe the western line, and to absolve the conscience of its electorate and hence maintain political legitimacy.

purchases from donor countries, and guard against recipient moral hazard through the close supervision of projects and the promotion of western capitalist values.[20] To obfuscate the underlying motives for assistance, agencies remain semi-independent organisations and are therefore subject to weak political control. As a result, like the Crown Agents, they are notoriously arrogant towards the officials of third world governments, excessively secretive and inevitably begin to act in their own interests, though their actions are largely compatible with the interests of their principals, who therefore tolerate them.[21] The higher-grade staff of the World Bank, like their late nineteenth-century counterparts, enjoy lavish lifestyles, partly justified by the need to attract quality employees and to increase the cost of opportunism and hence dismissal.[22] Whereas the Agents maximised quality, the World Bank concentrates on the quantity of loans raised, the only aspect of its service that can be effectively measured, and has been accused of 'pushing money', supporting unsound projects or schemes that could easily obtain funds in the open market.[23] Meanwhile, it has been claimed that the International Monetary Fund actively encourages self-interested behaviour on the part of recipients in order to maximise its lending and increase the spread of conditionality and its own power. Its provision of balance of payments finance at subsidised and concessionary rates supposedly prompts countries seeking such finance to pursue policies that create deficits, and its willingness to reschedule debt and to provide further funds makes indebted countries less willing to fully adopt adjustment programmes.[24]

To conclude, all organisations are subject to principal–agent problems, and adverse selection and moral hazard are ever present threats. The selfish be-

---

[20] More than 75% of UK bilateral aid is spent in the UK: May, Schumacher and Malek, *Overseas aid*, 225. Although the World Bank procures goods through competition, the international bidding process favours large multinationals and the leading industrialised countries: C. Payer, *The World Bank: a critical analysis*, London 1982, 20, 35–8. The bank monitors projects through progress reports and field visits. It also presses borrowers to offer liberal tax allowances in return for foreign investment, insists upon production for export, refuses loans to governments that have previously repudiated international debts or nationalised foreign property and opposes minimum wage laws and trade union activity: ibid. 20.

[21] T. Hayter and C. Watson, *Aid: rhetoric and reality*, London 1985, 74, 75.

[22] World Bank staff earn high salaries, which are exempt from US tax, and receive numerous perks, including free health and life insurance, the payment of school fees, paid home leave, first-class air travel, subsidised restaurants, access to gyms and sporting facilities and well-appointed offices: ibid; P. J. Nelson, *The World Bank and non-governmental organisations: the limits of apolitical development*, London 1995, 161.

[23] Payer, *World Bank*, 27; I. Vasquez and D. Bandow (eds), *Perpetuating poverty: the World Bank, the IMF and the developing world*, Washington 1994, 79–81. The bank helps borrowers to identify and prepare projects, which on completion are evaluated by an 'independent' department within the bank: Payer, *World Bank*, 74.

[24] Roland Vaubel and Thomas Willett, *The political economy of international organisations: a public choice approach*, Oxford 1991.

haviour of the Agents could only be said to have constituted real corruption in the latter part of the period covered by this book and almost pales into insignificance when compared to the activities of their counterparts in the City and modern day organisations, where laxer social and private moral standards are the norm. Moreover, it is quite clear that the benefits of the Agents' self-interested actions far outweighed the costs. Although the colonies paid high prices for public sector goods, they were rarely unsuitable or broke down and colonies were spared the real and opportunity cost of finding replacements. Many of the Agents' loans in the early 1900s were expensive. Yet, without the Agency, far less money would have been raised, broker moral hazard would have increased the cost of issues and poorer colonies would have had no access to overdraft or advance facilities. Similarly, although the actions of the Agents and their consulting engineers increased the capital costs, particularly of West African infrastructure, their promotion of construction ensured that many lines were built that otherwise would never have left the drawing board. The completed lines, of course, made a huge contribution to the economic growth of the colonies. The Crown Agents can therefore be seen as the linch-pin of crown colony development, and had they not existed economic growth in the colonies would almost certainly have been both slower and less significant.

The Crown Agents

Table 1
Personal histories of early Agents, 1798–1833

Colony	Agent	Period of service	Other appointments	Salary (per annum)
Berbice (1831 Agency combined with Demerera's)	George Baillie	1812–31	1810 Colonial Office clerk; 1824 senior clerk (head of the North American department); 1833 Joint Agent for the colonies	£200
Cape	William Huskisson	1798–1806	1794 Colonial Office chief clerk; 1795 under-secretary; 1827 secretary of state; first commissioner of woods, forests and land revenue	–
	Charles Agar	1806–11	not known	£600
	Robert Willimot	1811–12	Private secretary to the colonial secretary of state, 1809–12	£600
	Thomas P. Courtenay	1813–33	War Office clerk; 1800 Treasury clerk; 1802 Stationery Office cashier; 1811–32 MP for Totness; 1812–28 secretary to the Board of Control; 1828–30 vice-president of the Board of Trade; barrister and author	£600 (inclusive of office costs)
Ceylon	William Huskisson	1801–4	1794 Colonial Office chief clerk; 1795 under-secretary; 1827 secretary of state; first commissioner of woods, forests and land revenue	£1,200 (inclusive of office costs)
	Thomas P. Courtenay	1804–6	War Office clerk; 1800 Treasury clerk; 1802 Stationery Office cashier; 1811–32 MP for Totness; 1812–28 secretary to the Board of Control; 1828–30 vice-president of the Board of Trade; barrister and author	–

Colony	Agent	Period of service	Other appointments	Salary (per annum)
	William Huskisson	1806–22	1794 Colonial Office chief clerk; 1795 under-secretary; 1827 secretary of state; first commissioner of woods forests and land revenue	–
	Richard Penn	1824–33	1801 Colonial Office clerk; 1807–14 Colonial Office librarian; 1822 senior clerk; 1824 retired from Colonial Office; writer of humorous books	£800 (including £350 office allowances)
Curacao (1807 returned to Dutch)	Thomas Amyot	1807	1806 Colonial Office clerk; 1807 secretary of Lower Canada; 1819 registrar of colonial slaves (on resignation from Colonial Office); expert on archaeology and historical research	–
Demerera	Adam Gordon	1804–33	1791–5 Home Office clerk; 1794 Colonial Office clerk; 1801 sinecure of Trinidad naval officer; 1822 senior clerk; 1824 chief clerk; retired from the Colonial Office in 1833	£400 (later £0 owing to the 'distresses of the colony')
Gambia	George Baillie	1822–33	1810 Colonial Office clerk; 1824 senior clerk (head of the North American department); 1833 Joint Agent for the Colonies	£500 (for both Sierra Leone and Gambia)
Grenada	Purbec Langham	1764–70	not known	–
Lower Canada	Adam Gordon	1814–28	1791–5 Home Office clerk; 1794 Colonial Office clerk; 1801 sinecure of Trinidad naval officer; 1822 senior clerk; 1824 chief clerk; retired from the Colonial Office in 1833	–
Malta	Major-General Sir Henry Edward Banbury	1813–21	1794 army officer; 1805 quarter-master general for the Mediterranean; under-secretary for war and colonies; 1830–2 MP; author	£600 (inclusive of office expenses)
	Seymour Bathurst	1822–5	Possible relation of Henry Bathurst, colonial secretary of state, 1812–27	–
	Lt Col. William F. R. de Boos	1826–33	Army officer	£500 (inclusive of office expenses)
Mauritius	Richard Penn	1811–24	1801 Colonial Office clerk; 1807–14 Colonial Office librarian; 1822 senior clerk; 1824 retired from Colonial Office; writer of humorous books	£500 (inclusive of office expenses)

Colony	Name	Dates	Career	Salary
	Peter Smith	1824–33	1810 Colonial Office clerk; 1824 senior clerk (head of Mediterranean and eastern department); 1843 chief clerk; retired from the Colonial Office in 1860	£500
New South Wales	Edward Barnard	1822–33	1805 Colonial Office clerk; 1822 second-class clerk; 1822 retired from the Colonial Office; 1833 Joint Agent for the Colonies	£600
Newfoundland (1833 vacant)	not known	not known	not known	£300
Quebec (1828 abolished)	Richard Cumberland	1764–1811	1758 parliamentary grant agent for Nova Scotia	–
	Adam Gordon	1811–28	1791–5 Home Office clerk; 1794 Colonial Office clerk; 1801 sinecure of Trinidad naval officer; 1822 senior clerk; 1824 chief clerk; retired from the Colonial Office in 1833	–
St Lucia	Charles W. H. Bouverie	1826–33	Former army officer	£200
Sierra Leone	George Baillie	1822–33	1810 Colonial Office clerk; 1824 senior clerk (head of the North American department); 1833 Joint Agent for the Colonies	£500 (for both Sierra Leone and Gambia)
Trinidad	William Knox	1801–3	–	£800
	Charles Cameron (Colonial Office Agent)	1803–4	Commissioner to Malta; governor of Bahamas	–
	T. C Marling (Colonial Office Agent)	1804–10	–	£500
	Archibald Gloster (Colony Agent)	1804–6	Attorney-general for Trinidad	–
	Joseph Marryat (Colony Agent, Joint Agent)	1806–16	West Indian and North American merchant; 1789 Lloyds member; banker; MP for Sandwich; author	–

Colony	Agent	Period of service	Other appointments	Salary (per annum)
	Robert Willimot (Colonial Office Agent, Joint Agent)	1810–16	Private secretary to the colonial secretary of state, 1809–12	–
	Henry Cutler	1816–27	1806 Colonial Office clerk; retired from Colonial Office in 1816	–
	Henry Trevor Short	1828–33	1809 Colonial Office clerk; 1824 senior clerk (head of Eastern department); 1836 retired from Colonial Office.	£344
Van Diemens Land (Tasmania)	Edward Barnard	1822–33	1805 Colonial Office clerk; 1822 second-class clerk; 1822 retired from the Colonial Office; 1833 Joint Agent for the Colonies	0

Source: PP 1830–1, iv, 3; CO to Treasury 15 Mar. 1833, CO 324/147/139; G. F. R. Barker and Alan H. Stenning, *The record of old Westminsters*, i, London 1928.

Notes: n.d., CO 323/217/191; Treasury to CO, 7 Oct. 1833, CO 323/217/291; Gordon to Treasury, 24 June 1832, CO 323/217/191; PP 1822, xx; Barnard to CO, 4 Feb. 1851, CO 323/239/1004; Baillie to CO, 19 Mar. 1855, CO 323/245/2837; Treasury to CO, 10 Feb. 1832, CO 323/214/136; CAA, CA (M) 1; J. C. Sainty, *Office holders in modern Britain: colonial officials*, London 1976; *British biographical index*; Young, *The Colonial Office*; Penson, 'Origins of the Crown Agents' office', 197, 201; CO to Huskisson, 20 May 1804, CO 324/115, 64; T 64/86, 22, 35, 54; T 64/52, 4, 357.

Table 2

Personal histories of Crown Agents and other senior staff, 1880–1914

Agents	Period of service	Father's occupation	Education	Career prior to appointment	Sum left on death (£)	Directorships on retirement
George Baillie	1833–55	not known	not known	See appendix 1, table 1	not known	–
Edward Barnard	1833–61	not known	not known	See appendix 1, table 1	6,000	–
Sir Penrose Goodchild Julyan	1858–63	Royal Navy lieutenant	not known	1839 special commissioner of roads and bridges, Lower Canada; 1845 British army commissariat; 1848 assistant financial secretary, Board of Works, Ireland; 1852 director of the Royal Mint, Australia	36,620	
Sir William Charles Sargeaunt	1863–88	rector	Charterhouse	1848 Colonial Office supernumerary clerk; 1849 assistant junior clerk; 1853–8 colonial secretary of Natal; 1858 junior clerk: 1859–60 acting lieutenant-governor of St Vincent; 1860–2 assistant clerk	4,805	–
Sir Montague Frederick Ommanney	1877–1900	banker/ naval agent	Cheltenham College; Royal Military Academy, Woolwich	1864 commission in the Royal Engineers; 1866–70 architect at the War Office and Admiralty; 1871 instructor at the Royal Military Academy, Woolwich; 1874 private secretary to Lord Canarvon, colonial secretary of state	13,329	British N. Borneo Ltd; Kimanis Rubber Ltd; Anglo-African Plantations Ltd (Chair); Union Castle Mail Steamship Co Ltd
Sir Ernest Edward Blake	1881–1909	rector	Norwich Grammar School	1863 upper division exam (2nd in year); 1864 Colonial Office assistant junior clerk; 1869 junior clerk; 1872 second-class clerk and assistant private secretary to the earl of Kimberley, colonial secretary of state; 1874 private secretary to the earl of Kimberley; 1879 first-class clerk and head of general department	23,173	–

Agents	Period of service	Father's occupation	Education	Career prior to appointment	Sum left on death	Directorships on retirement
Sir Maurice Alexander Cameron	1895–1920	army lieutenant	Wellington College; Royal Military Academy, Woolwich	1874 lieutenant in the Royal Engineers; 1883–92 deputy colonial engineer and surveyor general of the Straits Settlements (also a member of the Straits executive and legislative councils); 1894 major in the Royal Engineers	14,969	–
Sir William Hepworth Mercer	1900–21	designer and gentleman	Wadham College, Oxford, BA in classics; bar exams, Inner Temple	1879 upper division exam (4th in year); 1894 secretary to the earl of Jersey in Ottawa and accompanied Sir Stanford Fleming to Hawaii; 1895 assistant private secretary to Lord Ripon and Joseph Chamberlain, colonial secretaries of state; 1896 first-class clerk and secretary to Pacific cable committee; 1898 principal clerk	8,041	British Controlled Oilfields Ltd; Century European Timber Corp. Ltd; Century Trust Ltd; Freeholds Trust Ltd; Trinidad Petroleum Co; Century Russian Syndicate Ltd
Sir Reginald Laurence Antrobus	1909–18	rector	Winchester College; New College, Oxford, BA in classics (second- class)	1877 upper division exam (2nd in year); 1880–2 assistant private secretary to the earl of Kimberley, colonial secretary of state; 1882–6 private secretary to successive secretaries of state; 1889–90 acting governor of St Helena; 1894 senior clerk; 1896 principal clerk; 1898 assistant under-secretary of state	7,266	Trans-Zambesia Railway Co. Ltd (gov. director); Church Schools Co. Ltd

Secretaries

Arthur Berriedale Keith	1903–5	advertising agent	Royal High School, Edinburgh; Edinburgh University, MA in classics (first-class); Balliol College, Oxford BA degree in classics mods. (first-class); bar exams, Inner Temple	1901 upper division exam (first in year); 1901–3 Colonial Office junior clerk	–	–
Sir Percy Herbert Ezechiel	1905–20 (CA 1920–37)	army officer	Bombay University BA; London University BA; Trinity College, Cambridge BA maths (first-class); bar exams, Middle Temple	1898 upper division exam (3rd in year); 1899 Colonial Office junior clerk	–	–

Head of engineering	Period of service	Father's occupation	Education	Career prior to appointment	Sum left on death	Directorships on retirement
Lt Col. Sir James Forrest Halkett Carmichael	1905–21 (CA 1921–32)	Indian civil servant	Clifton College; Royal Military Academy, Woolwich	1887 commission in Royal Engineers; 1889–1900 served in India, Aden, Somaliland and Burma; 1903 employed by the Ordinance Survey	–	–
Chief Clerk and accountant						
Edward Gream Antrobus	1879–20 (1879–93 assistant accountant)	rector	Charterhouse	–	–	–

Source: *British biographical index*; Abbott, *A short history of the Crown Agents*; Sainty, *Office holders*; J. A. Venn, *Alumni cantabrigienses: 1852–1900*, Cambridge 1940; Anon, *The historical register of the university of Oxford*, Oxford 1900; *Colonial Office list*, 1900; *The Times*, 29 Apr. 1907, 6; 8 Dec. 1920, 15; 22 Aug. 1925, 5; *Directory of directors*, 1907–30; PP 1864, xxx (3316); PP 1878, xxvii (177); PP 1879, xix (C 9435); PP 1880, xxi (C 2721); PP 1902, xxii (Cd 1203); SH, probate records; *Who was whom*.

Figure 1. Office organisation, 1902

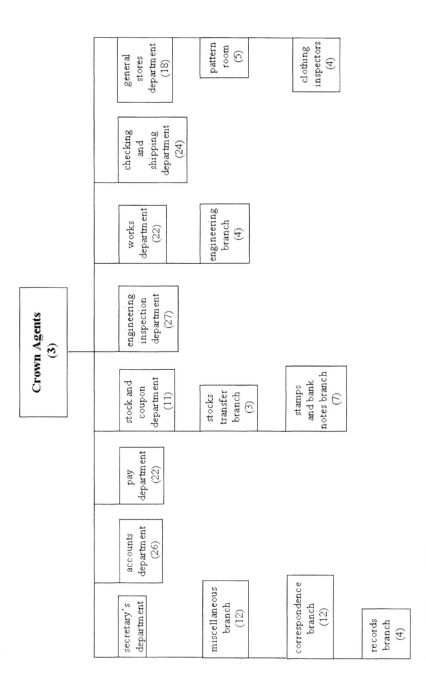

Crown Agents (3)

- secretary's department
  - accounts department (26)
  - pay department (22)
    - miscellaneous branch (12)
    - correspondence branch (12)
    - records branch (4)
- stock and coupon department (11)
  - stocks transfer branch (3)
  - stamps and bank notes branch (7)
- engineering inspection department (27)
- works department (22)
  - engineering branch (4)
- checking and shipping department (24)
- general stores department (18)
  - pattern room (5)
  - clothing inspectors (4)

Source: PPE, appendix 1.

Note: Established staff numbers in parenthesis.

Table 3
The Crown Agents' principals, 1833–1914

Antigua (1866–1914)

Bahamas (1857–1914)

Basutoland (1889–1914)

Bermuda(1848–1914)

British Bechuanaland/Bechuanaland Protectorate (1887–1914)

British Central Africa/Central Africa Protectorate (1896–1914)

British Colombia (1857–80; Loan management, 1880–91)

British East Africa/East Africa Protectorate (1896–1914)

British Guiana (1833–1914)

British Honduras/Honduras (1872–1914)

British Kaffraria (1857–65)

Cape (1833–80; loan management, 1880–91)

Central South African Railway (1903–7)

Ceylon (1833–1914)

Cyprus (1881–1914)

Demerara (1833–?)

Dominica (1872–1914)

Falkland Islands (1843–1914)

Federated Malay States/Malay States (1902–14)

Fiji (1876–1914)

Gambia (1833–1914)

Gibraltar (1833–1914)

Gold Coast (1851–1914)

Grenada (1859–1914)

Griqualand West (1875–81)

Heligoland (1844–90)

Hong Kong (1844–1914)

Jamaica (1857–1914)

Jelebu (1891–7)

Kedah (1913–14)

Newfoundland (1838–1914)

New South Wales (1833–58)

New Zealand (1841–80; loan management, 1880–91)

Niger Coast Protectorate/Southern Nigeria (1896–1914)

Northern Nigeria (1900–14)

Nova Scotia (1860–2)

Nyasaland (1908–14)

Orange River Colony (1901–8)

Pahang (1890–1901 when incorporated into the Federated Malay States)

Perak (1885–1901 when incorporated into the Federated Malay States)

Prince Edward Island (1857–79)

Queensland (1867–79)

St Helena (1836–?)

St Kitts (1859–1914)

St Lucia (1834–1914)

St Vincent (1867–1914)

Selangor (1885–1901 when incorporated into the Federated Malay States)

Seychelles (1878–1914)

Sierra Leone (1833–1914)

Somali Coast Protectorate (1900–14

South African Constabulary (1902–7)

South Australia (1842–58)

Straits Settlements (1867–1914)

Sungei Ujong (1885–97)

Swaziland (1908–14)

Tanjong Pagar Dock Board (1907–14)

Tobago (1872–1914)

Transvaal (1900–7)

Trinidad (1833–1914)

Turks Islands (1854–1914)

Kelantan (1913–14)

King African Rifles (1903–14)

Labuan (1845–90)

Lagos (1857–1914)

Leeward Islands federal government (1873–1914)

Malta (1833–1914)

Mauritius (1833–1914)

Montserrat (1872–1914)

Natal (1857–93)

Negri Sanbilan (1891–1902, when incorporated into the Federated Malay States)

Nevis (1873–1914)

New Brunswick (1834–71)

Uganda Protectorate (1896–1914)

Uganda Railway (1900–14)

Van Diemens land/ Tasmania (1833–80; loan management 1885–86)

Vancouver Island (1857–67)

Victoria (1857–69)

Virgin Islands (1872–1914)

Wei-hai-wei (1902–14)

West African Frontier Force (1900–14)

West Pacific High Commission (1913–14)

Western Australia (1833–80; financial duties 1880–91)

Zanzibar (1907–14)

Zululand (1891–7)

Source: *Colonial Office list*, 1862–1914; CAs to CO, 4 Feb. 1851, CO 323/239/1003; AO to Treasury, 10 June 1859, CO 323/254/7887; CAs to CO, 7 May 1858, CO 323/252/4453M; memo, 31 Oct. 1860, CO 323/256/10513; CAs to CO, 22 Feb. 1834, CO 323/219/246; CAA, CA (M) 4, average disbursements, 1857–62.

Table 4
Crown Agent and other government salaries, 1908

Organisation	Position	Salary (£ *p.a*)	Post-enquiry salary (£ *p.a*)
Crown Agents	senior Crown Agent	2,500	1,800–2,000
	second Crown Agent	1,500–1,800	1,500–1,800
	third Crown Agent	1,300–1,500	1,300–1,500
	class 1 clerk	450–600	550–700
	class 2 clerk	300–450	350–500
	class 3 clerk	90–300	100–350
	class 4 clerk	70–250	70–250
Colonial Office	secretary of state	5,000	
	permanent under-secretary	2,000	
	parliamentary under-secretary	1,500	
	assistant under-secretary	1,200–1,500 (after 5 years)	
	second assistant under-secretary	1,200	
	third assistant under-secretary	1,000–1,200 (after 5 years)	

Organisation	Position	Salary (£ p.a)	Post-enquiry salary (£ p.a)
	upper-division principal clerk	850–1,000	
	upper-division first-class clerk	600–800	
	upper-division second-class clerk	200–500	
	lower-division higher-grade clerk	250–350	
	lower-division lower-grade clerk	70–300	
India Office	director-general of stores	1,200	
	accountant-general	1,200	
	deputy director-general of stores	800–1,000	
	deputy accountant-general	800–1,000	
Board of Trade	president	2,000	
	permanent secretary	1,500–1,800	

Source: PPR, xxii–xxiii; PPE, appendix ii; PP 1909, lv (54), 111.

Table 5
Crown Agent and other links with the City

Crown Agent, employee or other contact	Link
Edward Gream Antrobus, CA accountant	Distantly related to Sir James Antrobus and his descendants, co-partners of Coutts Bank. Cousin to George Antrobus, an official of Cox's Bank.
Sir Reginald Antrobus, CA	Distantly related to Sir James Antrobus and his descendants, co-partners of Coutts Bank. Cousin of George Antrobus, an official of Cox's Bank.
Sir Ernest Blake, CA	Brother-in-law, Charles Cubit Gooch, was a partner of J. S. Morgan & Co., which issued loans for China, Argentina, Spain etc. Son, Edmund Christopher K. S. Blake, from 1906–8 was employed by J. and A. Scrimgeour as a clerk. From 1909 he was a broker in partnership with W. W. Fidgeon, another former J. & A. Scrimgeour clerk. Director of London Assurance and government director of the Pretoria & Pietersberg Railway Co. In 1901 his seven fellow Pretoria & Pietersberg Railway Co. directors held between them 45 directorships, many in the financial sector.

Villiers Blakemore, supplier	Director of the Union Bank of Birmingham
Miss A. E. Boddy, head of correspondence branch	Brother, Walter Randall Boddy, stockbroker.
Miss M. E. Boddy, lady clerk	Brother, Walter Randall Boddy, stockbroker
F. W. Deakin, clerk	Former employee of Messrs. Glynn Mills Currie & Co.
Sir Fortescue Flannery, consulting engineer	Director of the London and SW Bank
Sir Penrose Julyan, CA	Director of the London & Westminster Bank, 1879–90. From 1880 arranged loans for the Cape, Newfoundland and New Zealand. Director of the Bank of New Zealand, 1880–9.
J. Y. Kennedy, a friend of Sir Maurice Cameron, CA	Stockbroker
Sir Alfred Lyttelton, colonial secretary of state	Director of the London & Westminster Bank, 1903–5.
Sir George Murray, a friend of Sir Maurice Cameron, CA	Manager of the Mercantile Bank of India.
Sir Montague Ommanney	Uncle and father-in-law was Octavius Ommanney who was a partner of Ommanney & Son (from 1862 Hallett Ommanney & Co.), private bankers, naval agents, and, from 1866, a subsidiary of the London Joint Stock Bank. Octavius Ommanney was also a director of the National Bank of Ireland and Law Union & Crown Insurance Co. Friend of Harry Blunt, clerk and partner at J. and A. Scrimgeour. Director of London Assurance, many of whose directors had links with the City
Sir Edward Reed, consulting engineer	Director of the Royal Exchange Bank
Sir William Sargeaunt, CA	Son, Edward Woodbine Sargeaunt, from 1880–2 was employed by J. and A. Scrimgeour as a clerk. He then spent the rest of his career as a broker, specialising in the colonial market.
J. H. Thomson, manager of the CA City office 1886–96	Former Stock Exchange employee.

Sources and notes: For Ommanney see Francis G. Belton (ed.), *Ommanney of Sheffield: memoirs of George Campbell Ommanney, vicar of St Matthews Sheffield, 1882–1936*, London 1936, 14; *Banking almanac*, 1856; F. G. Hilton Price, *A handbook of London bankers with some account of their predecessors*, London 1890, 76; *The Times*, 17 May 1866, 6; GL, ms 17957, vol. 136. Octavius Ommanney provided Ommanney's Colonial Office third party security. Harry Blunt attended the weddings of Ommanney's son and daughter:

Barnes & Mortlake Herald, 18 Nov. 1899, in Shelford press cuttings; *Morning Post*, 13 July 1903. Sir George Aylwen, who joined Scrimgeours in 1896, regarded Blunt as 'rather lazy. His business contacts were few, and I would think it would be right to say that he added little to the material side of the firm. When I say that he was a very good chess player with a sardonic strain it will convey what I feel': Aylwen reminiscences, Scrimgeour papers.

For Antrobus see Antrobus, *Antrobus pedigrees*, 60–1, 82–3.

For Sargeaunt see GL, MS 17957, 1883; *Members of the Stock Exchange*, 1909–10.

For Blake see GL, MS 17957, 1906, 1909; Anon, *George Peabody & Co, 1838–1958*, Oxford 1958, for private circulation, 3, 8. Gooch provided Blake's Colonial Office third party security: CO 323/375b/6790, Blake to Meade, 29 Mar. 1889; *Stock Exchange official intelligence*, 1901; *Directory of directors*, 1901.

For Julyan see NWB, 12895/221; 12895/238; 12895/216; 1597, Mills to Julyan, 2 Nov. 1883; N. M. Chappell, *New Zealand bankers' hundred: a history of the Bank of New Zealand, 1861–1961*, Wellington 1961, 397.

For Boddy see SH, probate records; *Members of the Stock Exchange*, 1894.

For Cameron see Cameron memoirs, 11, 86.

For Lyttelton see *Directory of directors*, 1903–5.

For others see *Directory of directors*, 1880, 1889, 1899; CAA, O/SEC 12/3, 19; Deakin to CAs, 4 Sept. 1900, CO 323/797/55272.

Table 6
Links between Scrimgeours and the City

Person	Link
Charles Howard Atkinson, former clerk	Later clerk at Mullens Marshall
Hampton John Aubrey, former clerk	Founded the stockbroking firms Gunn & Aubrey and Aubrey & Russell
William Lavender Farrell, former clerk	Founded the stockbroking firm Farrell & Vaughan
Harry Panmure Gordon, former clerk and partner	Founded the stockbroking firm Panmure Gordon.
Alfred McNish, former partner	Founder of the stockbroking firm Alfred McNish & Co.
Frederick Henry Milbank, former clerk and partner	Founded the stockbroking firm Laurie Milbank.
Matthew Fletcher Oxenford, former clerk	Founder of the stockbroking firm Matthew Oxenford & Co.
Harry Robinson, former clerk and partner	Partner in the stockbroking firm Stewart & Whitmore
David Scrimgeour, nephew of founders	Union Bank of London employee.

R. S and J. S. Scrimgeour	Employees of Barings Bros., serving in Malta and Holland.
	Stockbrokers and shareholders of the Union Bank of London.
	Stockbrokers to Barings Bros.
	Stockbrokers to Credit Foncier of Mauritius.
Walter Wilson Scrimgeour, brother of founder	Deputy principal of the Bank of England discount office, 1808.
	General manager of the Union Bank of London, 1840–64.
	Director (1865–7) and shareholder of the Union Bank of London.
Alexander Boyce Stewart, former clerk	Founder of the stockbroking firm A. B. Stewart
Randolph Wix, former clerk	Became a partner in Panmure Gordon.

Source: NWB 11446/16; 3059, Union Bank of London, special report, 11 July 1860; Union Bank of London, annual reports, 34–8; Union Bank of London, list of proprietors, 1858, 1860; R. W. Munro and Jean Munro, *The Scrimgeours and their chiefs: Scotland's royal banner bearers*, Edinburgh 1980, (privately printed), 123; *Banking almanac and directory*, 1865; Purkis, 'Railway building in the Cape colony', 307; David Jeremy (ed.), *Dictionary of business biography*, London 1984; GL, MS 17957, 1865, 1870, 1875, 1886, 1889, 1891, 1896, 1909; *Members of the Stock Exchange*, 1885; *The United Kingdom stock & stockbrokers directory*, 1898–9, 1917.

APPENDIX 2

Railway construction

Table 1

West African railway construction, 1898–1914

Railway	Length (miles)	Gauge	Gradient/curves/rail weight	Cost per mile (£)	Date completed	Miles constructed per month	Under/overestimate (%)	Method of construction
Southern Nigeria								
Lagos–Ibadan	125	3' 6"	1 in 50; 10 chains; 55 lb per yard	9,967	Mar. 1901	2.049	+ 78	Dept.
Ibadan–Oshogbo	62	3' 6"	1 in 60 in, 1 in 80 out; 8 chains	6,905	Apr. 1907	2.3	+ 9	Dept.
Oshogbo–Illorin	61	3' 6"	1 in 80; 15 chains	7,883	Aug. 1908	3.05	+ 36	Dept.
Illorin–Jebba	60	3' 6"	not known	8,587	1910	3	not known	Dept.
Jebba–Minna	160	3' 6"	1 in 80 in, 1 in 100 out	8,693	1912	6.7	+ 65	Dept.
Average cost per mile £8,407								
Sierra Leone								
Freetown–Songotown	32	2' 6"	1 in 60; 5 chains; 30 lb per yard	6,061	Dec. 1898	0.97	+ 45	Dept.
Songotown–Rotifunk	23	2' 6"	1 in 50; 30 lb per yard	4,224	Mar. 1900	2.55	- 17	Dept.
Rotifunk–Bo	80	2' 6"	1 in 50; 30 lb per yard	3,988	Oct. 1902	3.5	+ 23	Dept.
Bo–Baiima	87	2' 6"	1 in 50	3,604	1905	not known	+ 0.4	Dept.
Mountain Railway	5.75	2' 6"	1 in 22	5,604	1904	0.38	+ 4	Dept.
Average cost per mile £4,696								
Gold Coast								
Sekondi–Tarkwa	40	3' 6"	1 in 40; 5 chains; 50lb per yard	9,162	May 1901	1.2	+ 53	Dept.
Tarkwa–Kumassi	130	3' 6"	as above	10,669	Sept. 1903	4.8	+ 89	Dept.

	Miles	Gauge	Gradient / rail weight		Date	Cost		Constructed by
Tarkwa–Broomassie	26.5	3' 6"	not known	6,101	1910	1.104	+ 20	Dept.
Accra–Akwapim	36	3' 6"	1 in 80; 45 lb per yard	9,856	1912	1.08	+ 47	Contractor
Average cost per mile £8,947								
Northern Nigeria								
Baro–Kano	355	3' 6"	1 in 60	3,915	Mar. 1911	8.07	+ 8	PWD
Bauchi line	90	2' 6" (3' 6" formation)	not known	2,000	Mar. 1912	6.43	0	PWD
Average cost per mile £2,957								
Nyasaland								
Shire River line	113	3' 6"	1 in 44; 5.5 chains; 41 lb per yard	5,854	1908	not known	not known	Private

Source and notes: 1 chain = 66'. The cost per mile figures given in PPP are inaccurate, and, where possible, therefore have not been used.
Lagos–Ibadan: CO 520/51/25175; CO 147/152/4983; CO 766/1; CO520/51/18323; CO 446/47/12976; Shelford, *Features of the West African railways*, 5. Cost includes the Carter/Denton bridges.
Ibadan–Oshogbo: CO 520/109/1087; CO 520/70/41397, Shelford to CO, 26 Nov. 1908.
Oshogbo–Illorin: CO 520/109/1087.
Illorin–Jebba: CO 766/1, CO evidence. Estimate only available.
Jebba–Minna: Hansard, 5th ser., 1923, clxv 1464/5; CO 520/51/25175.
Freetown–Songotown: PPP; CO 267/422/14724; CO 267/420/18005.
Songotown–Rotifunk: PPP; CO 267/434/26730; CO 267/470/13753.
Rotifunk–Bo: PPP; CO 267/464/52678; CO 267/470/13753.
Mountain railway: CO 267/474/23391; Shelford, *Features of the West African railways*, 3.
Sekondi–Tarkwa: CO 96/434/17000; PPP.
Tarkwa–Kumassi: CO 96/412/39660; PPP.
Tarkwa–Broomassie: CO 96/512/18603.
Accra–Akwapim: CO 96/524/14210; CO 96/461/31830.
Baro–Kano: CO 446/107/10210.
Bauchi line: Hansard, 5th ser. 1912, xliv. .2276; CO 766/1, CO evidence.
Shire River: FO 2/693, Schneider to Henderson, 8 Aug. 1902; CO 766/1, CO evidence. The company claimed that the line cost £7,500: ibid.

Table 2
French and German West African lines

Railway	Mileage (miles)	Gauge	Cost per mile (£)
French West Africa			
Ivory Coast	281	1 metre	6,417
Lome–Palime	63	1 metre	6,190
Cotonou–Save	162	1 metre	5,185
Konakry–Niger	93	1 metre	5,120–5,696
St Louis–Dakar	164	1 metre	5,120
Thies–Kayes	423	1 metre	4,624
Kayes–Niger	350	1 metre	4,224–4,800
Central Dahomey	204	1 metre	4,117
Lome–Atakpame	104	1 metre	3,456–5,309
Porto Novo–Pobe	47	1 metre	3,357
Lome–Anecho	27	0.75 metre	2,015

Average cost per mile £4,529–4,803

Railway	Mileage (miles)	Gauge	Cost per mile (£)
German West Africa			
Swakopmund–Windhoek	not known	1' 10.5"	3,114
Otavi RR	not known	1' 10.5"	2,010

Average cost per mile £2,562

Sources: Ivory Coast line: L. Wiener, *Chemins de fer de l'Afrique*, Paris 1930, 94.
Lome–Palime: Newbury, *The western slave coast*, 144.
Cotonou–Save: ibid. 144.
Konakry–Niger: CO 879/86/7650, no. 3. Wiener gives a 'pre-war' figure of £6,523 per mile: *Chemins de fer*, 83.
St Louis–Dakar: CO 879/86/7650, no. 3.
Thies–Kayes: Wiener, *Chemins de fer*, 85.
Kayes–Niger: CO 879/86/7650, no. 3. Wiener gives a 1913 figure of £6,232 per mile: *Chemins de fer*, 92.
Central Dahomey line: ibid. 101.
Lome–Atakpame: Newbury, quoting a 1921 French bulletin, gives a figure of £3,456 per mile: *The western slave coast*, 144. Wiener quotes a figure of £5,309 per mile: *Chemins de fer*, 98.
Porto Novo–Pobe: Wiener, *Chemins de fer*, 103–4.
Lome–Anecho: Ibid. 97.
Swakopmund–Windhoeck: *Railway Gazette*, 29 Nov. 1907, 649.
Otavi RR: ibid..

Table 3
Cost of other colonial lines, 1912–15

Colony	Mileage	Cost per mile (£)	Gauge	Method of Construction
Crown colony lines				
Cyprus	61	2,023	2' 6"	Dept.
British Honduras	25	5,291	not known	Dept.
Barbados	28	6,968	2' 6"	Private
British Guiana	98	7,023	2' 6"	Private
Natal	399	8,916	3' 6"	Contractor
Ceylon	577.75	11,038	83% 5' 6", 17% 2' 6"	33% contractor, 67% dept.
Straits/FMS	359	11,325	1 metre	Local
Trinidad	81.5	11,436	4' 8.5"	56% contractor, 44% dept.
Jamaica	184	13,804	4' 8.5"	79% private, 21% contractor
Mauritius	120	15,650	4' 8.5"	Dept.
Hong Kong	21.5	25,581 (includes tunnelling costs)	4' 8.5	Dept.
Non-crown colony lines				
Victoria (18 lines)	610	1,290–2,400	2' 6", 5' 3"	not known
Queensland (5 lines)	227	1,327–2,495	3' 6"	not known
South Australia (7 lines)	238	1,544–2,590	3' 6", 5' 6"	not known
Egyptian Delta line	303	1,708	2' 6"	not known
Rhodesia	1,937	5,008	3' 6"	Private
India	34,656	9,524	51% 5' 6", 42% 1 metre, 7% 2'/2' 6"	not known

Source: PP 1913, lviii (287); PP 1916, xxxii (Cd 8329); *Trinidad and Tobago blue book 1914/5*; *Mauritius annual report*, 1914, (Cd 8172); PP 1907, lvi (103); report, 15 July 1903, CO 67/136/28061; *Report of the general manager of railways and harbours for the year ending 31 December 1913*, Cape Town, South Africa, 10–11.

Notes: Natal's mileage figure only includes track constructed from 1894, when the colony became self-governing. The colony's cost per mile figure is for track built to 1907. In 1869 the average cost of Indian railways was £18,000 per mile largely because the 5 per cent government guaranteed return given to the private sector companies that built the lines encouraged extravagance: Kerr, *Railways of the raj*, 54; A. K. Banerji, *Finance in the early raj: investments and the external sector*, London 1995, 199.

APPENDIX 3

Finance

Table 1
Crown colony loans publicly-issued in London, 1860–82

Year	Colony	Amount (£)	Interest rate (%)	Price (£)	Average price (£)	Sinking fund rate (%)	Redem. date	Amount subscribed (£)	No. of applications	Purpose
1860	Cape	300,000	6	—	106.43	—	—	1,800,000	—	—
	Cape	200,000	6	—	103.525	—	1880 & 1883	1,000,000	—	H
1861	Natal	50,000	6	MP 102	102.45	3	1883	U	—	H
	Cape	150,000	6	CMP	105.95	N	1891	O	—	P
	Cape	25,000	6	—	103.925	—	1881	O	—	I
	Cape	200,000	6	—	—	—	1873	—	—	F
	Ceylon	100,000	6	—	104.63	—	1868	700,000	21	R
1862	Cape	29,500	6	—	—	—	1892	—	—	H
	Mauritius	200,000	6	CMP	107.72	—	1882	1,118,000	159	R
	Natal	50,000	6	MP 105	105.61	3	1885	161,500	39	H
1863	Brit. Colombia	50,000	6	MP 104	104.81	4	1883	41,200	—	P
	Cape	150,000	6	—	108.13	1	1891	O	—	P
	Cape	24,000	5.5	—	108	—	1884	O	—	H
	Ceylon	250,000	6	CMP (111)	112.05	—	1878	372,800 (at above CMP)	173	R
	Mauritius	200,000	6	MP 105	105.39	—	1873	111,600	—	R
	Mauritius	200,000	6	MP 106.5	107.47	—	1878	—	—	R

Year	Place									
1864	Vancouver	40,000	6	CMP (105)	105.4	4	1883	—	—	P
	Cape	20,000	6	—	100.17	—	1900	—	—	H
	New Zealand	1,000,000	5	MP 90	81.8	1	1914	40,000	—	M, I
1865	Antigua	3,000	6	MP 100	100.3	£1,000 pa	1885	U	8	P
	Brit. Colombia	100,000	6	MP 100	95.8	2.25	1894	11,000	—	P
	Cape	29,000	6	CMP	101.05	N	1894	—	—	H
	Cape	20,000	6	—		—	1900	—	—	H
	Cape	234,000	5	CMP (90)	91.62	1	1900	295,000 (at above CMP)	—	R/C
	Ceylon	100,000	6	CMP (104)	104.05	—	1872	10,300	67	R
	Mauritius	300,000		CMP (103)	103.8	—	1895	154,900 (at above CMP)	47	R
	Mauritius	100,000	6	CMP (100)	100.9	—	1896	177,400	39	R
	Natal	50,000	6	CMP (97)	98.74	2	1896	24,050	—	I
	Natal	10,000	6	—	—	—	1887	—	—	H
1866	Cape	20,000	6	—	—	—	1900	—	—	H
	New Zealand	500,000	6	FP 90	90.6	2	1891	281,700	—	M
	New Zealand	250,000	6	CMP (95)	95	2	1896	67,100	—	R/C
	New Zealand	100,000	6	—	92.25	—	1896	1,054,600	—	—
1867	Cape	200,000	6	MP 102.75	104.64	—	1900	474,400	58	P, F
	Ceylon	250,000	6	FP 108	107.49	—	1882	82,300	—	R
	Ceylon	100,000	6	CMP (108)	108.78	—	1883	572,200	97	R
	Natal	65,500	6	MP 100	103.86	3	1887	129,200	—	H
	Natal	50,000	6	CMP (100)	100.66	2	1896	—	—	I
1868	New Zealand	468,000	6	CMP	104.25	2	1891	2,648,000	—	R/C
	New Zealand	1,114,000	5	MP 97	97	1	1904	2,660,700	—	P, M, F
1869	Gibraltar	24,000	6	MP 100	100	30 9 (ann. installs)	1899	—	—	P

Year	Colony	Amount (£)	Interest rate (%)	Price (£)	Average price (£)	Sinking fund rate (%)	Redem. date	Amount subscribed (£)	No. of applications	Purpose
1870	Mauritius	100,000	6	MP 103	103.37	1	1878	53,700	43	P
	Jamaica	367,600	4	CMP (104)	104.25	2	1897 & 1922	300,000 (at above CMP)	34	–
1871	Antigua	2,500	6	–	–	£1,000 pa	1891	–	–	–
	New Zealand	1,200,000	5	CMP (95.5)	95.84	1	–	1,829,000	–	–
	Sierra Leone	25,000	6	MP 100	100	2	1896	96,450	37	P
1872	Cape	40,000	4.5	MP 97	97	1	1911	84,500	34	R
	Natal	55,000	5	CMP (100)	100	1	1909	97,600	18	–
1873	New Zealand	1,000,000	5	MP 100	100.52	1	–	1,353,500	–	–
	New Zealand	500,000	5	FP 102.5	102.5	1	–	1,447,800	–	–
	New Zealand	200,000	4	CMP (105)	103.5	N	1907	0 (at above CMP)	–	–
1874	Sierra Leone	25,000	6	MP 100	100	2	1898	25,000	44	P
	New Zealand	500,000	4.5	FP 98	97.36	N	5/30 yrs	369,500	–	P, I
	New Zealand	1,500,000	4.5	FP 98	98	N	5/30 yrs	673,400	–	P, I
	New Zealand	200,000	4	–	–	2	1907	–	–	P, I
1875	Trinidad	100,000	5	MP 100	103.4	1	1910	26,400	59	R
	Cape	109,000	4.5	CMP (100)	101.43	1	–	422,200	50	R
	Cape	1,000,000	4.5	CMP (98.5)	98.75	1	–	540,200	128	R
1876	Cape	300,000	4.5	MP 98	98.38	1	–	257,800	52	R
	Cape	650,000	4.5	MP 99	99.21	1	–	796,300	102	H, P
	Ceylon	100,000	4.5	MP 102	104.425	1	1920	503,700	54	H
	Mauritius	100,000	4.5	MP 99	100.39	1	1920	475,500	44	R
	Natal	350,000	4.5	MP 95.25	95.75	1	1919	100,000	75	R, I
	New Zealand	1,250,000	5	MP 100	100.04	N	5/30 yrs	200,000	–	P, I

1877	Cape	1,000,000	4.5	MP 100.5	101.88	1	–	3,432,300	223	R
	Natal	550,000	4.5	MP 96	96.26	1	1919	183,333	82	R,I
	Straits	100,000	4.5	MP 98	99.31	5.5	1891	291,600	37	P,M,F
1878	Cape	1,000,000	4.5	MP 98	99.54	1	–	2,975,900	356	R
	Cape	1,000,000	4.5	MP 96.5	97.57	1	–	2,266,000	370	R
	Cape	300,000	4.5	–	98.48	–	–	–	–	H,P
	Ceylon	100,000	4.5	FP 105	105	1	1920	100,000	16	H
	Natal	400,000	4.5	MP 92.5	93.35	1	1919	1,412,000	168	R,I
	Trinidad	100,000	5	MP 100	101.26	1	–	101,260	51	R
1879	Cape	2,615,600	4.5	MP 96.5	98.29	1	–	5,050,000	400	R,M
	Jamaica	100,000	4.5	MP 96	99.525	1	1922	302,200	–	R
	W. Australia	100,000	4.5	MP 96	98.8	1	1922	166,700	84	–
	W. Australia	100,000	4.5	MP 96	97.75	1	1922	149,100	72	–
1880	Cape	1,006,500	4.5	97.5	98.34	–	–	3,700,900	400	P,I
	Cape	535,400	4.5	101.5	103.054	–	–	1,890,100	142	P
	Ceylon	700,000	4	FP 98	98	–	–	4,718,100	73	R
	Trinidad	150,000	4	FP 96	96	–	–	6,320,400	122	R,H
1881	Cape	2,000,000	4	95.5	98.24	–	–	5,460,400	287	M
	Ceylon	575,000	4	102	103.68	–	–	2,641,000	50	R
	Fiji	150,000	4.5	98	99.98	–	–	654,200	62	P,I,F
	Jamaica	200,000	4	98	98.76	–	–	285,600	28	R
	Trinidad	100,000	4	100	101.75	–	–	316,400	17	R
	W. Australia	150,000	4	95/10	97.046	–	–	475,300	46	P,R,F
1882	Jamaica	509,000	4	98	99.042	–	–	327,800	33	R,R/C
	Natal	700,000	4	94	94.2	–	1926	258,600	84	R,P
	Trinidad	100,000	4	98	101.05	–	–	376,500	23	R

Source: CAA, M 60A; CA M 5; Loan memorandum book; Stock Exchange Official Intelligence, 1883, Stock Exchange year book, 1889, 31–3; GL, prospectuses; Fenn's Compendium of English and Foreign Funds, 1867, 1876; CAs to CO, 30 Sept. 1865, CO 54/408/9548; CAs to CO, 7 Sept. 1863, CO 167/455/6632; CAs to CO, 9 May 1863, CO 54/382/4605; CAs to CO, 15 Dec. 1865, CO 179/78/12293; CAs to CO, 26 Jan. 1860, CO 48/405/834;

schedule, 28 Nov. 1961, CO 54/364/10229; CAs to CO, 16 Sept. 1863, CO 60/17/9051; CAs to Antigua, 16 May 1865, CO 7/126/5158; schedule, 21 Nov. 1877, CO 273/92/14043; schedule, 26 July 1867, CO 48/439/7227; schedule, 1 Nov. 1862, CO 179/66/10879; schedule, 27 June 1869, CO 167/521/7340; schedule, 10 Jan. 1866, CO 167/494/346; schedule, 17 Nov. 1862, CO 167/444/11250; CAs to Ceylon, 26 Mar. 1867, CO 54/429/4764.

Notes: Price: MP = minimum price; CMP = concealed minimum price; FP = fixed price.
Sinking fund rate: N = none.
Amount subscribed: U = undersubscribed; O = obtained.
Purpose: P = public works; R = railways; H = harbour; I = immigration; M = military operations; F = internal finance; R/C = redemption/conversion.

Table 2

Crown colony loans publicly-issued in London, 1883–1914

Yr	Colony	Form	Issue type	Amount (£)	Discount (%)	Inter. rate (%)	Min. price (£)	Av. price (£)	Redem. date	Amount subscribed (£)	No. of applications	Purpose
1883	Ceylon	D	T	491,000	3	4	98.5	99.77	D/P	1,260,600	152	H,P
	W. Australia	D	T	254,000	3	4	96.5	96.79	D/P	100,000	28	P,H,R
1884	Natal	D	T	1,132,000 (230,200 re-issue)	4	5	98	100.97	10/40 yrs	6,059,900	1,381	R,P
	W. Australia	D	T	154,000 (re-issue)	3	4	96.5	97.25	D/P	257,500	–	P
1885	Bahamas	D	T	35,000	4	4.5	98	99.53	D/P	74,100	–	–
	Ceylon	D/S	T	100,000	3	4	99	100.55	D/P	392,800	–	H,P
	Jamaica	D	T	150,000	4	4	97.5	97.56	D/P	11,500	–	R
	Natal	D	T	536,500	3	5	100	101.83	D	1,148,300	173	R,P
	W. Australia	D/S	T	525,000	3	4	97.5	98.12	D/P	457,400	119	P
1886	Brit. Guiana	D	T	250,000	2.5	4	97	98.13	D/P	248,500	–	P
1887	Hong Kong	D	T	200,000	3	4	98	100.74	1892/1907	737,400	–	P
	Mauritius	D/S	T	102,900	3	4	100	100.46	D/P	–	–	R
	St Lucia	D	T	79,700	2	4.5	99	105.05	D/P	324,000	63	H,F

Year	Place												
1888	Natal	S	T	500,000	3.5	4	101	103.28	D/P	1,520,200	93	H,R,P
	Mauritius	S	T	209,800	3	4	101	107.76	D/P	1,285,500	100	P,R/C
1889	Natal	S	T	500,000	2.5	3.5	99	100.6	1914/39	1,048,500	111	R,P
	W. Australia	S	T	100,000	2.5	4	107.5	108.76	1934	136,900	21	P
1890	Ceylon	S	T	450,000	3	3	93	93.14	1940	300,500	–	R
1891	Natal	S	T	2,110,000	3	3.5	95.5	95.78	1914/39	2,466,800	376	R,P
1892	Grenada	S	T	64,500	2	4	100	101.41	1917/42	79,200	–	P,R/C
	Jamaica	S	T	180,000	2	4	103	103.54	1934	375,700	93	P
	Trinidad	S	T	100,000	3	4	101	102.19	1917/42	193,500	64	P
1893	Hong Kong	S	T	200,000	2	3.5	98	100.63	1918/43	625,500	–	P
	Mauritius	S (G)	T	600,000	2	3	101	105.39	1948	5,197,400	138	–
	Natal	S	T	890,000	3	3.5	94	95.27	1914/39	1,963,400	336	R,P
1894	Antigua	S	T	100,000	2	4	102	103.74	1919/44	279,700	–	H,P
	Ceylon	S	T	500,000	2	3	94.5	96.28	1940	1,472,300	133	H,R,P
	Ceylon	S	T	500,000	1	3	98.5	100.96	1940	3,739,000	180	H,R,P
	St Lucia	S	T	48,600	2	4	100	102.69	1919/44	79,500	43	P,I
1895	Barbados	S	T	375,000	1	3.5	99	102.35	1925/42	1,565,300	193	H,R,P
1896	Brit. Guiana	S	T	150,000	1	3	97	101.27	1906	1,117,400	–	I
1897	Jamaica	D	T	200,000	1	3	97.5	100.07	1922/44	607,900	73	–
	Trinidad	S	T	400,000	1	3	97.5	98.02	1922/44	562,900	34	R, P
1898	Brit. Guiana	S	T	150,000	1	3	96.5	96.82	1923/45	145,230	25	P
1901	Brit. Guiana	S	T	100,000	2	3	93	93	1923/45	26,700	18	P
	Zanzibar	D (G)	T	100,000	0	3	100	100	1916/31	107,300	–	–
1902	Ceylon	S	S	1,400,000	2.5	3	n/a	94.5	1940	–	–	R, P
	Gold Coast	S	S	1,035,000	3	3	n/a	91	1927/52	38,300	31	R
	Trinidad	S	T	200,000	2	3	93.5	93.54	1922/44	404,600	57	R, P
1904	Sierra Leone	10 yr cd	S	1,250,000	3	4	n/a	98	1929/54 (3.5% s.)	2,611,000	–	R

Yr	Colony	Form	Issue type	Amount (£)	Discount (%)	Inter. rate (%)	Min. price (£)	Av. price (£)	Redem. date	Amount subscribed (£)	No. of applications	Purpose
1905	Lagos	S	S	2,000,000	3	3.5	n/a	97	1930/55	708,000	–	R,P,F
	Mauritius	S	T	150,000	3	3.5	97	97.01	1930/55	57,000	29	R,P
1906	Brit. Guiana	D	T	70,000	3	4	100	100.85	1916	297,100	–	I
	Hong Kong	S	T	1,000,000	3	3.5	99	99.05	1918/43	353,100	–	F
1907	Straits	5 yr cd	S	5,000,000	3.5	4	n/a	99	1937/67 (3.5 % s.)	753,600	673	P,R/C
1908	S. Nigeria	4 yr cd	T	3,000,000	2	3.5	99	99	1930/55 (3.5 % s.)	385,600	–	H,R
1909	Ceylon	S	S	1,500,000	3	3.5	n/a	98.5	1934/59	150,000	–	R,H,P
	Gold Coast	4 yr cd	S	1,000,000	1	3.5	n/a	99	1934/59 (3.5 % s.)	4,330,000	–	H,R
1910	Straits	S	S	2,750,000	3.5	3.5	n/a	95.5	1937/67	175,500	–	H,R,PR/C
1911	S. Nigeria	5 yr cd	S	5,000,000	3.5	4	n/a	99.5	1930/55 (3.5 % s.)	2,528,100	–	H,P
1913	Sierra Leone	S	S	1,000,000	4	4	n/a	97	1938/63	31,000	–	H,R,R/C
1914	Ceylon	S	S	1,000,000	2.5	4	n/a	99	1939/59	8,693,500	–	H,R,P
	Gold Coast	S	S	1,035,000	2.5	4	n/a	98.5	1939/59	152,400	–	H,R,P
	Trinidad	S	S	550,000	2.5	4	n/a	99	1917/42	–	–	H,P

Source: CAA, M 60; Press advertisement book; GL, prospectuses; *Stock Exchange official intelligence*, 1880–1914; CAOG 9/2; 9/4; 9/7; 9/8; 9/10; 9/14; 9/17; 9/21; 9/29; 9/36; 9/65; 9/66; 9/71; 9/76; 9/94; CO 129/235/7249; CO 129/261/6994; CO 179/186/20549; CO 147/177/6936; CO 111/553/31194; CO 167/677/1700; CO 520/69/16505; CO 83/28/7032; CO 23/227/17817; CO 137/585/15238; CO 147/177/6936.

Notes: Form: D = debenture; S = stock; G = guaranteed; cd = debentures convertible to 3.5 % stock.
Issue type: T = tender; S = subscription.
Redemption date: D = drawing SF; D/P = drawing/purchase SF.
Purpose: P = public works; R = railway; H = harbour; R/C = redemption/conversion; M = military operations; F = internal finance.

Table 3
Purchasers of those loans with surviving allotment schedules, 1861–1906

Yr	Colony	Loan (£)	Lowest accepted price	Largest purchase/ purchaser	Price paid	Second largest purchase/purchaser	Price paid	Third largest purchase/ purchaser	Price paid
1861	Ceylon	100,000	104.117	35,000 (35%) (Revd. D. Blackwood)	104.875	19,100 (19.1%) (Oriental Bank Corp.)	104.117	15,000 (15%) (S. B. Worms)	75% 104.5, rest at 105
1862	Mauritius	200,000	107.65	101,500 (51%) (Scrimgeours)	107.65	50,000 (25%) (Linton & Clarke)	107.675	20,000 (10%) (Bragg & Stockdale)	107.7
	Natal	50,000	105.6	49,700 (99.4%) (A. A. Lightfoot)	105.6	300 (0.6%) (Henry P. Smith)	107	–	–
1863	Ceylon	250,000	112.05	246,700 (99%) (Scrimgeours)	112.05	2,000 (0.8%) (John Rankny)	112.275	1,300 (0.52%) (George Robinson)	112.05
	Mauritius	200,000	not known	107,100 (54%) (Scrimgeours)	not known	45,800 (23%) (Linton Clarke)	not known	10,000 (5%) (Sebag)	not known
	Mauritius	200,000	not known	145,300 (73%) (Scrimgeours)	not known	20,000 (10%) (Capt. W. Hopwood)	not known	10,000 (5%) (S. W. Waley)	not known
1865	Ceylon	100,000	104	25,000 (25%) (Samual Harris)	104	19,100 (19.1%) (CAs)	104	8,000 (8%) (S. M. Waley)	104
	Mauritius	100,000	100.25	75,000 (75%) (Sheppards Pelly)	101	10,800 (11%) (Mauritius Svngs Bank)	not known	3,000 (3%) (J. Briggs)	101
	Mauritius	300,000	103	112,000 (37.3%) (CAs)	104–104.75	34,900 (11.6%) (Sheppards Pelly)	103.05	26,500 (8.8%) (Scrimgeours)	62% 103.25, rest at 103
1867	Cape	200,000	103.9	80,000 (40%) (Sheppards Pelly)	105	60,500 (30%) (Hitchens Harrison)	99% 106	37,000 (18%) (Linton Clarke)	103.9

Yr	Colony	Loan (£)	Lowest accepted price	Largest purchase/ purchaser	Price paid	Second largest purchase/purchaser	Price paid	Third largest purchase/ purchaser	Price paid
1869	Mauritius	100,000	102	66,300 (66.3%) (Scrimgeours)	42% 103, rest at 103.25	13,700 (14%) (Mullens Marshall)	103	10,000 (10%) (James Duncan)	50% 106, rest at 103
1876	Mauritius	100,000	100.35	99,800 (99.8%) (Mullens Marshall)	100.35–100.425	200 (0.2%) (James Capel)	100.525	–	–
1877	Straits	150,000	99.025	45,400 (30%) (Scrimgeours)	74% 99.025	40,100 (27%) (Westgarths)	75% 99.025	10,000 (7%) (G. S. Brodie)	100.2
1879	W. Australia	100,000	96.575	51,000 (51%) (Westgarths)	98% 97	15,000 (15%) (Sheppards Pelly)	96.625	10,000 (10%) (J. Maynard)	98
1881	Fiji	15,000	99.525	60,600 (40%) (Sheppards Pelly)	34% 99.525	50,000 (33%) (L. Pounder)	99.875–100.125	25,000 (17%) (Linton Clarke)	99.775
	W. Australia	150,000	96.875	67,400 (45%) (Sheppards Pelly)	88% 96.875	50,000 (33%) (Kerr & Homan)	97.05	26,000 (17%) (Scrimgeours)	96% 97, 4% 97.05
1882	Natal	469,800	94	60,000 (13%) (Sheppards Pelly)	94.15	50,000 (11%) (Bnk of Brit. S. Africa)	94–94.25	50,000 (11%) (Westgarths)	94
1883	Ceylon	491,000	99.65	180,000 (37%) (Scrimgeours)	99.65	139,700 (28%) (Westgarths)	99.65	40,000 (8%) (Clayton & Ashton)	100.025–100.775
1884	Natal	1,132,000	100.8	159,900 (14%) (Brunton Bourke)	94% 100.8	131,000 (12%) (Scrimgeours)	100.8	80,000 (7%) (Sutton Millar)	various
1885	Jamaica	150,000	97.5	62,700 (48%) (Scrimgeours)	97.5	58,500 (45%) (Westgarths)	97.05	1,200 (1%) (James Ross)	98.1625–99.075
	Natal	536,500	101	81,000 (15%) (Neville)	101.775–102.625	60,000 (11%) (Cazenove & Akroyd)	92% 101.875	55,000 (10%) (Sheppards & Pelly)	101.675–102.175
	W. Australia	525,000	97.5	250,500 (48%) (Scrimgeours)	23% 97.5	80,000 (15%) (Sheppards Pelly)	12% 97.05	49,000 (9%) (Mullens Marshall)	various

Year	Colony	Amount	Price	Allotment 1	Price	Allotment 2	Price	Allotment 3	Price
1887	St Lucia	79,700	104.975	40,000 (50%) (Brunton Bourke)	105.075 & 105.125	20,000 (25%) (Blockey Bright)	105.075	19,700 (25%) (W. H. Gramshaw)	104.975
1888	Mauritius	209,800	100.375	136,600 (65%) (Brunton Bourke)	107.375	42,000 (20%) (CAs)	109.125	30,000 (14%) (Ellis & Co.)	107.625
1889	Natal	500,000	103.275	246,600 (49%) (Scrimgeours)	103.275	246,600 (49%) (Westgarths)	103.275	4,900 (1%) (Hecht & Behrins)	103.275
	Natal	500,000	100.45	229,400 (46%) (Scrimgeours)	100.45	160,000 (32%) (Ellis & Co.)	62% 100.625, 48% 100.65	50,000 (10%) (Charles Raphael & Kahn)	101.054–100.5
	W. Australia	100,000	108.575	83,000 (83%) (Scrimgeours)	108.575	5,000 (5%) (E. A. Maynard)	110	5,000 (5%) (L. C. Maynard)	110
1891	Natal	2,110,000	95.55	368,600 (17%) (Ellis & Co.)	95.65–96.5	202,600 (10%) (Neville)	95.575–95.95	189,600 (9%) (Sandeman Clark)	95.55–95.775
1892	Jamaica	180,000	103.3	97,300 (54%) (Scrimgeours)	103.3	18,600 (10%) (Ellis & Co.)	103.3	17,700 (10%) (Aubrey Brown & Hopkinson)	103.575–108
	Trinidad	100,000	102.175	97,900 (98%) (Scrimgeours)	102.175	1,000 (1%) (L. Smith)	103	600 (0.5%) (S. Bonus)	103
1893	Natal	890,000	95.1	163,000 (18%) (Ellis & Co.)	95.375	100,000 (11%) (Brunton Bourke)	95.125	80,600 (9%) (Scrimgeours)	63% at 95.1
1894	Antigua	100,000	103.5	68,900 (69%) (Steer Lawford)	60% 103.5	14,000 (14%) (Aubrey Brown & Hopkinson)	103.6–105.5	10,000 (10%) (H. Vigne & Sons)	104.525 & 104.275
	Ceylon	500,000	96.275	172,200 (34%) (Scrimgeours)	96% 96.275	120,000 (24%) (Pember Boyle)	96.275	96,700 (19%) (Linton Clarke)	96.275
	Ceylon	500,000	100.8	125,000 (25%) (Mullens Marshall)	100.875	109,800 (22%) (Brunton Bourke)	54% 100.8	44,900 (9%) (Scrimgeours)	100.8
	St Lucia	48,600	102.2	33,100 (68%) (Scrimgeours)	102.2	12,100 (25%) (Aubrey Brown & Hopkinson)	103.075–105.075	800 (2%) (Vivian Gray & Co.)	102.75

Year	Colony								
1897	Jamaica	200,000	99.775	62,200 (31%) (Scrimgeours)	99.775	25,000 (12%) (Stewart & Whitmore)	99.975 & 99.95	24,900 (12%) (Linton Clarke)	99.775
	Trinidad	400,000	97.8	228,300 (57%) (Scrimgeours)	97.8	65,300 (16%) (R. Nivison & Co.)	97.8	25,000 (6%) (Hichens Harrison)	98 & 98.275
1898	Brit. Guiana	150,000	96.65	113,400 (76%) (Scrimgeours)	96.65	20,000 (13%) (Birbeck Bank)	97.05–98.05	12,000 (8%) (Mullens Marshall)	97
1901	Brit. Guiana	100,000	93	73,300 (73%) (CAs)	93	24,000 (24%) (Scrimgeours)	93	2,000 (2%) (Neville)	93.175–93.275
1902	Gold Coast	1,035,000	91	418,800 (40%) (Mullens Marshall)	91	392,900 (38%) (Scrimgeours)	91	160,000 (15%) (CAs)	91
	Trinidad	200,000	93.525	80,400 (40%) (CAs)	93.525	52,900 (26%) (Scrimgeours)	93.525	25,000 (12%) (Lon. & SW Bank)	93.625 & 93.65
1905	Mauritius	150,000	97	138,200 (92%) (Scrimgeours)	75% 97	5,000 (3%) (Scottish Prov.)	97	3,000 (2%) (Francis & Praed)	97.05
1906	Hong Kong	1,000,000	99	965,300 (88%) (Scrimgeours)	81% 99	30,000 (3%) (Prudential)	99.175–99.3	25,000 (2%) (National d' Escompte de Paris)	100

Source: WASA, ACC 527/432; 527/1326; 527/2834; Sri Lanka Department of National Archives, 6/6649; NAN, NT/164/1824; 164/3944; 164/5529; schedule, 17 Apr. 1894 and schedule, 23 Nov. 1894, CAOG 9/4; schedule, 29 Jan. 1885, 9/7; schedule, 30 Sept. 1892, 9/8; schedule, 9/9; schedule, 9/10; schedule, 11 Aug. 885, 9/11; schedule, 1 Mar. 1888, 9/12; schedule, 23 May 1887, 9/17; schedule, 7 Apr. 1892, 9/18; schedule, 9/21; schedule; 9/25; schedule, 13 Mar. 1894, 9/54; schedule, 9/66; schedule, 1 Aug. 1901, 9/70; schedule, 28 Jan. 1898, 9/71; schedule, 21 Dec. 1905, 9/77; schedule, 9/86; schedule, CO 48/439/7227; schedule, CO 54/364/10229; schedule, CO 54/382/4605; schedule, CO 54/408/9548; schedule, CO 83/28/7032; schedule, 2 July 1897, CO 137/585/15238; schedule, CO 167/444/11250; schedule; schedule, CO 167/455/8111; schedule, CO 167/483/2243; schedule, CO 167/494/346; schedule, CO 167/570/6631; schedule, CO 179/66/10879; schedule, CO 273/92/14043; schedule, Feb. 1894, CO 321/156/4028.

Table 4
Crown Agent conversions, 1872–1914

Colony/loan	Amount to be converted (£)	Redemption date	Conversion rate (%)	New stock interest rate (%)	Amount converted (£)	Period of conversion
Natal 6% d., 1860 & 1864	263,000	1883–96	114	5 (d.)	97,400	8/5/72–11/10/75
NZ 8 % t.b.	not known	1866	not known	6 (d.)	111,400	1866
NZ 8% t.b.	144,600	Jun. 1867	99.75	6 (d.)	11,700	1867
NZ 8% t.b.	505,400	Dec. 1867	103.75	6 (d.)	36,800	1867
NZ Otago 8% & 10% d.; Canterbury 8% d.; Wellington 8% d.; Nelson 10% d.; Teranaki 7% d; Auckland, Canterbury, Otago & Hawkes Bay 6% d.; general gov. 5% & 6% d.	–	1868–1914	99.5–128.5	5 (d.)	3,308,000	1/5/68–15/6/71
Cape 5%, 5.5%, & 6% d.	1,523,000	1873–1900	101–20	4 (d.)	–	–
Mauritius 6% d., 19 of 1862 & 6% d., 15 of 1864	600,000	1882–1896	108–18	4 (d.)	173,000	15/3/80–31/12/80
Mauritius 6% d., 19 of 1862 & 6% d., 15 of 1864	431,200	1882–1896	104–16 (c.)	4 (d.)	42,600	17/1/81–11/7/81
Natal 4% d., 35 of 1880	469,800	1927	100	4 (m./n.)	231,800 (1887)	22/2/83–n.c.d
Natal 5% d., 35 of 1880	1,130,000	1894/1924	115	4	987,000 (1887)	15/5/84–15/6/86
Ceylon 4% d., 3 & 4 of 1885; 4% d., 7 of 1879; 4% d., 1 of 1876; 4% 1 of 1881; 4% d., 9 of 1878; 4% d., 8 & 12 of 1881	1,865,000	D	100	4	702,000	27/6/85–1/1/87
W. Aust. 4% d., 26 of 1884, 4% d., 22 of 44 of 1881; 4% d., (46 Vict.) 22 of 1882	929,000	D	100	4	493,000	27/6/85–1/1/87
Jamaica 4% d., 17 0f 1882; 4% d., 8 & 17 of 1880; 4% d., 19 0f 1880	839,000	D	100	4	158,800	27/6/85–1/1/87
Natal 5% d., 44 of 1884	536,500	1895/ 1925	115	4	465,200	7/8/85–15/6/86

Colony/loan	Amount to be converted (£)	Redemption date	Conversion rate (%)	New stock interest rate (%)	Amount converted (£)	Period of conversion
Brit. Guiana 4% d., 4 of 1886	250,000	D	100	4	194,500	15/11/86–14/5/91
Natal 6% d., 8 of 1860; 6% d., 15 of 1864; 5% d., 16 of 1871; 5% d., 35 of 1880; 5% d., 44 of 1884; 4.5% d., 5 of 1875; 4.5% d., 1 of 1876; 4.5% d., 19 of 1876; 4% d., 35 of 1880; 4% s. (m./n.), 35 of 1880 & 44 of 1884.	3,908,000	1887–1927	100–120	4 (a./o.)	2,432,000	16/4/87–31/10/87
Mauritius 4% d., 1887	102,900	D	100	4	99,200	7/87–1/2/88
Ceylon 4% d., 7 of 1879; 4% d., 1 of 1876 & 1 of 1881; 4% d., 9 of 1878; 4% d., 8 & 12 1877	1,175,000	D	100	4	374,100	Ad hoc
Mauritius 6% d., 15 of 1864; 4.5% d., 10 of 1876; 4% d., 10 of 1879; 4% d., 2 of 1887	633,500	D & 1895, 1896	100–112	4	331,200	14/3/88–30/6/88
W. Aust. 6% d., 3 of 36 Vict.; 5% d., 19 of 37 Vict.; 5% d., 21 of 39 Vict.; 4.5% d., 22 of 1878; 4.5% d., 32 of 1879; 4% d., 26 of 1884; 4% d., 22 of 44 Vict. of 1881; 4% d., (46 Vict.) 22 of 1882	788,500	D & 1901, 1902, 1905	98.5–113	4	At least 349,700	19/2/89– 19/11/94
Jamaica 4.5% d., 12 of 1879; 4% d., 8 & 7 of 1880; 4% d., 19 of 1880; 4% d., 17 of 1884	538,900	D	99–104	4	366,200	19/2/89–19/11/94
Grenada 4.5% d., 1888/9	40,000	D	103	4	23,390 (1909)	Ad hoc
Hong Kong 4% d., 11 of 1887	140,000	1892/1907	100	3.5	140,000	2/94–30/4/94
Natal 5% d., 35 of 1880	180,800	1894/1924	98.5	3.5	89,500	8/94–15/10/94
Natal 5% d., 44 of 1884	31,000	1895/1925	97.5	3.5	14,400	11/94–15/12/94
St Lucia 4.5% d., 1888	17,300	1933	102.25	4	17,300	1894
W. Aust. 4.5% d., 22 of 1878 & 32 of 1879; 4% d., 26 of 1884; 4% d., 22 of 1878 & 32 of 1879	238,500	D	100 & t.s.	4	47,900 (30/11/14)	19/11/94– n.c.d.

Colony/loan		Redemption date	Conversion rate (%)	New stock interest rate (%)		Period of conversion
Trinidad 5% d., 7 & 15 of 1873; 5% d., 1 of 1878; 4% d., 8 of 1880; 4% d., 1 of 1882	448,880	D	91–97	4	346,200	13/8/96–31/10/96
Jamaica 4% railway bonds	1,493,000	D	100	3.5	1,493,600	1899/1900
Sierra Leone 4% 10 yr c.d.	1,250,000	1914	100–5	3.5	739,600 (30/11/14)	3/6/1904–1/6/14
Straits 4% 5 yr c.d., 1 of 1882	5,000,000	1912	101–5	3.5	3,969,900	25/5/1907–15/2/12
S. Nigeria 4% 4 yr c.d., 7 of 1908	3,000,000	1912	101–4	3.5	1,090,200	2/5/1908–15/8/11
Gold Coast 3.5% 4 yr c.d. 4 of 1908	1,000,000	1913	101–3	3.5	1,000,000	26/5/1909–1/10/12
British Honduras, 4% 10 yr c.d.	160,000	1921	100	4	116,900 (30/11/14)	1911–21
Jamaica 4% railway bonds	38,100	D	100	3.5	38,100	1912
S. Nigeria 4% 5 yr c.d., 1904 & 1911	5,000,000	1916	103–104.5	3.5	777,200 (30/11/14)	10/11/1911–15/8/15

Source: This table was compiled from a wide range of adverts, correspondence, memos and schedules to be found in CAA: Press advertisement book; GL, prospectuses; CAOG 9/2; 9/3; 9/7; 9/9; 9/10; 9/13; 9/20; 9/21; 9/32; 9/48; 9/50; 9/65; 9/68; 9/70; 9/73; 9/74; 9/76; 9/100; CO 167/598/814; CO 137/507/12161; CO 321/144/10204; CO 179/173/3190; Stock Exchange official intelligence, 1880–1914.

Note: Colony/loan: t.b. = treasury bill; d. = debentures; c.d. = convertible debentures; s. = stock.
Redemption date: D = Drawing sinking fund.
Conversion rate (%): t.s. = terms set by CAs; c = cash.
New stock interest rate (%): d = debentures; m./n. = May/Nov. debentures or stock; a./o. = Apr./Oct. debentures or stock.
Period of conversion: n.c.d. = no closing date

Table 5
New advances made by the Bank of England, 1873–1914

Year	Colony	Amount advanced (£)	Interest rate (%)
1873	New Zealand	250,000	4.5
1874	New Zealand	718,000	3.5–6
	–	127,000	3–5
1875	New Zealand	240,000	3–6
	Cape	207,000	2.5–3.5
	–	336,000	2–4
1876	New Zealand	105,000	2–4
	–	144,000	2–4
1877	Griqualand	90,000	4
	New Zealand	70,000	3
	–	240,000	2–4
1878	New Zealand	220,000	4.5–5
	–	90,000	5
	Cape	375,000	2–3
1879	New Zealand	1,820,550	2–5
	Cape	234,000	2.5
	–	111,000	2–4
1881	New Zealand	100,000	4
1883	Ceylon	140,000	BR
1885	Ceylon	70,000	BR
1886	–	26,500	BR
1887	Mauritius	67,000	BR
	–	8,500	BR
1889	Dominica/St Lucia	25,660	BR
1890	Ceylon	100,000	BR
1892	Trinidad	50,000	BR, minimum 3%
1899	Zanzibar	83,000	1% under BR, minimum 3%
	Barbados	7,000	1% under BR, minimum 3%
	St Vincent	5,000	1% under BR, minimum 3%
1900	Ceylon	155,000	BR, minimum 3%
1901	Zanzibar	13,000	BR, minimum 3%
	Ceylon	790,000	BR & BR, minimum 3%
1902	Uganda railway	242,000	BR
	–	125,000	BR
1903	Mauritius	208,000	BR
	Trinidad	125,000	BR
	Transvaal	2,515,000	BR & BR minus 1/2%
	–	10,000	BR

	–	15,000	BR
1914	East Africa Protectorate	150,000	BR
	Federated Malay States	350,000	BR

Source: BE, C 58/1; C 58/2; C 58/3; C 58/4; C 58/6; C 58/6; C 58/8; C 58/12; C 62/7; C 62/8; C 62/9; C 62/10; C 62/12; G 8/43/116–7.

Note: BR = Bank rate.

Table 6
New advances made by London and Westminster Bank, 1880–1902

Year	Colony	Amount advanced (£)
1880	Cape	350,000
	Natal	50,000
1881	–	100,000
	Cape	1,285,000 – 1,385,000
	Isle of Man	15,000
1882	Cape	500,000
1884	Natal	526,000
1890	–	415,000
1892	British Honduras	11,000
1893	Antigua	35,000
	British Honduras	6,000
1898	British Guiana	48,500
	Federated Malay States	500,000
	Gold Coast	35,000
	Lagos	119,500
	Trinidad	30,000
1899	British Guiana	25,000
	Gold Coast	40,000
	Federated Malay States	101,000
	Jamaica	20,000
	Lagos	165,000
	Sierra Leone	73,000
	Trinidad	45,000
1900	Federated Malay States	35,000
	Gold Coast	20,000
	Jamaica	20,000
	Lagos	50,000
	Sierra Leone	70,000
1902	–	100,000

Source: CAOG 9/49; 9/54; NWB, 12895; 12909; 12911–3.

Note: This list is incomplete.

Table 7
Treasury loans, 1899–1914

Year	Colony	Purpose	Amount (£)	Interest rate (%)
1899	Barbados	Hurricane relief	11,649	2.75
1900	Cyprus	Harbour, railway and irrigation	51,000	3.00
	Jamaica	Public works	85,000	3.50
	Jamaica	Revenue	20,000	2.75
	Jamaica	Railway	44,000	2.75
	Jamaica	Railway debenture interest	88,000	2.75
	Lagos	Railway	792,500	3.25
	St Vincent	Hurricane relief	16,077	2.75
	Seychelles	Road construction	20,000	2.75
1901	Cyprus	Harbour, railway and irrigation	9,000	3.00
	Jamaica	Railway	22,000	2.75
1902	Cyprus	Harbour, railway and irrigation	2,500	3.25
	Jamaica	Railway	44,000	2.75
1903	Cyprus	Harbour, railway and irrigation	18,500	3.00
1904	Cyprus	Harbour, railway and irrigation	59,000	3.25
1905	Cyprus	Harbour, railway and irrigation	134,000	3.25
1906	Cyprus	Harbour, railway and irrigation	58,500	3.25

Source: PP 1902, lv (143), 258; PP 1917–18, xix (17), 232.

APPENDIX 4

Coinage and currency

Table 1
Imperial coinage issued to the Crown colonies, 1872–1913 (£)

Colony	Silver coin issued	Silver coin withdrawn	Bronze coin issued
Cyprus	29,300	702	200
Falkland Islands	34,550	–	75
Fiji	10,000	–	–
Gibraltar	38,900	–	2,800
Malta	296,700	17,718	5,830
Mauritius	10,000	1,722	1,300
St Helena	13,245	1,475	300
West Africa	8,320,000	153,995	22,530
Bermuda, British Guiana and West Indies	2,460,000	144,425	32,245

Source: PP 1914, xliii. 67, 69.

Table 2
Colonial currency issued by the Royal and Birmingham Mints, 1854–1913

Colony	Royal Mint issue			Birmingham Mint issue		
	Silver (£)	Bronze (£)	Nickel/ nickel bronze/ aluminium (£)	Silver	Bronze	Nickel/ nickel bronze/ copper
British Guiana	13,450	–	–	–	–	–
British Honduras	32,896	906	312	–	£312	£208
West Africa	667,000	11,810	–	£310,800	–	£19,000
Ceylon	374,604	20,000	–	RS 500,000	£13,333	–
Cyprus	75,000	12,218	–	–	£850	–
Hong Kong	6,735,000	46,875	–	$7.9 m £33,916	$120,000 £2,083	–
Jamaica	–	–	16,650	–	–	–

325

Colony	Royal Mint issue			Birmingham Mint issue		
	Silver (£)	Bronze (£)	Nickel/ nickel bronze/ aluminium (£)	Silver	Bronze	Nickel/ nickel bronze/ copper
Malta	–	700	–	–	–	–
Mauritius	17,446	9,720	–	106,000 rps £10,000	45,000 rps	–
Nigeria	–	–	43,984	–	–	£18,000
Straits	2,945,000	18,549	–	$5.74 m £27,291	–	£76,339

Source: PRO, MINT 26/1–11.

Bibliography

Unpublished primary sources

AUSTRALIA

Perth, Western Australia, West Australian State Archives
ACC 527/432, 1326, 2834

GREAT BRITAIN

Bramley, Surrey, Alexander Scrimgeour, Thorncombe House

Scrimgeour papers
Profit figures
Reminiscences of Sir George Aylwen

Bromyard, Herts, Lt Col. J. A. Cameron, 22 Butterfield House
Memoirs of Sir Maurice Cameron, typescript *c.* 1914

Cambridge, Churchill College
Chur 10/7–53 Winston Churchill papers

Cardiff, Companies House
578272, V. & R. Blakemore Ltd accounts

Edinburgh University Library
Arthur Berriedale Keith papers Gen 144/2–3

London, Bank of England
AC 14 Borrowing bodies
AC 18 Loan issues
AC 19 Colonial issues
AC 30 Colonial issues
ADM 7 General register
ADM 19 Stock estimates
C 16
C 23 Drawing office
C 58 Temporary advances
C 62 Temporary advance
C 98/7202, 7211–12, 7221–2, 7227
CA General accounts
G 4 Court of directors
G 8 Committee of treasury

G 23 Letter books
M/21

London, Baring Brothers & Co., 60 London Wall
AC 21 Consol receipts
HC 15.2.1 House correspondence relating to the 1882 Cape loan
101812–21 Loans and stock registers

London, British Library
India Office records
LAG 14/14/1–2 Accounting general's papers

London, British Library of Political and Economic Science, London School of Economics
E. D. Morel papers

London, British Museum
Philately collection
G/1736a
M/coins

London, Guildhall Library
Ashanti Goldfields Corporation papers, MSS 14164/1–2; 14168/2–3; 14172
Bank of British West Africa papers, MS 28534
City and Guilds Institute papers, MS 21899
Foster & Braithwaite papers, MS 14271, vols i–ii
London Assurance papers, MS 18728, vols 49–51; MS 18316, vol. ix
Mullens Marshall papers, MSS 29104, 29117
Stock Exchange papers, MSS 17957, 19516, 29787

London, Metropolitan Archives, Clerkenwell
ACC 1037/92–4 Howard & Son papers
Board minutes

London, National Postal Museum
De La Rue correspondence, vols 1–57

London, National Westminster Bank, 41 Lothbury
1597 Cape papers
3059 Union Bank of London papers
9044 Colonial and other loans committee
10066 Private minute book, 1836–90
10083 Register of officers
12894 Board minutes
12895 Board minutes
12908–17 Daily committee minutes
13354 Directors' private notes

London, Public Record Office, Chancery Lane
Census records, RG 12/548

London, Public Record Office, Kew

Audit Office papers
AO 25

Colonial Office papers
CO 18 Western Australia
CO 23 Bahamas
CO 28 Barbados
CO 48 Cape
CO 54 Ceylon
CO 59 Ceylon miscellanea
CO 67 Cyprus
CO 83 Fiji
CO 87 Gambia
CO 96 Gold Coast
CO 107 Griqualand West
CO 111 British Guiana
CO 123 British Honduras
CO 129 Hong Kong
CO 131 Hong Kong sessional papers
CO 137 Jamaica
CO 146
CO 147 Lagos
CO 152 Leeward Islands
CO 167 Mauritius
CO 179 Natal
CO 209 New Zealand
CO 247 St Helena
CO 267 Sierra Leone
CO 273 Straits
CO 287 Tobago
CO 291 Transvaal
CO 295 Trinidad
CO 309 Victoria
CO 321 Windward Islands
CO 323 General correspondence
CO 324 Colonies general (entry books series)
CO 378 Register of general correspondence
CO 384 Emigration
CO 431 Accounts
CO 446 Northern Nigeria
CO 520 Southern Nigeria
CO 525 Nyasaland
CO 536 Uganda
CO 537 Supplementary correspondence

CO 554 West Africa
CO 614 Uganda Railway
CO 766 Evidence to the Private Enterprise Committee
CO 879 Confidential prints, Africa
CO 882 Confidential print, Eastern
CO 883 Confidential print, Mediterranean
CO 884 Confidential print, West Indies
CO 885 Confidential prints, miscellaneous

Crown Agent papers
CAOG 9 Finance
CAOG 10 Engineering
CAOG 11 Shipping
CAOG 12 Purchasing
CAOG 13 Appointments and passages
CAOG 14 Relations with principals
CAOG 15 Pay office
CAOG 16 Personnel
CAOG 17 Miscellaneous
CAOG 18 Investigations by Messrs Cooper & Lybrand
CAOG 19 Contract documents

Foreign Office papers
FO 2 Africa
FO 881 Foreign Office: confidential print

Inland Revenue papers
IR 79 Director of Stamping: miscellanea

Royal Mint papers
Mint 4
Mint 9 Coinage, imperial
Mint 13 Coinage, colonial and foreign
Mint 20
Mint 21 Registers of correspondence
Mint 26 Annual reports of the deputy master and comptroller
Mint 28

Treasury papers
T 1 Treasury Board
T 64 Miscellaneous papers

War Office papers
WO 254 Purchase decisions

London, Rothschild archive, New Court, St Swithin's Lane
xi/3/154 New Zealand 1875 loan
xi/109/118 Private correspondence

London, Somerset House
Probate records

Oxford, Bodleian Library
MSS Afr. s. 141 Earl of Selborne papers
MSS Asquith Herbert Asquith papers
MSS Milner Lord Milner papers
MSS Southborough Sir Francis Hopwood papers

Oxford, Nuffield College
MSS Mottistone 1–36 Sir John Seely papers

Oxford, Rhodes House
MSS Afr. s. 26 Sir M. Ommanney papers
MSS Afr. s. 85–101 Earl of Scarborough papers
MSS Afr. s. 1525, 1657 John Holt & Co. papers
MSS Afr. s. 1865 Sir P. Girouard papers
MSS Brit. Emp. s. 62 Lord Lugard papers
MSS Nathan 231–656 Sir Matthew Nathan papers
A. R. Seymour, 'Tropical railway', typescript c. 1925
Frederic Shelford, album of press clippings

Sutton, Surrey, Crown Agents' Archive
Accounts, 1880–1941
British Guiana (Demerara railway) 4% loan stock register
CA circulars and papers, list of current prices
CA 73/4
CA M 1 Various early papers
CA M 4 Average disbursements, 1857–62
CA M 5 Memorandum on the procedures followed in connection with the issue
    of Crown colony loans, 1919
CA M 9, 16, 38, 60, 64, 68, 70, 82, 120, 202
CAOG 18 Miscellaneous reports
CAOG 19 Engineering contracts
CS 4 SL
EM 261
Files 20, 21, 53, 99
G 844/5 List of standard patterns
General guard book
Hayes papers
Jeffries, A., 'A short history of the Crown Agents' insurance fund', typescript, c.
    1960
MC 77
Office memorandum book

O/SEC 12/3, 19
Press advertisement book
Prospectuses
Record of inspectors
S/Gen
S 203/5
Security bond file
Staff register, vol. 1
Weeded files (summaries of the contents of files that were subsequently destroyed)

SOUTH AFRICA

Pietermaritzburg, National Archive of Natal
NT/164/1824, 3944, 5529

Simonstown, J. A. Sibbald, 7 Wilfred Street
Various papers associated with Sir Ernest Blake, including Herbert to Blake, 28 Jan. 1881

SRI LANKA

Colombo, Department of National Archives
6/6649

UNITED STATES

Durham, North Carolina, Duke University
Correspondence of Sir Montague Ommanney 3–8–67

Published primary sources

Official documents and publications
British parliamentary papers (in chronological order)

A statement showing the years for which the commissioners of audit have audited the accounts of the colonies of Ceylon, Mauritius, Malta, Trinidad, and the Cape, 1820, xii

An abstract of the net annual revenue and expenditure of the colonies of Ceylon, Mauritius, Malta, the Cape and Trinidad, 1816–19, 1821, xiv

Colonial Agents: returns of the names of the agents for the new colonies, 1822, xx

Return showing the amount of expenditure in the new colonies of Ceylon, Mauritius, Trinidad, Cape, Malta and other places, 1822, xx

Accounts of the receipts and disbursements of Trinidad, Malta, Mauritius, Cape and Ceylon, 1823, xiv

Accounts of the receipts and disbursements of Trinidad, Malta, Mauritius and Ceylon, 1824, xvi

Accounts of the receipts and disbursements of Trinidad, Malta, Mauritius, and Ceylon, 1825, xix

Report of the commissioners appointed 21 June 1830 to inquire into the receipt and expenditure of the revenue of the colonies and foreign possessions, 1830–1, iv

Agents for colonies: return of the names of agents for colonies at present acting in Great Britain, 1845, xxxi

Tenth report of the Civil Service Commissioners with appendix, 1864, xxx (3316)

Statistical abstract for the several colonies and other possessions of the United Kingdom in each year from 1851 to 1864, 1866, lxxiii

Report from the Select Committee on Loans to Foreign States together with the proceedings of the committee, minutes of evidence, appendix and index, 1875, xi (367)

Twenty–third report of the Civil Service Commissioners with appendix, 1878, xxvii (177)

Royal Commission into the Stock Exchange, evidence, 1878, xix (C 2157)

Estimates for civil service and revenue departments for the year ending 31 March 1880, 1880, xlv (161)

Twenty–fifth report of the Civil Service Commissioners with appendix, 1880, xxi (C 2721)

Papers explanatory of the functions of the Crown Agents for the Colonies, 1881, lxiv (C 3075)

Statistical abstract for the several colonies and other possessions of the United Kingdom in each year from 1866–80, 1882, lxxiii

Statistical abstract for the several colonies and other possessions of the United Kingdom in each year from 1877 to 1891, 1892, lxxxvii (C 6719)

Statistical abstract for the several colonies and other possessions of the United Kingdom, in each year from 1880 to 1894, 1894, xcii (C 7526)

First report of the Royal Commission on the Administration of the Expenditure of India, evidence, volume 1, 1896, xv (Cd 8258)

Report from the Select Committee on War Office Contracts with the proceedings of the committee, minutes of evidence, appendix and index, 1900, ix (313)

Report of the Committee on the War Office Organisation, 1901, xl (Cd 580)

Committee on the War Office Organisation, evidence, appendices, digest and index, 1901, xl (Cd 581)

Statistical abstract for the several colonial and other possessions of the United Kingdom, 1886–1900, 1901, lxxxvi (Cd 751)

Forty-sixth report of the Civil Service Commissioners with appendix, 1902, xxii (Cd 1203)

Local loans fund accounts for the year ending 31 March 1901, 1902, lv (143)

Despatch from the Secretary of State for the Colonies relating to the commercial business of the Crown Agents for the Colonies, 1904, lix (Cd 1944)

Review of the trade of India, 1898/9 to 1902/3, 1904, lxvii (Cd 1915)

Return showing how many firms were invited by the Crown Agents to tender for the supply of each of the following articles . . ., 1904, lxxviii (Cmd 194)

Return showing the total amount, including loans, on which any commission was charged or received by the Crown Agents during each of the last five years, 1904, lxxviii (264)

Papers relating to the construction of railways in Sierra Leone, Lagos and the Gold Coast, 1905, lvi (Cd 2325)

Statistical abstract for the several colonial and other possessions of the United Kingdom, 1890–1904, 1905, xcvi (Cd 2679)

Remuneration of the consulting engineers to the Crown colonies and protectorates, 1907, lvi (103)

Railways in British protectorates, leased territories and colonies not possessing responsible government, 1907, lvi (336)

Review of the trade of India, 1902/3 to 1906/7, 1908, lxxv (Cd 3969)

Report by the Hon. Reginald Lister, HM Minister in Paris, on the French colonies, 1908 cviii (Cd 3883)

Report of the Committee of the Enquiry into the Organisation of the Crown Agents Office, 1909, xvi (Cd 4473)

Enquiry into the Organisation of the Crown Agents Office, evidence and appendices, 1909, xvi (Cd 4474)

Royal Commission on Shipping Rings: evidence, 1909, xlvii (Cd 4668)

Estimates for the civil service for the year ending 31 March 1910, 1909, lv (54)

Report of the Committee on Emigration from India to the Crown Colonies and Protectorates, part iii, papers laid before the committee, 1910, xxvii (Cd 5194)

Accounts of the Crown Agents office funds for the year 1909, 1910, lxvi (Cd 5391)

Accounts of the Crown Agents office funds for the year 1910, 1911, liii (Cd 5744)

Annual report of Nigeria, 1910/11, 1912/13, lviii (Cd 6007)

Accounts of the Crown Agents office funds for the year 1911, 1912/13, lx (Cd 6279)

Review of the trade of India, 1907/8 to 1911/12, 1913, xlviii (Cd 6783)

State railways (British possessions and foreign countries), 1913, lviii (287)

Minutes of evidence taken before the Royal Commission on Indian Finance and Currency, 1914, xix (Cd 7069)

Royal Commission on Indian Finance and Currency: appendices to the interim report of the commissioners, volume one, 1914, xx (Cd 7070)

Royal Commission on Indian Finance and Currency: appendices and interim report of the commissioners, volume two, 1914, xx (Cd 7071)

Estimates for the civil service for the year ending 31 March 1915, 1914, lv (132)

Accounts of the Crown Agents office funds for the year 1913, 1914, lx (Cd 7510)

Statistical abstract for several British self-governing dominions, colonies, possessions and protectorates for each year from 1899–1913, 1914–16, lxxix (Cd 7786)

Accounts of the Crown Agents office funds for the year 1914, 1914–16, xlv (Cd 7973)

Review of the trade of India 1910/1 to 1914/5, 1916, xxi (Cd 8343)

Statistical abstract for the several British self–governing dominions, colonies, possessions and protectorates in each year from 1900 to 1914, 1916, xxxii (Cd 8329)

Local loans fund accounts for the year ending 31 march 1916, 1917/8, xix (17)

Statistical abstract for the several British colonies, possessions and protectorates, 1901–1915, 1918, xxv (Cd 9051)

Private enterprise in British tropical Africa, 1924, viii (Cmd 2016)

Report of the work of the India store department for the year 1924–5, 1924–5, xxi (711)

Report by the Advisory Committee on the Crown Agents (Stevenson Committee), 1977/8, viii

Report of the committee of enquiry appointed by the minister of overseas development into the circumstances which led to the Crown Agents requesting financial assistance from the government (Fay Committee), 1977/8, viii

Report of the tribunal appointed to enquire into certain issues arising out of the operations of the Crown Agents as financiers on their own account, 1981/2, 364

Colonial Office list
Hansard

Cape papers
*Joint report by Sir P. Julyan and Captain Mills on the floating of a loan of £4,837,500,
    parliament notes and proceedings*, appendix 1, vol. 1, A3–84

Ceylon papers
Papers laid before the legislative council of Ceylon, 1895, 1896, 1903, 1904, 1912–13,
    1914–15

Mauritius annual report, 1914 (Cd 8172)
New Zealand parliamentary debates, ix, xxxii
Trinidad and Tobago blue book, 1914/15
*Report of the general manager of railways and harbours for the year ending 31
    December 1913*, Cape Town, South Africa, 10–11

Newspapers and periodicals
The Argosy (London)
Banker's Magazine (London)
Board of Trade Labour Gazette (London)
British and South African Export Gazette (London)
British Trade Journal (London)
Cape Argus (weekly edition) (Cape Town)
Civil Service Gazette (London)
Credit Index (London)
Crown Agents' Quarterly (London)
Crown Colonist (London)
Daily Chronicle (London)
Daily Graphic (London)
Daily List (London)
Daily Mail (London)
Daily News (London)
Demerara Daily Chronicle (Demerara)
Economist (London)
Empire Review (London)
The Engineer (London)
The Financier (London)
Gibbon's Stamp Weekly (London)
Jamaica Daily Telegraph (Kingston)
Journal of the Royal Society of Arts (London)
Liverpool Daily Post (Liverpool)
Manchester Guardian (Manchester)
Minutes of the Proceedings of the Institution of Civil Engineers (London)
Pall Mall Gazette (London)
Railway Gazette (New York)
Sell's Commercial Intelligence (London)
The Standard (London)
The Statist (London)

Straits Times (Singapore)
The Times (London)
Transvaal Leader (Pretoria)
West Africa (Liverpool)
West African Mail (Liverpool)
Westminster Gazette (London)

Contemporary books and articles

Anon, *The City or the physiology of London*, London 1845

Antrobus, Sir Reginald L., *Antrobus pedigrees: the story of a Cheshire family*, London 1929

Barker, G. F. R. and Alan H. Stenning, *The record of old Westminster*, i, London 1928

Bastable, E. F., *Public finance*, London 1892

Belton, Francis G. (ed.), *Ommanney of Sheffield: memoirs of George Campbell Ommanney, vicar of St Matthews Sheffield, 1882–1936*, London 1936

Bruce, B., *The broad stone of empire*, London 1903

Calthrop, E. R., *The economics of light railway construction*, Leeds 1896

────── 'Light railways in the colonies', *Proceedings of the Royal Colonial Institute* xxix (1897–8), 98–103

Chatley, Herbert, *Pioneering railway engineering*, London 1916

Cordingley, W. G., *Cordingley's guide to the Stock Exchange*, London 1893

Davey, F., *A student catechism on bookkeeping*, London 1910

Foster, John, *Oxford men, 1880–92*, Oxford–London 1893

Giffen, Robert, *Stock Exchange securities: an essay on the general fluctuations in their price*, London 1879

Lowenfeld, Henry, *All about investment*, London 1909

Mills, William, *Railway construction*, London 1898

Morel, E. D., *Affairs of Africa*, London 1902

────── *Nigeria: its peoples and its problems*, London 1908

Price, F. G. Hilton, *A handbook of London bankers with some account of their predecessors*, London 1890

Raymond, William G., *Elements of railway engineering*, London 1908

Searles, William. H., *Field engineering: a handbook of the theory and practice of railway surveying*, London 1915

Shelford, Anna E., *The life of Sir William Shelford*, London 1909 (privately printed)

Shelford, F., 'The development of West Africa by railways', *Proceedings of the Royal Colonial Institute* xxxv (1903–4), 248–80

────── *Pioneering*, London 1909

────── *Some features of the West African railways*, London 1912

Talbot, F. A., *Railway wonders of the world*, i, London 1913

Tovey, Philip, *Prospectuses: how to read and understand them*, London 1912

Webb, Walter L., *Economics of railway construction*, London 1910

de Worms, Percy (ed.), *Perkins Bacon records extracted*, London 1953

Directories and works of reference

The banking almanac & directory (London)
British biographical archive, London 1984
British biographical index, London 1990
City of London directory (London)
Dictionary of national biography, Oxford 1901, 1912, 1927, 1993
Dictionary of national biography: missing persons, Oxford 1993
Dictionary of stock market terms, London 1915
Directory of directors, London 1889, 1901, 1904 1908
Fenn's compendium of English and foreign funds (London)
The historical register of the University of Oxford, Oxford 1900
Institution of civil engineers: list of members, London 1895–1905
Jeremy, David (ed.), *Dictionary of business biography*, London 1984
Law list (London)
Members of the Stock Exchange (London)
Mitchell, B. R., *British historical statistics*, Cambridge 1988
Stock Exchange official intelligence (London)
The United Kingdom stock and stockbrokers directory (London)
Venn, J. A., *Alumni cantabrigienses: 1852–1900*, Cambridge 1940
War Office vocabulary (London)
Whitaker's almanac, London 1898, 1915
Who's who, London 1849, 1936
Who was whom (CD–ROM)

Secondary Sources

Abbott, A. W., *A short history of the Crown Agents and their office*, London 1959 (privately printed)
——— 'Oversea Q Ltd', *Army Quarterly and Defence Journal* lxxxvii (1964), 225–8
Acres, W. Marston, *The Bank of England from within*, London 1931 (privately printed)
Ainslie, George, 'Beyond microeconomics: conflict among interests in a multiple self as a determination of value', in Elster, *Multiple self*, 139–43
Anon, 'A century of development: the growth of the functions of the Crown Agents from 1833–1933', *Crown Colonist* (August 1933), 341–4
——— 'The work of the Crown Agents', *Crown Colonist* (August 1933), 345–50
——— *The Crown Agents for the colonies*, London 1933 (privately printed)
——— 'The cares of the Crown Agents', *West African Review* (May 1954), 385–9
——— *George Peabody & Co., J. S. Morgan & Co., Morgan Grenfell & Co., Morgan Grenfell & Co. Ltd, 1838–1958*, Oxford 1958 (privately published)
——— *The McNamara years at the World Bank: major policy addresses of Robert S. McNamara, 1968–81*, London 1981
Aoki, M., Bo Gustafsson and Oliver E. Williamson (eds), *The firm as a nexus of treaties*, London 1990
Avery, R. W., 'The Crown Agents keep the link', *New Commonwealth* xxxi (1956), 329–32

Axelrod, Robert, 'An evolutionary approach to norms', *American Political Science Review* lxxx (1986), 102–7

Baker, E. C., *Preece and those who followed: consulting engineers in the twentieth century*, Brighton 1980

Banerji, A. K., *Aspects of Indo–British economic relations, 1858–1898*, Oxford 1982
—— *Finance in the early raj: investments and the external sector*, London 1995

Barlow, H. S., *Swettenham*, Kuala Lumpar 1995

Baron, D. and D. Besanko, 'Monitoring, moral hazard, asymmetric information and risk sharing in procurement contracting', *Rand Journal of Economics* xviii (1987), 509–32

Baster, A. S. J., 'A note on the Colonial Stock Acts and dominion borrowing', *Economic History* ii (1933), 602–8

Becker, Gay S., 'Altruism, egoism and genetic fitness: economics and socio-biology', *Journal of Economic Literature* xiv (1976), 817–26

Berman, H. D., *The Stock Exchange*, London 1966

Best, J. R., *A history of the Sierra Leone railway, 1899–1949*, London 1949

Binnie, G. M., *Early Victorian water engineers*, London 1981

Blakely, B., *The Colonial Office, 1868–92*, Durham, NC 1972

Blackstock, Raewyn, 'Sir Julius Vogel, 1876–80: from politics to business', *New Zealand Journal of History* v (1971), 150–70

Bland, E. M., 'A colonial view of the Crown Agents' work', *Crown Colonist* (Aug. 1933), 356–8

Bourne, J. M., *Patronage and society in nineteenth century England*, London 1986

Bunt, J. P., *The De La Rue definitives of the Falkland Islands, 1901–29*, Truro 1986

Burchill, B. and F. Wilkinson, *Trust business relationships and the contractual environment* (ESRC Centre for Business Research, University of Cambridge, working paper, no. 35)

Burk, K., *Morgan Grenfell, 1838–88: the biography of a merchant bank*, Oxford 1989

Burton, Ann, ''Treasury control and colonial policy in the late nineteenth century', *Public Administration* xliv (1966), 169–92

Burton, Anthony, *The railway empire*, London 1994

Busschau, W. J., 'Some aspects of railway development in Natal', *South African Journal of Economics* i (1933), 405–20

Butler, Jeffery, *The Liberal Party and the Jameson raid*, Oxford 1996

Butlin, N. G., *Investment in Australian economic development, 1861–1900*, Cambridge 1964

Cain, P. J. and A. G. Hopkins, *British imperialism: innovation and expansion, 1688–1914*, London 1993
—— *British imperialism: crisis and deconstruction, 1914–90*, London 1993

Carland, J. M., 'Public expenditure and development in a Crown colony: the Colonial Office, Sir Egerton Walter and southern Nigeria, 1900–12', *Albion* xii (1980), 368–86
—— *The Colonial Office and Nigeria, 1898–1914*, London 1985
—— 'The Colonial Office and the first West African note issue', *International Journal of African Historical Studies* xxiii (1990), 495–502

Carlos, A. M., 'Principal – agent problems in the early trading companies: a tale of two firms', *American Economic Review* lxxxii (1992), 140–5

Cassis, Youssef, *La City de Londres, 1870–1914*, Paris 1987
—— *City bankers, 1890–1914*, Cambridge 1994

—— (ed.), *Finance and financiers in European history, 1880–1960*, Cambridge 1992

Casson, Mark, *Corporate culture and the agency problem* (University of Reading, Department of Economics, discussion papers in economics, no. 238, 1991)

Chappell, N. M., *New Zealand banker's hundred: a history of the Bank of New Zealand, 1861–1941*, Wellington 1961

Child, John, *Organisation: a guide to problems and practice*, London 1984

Church, R. J. Harrison, *The evolution of railways in French and British West Africa*, Lisbon 1952

Churchill, Randolph S., *Winston Churchill*, ii, London 1969

Clapham, Sir John, *The Bank of England*, ii, Cambridge 1958

Cline, Catherine Ann, *E. D. Morel, 1873–1924: the strategies of protest*, Belfast 1980

Cocks, F. Seymour, *E. D. Morel: the man and his work*, London 1920

Cottrell, P. L., *British overseas investment in the nineteenth century*, London 1975

Dalziel, Raewyn, *Julius Vogel: business politician*, Oxford 1986

Daunton, Martin, 'Payment and participation: welfare and state formation in Britain, 1900–1951', *Past and Present* cl (1996), 167–216

Davies, P. N., *The trade makers: Elder Dempster in West Africa, 1852–1972*, London 1973

—— *Sir Alfred Jones, shipping entrepreneur par excellence*, London 1978

Davis, L. E. and R. A. Huttenback, *Mammon and the pursuit of empire: the political economy of British imperialism, 1860–1912*, Cambridge 1986

Dawkins, Richard, *The selfish gene*, London 1978

Day, John R., *Railways of South Africa*, London 1963

Drew, Bernard, *The London Assurance: a second chronicle*, London 1949

Dummett, R. E., 'Joseph Chamberlain, imperial finance and railway policy in British West Africa in the late nineteenth century', *EHR* xc (1975), 287–321

Dunleavy, Patrick, *Democracy, bureaucracy and public choice: economic explanations in political science*, London 1991

Ebers, Mark (ed.), *The formation of inter-organisational networks*, Oxford 1997

Edelstein, M, 'Realised rates of return on UK home and overseas portfolio investment in the age of high imperialism', *Explorations in Economic History* xiii (1976), 283–329

Elster, Jon, *The multiple self*, Cambridge 1986

—— 'Social norms and economic theory', *Journal of Economic Perspectives* iii (1989), 91–111

Farrell, J. and Carl Shapiro, 'Optimal contracts with lock-in', *American Economic Review* lxxix (1989), 51–68

Federated Malay States Railways, *Fifty years of railways in Malaya, 1885–1935*, Kuala Lumpar 1935

Feis, H., *Europe: the world's banker*, New York 1930

Fiddes, G. V., *The dominions and Colonial Offices*, London 1926

Frankel, S. H., *Capital investment in Africa*, Oxford 1938

Frece, Sir W. de, *The failure of officialdom: the disastrous record of government railway building*, London 1923

Fry, Richard, *Bankers in British West Africa: the story of the Bank of British West Africa Ltd*, London 1976

Fukuyama, Francis, *Trust: the social virtues and the creation of prosperity*, London 1995

Gaerner, W. and Y. Xu, *Rationality and external reference* (University of Nottingham, discussion papers on economics, no. 96/17, May 1996)

Gann, L. H. and P. Duignan, *The rulers of British Africa, 1870–1914*, Stanford 1978

Gilbert, R. S., 'London financial intermediaries and Australian overseas borrowing, 1900–29', *Australian Economic Review* xi (1971), 39–47

Goodhart, C. A. E., *The business of banking, 1891–1914*, London 1972

Gould, Peter, *The development of the transportation pattern in Ghana*, Evaston, Illinois 1960

Green, Donald P. and Ian Shapiro, *Pathologies of rational choice theory: a critique of applications in political science*, London 1994

Gregory, T. E., *The Westminster Bank through a century*, i, Oxford 1936

Guest, B. and J. M. Sellers (eds), *Enterprise and exploitation in a Victorian economy: aspects of the economic and social history of colonial Natal*, Pietermaritzburg 1985

Gunasekera, H. A. de S, *From dependent currency to central banking in Ceylon: an analysis of monetary experience, 1825–1957*, London 1962

Hall, A. R., *The London capital market and Australia, 1870–1914*, Canberra 1963
―――― (ed.), *The export of capital from Britain, 1870–1914*, London 1968

Hay, Donald A. and Derek J. Morris, *Industrial economics and organisation: theory and evidence*, Oxford 1991

Hayter, T. and C. Watson, *Aid: rhetoric and reality*, London 1985

Headrick, Daniel, 'The tools of imperialism: technology and the expansion of European empires in the nineteenth century', *Journal of Modern History* li (1979), 231–63

Heap, Simon, 'The development of motor transport in the Gold Coast, 1900–39', *Journal of Transport History* xi (1990), 19–37

Heimer, A. and A. L. Stinheombeleds, *Organisation through project management*, London 1985

Hennock, E. P, *Fit and proper persons: ideal and reality in nineteenth century urban government*, London 1973

Heussler, R, *The British in Northern Nigeria*, London 1968

Higgins, G. C., *A history of Trinidad oil*, Port of Spain 1996

Hill, M. F., *Permanent way: the story of the Kenya and Uganda railway*, London 1950

Hitchens, F. H., *The Colonial Land and Emigration Commission*, London 1931

Hollett, David, *The conquest of the Niger by land and sea: from the early explorers and pioneer steamships to Elder Dempster*, Abergavenny 1995

Holmstrom, B. and P. Milgrom, 'Multi-task analysis: incentive contracts, asset ownership and job design', *Journal of Law, Economics and Organisation* vii (1991), 24–52

Hopkins, A. G., 'The creation of a colonial monetary system: the origins of the West African Currency Board', *International Journal of African Historical Studies* iii (1970), 101–32
―――― *An economic history of West Africa*, London 1973

Houseman, Lorna, *The house that Thomas built: the story of De La Rue*, London 1968

Hyam, R., *Elgin and Churchill at the Colonial Office*, London 1968

Jaekel, Francis, *The history of the Nigerian railway*, i, ii, Ibadan 1997

Jarvis, R., The Crown Agents' offices: past, present and future', *Crown Agents' Review* i (1985), 17–20

Jeffries, C., *The colonial empire and its civil service*, Cambridge 1938

Jessop, David, 'The Colonial Stock Act of 1901: a symptom of new imperialism', *Journal of Imperial and Commonwealth History* iv (1976), 154–63

Joyce, R. B., *Sir William MacGregor*, Oxford 1971

Kerr, J., *Building the railways of the raj, 1850–1900*, Oxford 1995

Kesner, R. M., 'Builders of empire: the role of the Crown Agents in imperial development, 1880–1914', *Journal of Imperial and Commonwealth History* v (1977), 310–29

———— *Economic control and colonial development: Crown colony financial management in the age of Joseph Chamberlain*, Oxford 1981

Kramer, R. M. and T. R. Tyler, *Trust in organisations: frontiers of theory and research*, London 1996

Kreps, Richard M., *A course in macroeconomic theory*, London 1990

Kubicek, Robert V., *The administration of imperialism: Joseph Chamberlain at the Colonial Office*, Durham, NC 1969

———— 'The design of shallow draft steamers for the British empire, 1868–1906', *Technology and Culture* xxxi (1990), 427–50

Kynaston, D., *Cazenove & Co.*, London 1991

———— *The City of London: a world of its own, 1815–90*, London 1994

———— *The City of London: the golden years, 1890–1914*, London 1995

Lavington, F., *The English capital market*, London 1929

Leitzel, Jim and Jean Tirole (eds), *Incentives in procurement contracting*, Oxford 1993

Leubuscher, C., *The West African shipping trade, 1909–59*, London 1963

Loynes, J. B. de, *The West African Currency Board, 1912–62*, London 1962

———— *A history of the West African Currency Board*, London 1974

Lubbock, Basil, *Coolie ships and oil sailors*, Glasgow 1955

Lugard, Lord, *The dual mandate in British tropical Africa*, London 1922

Luntinen, P., *Railway on the Gold Coast: a meeting of two cultures*, Helsinki 1996

MacDermot, B. H. D., *Panmure Gordon and Co.*, London 1976 (privately printed)

MacFee, R. P. and J. MacMillan, 'Auctions and bidding', *Journal of Economic Literature* xxv (1987), 699–738

Macinnes, C. M, *An introduction to the economic history of the British empire*, London 1935

MacLeod, Roy, *Government and expertise: specialists, administrators and professionals, 1860–1919*, Cambridge 1988

MacLeod, W. B. and J. Malcolmson, 'Reputation and hierarchy in dynamic models of employment', *Journal of Political Economy* xcvi (1988), 832–54

Makepeace, Walter, Gilbert E. Brooke and Roland Braddell (eds), *One hundred years of Singapore*, ii, London 1921

Maskin, E. and J. Tirole, 'The principal–agent relationship with an informed principal: a case of private values', *Econometrica* lviii (1990), 379–409

May, R. S., D. Schumacher and M. H. Malek, *Overseas aid: the impact on Britain and Germany*, London 1989

Michie, R. C., *The City of London*, London 1992

Milgrom, Paul and John Roberts, *Economics, organisation and management*, Princeton, NJ 1992

Miller, Charles, *The lunatic express: an entertainment in imperialism*, London 1971

Moore, C. and E. Newbigging, 'Environmental change and public enterprise: the dilemma of the Crown Agents', *Journal of General Management* viii (1982), 70–81

Munro, R. W. and Jean Munro, *The Scrimgeours and their chiefs: Scotland's royal banner bearers*, Edinburgh 1980 (privately printed)

Musgrove, F., 'Middle class education and employment in the nineteenth century', *Economic History Review* xii (1959), 99–111

Nelson, P. J., *The World Bank and non-governmental organisations: the limits of apolitical development*, London 1995

Nelson, W. Evan, 'The gold standard in Mauritius and the Straits Settlements between 1850 and 1914', *Journal of Imperial and Commonwealth History* xvi (1987), 48–76

Newbury, C., *The western slave coast and its rulers*, Oxford 1961

Newlyn, W. T and D. C. Rowan, *Money and banking in British colonial Africa*, Oxford 1954

Nworah, K., 'The Liverpool sect and British West African policy', *African Affairs* lxx (1971), 349–64

Offer, Avner, 'Empire and social reform: British overseas investment and domestic politics, 1908–14', *Historical Journal* xxvi (1983), 119–38

——— 'Between the gift and the market: the economy of regard' (University of Oxford, discussion papers in economic and social history, no. 3, 1996)

Ofonagoro, W. I., *Trade and imperialism in Southern Nigeria, 1881–1929*, New York 1979

Osborne, Thomas, 'Bureaucracy as a vocation: governmentality and administration in nineteenth century Britain', *Journal of Historical Sociology* vii (1994), 289–93

Oshin, O., 'Road transport and the declining fortunes of the Nigerian Railway, 1901–50', *Journal of Transport History* xii (1991), 11–36

Owen, R. and B. Sutcliffe (eds), *Studies in the theory of imperialism*, London 1972

Oyemakindo, W., 'Railway construction and operation in Nigeria, 1895–1911: the labour problems and socio-economic impact', *Journal of the Historical Society of Nigeria* vii (1974), 303–24

Pauling, George, *The chronicles of a contractor*, London 1926

Payer, C., *The World Bank: a critical analysis*, London 1982

Penson, L. M., *The colonial agents of the British West Indies*, London 1924

——— 'The origins of the Crown Agents' office', *EHR* xl (1925), 196–206

Perera, G. F., *The Ceylon railway: the story of its inception and progress*, Colombo 1925

Perham, Margery, *Lugard: the years of authority*, London 1960

Platt, D. C. M. (ed), *Business imperialism, 1840–1930*, Oxford 1977

Ponko, Jr, Vincent, 'Economic management in a free trade empire: the work of the Crown Agents for the colonies in the nineteenth and early twentieth centuries', *Journal of Economic History* xxxi (1966), 363–77

——— 'The history and methodology of public administration: the case of the Crown Agents for the colonies', *Administration Review* xxvii (1967), 1–9

———— 'The Colonial Office and British business before World War One: a case study', *Business History Review* xliii (1969), 39–58

Porter, A., 'Britain, the Cape Colony and Natal, 1870–1914: capital, shipping and the imperial connection', *Economic History Review* xxxiv (1981), 554–77

———— *The Victorian shipping business and imperial policy: Donald Currie, the Castle Line and Southern Africa*, London 1986

Porter, Bernard, *Critics of empire: British radical attitudes to colonialism in Africa, 1895–1914*, London 1968

Porter, D. H. and G. C. Clifton, 'Patronage, professional values and Victorian public works: engineering and contracting the Thames embankment', *Victorian Studies* xxxi (1988), 319–49

Powell, W. W., 'Trust based forms of governance', in R. M. Kramer and T. R. Tyler (eds), *Trust in organisations: frontiers of theory and research*, London 1996

Pratt, J. W. and Richard Zeckhauser (eds), *Principal agent theory: the structure of business*, Boston 1984

Raftery, John, *Risk analysis in project management*, London 1994

Rasmusen, Eric, *Games and information: an introduction to game theory*, London 1995

Ratcliffe, Barrie, 'Commerce and empire: Manchester merchants and West Africa, 1873–1895', *Journal of Imperial and Commonwealth History* vii (1979), 293–320

Rennie, Sir John, *An autobiography of Sir John Rennie*, London 1925

Righi, A. G. Rigo de, *Postage stamps of De La Rue*, London 1970

Robb, George, *White collar crime in modern England: financial fraud and business morality, 1845–1929*, Cambridge 1992

Robinson, Ronald, John Gallagher and Alice Denny, *Africa and the Victorians*, Garden City, NY 1968

Sainty, J. C., *Office holders in modern Britain: colonial officials*, London 1976

Sammut, J. C., *From scudo to sterling: money in Malta, 1798–1887*, Malta 1992

Sappington, David, 'Incentives in principal–agent relationships', *Journal of Economic Perspectives* v (1991), 45–66

Saul, S. B., 'The economic significance of constructive imperialism', *Journal of Economic History* xvii (1957), 173–92

Saunders, Kay, *Indentured labour in the British empire*, London 1984

Sayers, R. S., *Bank of England operations, 1890–1914*, London 1936

———— *The Bank of England, 1891–1944*, Cambridge 1944

Schmitz, Hubert, 'From ascribed to earned trust in exporting clusters', *Journal of International Economics* xlviii (1999), 140–50

Schumpeter, J. A, *Imperialism and social class*, New York 1951

Searle, G. R., *Corruption in British politics, 1895–1930*, Oxford 1987

Sherwood, M., 'Elder Dempster and West Africa, 1891–1940: the genesis of underdevelopment', *International Journal of the African Historical Society* xxx (1997), 253–76

Shinn, Ridgway F., Jr, *Arthur Berriedale Keith, 1874–1914*, Aberdeen 1990

Simon, M, 'The pattern of new British portfolio foreign investment, 1865–1914', in Hall, *Export of capital*, 18–36

Skocpol, T., D. Rueschemeyer and P. Evans (eds), *Bringing the state back in*, Cambridge 1985

Stahl, Kathleen M., *The metropolitan organisation of British colonial trade*, London 1951

Suzuki, Toshio, *Japanese government loan issues on the London capital market, 1870–1913*, London 1994

Tamuno, Takema N., 'Genesis of the Nigerian railway', *Nigeria Magazine* lxxxiii (1964) 279–92; lxxxiv (1965), 31–43

—— *The evolution of the Nigerian state: the southern phase, 1898–1914*, London 1978

Vasquez, I. and D. Bandow (eds), *Perpetuating poverty: the World Bank, the IMF and the developing world*, Washington 1994

Vaubel, Roland and Thomas Willett, *The political economy of international organisations: a public choice approach*, Oxford 1991

—— 'A public choice approach to international organisations', *Public Choice* li (1999), 39–57

Wainwright, David, *Government broker: the story of an office and of Mullens & Co.*, London 1990

Walton, C., 'Broker to the Bank of England', *Goldsmiths Review* ix (1988/9), 10–19

Watson, Garth, *The civils: the story of the Institution of Civil Engineers*, London 1988

Whymes, David K., 'Can performance monitoring solve the public service's principal – agent problem?', *Scottish Journal of Political Economy* xl (1993), 434–46

Wiener, L., *Chemins de fer de L'Afrique*, Paris 1930

Williamson, Oliver E. (ed.), *Organisation theory*, Oxford 1995

Wintrobe, R. and A. Breton, 'Organisational structure and productivity', *American Economic Review* lxxvi (1986), 530–8

Young, D. M., *The Colonial Office in the early nineteenth century*, London 1961

Unpublished theses

Attard, B., 'The Australian high commissioners office', DPhil. diss. Oxford 1991

Breckin, Michael, 'Colonial Office policy toward the economic development of the Leeward and Winward Islands, Barbados and British Guiana, 1897–1921', PhD diss. London 1978

Buckley, E. V., 'Colonial Office policy to constitutional change in Cyprus, Hong Kong, Mauritius and Ceylon, 1878–90', PhD diss. London 1974

Bush, D. D., 'The Colonial Office and the making of British policy towards Sierra Leone, 1865–98: a case study in the bureaucracy of imperialism', PhD diss. Cambridge 1978

Crosby, Cynthia, 'A history of the Nyasaland railway, 1895–1935: a study in colonial economic development', Phd diss. Syracuse 1974

Gertzel, C., 'John Holt: a British merchant in West Africa in the era of imperialism', DPhil. diss. Oxford 1959

Hargrave, J. F., 'Competition and collusion in the British railway track fittings industry: the case of the Anderton foundry, 1800–1960', PhD diss. Durham 1992

Hatton, P. H. S., 'British colonial policy in Africa, 1910–14', PhD diss. Cambridge 1971

Kynaston, David, 'The London Stock Exchange, 1870–1914: an institutional history', PhD diss. London 1983

Nelson, W. Evan, 'The imperial administration of currency and British banking in the Straits Settlements, 1867–1908', PhD diss. Duke, NC 1984

Nworah, K. K. D., 'Humanitarian pressure groups and British attitudes to West Africa, 1895–1915', PhD diss. London 1964

Page, A., 'The supply services of the British army during the South African War, 1899–1902', DPhil. diss. Oxford 1976

Pflaumer, Walter, 'The politics of transport policy in Nigeria, 1890–1914: a case study of economic planning in the colonial period', PhD diss. Yale 1982

Purkis, A. J., 'The politics, capital and labour of railway building in the Cape Colony, 1870–85', DPhil. diss. Oxford 1978

Shiels, R., 'Indentured immigration into Trinidad, 1891–1916', BLitt diss. Oxford 1967

Sunderland, David, 'Agents and principals: the Crown Agents for the colonies, 1880–1914', DPhil. diss. Oxford 1997

Tsey, Christian F., 'Gold Coast railways: the making of a colonial economy, 1879–1929', PhD diss. Glasgow 1986

Index

Lightning Source UK Ltd.
Milton Keynes UK
UKHW022152190820
368508UK00003B/94